Self and Sequence

THE POETRY OF D. H. LAWRENCE

Self
and Sequence

THE POETRY OF D. H. LAWRENCE

HOLLY A. LAIRD

UNIVERSITY PRESS OF VIRGINIA
CHARLOTTESVILLE

To my parents

THE UNIVERSITY PRESS OF VIRGINIA
Copyright © 1988 by the Rector and Visitors
of the University of Virginia
First published 1988

Library of Congress Cataloging-in-Publication Data
Laird, Holly A., 1953-
  Self and sequence.
  Includes index.
  1. Lawrence, D. H. (David Herbert), 1885–1930—
Poetic works.   2. Lawrence, D. H. (David Herbert),
1885–1930—Chronology.   3. Self in literature.   I. Title.
PR6023.A93Z6397   1988   821'.912   87-23047
ISBN 0-8139-1147-8

Design by Joanna Hill

Printed in the United States of America

Frontispiece: self-portrait, frontispiece to *Pansies* (June 1929).
Reproduced with permission of Laurence Pollinger Ltd.

Contents

Preface

But what fascinates me about the poems of Lawrence's which I
like is that I must admit he could never have written them had
he held the kind of views about poetry of which I approve.
                                                    —W. H. Auden

Lawrence's poetry is barely acknowledged by the scholarship of modernism. It advertised its own unorthodoxies, yet it was in some ways even
more rooted in the traditions and forms of its immediate predecessors than
that of a central modernist like Eliot. A late Romantic who resisted any
formal tradition he recognized, Lawrence sometimes seemed to write verse
against his own grain. Critical appreciations have come to grant him a
place among post-Romantic writers of the epiphany, but this assimilation
into an accepted poetics accommodates too smoothly the self-dramatizing
rhetoric of his poems, what one of I. A. Richards's Cambridge students
called the "appalling risk of sentimentality."[1] Lawrence's poetry is also recognizably part of his polemical writing in that it imposes his opinions on
us. We might sum up the problem by saying that Lawrence's poems em-
barrass criticism in their direct presentation of self; theirs is an autobiographical, narrative, "impure" lyricism. Moreover, Lawrence shows little
respect for the formal boundaries of lyric. Most of the poems ("bits" he
called them) are brief, composed in groups rather than alone, each a passing, emotional episode pressing forward into other poems. Thus the poetry presents a problem of specification or taxonomy: What is the proper

unit of analysis? In what follows I argue that Lawrence's restless search for himself, as he forever backed off from what he called old lives, found its productive vehicle in the poetic sequence.

Nothing can be more familiar to a reader of Lawrence than his reiterated tales of a new self emerging from the old. He typically breaks out of, rejects, and moves on from a habituated form to envisage an ego with no ego boundaries, what Lawrence termed in his letters a metamorphic "single element." Old and new selves are antagonistic to each other, but there is conflict as well between the new self's halves. Lawrence had projected a change in self, to arrive at a self in flux: "the blood-stream is one, and unbroken, yet storming with oppositions and contradictions."[2] To think of and *in* such patterns was to locate himself already amidst a sequence of identities.

When Lawrence was gathering his verse books, he often referred to them as embodying "essential stories of the soul." He betrayed his concern to find *one* essential soul story when he spoke of the "Study of Thomas Hardy" (1914), his first philosophic work, in similar terms, as a *"Story of My Heart:* or a Confessio Fidei."[3] Upheld by previous scholars as a crucial link in his development as a novelist, the "Study," I propose, also suggests the underlying argument of Lawrence's first books of poems. The "cycle" of the "dance" of male and female—that metaphor for the dynamic, doubled self—crosses three biblical analogues, of David, Solomon, and Job: narratives of yearning, rapturous possession, and agonized remembrance. Man approaches the other, grasps her hand, then must leave her again.[4] Such is the argument of the "Study." But Lawrence's works are rarely as happy as his philosophy. The "story" of the poetry is closer to Job's innocent suffering than to Solomon or David in their glory: with man severed from old connections, wrestling with society and against himself, to encounter the unknown God. And like the ancient poem of Job, Lawrence's verse arguments possess only an implied beginning and end, breaking the Aristotelian curve to detail a perpetually repeated series of contests, setting a pattern that evades patterning. Once this creative scheme is recognized, it is easy to identify a series of stories Lawrence told about himself in successive books, his original, provisional story line becoming increasingly flexible in later works. The greater part of *Self and Sequence* is devoted to tracing these stories and describing their evolution.

Chapter 1 begins by setting forth Lawrence's typical autobiographical methods. It then reviews four contexts from which the verse emerged: the literary traditions, the biography, the philosophy, and the career. My study is primarily descriptive and contextual because the grouped and fragmented character of the poetry needs to be understood before any particular poem is evaluated. Since Lawrence typically wrote his verse in groups and sequences, and then rewrote and reordered in the same way, an understanding of these larger orders may usefully precede close reading of separate poems. Brilliant though individual poems frequently are, no poem of Lawrence stands alone as a well-wrought urn. As Paul Zietlow said of Hardy, the innovative nature of Lawrence's poems "place[s] a heavy demand on the reader's initial willingness to meet them halfway."[5] Moreover, because of their polemical contexts and methods, the poetry presents a special problem for evaluation. Questions of relevance rather than predetermined or absolute criteria are even more necessary than usual to judgment of this poetry. The second part of chapter 1 presents some criteria for Lawrencean success drawn from the poetry itself and suggests how a poem may stand or fall by these measures.

The chapters that follow take up in chronological order the making of the sequences and books. I divide the career into periods bounded by crises Lawrence experienced, since he made these crises the subjects of his verse books. At the same time he fictionalized actual events, to represent his life as constantly self-regenerating. His adaptations of the poetic sequence to record and to reimagine his life deliberately avoid a clear teleological development, in order to project the movements of a self in flux. While Lawrence frequently provided prefaces that attached arguments of various sorts to his poems, he did not make it easy for us to find our way. On the contrary, he complicated the reading process, fragmenting sequences where they seemed too orderly.

After the introductory discussion of Lawrence's method in Chapter 1, I treat the sequences in turn, beginning with the earliest sequences Lawrence wrote—sequences recorded in his manuscripts but left unpublished. The first published book he designed was not *Look! We Have Come Through!* but his book of elegies, *Amores,* which he conceived as a secular book of hours. After publication of *Amores,* the designs for his books became increasingly sophisticated. *Birds, Beasts and Flowers* is a book of books, containing nine sequences and perhaps best understood in relation to the several generic kinds it draws on: from the fantasia to the travel novel. In his *Collected Poems* (Secker, 1928) Lawrence reworked all these poems, shuffling and reordering his books to reshape his career, suggesting that instead of the many stages of struggle he had faced in developing his poetry, he had endured only one great crisis, breaking through from the *Rhyming Poems* of volume 1 to the *Unrhyming Poems* of volume 2. By the time Lawrence wrote his *Last Poems,* sequential composition had become instinctive. If he had lived to publish these, it is unlikely that he would have altered them substantially from their final state in manuscript.

I have devoted ample space in this study to a narrative description of the making of each book. If one believes, as I do, that the sequence is, like the individual poem, a fundamental unit of poetic composition for Lawrence, then it is obviously important for students of the poetry to know exactly what he did in arranging and rearranging his sequences when they assess any group of poems. I intend these descriptive sections on each book to be useful as a scholarly resource to critics writing about Lawrence's poems and sequences. My own critical arguments might have been presented by way of a more selective discussion of the sequences, but I have chosen to be inclusive, in part because for students of Lawrence's poetry, there is and will be no other access to the information I have collected, short of repeating my own efforts. The variorum edition of the poems now in preparation does not make the evolution of Lawrence's ordering of poems automatically clear to students. I hope, then, that my book will be read both as a whole and selectively, as students of particular poems try to fit them into the sequences that enhance them and sometimes give them their meaning.

The chronological organization of this study makes it possible to examine the original shape of Lawrence's career as a poet, to consider the areas in which it overlapped with, or even took precedence over, his career as novelist, and to uncover the autonomy and continuity in Lawrence's poetic development. Because he tended to move from periods of experimentation to later periods of mastery over a new style of verse, it becomes convenient to consider often-neglected pockets of writing before discussing the major works. So each chapter in this study is divided into two parts, the first discussing little-known materials, the second the major sequences to which they are related. In part I of chapters 2–6, I examine Lawrence's juvenilia, the war poetry, the poems in *The Plumed Serpent,* and his satiric books, *Pansies,* and *Nettles,* while reserving part 2 for his major books: *Love Poems and Others, Amores, Look! We Have Come Through! Birds, Beasts and Flowers, Collected Poems,* and *Last Poems.* One thing is clear in the shaping of his long and various career as a poet: because, with each project, Lawrence was intent upon transcending its predecessor—like Yeats remaking himself—all could never cohere into a single harmonium. Each new book reveals the last as insufficient; with each work, as Lawrence believed even in his last poems, "the whole thing starts again" ("The Ship of Death").[6]

While I am deeply indebted to the work of others who have written biographical and critical studies of Lawrence (especially to Emile Delavenay, Paul Delany, Harry T. Moore, Edward Nehls, and Sandra Gilbert) and to the editorial labors of Vivian de Sola Pinto, F. Warren Roberts, and Carole Ferrier (Ferrier's scholarly dissertation will form the basis for the Cambridge Poems, edited by Ferrier and Christopher Pollnitz), most of what I argue below is new. I offer a fresh account of the autobiographical patterns in Lawrence's poetry, one that relies on thorough examination of his life, letters, and poetry, without placing complete faith in his claims in various famous prefaces to his poems. This description enables me to view Lawrence's poetry from a neutral position, assuming neither that he is an artist fascinated by extreme or "perverse" states of being nor that the "new" worlds he describes are necessarily better or even radically different from the "old." Old and new depend inexorably on each other in a single, central dualism. This means that while I see a kind of heroism in Lawrence's effort to reject absolutes and embrace the processes of change, a heroism that many of Lawrence's readers have found inspiring, I also believe that this effort became an absolute in its own right, that Lawrence eventually insisted on change for its own sake, and that this feature of his thought accounts for the repetition of strategy, theme, and phrase that has worried his readers.

In my view, Lawrence as an autobiographer has three aims: self-expression, self-transformation, and the transformation of the reader. The articulation of the third aim is itself an important new emphasis in this descriptive model; for while it is normal for critics of autobiography to describe the interesting twofold process by which artists express and transform their lives in their works, the critics rarely see rhetorical designs as intrinsic to, or aesthetically intriguing aspects of, poetic autobiographies. I argue that this triple aim informs not only each act of writing, but also the relationship between Lawrence's poems and their contexts in the life, the philosophy, and the poetic tradition. This complex model enables me, finally, to present a full description both of the poetic sequence as a form of autobiography and of Lawrence's experimentation with it. Since the poetic sequence as a genre has drawn astonishingly little attention, my discussion of Lawrence's sequences should be of use to students attempting a comprehensive approach to the verse sequences and books of other poets.

I offer a history of Lawrence's poetic career that differs from that of previous scholars by basing its divisions on the books of poems in the original order in which Lawrence wrote, revised, and published them, rather than making the *Collected Poems* the sole basis for generalization about his development. In the process of detailing this history, *Self and Sequence* offers a fresh and precise description of the connections between his books of poems and major events in his life and thought. In addition, it offers an account of numerous influences in Lawrence's reading, such as those of Richard Jefferies and Rachel Annand Taylor on the "story of my soul" or that of Andrew Lang on Lawrence's defense of autobiography in the Note to *Collected Poems*, which have previously gone unnoticed or unexplored.

I hope this book will speak to three audiences. Professional Lawren-ceans will find in it an account of Lawrence's patterns of repetition and variation as a poet that may be of use in accounting for similar patterns in Lawrence's fiction. Students working on particular poems or groups of poems will find in it an account of the history of sequential placements and arrangements of important poems. And students of the autobiographical impulse in modern literature will find an account of Lawrence's extraor-dinarily original solutions to widely felt problems of expression.

It is a pleasure to acknowledge the help I have received in writing this book. For their gracious assistance with the manuscripts of Lawrence, I would like to thank Robert Bertholf of the Poetry / Rare Books Collec-tion at SUNY Buffalo; Cathy Henderson of the Humanities Research Center at the University of Texas, Austin; M. A. Welch, formerly Keeper of the Manuscripts at the University of Nottingham Library; Lola Szladits of the Berg Collection at the New York Public Library; and the staff of the Bancroft Library at the University of California, Berkeley. Permissions to publish copyrighted materials are acknowledged specifically in the Notes; Mr. Gerald Pollinger has made my many dealings with the Lawrence estate a pleasure.

Keith Cushman made invaluable suggestions for revision and supported this project at important moments in its development. I am indebted to L. D. Clark for his thoughtful response to my treatment of *The Plumed Serpent*. I thank Robert Langbaum, Daniel Albright, and Anthony Winner for their very useful suggestions at an earlier stage. Samuel Hynes and A. Walton Litz generously watched over its progress from its earliest in-ception. The Whiting Foundation assisted with a fellowship year in which some of the initial research was done; the University of Virginia granted me a Sesquicentennial Associateship during which final revisions were completed. I am deeply grateful to several friends: to Lars Engle and John Kidd for kindness and for editorial help, to Mark Edmundson and Clare Kinney for encouragement, and to John Lynch for his aid in proofreading and indexing. The infelicities and faults still to be found are, of course, my own. For his warm support and interest in the progress of my work (espe-cially of shorter pieces developed alongside this book), I want to thank Dennis Jackson. The guidance of my undergraduate professors, especially Sandra Berwind and Laurence Stapleton of Bryn Mawr College, has been with me throughout this project and remains with me now. This book is dedicated to my parents and dearest friends, Joseph and Shirley Eder Laird.

Self and Sequence

THE POETRY OF D. H. LAWRENCE

Abbreviations for Titles of Books of Poems

AM   *Amores*

B   *Bay*

CP   *The Complete Poems of D. H. Lawrence*

LP   *Love Poems and Others*

NP   *New Poems*

RP   *Rhyming Poems*, vol. 1, *Collected Poems*

UP   *Unrhyming Poems*, vol. 2, *Collected Poems*

—

CHAPTER ONE

Introduction

AN AUTOBIOGRAPHICAL METHOD

In addressing even his most private thoughts he addresses a
stranger and must needs find a common tongue between them.

—R. P. Blackmur

Part I: Lawrence's Poetic Autobiographies

The introductory Note to the *Collected Poems* (1928) contains one of
Lawrence's most memorable self-portraits, brief though it is. He describes
his first attempts to write verse as the jejune efforts of an earnest poetaster
who, despite himself, is shaken by a fierce creative demon:

> The first poems I ever wrote, if poems they were, was when I was nineteen:
> now twenty-three years ago. I remember perfectly the Sunday afternoon
> when I perpetrated those first two pieces: "To Guelder-Roses" and "To
> Campions"; in springtime, of course, and, as I say, in my twentieth year.
> Any young lady might have written them and been pleased with them; as I
> was pleased with them. But it was after that, when I was twenty, that my real
> demon would now and then get hold of me and shake more real poems out
> of me, making me uneasy. I never "liked" my real poems as I liked "To
> Guelder-Roses." (Note, *CP,* p. 27)

This self-portrait offers a condensed version of typically Lawrencean dualisms: the conventional versus the subversive, complacent self-control versus uneasy transport, young ladies versus demons. But Lawrence gives his creed a special form as a fable of his early writing experience. His anecdote is a myth of the primal poet: the "real" man at the back of the writing, the figure of a "demon" beyond the timid "I." This is also a mocking portrait: Lawrence diminishes his younger self to magnify his intense demon. Mocking himself, he mocks his readers: he undercuts our desire for a proud, self-controlled author, ridicules our powers of judgment, and scandalizes our sense of what is equitable (especially if we are young ladies). He challenges readers to overturn conventional ideas of the good and the known and admit a deeper knowledge.

Further on, the Note informs us that the poems are autobiographical, forming a record of the "sayings" of Lawrence's demon: "many of the poems are so personal that, in their fragmentary fashion, they make up a biography of an emotional and inner life" (*CP*, p. 27). He describes his collection almost as if it were a novel with changes in scene, characters, and a full history of crises and climaxes (pp. 27–28). But the *Collected Poems* is no more a strict chronicle of the life than the figure of the possessed poet is a portrait of the young man. Lawrence ordered the poems in his collection to give his autobiography a significant, symbolic shape.

This Note should be read as we would a Henry James preface: as an anecdote anterior to the work, which predicts its strategies. Lawrence splits himself twice, rejecting an old self in favor of a new, and envisaging that new self as a dynamic double being, a self in communication with its deeper, better half. While the young Lawrence of the Note is self-controlled and dwells in an easy, bounded world of Sunday parlors, the demon-shaken poet within him is disoriented, yet empowered by the unknown. These old and new selves are antagonistic, and there is conflict between the new self's two halves as well. Lawrence demands a change in self that will result in a self-in-flux; to think this way was to commit himself to a sequence of inevitably partial representations of identity.

Lawrence's tales of a new self emerging from the old are very familiar to his readers. One may recall, for instance, his famous letter to Edward Garnett in 1914 about *The Wedding Ring* (an early study for *The Rainbow*), in which he claimed to have revolutionized the structure of character in his novels. The "old stable ego" of the traditional character must be rejected for a new type that can scarcely be defined except through metaphor: "You mustn't look in my novel for the old stable ego of the character. There is another ego according to whose action the individual is unrecognisable, and passes through, as it were, allotropic states which it needs a deeper sense than any we've been used to exercise, to discover are states of the same single radically unchanged element. (Like as diamond and coal are the same pure single element of carbon.)" (*Letters*, 2:183). Lawrence's new "ego" has no ego boundaries, only a deeper, imperceptible "single element," and this ego is metamorphic. This pattern even overtakes the rhythm of Lawrence's prose (and that of his explicators); the syntactic structure "not only . . . but also" appears everywhere in his works. At times Lawrence's projections of the wished-for kingdom of self appear to double back on themselves; ideal oneness becomes a state of siege, as in the late work *Etruscan Places* (1927–28): "All emerges out of the unbroken circle with its nucleus, the germ, the One, the god, if you like to call it so. And man, with his soul and his personality, emerges in eternal connexion with all the rest. The blood-stream is one, and unbroken, yet storming with oppositions and contradictions" (p. 168). Lawrence was in no simple sense a utopian thinker. While he normally had in mind some scheme for a paradise on earth, he rarely imagined it static or unvexed. He conceives the movement toward fulfillment as a threefold "utterance" in his Hardy essay of 1914: the self is moved out of "agonized remembrance" of the past by the "touch" of another, for whom it forever after "yearns," "hailing" the other's approach (*Phoenix*, pp. 449–50).

These habits of autobiography perform at least three functions: recording personal crises, creating fictions of transcendence, and shaking the audience by challenging and reforming received wisdom. The Note records an early crisis in which the poet was overwhelmed by a shadow self, and this crisis retrospectively becomes a fictional battle, as the primal poet triumphs over his more timid everyday nature. The reader is pressed into the role of this timid self, whom the mature narrator (who comprehends both demon and young man) deliberately provokes. This is, of course, neither accurate autobiography nor practical philosophy. Lawrence creates instead an art in which he redefines and extends himself, not to convert others, but to awaken their instinct for conflict.

Both Lawrence's champions and his detractors have taken him at his word in his Note and, without considering it a possible example of his methods, have interpreted it as a literal (if incomplete) description of his principles of composition and technique. In a damning essay on the poetry, R. P. Blackmur decided that "the young man in the quotation [is] just what Lawrence thought he was not, the poet as craftsman, and the demon was exactly that outburst of personal feeling which needed the discipline of craft to become a poem." Vivian de Sola Pinto and Sandra Gilbert, two staunch defenders of Lawrence, decided that Blackmur had misinterpreted the "young lady," that Lawrence meant—not the skilled, but the derivative poet working with old-fashioned techniques. Pinto and Gilbert, joined by Harold Bloom, invoke Romantic criteria of praise to judge Lawrence as a mythopoeic, organicist, and visionary poet.[1] But Lawrence's Note is not explicitly about technique, nor does it place this poet snugly within a Romantic tradition. A more recent study by Gail Mandell makes an impressive effort to uncover the patterning of the *Collected Poems,* but her book follows the Note word by word, allowing it to dictate her understanding of Lawrence's poetic development.[2]

Lawrence's Note is, I believe, simply another of his autobiographical fictions. Like his poetry, it needs to be interpreted in four contexts: the poetic tradition Lawrence recognized, his biography, his philosophy, and his career as a publishing poet who knew and cared about his audience. In the following pages, I will review each of these contexts to establish how they condition Lawrence's art.

Lawrence persistently defined himself against tradition, against classics and romantics, Victorians and contemporaries. The "changeless" art of tradition was his express antagonist. Only late in his career did he develop a model that assimilated the poetry of his predecessors to his own, and here the chief antagonist (for every artist) was the reader, whom Lawrence accused of conventionalizing art. Bloom and Gilbert wrote on Lawrence before they developed their revisionist theories of literature, though more recently Gilbert has enlarged her view of *Birds, Beasts and Flowers* to examine its redaction of Blake, and Ross Murfin has argued for a Lawrence haunted by precursors.[3] I differ from both, however, in that I see Lawrence's antitraditionalist aesthetic as a conscious procedure that angles eclectically in all directions, against contemporaries and readers, as well as against his predecessors. Revisionism is so inseparable from Lawrence's art that his controversiality, engaging T. S. Eliot and Auden, Blackmur and Bloom, becomes a sign of his talents.[4]

Lawrence read and reviewed constantly, trying on many writers, but was far more likely to acknowledge and push minor poets than major ones—he praises Rachel Annand Taylor, Robert Nichols, and Harry Crosby, among others. His desire to magnify lesser poets should be taken as seriously in assessing his relations to other writers as his penchant for diminishing the greats. But in general he put all fellow artists behind him to project something beyond everything known. Since so many other artists engage in comparable pilgrimages, however, their muses sometimes emerge, demonlike, to wrestle with the mere Lawrence. Shelley took pride of place in the "Study of Thomas Hardy" (1914), and his influence surely inspired the last poem of *Look! We Have Come Through!* (1917), where "Ode to the West Wind" found its Lawrencean complement in "Craving for Spring," but Shelley was then peremptorily dismissed in "Poetry of the Present" (1919).

Whitman stands out from the other influences. The American offered an example of iconoclasm more suitable to Lawrence's needs than that of Swinburne, Shelley, or even Blake. Whitman set a precedent by leaping altogether past the British Romantic and the Puritan traditions to stride into Elysian fields of the flesh. Whitman's towering importance further explains the general neglect of Lawrence's poetry; what once roused James Miller's indignation—that Whitman had been neglected in favor of a rationalist tradition—is even truer of his descendants.[5] Lawrence's essay on Whitman in *Studies in Classic American Literature* (1923) is the most representative sample of his response, for while philosophizing over the "postmortem effects" of Whitman's corpus, Lawrence retraced the steps by which he established a separate identity. Devoting the first half of the essay to vivisecting Whitman, whom he judges consumptively lovesick, he then resurrects Whitman's remains. Whitman's "sympathy" makes up half a man, says Lawrence. To possess "integrity" (as Whitman did not), a poet must sympathize but separate himself from the crowd. Thus Lawrence defined his "whole" poet as he defined himself, split by revulsion from, yet linked by sympathy for, his greater half.[6]

In prose and poetry alike, Lawrence took his pose as something less than, yet beyond, Whitman. He tore down what he termed in his essay the "Mystic Evolution" and mighty "Myself" of Whitman and then looked in the fragments for a new mystic grace. As an example of this relationship in the poetry, compare the "autograph" that heads *Leaves of Grass* with the headpiece to Lawrence's *Collected Poems*. Whitman writes:

> *Come, said my Soul,*
> *Such verses for my Body let us write, (for we are one,)*
> *That should I after death invisibly return,*
> *Or, long, long hence, in other spheres,*
> *There to some group of mates the chants resuming,*
> *(Tallying Earth's soil, trees, winds, tumultuous waves,)*
> *Ever with pleas'd smile I may keep on,*
> *Ever and ever yet the verses owning—as, first, I here and now,*
> *Signing for Soul and Body, set to them my name,*
> > *WALT WHITMAN*[7]

In "The Wild Common," Lawrence violates the conditions set in Whitman's signature. In the little drama between body and soul, as he gazes at his shadow in water, he is at first unable to see his shadowy soul as other than a doglike substance,

What if the waters ceased, where were the marigolds then, and the gudgeon?
What is this thing that I look down upon?
White on the water wimples my shadow, strains like a dog on a string, to run on.

How it looks back, like a white dog to its master! (*CP,* pp. 33–34)

but then imagines the joyous, prolific merging of his shadow self with the bodily water,

Oh but the water loves me and folds me,
Plays with me, sways me, lifts me and sinks me, murmurs: Oh marvellous stuff!
No longer shadow!

Thus Lawrence rejects the initial, puritan dualism, for an Edenic, Whitmanesque immediacy. The temporal scheme, the syntax of Whitman's proposition, too, is altered. For Whitman's smooth, discursive, conditional statement, "should I after death invisibly return," then "I may keep on, / Ever and ever," Lawrence adopts an elliptical, nondiscursive sequence of clauses: "What if the gorse-flowers shrivelled, and I were gone? / . . . But how splendid it is, to be substance, here!" (*CP,* pp. 33–34). Lawrence's syntax implies a rejection of orthodox beliefs in any kind of afterlife (expressed by "and when I die, I will live again"), reasserting the present condition as fact ("but the water loves me"). Instead of the smooth extension of self from here to hereafter, he proposes a shift here and now in attitudes: time passes in a split second in the speaker's perception, as he sees one world break into another.

Even Lawrence's career as a poet retraced Whitman's steps, modifying them as he proceeded. In his earliest philosophical sequences (manuscript poems as yet unpublished), he rejected a Romanticist poetics in favor of the Whitmanesque. Then with the collection of his books, he began to trace Whitman's evolution: matching Whitman's concern with self-identity in "Song of Myself" with his own in *Amores;* exploring the relationship between man and the world of men as in Whitman's "Calamus" with *Birds, Beasts and Flowers.* Lawrence alluded to Whitman's precedent even in his last works—recapitulating "Sands at Seventy" in *Pansies* and *Nettles;* celebrating the "great poet, of the end of life" ("Whitman," *Studies,* p. 179) in his *Last Poems,* especially in "The Ship of Death" and "Song of Death." He also placed obviously Whitmanesque poems at the end (or near the end) of several sequences, notably "Dreams . . . Nascent" in volume i of *Collected Poems,* "Blue" and "The Mystic Blue" in *Amores,* "Manifesto" in *Look! We Have Come Through!* "The American Eagle" in *Birds, Beasts and Flowers,* and "Leaves of Grass, Flowers of Grass" in *Nettles.* But Lawrence also found his way by tracing a path of opposition to that of his predecessor, since in theme and structure these poems implicitly criticize Whitman. Lawrence discards Whitman's evolutionary expansionism both as a heroic ideal and as a principle of form, choosing instead the mystic process of Dionysiac self-renewal.

Because his connections to other poets are so diverse, however, my concern will be less with Lawrence's affinities than with placing his poetry in the more immediate contexts of his life and career. Lawrence's life has often been used to gloss his art, but it might as easily be argued that he lived life as if it were material for novels. Like Wordsworth, Shelley, or Browning, he saw his life as an exemplary form, his mission to "sift the vital fact" from experience.[8] The vital fact for Lawrence announced itself in eruptive change. He began early in youth to seek change for its own sake; his life history is characterized by a profound restless eagerness to have done with one situation and begin the next. Periods in his life are more or less neatly marked by his comings and goings, and he made these his subject: his turbulent adolescence in the earliest sequences, his mother's death in *Amores,* his elopement with a married woman in *Look! We Have Come Through!* the nightmarish war years in *Bay,* the anxious quest for a Utopian frontier in *Birds, Beasts and Flowers,* his brief, stormy mission in America in the poems of *The Plumed Serpent,* the battle with censorship and his British public in *Pansies,* death in *Last Poems.* Crisis in these books was as much an occasion for self-discovery as of restless indecision or struggle.

But if change afforded a rule for life, it also established rules for art. Lawrence mythologized the actual circumstances of his life and rearranged the original records of his verse, to reconstruct the "vital facts." His earliest work turns the accounts of youth into myths of a poet's genesis. With the single exception of his first book, *Love Poems and Others,* which Lawrence did not design himself, each of the poetic books is (like the novels) a fictionalized sequence. The poems in *Amores* and *Look! We Have Come Through!* were revised and collected several years after the recorded events took place, and he reorganized these into stories of initiation into manhood. Similarly, *Bay* and *Birds, Beasts and Flowers* were written and organized as histories of world apocalypse: directed toward destruction in *Bay,* toward resurrection in *Birds, Beasts and Flowers.* Even *New Poems* (which contains revised, old poems, and was given its misleading title by its publisher) took as its theme a mythic moment in history when cities and people might "come awake" (*Letters,* 3 : 254). When Lawrence returned to these books to collect his poetry in one edition, he reshaped his entire career around a single crisis. The reorganization created a simple development from old-world English experience recorded in Lawrence's early love poems, elegies, and war verse into new-world experience (not restricted to any single geo-graphical location, but traveling around the world) heralded in *Look! We Have Come Through!* and *Birds, Beasts and Flowers*. *The Plumed Serpent* left realism almost entirely behind to erect hero-gods on earth. Finally, in *Pansies* and *Last Poems* he imagined the death of the mind and its afterlife. These reorganizations simplified Lawrence's history by establishing bound-aries and progressive triumphs for individual periods of his life, but he was also concerned to reinvent the fragmented character of his experiences. Each book tells of a search for self-renewal that seems to hover within grasp, yet is perpetually delayed.

Behind these books is a fund of metaphysical thought that Lawrence revised as often as he changed his story. Here again there is no simple translation of philosophy into art, nor any evasion of Lawrence's revision-ary impulse. He made contradictory assessments of his philosophy, on the one hand deriving his "pollyanalytics" after the fact from his experiences and art, on the other hand claiming that he needed a metaphysic before he could write.[9] Both claims make sense when the philosophy is viewed as a transitional stage, in which he elaborated principles from previous works and developed further arguments, hence preparing fresh creative experi-ments. The independent merit of Lawrence's metaphysics remains in dis-pute, but in any case it is a mistake to read his philosophical texts either as logically coherent treatises or as statements of final meaning for the novels and poems. They are discursive versions of Lawrence's imaginative work.

The relationship between the prose and the poetry is close enough to require special attention: the arguments of one predict those of the other. It was only after Lawrence had composed his first major philosophical work that he began to design his books of poems. "The Study of Thomas Hardy" set man and woman at the center of his philosophy. Standing face to face in eternal opposition, male and female define the boundaries of each other's egos, and their changing relations to each other give the curve of history, or a man's life. Lawrence's sexual exemplum displays the Her-aclitean paradox of an order based on the acausal, spontaneous conflict of antithetical elements—a concept he cites as a classical analogue of his en-terprise when writing *Birds, Beasts and Flowers*. He also called up ancient analogies in revising the story of Christ, replacing Christ's spiritualized fig-ure with earthier characters like Job. Progress is made, not by working toward the death of the body and the reward of resurrection of the soul, but by submitting to the living moment when man is tested by ecstatic suffering.

As Lawrence's philosophy developed, its themes registered the changing focus of his interests. The stories in *Amores* and *Look! We Have Come*

Through! hinge on the relationship between man and woman, elaborated in his "Study of Thomas Hardy." In *Birds, Beasts and Flowers* he rediscovered the theories of relationship between men described in *Fantasia of the Unconscious*. Even before he wrote the "Study of Thomas Hardy," Lawrence's verse had its ideological dimension, recorded in his first paper on aesthetics, "Art and the Individual," and in his letters. Then in addition to these intersections between his prose and poetry, prefaces to his works outline arguments for each book. His prefaces provide "arguments" in the old-fashioned sense of that word, synopses that both suggest an ethical standard of conduct and preview the book that follows. I will use the term *argument* at times interchangeably with *story* to refer, as Lawrence does, to the specific ethical plots of his books. Beyond the guidelines for reading they offer, these prefaces and the other prose writings about poetics offer a widely applicable apology for poetry, for its autobiography, its fragmented character, its revisionism, its sheer diversity.

While instructing us how to read his books, however, Lawrence does not make reading the poems easy. On the contrary, he complicated the reading process. His prefaces provide guiding arguments, but they also provoke the reader into active participation, demanding that we link these arguments to the poems, and particular poems to each other, in a pilgrim's progress. Modernist concerns with tradition and technique led critics not only away from "expressive form" but from this major aspect of Lawrence's poetry: the art of the verse cycle, the poetic book of moments.[10] Although each poem has its own integrity, Lawrence had no interest in creating the perfect poem; he wanted something as incomplete, vexed, fluid as himself, the fleeting gestures and episodic pieces of his inner story. These he gathered into sequences and books to reembody the order of the fluctuant self.

There exists abundant evidence of Lawrence's intentions, ranging from the statements of intention that appear in the prefaces to the manuscript evidence of his work of arrangement and revision. The most remarkable document of this kind is a table of contents for *Rhyming Poems*, volume 1 of *Collected Poems*, that Lawrence worked and reworked in the pages of his copy of *Love Poems and Others*, now held in The Poetry/Rare Books Collection of the University of Buffalo (see transcription of holograph list in Appendix B).[11] Lawrence did not construct his books upon an elaborate score, as T. S. Eliot did *Four Quartets*, for example. Rather, Lawrence built up his books by gathering together poems springing from a specific experience in his life so that they formed core groups; less frequently, poems originally long in their manuscript forms became, as Gail Mandell demonstrates, the source for clusters of shorter poems.[12] Lawrence then rearranged the core groups in sequences simulating the actual and symbolic order of his experience. The final arrangements for the books vary from one to the next, from the story form of *Look! We Have Come Through!* to the many-storied *Birds, Beasts and Flowers* or the two-part *Collected Poems*—shaped to mime a single crisis—until he reached the ritualism of *Last Poems.* Since Lawrence disliked set patterns, he also disrupted such orders; any calendar or map constructed from his works would be full of gaps and inconsistencies. The most elaborate of the books, *Birds, Beasts and Flowers,* is broken into nine individual sections, each in turn prefaced by several prose arguments. The reader must sort multiple instructions. Volume 1 of *Collected Poems—Rhyming Poems* (a rearrangement of *Love Poems and Others, Amores, Bay,* and *New Poems*)—was worked over as strenuously as any of these others, and the result reflects the intriguing encounter between the elder Lawrence and his ghostly, younger self. Every one of these volumes shows signs of the dialectic by which it was produced, a process of intensive revision and rearrangement that intervened between the fragmented state in which its poems were first written and the orderly history Lawrence discovered in that part of his life, then again between this projection and the fragmented condition he reimposed on the final, published version.

The poems acquire power and significance cumulatively as they gather in sequences. But what happens to the individual poem in the process of reading a book? The framing poems, or those that record crucial episodes in a story, usually reward attention in themselves. Poems that are already widely known, like "Piano," and poems that are rarely mentioned, like "Narcissus," acquire greater implication when placed in the larger drama of the sequences. Appreciation of any poem follows rapidly when we consider what it brings to the reading of a book. In addition, the structure of separate poems often mirrors that of individual books. Amid all their differences the poems have certain common features that make each of them genuinely representative. Closure, for example, of a provisional kind is obtained, not through formal construction (as in a sonnet), not through a complete, logical proposition (as in a metaphysical poem), and rarely through unity of plot, but through the illusion that some emotional crisis has been passed. Lawrence described this vaguely as getting "an emotion out in its own course" (*Letters,* 2:61). More precisely, he induces emotional crises by juxtaposing images or expressions of speech that possess opposite emotional values. The endings of such poems seem tentative, as if he had reached one more difficult precipice, one last twist in the course of the emotion. Though rarely rewarding the reader with the sense of a final ending, these twists and turns propel the reader through one poem and into the next; and they combine into a book that is as provisionally closed, as contradictory in nature, as its individual pieces. The relationship between a book and its poems epitomizes a favorite dualism of Lawrence: "That which is whole, torn asunder, / That which is in part, finding its whole again throughout the universe" ("Tortoise Shout," *CP,* p. 367).

The poems of *The Plumed Serpent* stand apart from Lawrence's general pattern of production. Here, in Lawrence's boldest experiment with poetry, he used the verse sequence to record the mythic utterances of Mexican hero-gods in their war against Christianity. The sequence evolves within the novel, so that its poetry carries the inner history, not of a single man, but of a national soul. The poems must be examined, then, not only in relation to each other, but in relation to the developing narrative. *The Plumed Serpent* bears special witness to Lawrence's belief in verse as the vehicle for men's most significant crises. A close examination of the relationship between all the novels and the poetry lies beyond the scope of this project, but I have indicated parallels where they appear most relevant. Lawrence became ambitious quite early in his career to unite the different strengths of the "lyric" and the "dramatic" writer. The proof of his success depends on our judgments of his individual works, but throughout this study it will be my contention that his great contribution in poetry, as in the novel, derives less from an attempt to exploit the differences between the genres than from his effort to recombine their different subjects, methods, and purposes.

Lawrence's career itself was something that he made consciously if unorthodoxly. He was both critical of literary establishments and patterns and committed to an ideal of poetic greatness in a way suggested by a comment of Lawrence Lipking's in *The Life of the Poet:* "The attack on careerism does not preclude the poet's need to shape some sort of career, some sense of destiny or vocation. Propertius and Pound, Winters and Graves, are not modest authors. Their contempt for 'official' poetry and 'heroic' careers implies a reverse ambition: a self-consuming devotion to craft. Indeed, one might argue that resistance to orthodox definitions of greatness and public careers itself constitutes a career ideal." [13] A career includes the very worldly consideration of publication; the poet who lives by writing not only must wrestle with his personal sense of destiny but must confront and somehow create his public audience. From the beginning Lawrence's books were intended to interest and arouse a public that knew and reacted daily to him in the marketplace. Contrary to the myth of a Lawrence recklessly indifferent to public approval, he was actually highly sensitive to public response even when in later years an angry superiority became his public stance. The almost immediate recognition he enjoyed as a young writer propelled him with enviable speed through his apprenticeship and into a fully established position as the author of *Sons and Lovers* and *Love Poems and Others,* "a volume of verse—my dearest treasure" (*Letters,* 1:313). His career changed shape during the war, when his novels were censored and he was reduced to producing books of poems for financial and emotional suport, books that present him as a man exiled in his own nation. Lawrence had from his youth been swayed by Carlyle's romantic notion of the book as a heroic field of action, and difficulty spurred him into the increasingly daring experiments of his "leadership" novels (so-called by critics—*The Lost Girl, Aaron's Rod, Kangaroo,* and *The Plumed Serpent*) and his finest verse book, *Birds, Beasts and Flowers.* His close brush with death in 1925 reinforced his desire to shape his work for present and future readers. In 1927–28, recognizing the range of his achievements, he consolidated his career in *Collected Poems.* And in the midst of censorship of his paintings and *Lady Chatterley's Lover,* he produced hundreds more *pensées,* which eventually found their way into satiric volumes aimed directly at the public. Only his *Last Poems* stands beyond the marketplace—a notebook that Lawrence did not live to revise, reshape, and publish, but that, with undiminished eloquence, gave him a last word on his own death.

Previous studies have relied on Lawrence's own organization of the career in *Collected Poems,* and have, by retracing the order of that anthology rather than of his actual production of the poems it contains, found him improving in a relatively steady progress. Lawrence's career had, however, no clear telos. One finds him working on different kinds of poetic productions at different times: first, a long period in which he produced massive quantities of verse, chiefly in manuscript; then, another long period in which he wrote little, but revised a great deal and collected several books; then, a few years when he wrote and designed books simultaneously; and so forth. But perhaps because he was always repeating himself, there is a strong correlation between his biography and his technical development. In every period he wrote of life as a Jobian struggle, but his repeated passages through crisis meant that he tended to begin new projects, and to choose fresh methods, with each major change in his life. It seems too that he experimented most in times of hardship, and this then enabled him in subsequent periods to compose in a matured confident style. He consolidated the work of his youth, for example, in books he designed as a married man. This pattern tended to produce sequels and even companion books: each new work takes up somewhere near the point at which the last ended and advances beyond it. The borders of these periods, however, overlap: Lawrence's collection of poems in *Look! We Have Come Through!*

melded the work of previous years; yet this volume ends with newer poems and a changed vision of the world preparatory to *Birds, Beasts and Flowers*. This complex progression might be visualized as the combined motion of wave and tide up a sloping beach. To reflect these fluctuations, each chapter of my study divides in two, tracing Lawrence's developments back and forth from new to mature endeavor; and every chapter overlaps in subject and chronology with the beginning of the next (brief chronologies are positioned at the head of each chapter to aid the reader in following these progressions). Repetition and cleavage marked every step in this career.

Part II: The Problem of Evaluation

Although the criticism is scanty, Lawrence's poetry has elicited strongly felt responses—mixed, adverse, or intensely loyal. The bad marks assigned the poetry are numerous, and they target its foremost characteristics: that its biographical elements are not sufficiently dramatized; that it is more interested in message than in making; that it is fragmented, not self-sufficient; that its formal elements of rhyme and meter are (when present) perfunctory; that is uses banal or conventional language or dead poetic diction; that it is nearly indistinguishable from prose. Against these, critics have argued for the poetry's Romantic originality: the honesty, intensity, and original sensibility of Lawrence; his powers of observation and insight; his mythopoeia; the emerging character of his free verse, which relies on parallelism or other forms of repetition and a kinetic verse line.[14] But even among defenders of Lawrence, a tendency to shy away from the polemical elements in his poetry seems to have led to neglect of other important features. His poetic language, for example, is rarely mentioned or described. Lawrence deserves critical description as a serious craftsman attentive to the currents of his time even when he swims against them: few poets have been more conscious of the aesthetic climate in which they wrote or more deliberate in flouting or modifying its conventions.

In one of his wittiest passages on this matter in "Pornography and Obscenity" (1929), Lawrence reflects cheerfully on the transience of contemporary public standards and teases his critics with the fact that "taste" is not only variable, but is a notoriously poor judge of the value of contemporary productions:

> [Take] the word *obscene:* nobody knows what it means. Suppose it were derived from *obscena:* that which might not be represented on the stage; how much further are you? None! What is obscene to Tom is not obscene to

Lucy or Joe, and really, the meaning of a word has to wait for majorities to decide it. If a play shocks ten people in an audience, and doesn't shock the remaining five hundred, then it is obscene to ten and innocuous to five hundred; hence, the play is not obscene, by majority. But *Hamlet* shocked all the Cromwellian Puritans, and shocks nobody today, and some of Aristophanes shocks everybody today, and didn't galvanize the later Greeks at all, apparently. Man is a changeable beast, and words change their meanings with him, and things are not what they seemed, and what's what becomes what isn't, and if we think we know where we are it's only because we are so rapidly being translated to somewhere else. (*Phoenix*, p. 170)

"Shock" will fade with time, and literature become acceptable; Aristophanes, *Hamlet,* and even Lawrence himself are now canonical; and canonical works—even those canonized as shocking—are to some extent insulated from audiences by their canonicity. But Lawrence did not think this a desirable goal, except isofar as it makes room for new authors to plow up emotion again, as he explained in another essay of 1929, his introduction to Harry Crosby's *Chariot of the Sun.* While poetry "is a matter of words," strung into a "ripple and jingle," an "interplay of images," and the "iridescent suggestion of an idea," it has yet more to do:

Man fixes some wonderful erection of his own between himself and the wild chaos, and gradually goes bleached and stifled under his parasol. Then comes a poet, enemy of convention, and makes a slit in the umbrella; and lo! the glimpse of chaos is a vision, a window to the sun. But after a while, getting used to the vision, and not liking the genuine draught from chaos, commonplace man daubs a simulacrum of the window that opens on to chaos, and patches the umbrella with the painted patch of the simulacrum. That is, he has got used to the vision. . . . But alas! it is all simulacrum, in innumerable patches. Homer and Keats, annotated and with glossary. . . . Till another poet makes a slit on to the open and windy chaos. (*Phoenix*, pp. 255–56)

And so Lawrence attempts to keep his poetry functioning as a "slit," offering not only a view of chaos but a draft from it. In this he succeeds, and succeeds by craft. Readers will probably remain sensitive to the shocks of these poems because Lawrence built them into the elements of his verse: in his choice of subjects, in incongruous or even mixed metaphors, in direct rhetorical address and jagged rhythms and rhymes. He stressed diction rather than *le mot juste* and, above all, chose contrasting types of diction that produce the sound of competing voices. Similarly, he contrasted different rhythms within, and instead of, orthodox meters. Together, these characteristics generate the illusions of authenticity, passionate conflict, and transience, a "poetry of the present." *Shock* is often a pejorative term; yet such unconventionalities helped Lawrence seem sincere, brutally honest, energetic, or, in more recent terms, a poet of defamiliarization. One or two critics have defended the polemical element of the poetry, pointing out that modernist irony avoids commitment, whereas the admission of a special interest or "*parti pris*" (as Ellmann expresses it) fully engages a reader's interests.[15] But the poetry's passion for ideas has also succeeded in distracting from its other ways and means. If Lawrence seems more frank or original than other poets, language makes him so. A great deal more could and should be said about his prosody, rhetoric, diction, and tropes. The poetry will reward highly technical discussion, but not until its obvious elements have been identified. The following brief discussions of a few poems may at least indicate where and how these devices are at work.

Criticizing "Snake" (*CP,* pp. 349–51), Ellmann writes, "His dignity can become ministerial; and his understanding of animals and flowers can lead him to lambaste discursively 'the voice of his education' which puts him out of tune with them. . . . the description of the 'Snake' is excellent: . . . [the speaker], 'in pyjamas for the heat,' is bathetic and oppressively moralistic."[16] Yet these two sets of contrasts, between the noble snake and the bathetic speaker, a voice of reverence and the "voice of his [moralizing] education," are exactly what Lawrence meant to produce, not merely to create two opposed worlds of the civilized and the dark unknown, but more delicately to reveal their overlay, the difficulty in discovering the connections between them—a snake that can be at once "horrid" and "a king" (*CP,* p. 351), a speaker moralizing, yet reverential—the possibility for a transformative crossing from one to the next. If these are experienced as a clash between incongruous emotional states, that is all to the good, for this is not merely a conflict in theory. It is a struggle in which anyone, including the speaker, can humbly fail:

> And so, I missed my chance with one of the lords
> Of life.
> And I have something to expiate;
> A pettiness.

(CP, p. 351)

The tension between the lofty and the low is played out to the bitter end in theme and lineation, with the worst crunch in the clipped last line, which appears to be exactly what it confesses, "A pettiness." At the moment that it defeats our expectation of romantic closure, an elevated conclusion, this last line follows inevitably from the difficult logic of this poem as an envenomed final bite.

In earlier, more directly autobiographical verse, Lawrence built himself into his poetry through similar methods. Ronald Draper noticed in "Bei Hennef," for example, that "certain lines . . . taken out of their context, would seem overemphatic, but . . . really belong to the confidence and exaltation of one particular time and place . . . created in the first half dozen lines."[17] In fact, very little need be known about the place and time as long as a sense of the occasion emerges, its "confidence and exaltation." Lawrence built his moment in the same way his predecessors had, through tense-formation and deictics. The latter term, which I take from Jonathan Culler,[18] is especially helpful in describing poems written within the Romantic tradition (in which "deictic" words like *here* and *there, you* and *I, this* and *that* orient the reader). In "Bei Hennef" (*CP,* p. 203), the "twilight" is oriented by such terms and set parallel to "sky" and "river," as if to suggest it were a place ("pain / Gone under the twilight") that might last forever. But the sense of his occasion is also produced, as before, through contrasting diction. The first line is almost cute in the familiar diminutive, the onomatopoeia, and the internal sound-echoes that evoke the river's birdlike chatter, "The little river twittering in the twilight"; the second line is carefully poetic, using poetic convention to suggest the frailty of both mood and expression, "The wan, wondering look of the pale sky"; closing this brief verse paragraph, the third line merges the humble "littleness" of the first with the deliberate lyricism of the second in a plain, bold, yet modest assertion that "This is almost bliss." From this cautiously sentimental mood, the poem rises into an expansive declaration of faith, but always in a common idiom, in everyday terms and simple declarative statements until, in the fifth verse paragraph, it produces a replica of dialogue between "you" and "I":

> *You are the call and I am the answer,*
> *You are the wish, and I the fulfillment,*
> *You are the night, and I the day.*   (ll. 14–16)

The famous last lines break off at a sharp angle from the growing burden of this easy chorus: "What more————? / Strange, how we suffer in spite of this!" Without this last act of severance (shared, at last, in "we"), the former caution and increasing lyricism would be far less credible. Other effects in the poem's conclusion work less visibly, reinforcing the illusion of dialogue within the speaker's mind, between two lovers, between a lover and the unknown, dramatizing his effort to reach for bliss.

"Snake" and "Bei Hennef" are two well-known poems that succeed according to their own devices. Both come from books included in volume 2 of *Collected Poems, Unrhyming Poems:* "Snake" from *Birds, Beasts and Flowers,* and "Bei Hennef" from *Look! We Have Come Through!* The problem of evaluation is most severe, however, for the poetry of *Rhyming Poems*. *Rhyming Poems* represents a 1928 revision of poetry written in several stages in Lawrence's career from 1906 to 1918, and though it is a carefully arranged volume, it has drawn more confusingly various judgments than any other work as a result of inconsistencies among its individual pieces. Critical evaluations of *Unrhyming Poems* are, on the whole, both more consistent and more favorable, and objections to *Unrhyming Poems* are more thoroughly worked out. I will therefore look more closely at two *Rhyming Poems* to suggest how even these may be judged. Auden once claimed that unlike other writers, Lawrence was not able to develop a style until quite late.[19] The term *style* may not be a particularly useful one, especially in the case of Lawrence, who tried out numerous modes and manners. Yet there is a coherent set of characteristics that he came upon as early as any other poet. In the following chapters, I will indicate some highs and lows in his successive books and suggest when and how Lawrence's methods shifted along with his concerns.

"The Appeal" and "Under the Oak" were one poem in manuscript, and though they are separated by much verse in *Rhyming Poems,* both are invocational "appeals" and share symbols of the golden bough. But "The Appeal," originally published in Lawrence's first book, *Love Poems and Others* (1913), is not among its best lyrics of passion; while "Under the Oak," published in *New Poems* (1918), is a successful example of the revisions undertaken for that book, incorporating mythic elements into its amorous landscapes. Neither poem was further revised for *Collected Poems,* except in minor matters of punctuation. Since Lawrence wrote some fine poems in 1913, the difference here is not a matter of timing, but of the ways in which he succeeded or failed at the same game.

"Under the Oak" (*CP,* pp. 130–31) begins with direct address and domestic terms of reproof, incorporating moralism into a realistic conversation. Its second line introduces the contrasting language of mythology. By the end of the first stanza, however, Lawrence has forged these two strains into something more potent than either and has had his speaker rename our categories of language: words like "wonderful" are banal chatter, while the "sensible" are aware of the presence of "dreadful" myth:

> *You, if you were sensible,*
> *When I tell you the stars flash signals, each one dreadful,*
> *You would not turn and answer me*
> *"The night is wonderful."*

His rhythms here are also varied between the short, iambic lines 1, 3, and 4 and the long, loosely anapestic line 2, to underpin the contrast between the common "wonderful," and the unconventional or difficult "dreadful."

In the next stanza (ll. 5–8) Lawrence elaborates his antithesis between the conventional you and the darkly aware I:

Even you, if you knew
How this darkness soaks me through and through, and infuses
Unholy fear in my essence, you would pause to distinguish
What hurts from what amuses.

He jars us here more harshly with two long, run-on median lines and with dissonant end-words—the half-rhyme "you knew" and unrhyming "distinguish" clashing with "infuses" and "amuses." After this the contrast rises into a more consistent rhetoric of urgency as in "Bei Hennef," with distinctions pointed between the insistent storyteller and his song: that is, between direct address in the short initial line and the "story" told at length in stanza 3,

For I tell you
Beneath this powerful tree, my whole soul's fluid
Oozes away . . .

(ll. 9–11)

and, in stanza 4, between his emotion and the facts confronting him, "I tell you my blood runs out on the floor of this oak, / Gout upon gout" (ll. 15–16). Finally, in stanza 5 the conflicts of self with history bear fruit, "Above me springs the blood-born mistletoe / In the shady smoke" (ll. 17–18). The rhymes become pure and simple in this fifth stanza, a b a b, yet not predictable: "mistletoe"/"to and fro," "smoke"/"oak."

But in the meantime, "you" has been left behind; only in the bottom half of this fifth stanza is she again condescendingly remembered, "But who are you, twittering to and fro / Beneath the oak?" (ll. 19–20). The anger expressed at the outset has risen through conflict and misery into cool acknowledgment. Readers may object to anger itself or consider it inappropriate in verse, but the curve of rage has been successfully articulated, and not for the sake of self-expression alone. Rather, the speaker has enacted his own initiation, so that at the end he may earn the right to preach and prophesy. In the last stanza (ll. 21–24) his tone rises again, lifting, not, however, from annoyance to anguish, but from active contempt into an ancient poetic mode, combining visionary retort with demand:

What thing better are you, what worse?
What have you to do with the mysteries
Of this ancient place, of my ancient curse?
What place have you in my histories?

Moreover, this rhetoric has been used not merely so that the speaker may roll into himself, setting externals aside for his inner progress, but so that he may reach "you" and answer the urgent question of where she may be found in his histories. Without you/she these "mysteries" cannot even get off the ground; the initiate requires the contrasting example of the uninitiated, the priest requires the prod of the unenlightened. But it is necessary that the other also define herself dynamically, in opposition to him, "better" or "worse." In each of these aspects, "Under the Oak" is confirmed and extended by the other *Rhyming Poems*. The rage and grief of mourning are expressed in love poems such as this more intensely than in many of the elegies. The speaker of *Rhyming Poems* must recover himself before he will ever find the "hell-queen" of "Autumn Sunshine" (*CP*, p. 177), and he must do so through conflict with and between the living and the dead.

"The Appeal" fails to produce any such mood of conviction or, as Lawrence called it, a "curve of emotion"—a failure, not in prosody, but in diction and metaphor:

> *You, Helen, who see the stars*
> *As mistletoe berries burning in a black tree,*
> *You surely, seeing I am a bowl of kisses*
> *Should put your mouth to mine and drink of me.*
>
> *Helen, you let my kisses steam*
> *Wasteful into the night's black nostrils; drink*
> *Me up, I pray; oh you, who are Night's bacchante,*
> *How can you from my bowl of kisses shrink?*

(*CP*, p. 86)

Here we again find the aggressive dialogue with "you," and there are contrasts in line and rhyme (parallel in the two stanzas): a short quasi-iambic initial line in each stanza, two ragged pentameters, and a smoothly iambic pentameter terminal line in each stanza, with a contrasting rhyme scheme of a b c b, d e b e. These and the juxtapositions of lines in the second stanza add some interest to the frustration expressed in this poem. But this structure does not support any strong contrast in subject or diction. Lawrence unravels a single rhetoric of complaint, in which the first imperative stanza—"You, Helen, who see the stars / . . . , Should put your mouth to mine and drink of me"—is repeated three times in the second stanza, by a declarative statement, another imperative, and a complaining question. Orthodox rhetoric like this catches nothing of plainspoken conversation, nor is it varied by contrast. The awkward and artificial poetic inversion also of the last line, which helps him out with a rhyme, is not justified by anything else in the poem—it might end more believably with a "shriek" than "shrink." So the reader attends only to the mix of imagery—the golden bough, the grail of kisses, the dark beast of night, the bacchante. This mix is no failure in itself. In "Under the Oak" Lawrence brought together the mistletoe and the dying priest more coherently and more faithfully to the original myths than is his normal practice. More often, he conjoined mythic references, contrasting and subduing those also to his history (as in "Snake": "king in exile," "albatross," "god, unseeing," "lord of life"). As it happens, all the images of "The Appeal" show up elsewhere in these poems to greater effect, and they collaborate in the larger mythology of *Rhyming Poems*, but they do not cohere in this instance. An even briefer poem could have been desirable, so that as in Lawrence's imagistic verse (such as "Aware," "A Pang of Reminiscence," or "A White Blossom"), the contrast between what is stated and what is not could become an expressive effect.

For all that, I would not dismiss "The Appeal" from Lawrence's collection. The uneven character and quality of his verse have drawn much criticism, and several defenders of Lawrence's poetry agree that he had "too much to say" to round his ideas into "formal utterance,"[20] or that he "wrote too many poems,"[21] and published "practice verses," "honed and refined to brightness in successful poems on the same subject."[22] Pinto offers the highest praise on this score: "like Wordsworth's, even his bad poems are important, because they are the experiments of a major poet groping his way towards the discovery of a new kind of poetic art" (Introduction to *CP*, p. 21). Lawrence revised and arranged, and meanwhile eliminated, poems even more assiduously than Pinto knew. All the verse of *Rhyming Poems* endured two and sometimes three such tests; and each poem has a place in the final collection, the low points as functional as the high. Like the many lesser poems of Yeats, these ring changes on the symbolism in his books, making it more accessible; while we brood over Yeats's central poems, we also search out the larger weaves of roses or wind. In *Rhyming Poems*, contrast is as necessary to the collection as to its individual pieces, shaping the different "moods" and stages in a history. While anticipating "Under the Oak," "The Appeal" is the pendant of "Return," and together with other invocational and frustrated poems to "Helen" (*CP*, p. 27), it raises the sound of conflict and need just before the central event in this volume, his mother's death. As I will argue below, a coherent mythology, a sense of his place in these "mysteries," jelled only after she died, and that fact finds expression in the final sequence of *Rhyming Poems*.

CHAPTER TWO

—

Youth

EARLY SEQUENCES AND
LOVE POEMS AND OTHERS

CHRONOLOGY:

Student in Nottingham University	1906
First college notebook	1906–8
Teaching post in Croydon	1908
Poems published in the *English Review*	1909
Second college notebook	1909–11
Elopement with Frieda Weekley	1912
"The Schoolmaster" published in the *Saturday Westminster Gazette*	1912
Poems in *Look! We Have Come Through!* to Frieda composed	1912–14
Love Poems and Others published	1913
Marriage	1914

Lawrence wrote his first poetry as a young man unready to leave home, yet anxious to take up the "task of living":

Ah, never let it be said I was poltroon
At this my task of living, this my dream,
This me which is risen out of the spell of sleep,
In white flesh robed to drape another dream.

(from the Juvenilia, CP, p. 870)

The wrestle with his mother's influence began before he entered college in Nottingham in 1906; at his teaching post in London in 1908, he suffered severe homesickness. And such conflicts were exacerbated by his mother's death in 1910. The long melancholy following her death dissipated only when he entered the last struggle of these years—his elopement with Frieda von Richthofen Weekley and her divorce and remarriage in 1914 to Lawrence. Long before these last events, Lawrence had believed himself freed from his mother's parochial orthodoxies and ready to enter a brave new world of sexual and antagonistic partnerships. He had not imagined how difficult it would be, or that the past would haunt him through life. From the start he shaped his art and his life according to a dream of resurrection that would be with him to the end, "this me which is risen."

During the years 1906–14, Lawrence wrote his early love poems, his elegies, and most of the love poems to Frieda, and he published his first book *Love Poems and Others* (1913). Readers of Lawrence in the past have had difficulty negotiating a path through the early poetry, chiefly because they viewed *Rhyming Poems* (volume 1 of *Collected Poems*) as the reflection of a coherent first period. No variorum edition existed, such as is now being compiled by Carole Ferrier and Christopher Pollnitz, to reveal the prior stages of composition. Lawrence's many revisions of the juvenilia, accomplished in a series of stages after 1910 and culminating in *Collected Poems* (1928), require separate study; I will indicate representative cases here.[1] Whereas *Rhyming Poems* includes poems previously revised for publication in four books from 1913 to 1919, and revised again in 1928 for *Collected Poems*, our records of Lawrence's actual production from 1906 to 1914 consist of two college notebooks (Ferrier MSS 1 and 5; Vasey MSS E317 and E320.1), containing late drafts and fair copies of the love poems and elegies, recorded in an unchronological sequence; his first two or three journal publications; and a published book of miscellaneous poems. A third notebook of poems to Frieda is lost. Among dozens of lyrics, Lawrence's notebooks contain his first sequences, mythologized stories of his earliest experiences.[2] The prose writings of these years are interspersed with aesthetic discussions, fledgling efforts to create a "new" subject and form for poetry. Together, these lyrics, verse sequences, and poetics form a coherent period in Lawrence's development, ending in his debut as a published poet.

The juvenilia reveal Lawrence's autobiographical strategy already at work. The earliest versions of his myth are blithely optimistic stories in which he easily transcends the past, and his first experiments in the poetic sequence express the optimism of this story about himself and may be generated by it. Obviously a sequence of lyrics largely complete in themselves, but fitting together to trace an evolution unforeseen by their speaker, is a particularly suitable form in which to treat the transformation of a self.

Lawrence's early sequences and mythic arguments, which have received no critical attention, signal his first steps toward maturity as a poet. By 1914 he was writing a new kind of spiritual autobiography: one that was more compelling in its subject matter, the eruptive moments of passion in which a person changes at the touch or influence of another, and more compelling in poetic method, the alogical, fragmentary verse forms he developed as he entered the literary world of prewar London. In his individual love poems and one late sequence, "The Schoolmaster," he showed himself unafraid to reproduce the rough actualities of his early relationships. Lawrence did not design his first book, *Love Poems and Others,* but he felt it represented him at his best, closing off a cycle in his life, and there is more order to this miscellany than one might expect. *Love Poems and Others* forms a protostory of the poet, a story of repeated crisis.

Part I: Myths of Genesis

To become a writer, Lawrence had first to imagine an immense change in himself. Jessie Chambers records in her memoir the moment when he declared himself a poet:

> Then looking at me with his eyes alight, he said softly:
> "It will be *poetry.*"
> I took fire at that.
> "Well, isn't that the very greatest thing?"
> "Ah, *you* say that," he replied. "But what will the others say? That I'm a fool. A collier's son a poet!"[3]

Even in Jessie's simple narrative, we find Lawrence's ambition for himself laced with self-irony. Later, as a London schoolteacher, he called his college writing "crudely sentimental." (Although he was probably writing poems as early as 1905, the extant poetry dates from the 1906 fair copies in a college notebook.) He believed that this writing harkened back to the past, and that he had gotten beyond all that, as he told Blanche Jennings in a letter of 1908: "When my boyhood—and I was a born boy, cut out for eternal boyishness—began to drop from me as the grains drop one by one from a head of oats, or ten at a time when rudely shaken, then I began to write. Consequently I wrote with crude sentimentality, being sick, having lost the health of my laddishness, all the humour that was the body of my mind's health dead" (*Letters,* 1:50). Anticipating the Note to *Collected Poems* by twenty years, these first comments on writing represent Lawrence engaged in a struggle with the past, in skirmishes that had defeated him as a boy, but that he was besting as a young adult. His self-portrait presents a dual Lawrence, trying to bridge two times in himself, and this image informs all the early autobiographical writings, including any he might have condemned as "sentimental": the mocking mature writer puts behind him a pathetic and defeated youth.

Lawrence had not outgrown the agonies of his youth; on the contrary, he continued throughout these years to be "rudely shaken" growing up. But he wrote many poems that deliberately fictionalized his experience, particularly in his first sequences. These would later be broken up into separate poems for publication, but though mechanical in structure, the sequences experiment with optimistic descriptions of a man's growth. In opposition to Christian pathos and the Wordsworthian myth of memory, Lawrence espoused a doctrine of joyous physical touch and evolved his own myth of child growth, in which man mystically renews himself, shedding his past.

The companion poems "Dreams Old and Nascent: Old" and "Dreams Old and Nascent: Nascent" offer a paradigmatic example. These have an important place in Lawrence's career, for they were among his earliest published work and brought him to the center of literary London. Ford Madox Hueffer, editor of the young, innovative *English Review,* "discovered" Lawrence upon receipt of several school poems combined under the title "A Still Afternoon" (though it was not until Hueffer read the story "Odour of Crysanthemums" that he proclaimed Lawrence a genius).[4] The first of these were "Dreams Old and Nascent," two pieces Lawrence would never neglect. When he revised them for *Collected Poems,* he placed "Dreams Old and Nascent: Nascent" among the last three poems in volume 1, as a manifesto for his countrymen. Together the original poems chart the poet's departure from childhood and resurrection into manhood.

In their published version in the *English Review* (November 1909; reprinted in *CP,* pp. 908–11), the poems divide the story of his growth neatly into two contrasting portraits of himself as a schoolmaster. In "Dreams . . . Old," the young schoolmaster leans on a windowsill and dreams of himself as a lad, who dreams in turn of romantic past lives:

> *among the misty indefinite dreams that range*
> *At the back of my life's horizon, where the dreams from the past lives crowd.*

Over the nearness of Norwood Hill, through the mellow veil
Of the afternoon, glows only the old romance of David and Dora.

(*CP*, p. 908)

This onion-layered moment of introspection, in which imagination is shaped by literature and "old romance," is superseded by the more immediate vision in "Dreams . . . Nascent" of men working in rhythmic unison just outside the window and schoolboys sitting before him: men and boys become a nascent dream "in the flesh":

Here in the subtle, rounded flesh
Beats the active ecstasy, suddenly lifting my eyes
Into quick response.
The fascination of the restless Creator, through the mesh of men
Moving, vibrating endlessly in the rounded flesh
Challenges me, and is answered.

(*CP*, p. 909)

Whereas old dreams remain distant no matter how frequently they are repeated or how much they "crowd" him (*CP*, p. 908), he can find palpable ecstasy in "rounded," shapely flesh.

The space between the two poems implies, but leaves unexplored, complex biographical changes from a sentimental, idealistic, and orthodox past to an ambitious, active, vital present. Lawrence often referred to himself when younger as an idealistic child, governed by his Nonconformist upbringing, and this is the dreamy lad of "Dreams . . . Old." The last lines of that poem say an ironic farewell to his Nonconformist youth: "An endless tapestry the past has woven, drapes / The halls of my life, and compels my soul to conform" (*CP*, p. 909). In contrast, "Dreams . . . Nascent" expresses a fierce pleasure in his portrait of himself in the midst of change. He is "also dream stuff, diffusing myself in the pattern, / Flowing I know not how," in "the power of the melting, fusing force" (*CP*, p. 910), half master of a new generation. Lawrence's typical self-description appears here, as he puts behind his orthodox, nostalgic youth to embrace a self with flexible boundaries, intermingling with mystic Others.

Most readers of Lawrence know of his term as schoolmaster only indirectly through the episodes of *The Rainbow*, where his protagonist Ursula endured the most painful and profound phase of *her* education as a schoolteacher. Lawrence's teaching experiences, however, encouraged him in thinking he possessed a special mission. The briefer schoolroom scenes in the "Class-Room" chapter of *Women in Love* reveal this side of Lawrence, absorbed in teaching "vital facts": "Then he went in among the desks, to see the scholars' books. Ursula watched his intent progress. . . . 'Give them some crayons, won't you?' he said, 'so that they can make the gynae-cious flowers red, and the androgynous yellow. I'd chalk them in plain, chalk in nothing else, merely the red and the yellow. Outline scarcely matters in this case. There is just the one fact to emphasise.'" The young schoolmaster was no less ready to give advice in his poetry. Ursula called his fictional descendant a "priggish Sunday-school" teacher when his ex-positions became too long,[5] and Lawrence's early verse sequences all have a didactic, preacherly enthusiasm.

Underlying Lawrence's myth of relationship in "Dreams . . . Nascent" was his belief that man was fundamentally a communal creature or, as he phrased it in his prose, a creature existing in "sympathy with and submis-sion to the great impulses," conveyed through "feeling." In its naive form, this doctrine states that man achieved bliss by touching someone. In a letter of 1908 to his confidante Blanche Jennings, Lawrence urged her not "to fall out with the homilies of so old a writer as Balzac" when he argued for "touch." So Lawrence sermonized,

> Such a touch is the connection between the vigorous flow of two lives. Like a positive electricity, a current of creative life runs through two persons, and they are instinct with the same life force—the same vitality—the same I know not what—when they kiss on the mouth—when they kiss as lovers do. . . . Then a certain life-current passes through them which changes them forever; another such effect is produced in a mother by the continual soft touchings of her baby. Somehow, I think we come into knowledge (uncon-scious) of the most vital parts of the cosmos through touching things. (*Letters* 1:99)

Although Lawrence later became notorious by condemning the eyes and mouth as the defenses of chastity, in 1908 the kiss had the highest value for him, and he felt bold to say so. In his early mythic poems simple touch satisfied.

Lawrence restated this doctrine of sympathy in a paper on aesthetics, "Art and the Individual" (1908), delivered in Eastwood and Croydon to groups of intellectuals interested in literature and social reform. Defining the purpose of education as "to gain a wide sympathy, in other words, a *many-sided interest,*" Lawrence gave art the correlative mission "to bring us into sympathy with as many men, as many objects, as many phenomena as possible."[6] He summarized much aesthetic thought in this paper, dividing theories of art into two ideas, the "mystical" (represented by Hegel) and the "sensual" (represented by Darwin, Schiller, and Spencer). To these he added a third, art as the medium of feeling, and this third idea rapidly sup-planted the former two, to become an encyclopedic possibility, culminating in universal understanding among men. Lawrence's infinitely mobile art allowed him everything: the poet exemplified a variety of heroisms, both serving and mastering mankind.

In its optimistic form this doctrine omitted the problem of pain. The Christian God diffused himself into a "luminous purpose" and immanent "direction," which Lawrence picked up from Buddhist doctrine ("Corot," *CP,* p. 68). In a letter of 1911 consoling his sister for her loss of faith (following their mother's death), he urged her to believe that "There still remains a God, but not a personal God: a vast, shimmering impulse which wavers onwards towards some end, I don't know what—" (*Letters,* 1:256).[7] Instead of a fatalist separation of God and man, he imagined a vitalist impregnation of man with "unknowable" life and "ultimate purpose." Lawrence's new man, like his new God, was God-in-man.

In keeping with that God, he revised the story of Genesis, to smooth the fall and recover the paradise of physical well-being. In an ambitious manuscript sequence of seven numbered poems entitled "Tranformations" (of which the fourth is a miniseries of three, so that the series actually contains a total of nine poems), the artist has the leading role (Ferrier MS 5; Vasey MS E320.1).[8] A bardic voice urges, then narrates, the dissolution of an urban landscape and the emergence of a new heaven and earth. Lawrence later dismantled the sequence, to retain in *Collected Poems* four middle poems in succession ("Morning Work" followed by "Transformations: I. The Town, II. The Earth, III. Men") and the two last poems as pendants ("Corot" and "Raphael," the latter more accurately retitled "Michael Angelo"). All six had been accomplished enough to be included in *Love Poems and Others,* while the other three titles from the original sequence waited until *New Poems* in 1918. In their final state, these poems record nine, scattered, "inanimate" and "animate," earthly and unearthly episodes. The rearrangement disrupted what had been a fantasial evolution from four poems about modern industrial landscapes, to threefold transformations, and concluding with portraits of earth and men as Corot and Raphael had imagined they could be.

Poems no. 1 through 4 of the original sequence evoked a state of anticipation, owing as much to fairy tale—

> *The red-gold spools of their hands and their faces swinging*
> *Hither and thither across the high crystalline frame*
> *Of day: trolls at the cave of ringing cerulean mining*
>
> ("Morning Work," *CP,* p. 72)

—as to his own creation of a vegetable cityscape, "The new red houses spring like plants . . . / Of reddish herbage that bristles and slants" ("Flat

Suburbs, S.W., in the Morning," *CP,* p. 50). In the central triad he arrived at Whitman's vision of a humanized world:

> Oh labourers, oh shuttles across the blue frame of morning!
> You feet of the rainbow balancing the sky!
>
> . . . . .
>
> Who curl in sleep like kittens, who mass as a swarm
> Of bees that vibrate with revolt; who fall to earth
> And rot like a bean-pod; what are you, oh multiform?
>
> (*CP,* p. 73)

Lawrence's God is multiform, and only the artist can conjure him up, by impassioned prayer in the original version,

> God, give our sunsets a stain of red,
>   Let us pass through the twilight blazed
> With a crimson of anguish
>
> (MS poem no. 1, "Evening")

or by asking, with Blake,

> How is it Someone can conjure thus with you,
>   Whose are the fingers that touched you,
> Whose the mouth that breathed thus into you?
>
> (MS poem no. 4, "The Inanimate that Changes Not in Shape").[9]

The last two poems of the original sequence became in revised forms two of Lawrence's most admired early pieces. In the name of "Corot," he applied Buddhist "immanence" to the earth's portrait:

> The trees rise taller and taller, lifted
> On a subtle rush of cool grey flame.
>
> . . . . .
>
> The grey, plasm-limpid, pellucid advance
> Of the luminous purpose of Life shines out.
>
> . . . . .
>
> Is heard in the windless whisper of leaves,
> In the silent labours of men in the field,
> In the downward-dropping of flimsy sheaves.
>
> . . . . .
>
> Ah listen, for silence is not lonely!
> Imitate the magnificent trees
> That speak no word of their rapture, but only
>   Breathe largely the luminous breeze.
>
> (*CP,* pp. 68–69)

Although the language of this poem is at times heavy with Lawrencean doctrine, its stanzas advance with an effectively controlled repetition that is rare among the juvenilia. Lawrence makes silence "breathe largely" in lines reminiscent of Shelley's "Ode to the West Wind": "In the tapping haste of a fallen leaf, / In the flapping of red-roof smoke" (*CP*, p. 68). But in "Corot" we are asked only to "imitate" the trees; in "Raphael" we become men. These lines took on the Blakean rhetoric of poem no. 4 when Lawrence revised them for *Collected Poems:* "Who shook thy roundness in his finger's cup? / Who sunk his hands in firmness down thy sides?" (*CP*, p. 69). In the original version, Adam gave birth by touch alone to an un-Darwinian succession of manly men. Created by God with a kiss and producing the generations in direct descent, this Adam transvalues the culpable kiss and elides the fall.

In addition to changing Genesis, these poems offer a revisionary aesthetic, drawing upon other artists where they are useful, otherwise correcting them. The manuscript sequence "Movements" (Ferrier MS 1; Vasey MS E317) openly alters Wordsworth's account of child growth. As in "Dreams Old and Nascent" the five-poem sequence offers a neat scheme of evolution from boy to man. But here Lawrence portrays five perfect moments in human intercourse: the speaker dandles a baby in two poems and in the third discovers his own body, then in poem no. 4 a man distinct from the speaker playfully intercepts a woman, and in poem no. 5 a host of men responds univocally to their general.[10] The evolutionary schemes of "Dreams Old and Nascent," "Transformations," and "Movements" all substitute Whitman's immediate sensual relationships for nostalgic and desirous connections in memory. Man spirals outward into community, rather than mourning his ever-greater distance from the womb.

When Lawrence revised the second poem of "Movements" for publication with "Dreams Old and Nascent" in the *English Review*, he laid bare its allusion to Wordsworth by titling it "'Trailing Clouds.'" A baby, who in the first poem of "Movements" appeared lightly kicking up her heels, in this poem hangs limply on the narrator's arm. A similar allusion appears in Lawrence's first novel, *The White Peacock*, where he teases the child Emily (a fictionalization of Jessie Chambers) in one of her gloomy moods, classifying her as one of those people who, not trailing "clouds of glory, trail clouds of shadow."[11] Next to that plain and unironic glance at Wordsworth's great ode, Lawrence's allusion in "Movements" is poised with complex ironic intent. The baby's limp body is an image of ripe vegetable pathos, as palpable as the baby at play:

> She who has always seemed so light
>> Sways on my arm like sorrowful, storm-heavy boughs,

Even her floating hair sinks like storm-bruised young leaves
Reaching downwards:
    As the wings of a drenched, drowned bee
    Are a heaviness, and a weariness.

(CP, p. 916)

Wordsworth's happy egotistical baby is corrected by Lawrence into a baby with an intimate and changeable responsiveness. Wordsworth's baby is a portentous image of a lost, harmonious past; Lawrence's little girl is an image of herself, her present glory or her sudden thoughtless fall. Nor does Lawrence adopt Wordsworth's distanced meditative stance; his persona participates, enchanted, watching the child lingeringly in the first poem, fondling her in the second.

Lawrence cut apart the sequence of "Movements," abandoning its easy evolutionism and transforming its pieces into frankly personal anecdotes. Set within "Movements," "'Trailing Clouds'" is a stage in every man's education. Returned to its first title, "A Baby Asleep after Pain," and placed in the autobiographical *Amores* and *Collected Poems*, it becomes a snapshot of the motherless, childless Lawrence, bent over his landlord's baby. ("A Baby Running Barefoot," and "'Trailing Clouds'" were originally published with "Dreams Old and Nascent" and with "Discipline," another schoolroom story, in the *English Review*.) The third piece, "The Body Awake" (later "Virgin Youth"), achieved the greatest notoriety of the bunch when, following publication of *Lady Chatterley's Lover*, Lawrence revised it into a festive phallic rite.

Poems no. 4 and 5 received no such attention. The fourth, "A Man at Play on the River," was abandoned, a rare gesture of omission, while Lawrence kept the fifth waiting until 1918, when he renamed it "Guards" and revised it to fit into the impersonal war poetry of *Bay*. It is impossible to know why he distanced himself from these poems: perhaps he was uneasy about their debt to Whitman. So close are they to the parent artist, they may have struck him as derivative. Sandra Gilbert demonstrated this affinity in the fourth piece, the whimsical "A Man at Play on the River."[12] Two sentences in Lawrence's poem divide between them forty-one lines like the following:

Flashing his bright, brown arms as he leans on the pole,
His blue shirt glimmering in the water among the shadow of trees,
Threading the round joy of his white-flanneled hips full of play,
Up the river, under the trees,
Down the river, in the gleam of the sun,

Across the river, bending low
In one swift bound to the house-boat.

(*CP*, pp. 866–67)

"Whitmanesque" was Lawrence's own term for poems like these, and as Jessie Chambers remembered: "Whitman's *Leaves of Grass* was one of his great books."[13] In its original form, the fifth poem, "The Review of the Scots Guards," bares its allegiance to Whitman even more overtly than "A Man at Play on the River":

Yet the soldiers move more sweetly, they are like the singing murmur of trees
They gather like the sound of trees all swinging to the wind,
They waver like the scent of honeysuckle spreading abroad at night,
They vibrate nearer, till the red blood in the veins
Reels under the rhythm of their approach
And the heart beats in time to them, and the blood sways to the beat.[14]

The myth of sensual vitalism, which Lawrence chose as a basis for human development, healing the individual and collective mind, was derived in these poems from Whitman.

Lawrence's descriptions of child and social development simplified, of course, the problems explored by the Romantics when they redefined their relationship to nature. He gained a sense of immediacy in "Movements" and "Dreams Old and Nascent" by smoothing over dissonant thoughts that Wordsworth faced. The baby's experience of a fall in "Movements" occurs (as in "Dreams Old and Nascent") in the blank space between the first two poems. The relationships between man and woman, man and man, are unblemished. But as a young writer in Edwardian England, Lawrence was reacting primarily to late Victorian romanticism, not to the great Romantics. He could gaily correct Wordsworth because Lawrence's struggle lay closer to home: "I want to write live things, if crude and half formed, rather than beautiful dying decadent things, with sad odors" (*Letters*, 1:108). If Lawrence's way of dealing with loss was to ignore it, turning his back on the past, this response nonetheless freed him to develop his own subjects for poetry and his own theories of form. Lawrence's criticisms late in 1910 of the minor Pre-Raphaelite Rachel Annand Taylor reveal a reasoned rejection of her "old dreams." Taylor has "begun to dream of her past life" and

to tell her dreams in symbols which are not always illuminating. She is esoteric. Her symbols do not show what they stand for of themselves: they are cousins of that Celtic and French form of symbolism which says—"Let X = the winds of passion, and Y = the yearning of the soul for love"

Now the dim, white petalled Υ
Draws dimly over the pallid atmosphere
The scalded kisses of X.

This "may claim to sound well, but to me it is meaningless" (*Phoenix II*, 219). A comment made directly to Taylor discloses the deeper object behind his distrust of late-Victorian forms: "Why do you persist in separating soul and body? I can't tell, in myself, or in anybody, one from the other" (*Letters*, 1:185).

Lawrence eventually faced the problem of discord and pain in his mythic poems. His earliest attempts in 1908 to explain relationships to Blanche Jennings in terms of "harmonies" and "discords" expressed the usual optimism: "Love is much finer, I think, when not only the sex group of chords is attuned, but the great harmonies, and the little harmonies, of what we call religious feeling," but he doubted whether "the chords of sex, and the fine chords of noble feeling do not inevitably produce a discord" (*Letters*, 1:66–67). Although the most unusual of his manuscript sequences, "A Life History in Harmonies and Discords" (Ferrier MS 5; Vasey MS E320.1), is illegible at many points, this long poem appears to be a remnant sample of a more elaborate philosophy he was working out for himself, drawn chiefly from the physiological descriptions of Francois Bichat.[15] Only "Discord in Childhood" and "Twenty Years Ago" survived Lawrence's cancellations of "A Life History," and he regretted the loss, recalling it in the first draft of his Note to the *Collected Poems:* "I must have burnt many poems that had the demon fuming in them. The fragment *Discord in Childhood* was a long poem, probably was good, but I destroyed it" (*CP*, p. 850). Lawrence also refers to it in his play *A Collier's Friday Night*, where he recreates a scene from his youth, discussing with Jessie Chambers verses he had just written:

ERNEST: That one, "A Life History," is the best.
MAGGIE (wondering): Yes?
ERNEST (smiling): It is. It means more. Look how full of significance it is, when you think of it. The profs. would make a great long essay out of the idea. Then the rhythm is finer: it's more complicated.[16]

"A Life History in Harmonies and Discords" (eleven poems) illustrates a doctrine that would become the cornerstone of Lawrence's later philosophic views: that fluctuating forces of destruction and creation are conveyed in the blood. Because key words and lines in every poem are heavily blacked over, it is impossible to reconstruct the entire sequence, but it is clear that he wished to fit his life history into a symbolic framework. The pathos of "Third Harmony" (which became "Twenty Years Ago" in *New Poems*)—"At a mother's knees, the trouble / Lost all its meaning" (*CP*, p. 152)—is swept aside in "Discord" (retitled "Discord in Childhood" in *Amores*), which immediately follows. "Discord in Childhood" is well known for its parallel to a scene in *Sons and Lovers*. Even in its unfinished state in "A Life History," this narrative of parental discord, overheard by the son, is unsettling—no less so when, in this version, his mother appears unconquered:

> *a swift thin lash*
> *Whistling, and a thick lash sweeping with a booming dreadful . . .*
> *Hoarser roared the heavy anger*
> *Hoarser after each hiss and bite*
> *Frayed, . . .*
> *. . . unable to requite.*[17]

A simple philosophic paradigm governs all fluctuations throughout the sequence:

> *Hastening always urgent to the new dark Cherubim*
> *Came the scalding blood, gladly, to the service of the Dim One, and drowned it*
> *In a passionate scarlet flood.*
>
> ("*First Harmony*") [18]

Lawrence's sequence alternates poems of "harmony" with poems of "discord," recording childhood as an oscillation between states of the blood. His narration stops just short of representing his maturer creed of a communion in strife.

After the "Last Harmony" another poem appears in the notebook, fortunately legible, which Lawrence may have intended to replace a middle poem. "Kiss" stands, unpublished by Lawrence and without comment (retitled "A Kiss" in *CP*), a cheerful last word to "A Life History." In "Kiss" opposites merge in a state of blissful touch:

> *A red flower falls to its red reflection,*
> *The shadow dances up in affection,*
> *And two are one in sweet connection,*
> *—Never a sound was heard.*
>
> (*CP*, p. 892)

Like body and soul, the antinomies meet, becoming palpable halves of one whole. The Eastern influence is rarely visible in Lawrence's actual poetic practice. Japanese poetry did not have the positive impact that it had on Pound, because Lawrence's acquaintance was more superficial. Writing in

1913 to Edward Marsh, Lawrence broadcast a debt to Noguchi, who was a popular but insubstantial writer, one who must have encouraged Lawrence in the development of a spare style, but could not guide his way. Yet Lawrence called him a Japanese Whitman (*Letters,* 2:61). The effects in Lawrence's "Kiss" have an Eastern simplicity, eliminating discord. A perfect closure is obtained through counterpointed imagery: a flower falls, and its shadow dances up in instant response.

The moment is curiously narcissistic: an image communes with itself. Lawrence was aware of such narcissism in his verse and again rewrote the myth—stopping with the moment when Narcissus touches water and substituting for the old story of fatal opposition his own faith in relationship. In an early version of the poem "Narcissus," the speaker recalls his boyhood "sensation of playing in fellowship with the minnows," and in contradistinction to Wordsworthian memory, he claims that

> *those wistful, childish rambles*
> *Took me further into the run of life than all these reflections.*
>
> *Robes falling in sumptuous fold*
> *Hang dignity round a naked man;*
> *Vestment of knowledge and thought hold*
> *The free-leaping soul, which untrammeled began.*[19]

"The free-leaping soul" is equated here with the naked body of a man. In Lawrence's new myth, soul may be made flesh, opposites may reunite, an attitude of defeatism may be reversed, and change may result in the accretion, not the loss, of tangible joys.

Part II: Crude Forms of Love

Although there are glimpses of great energy in the early sequences, the myths Lawrence invented at this time were mostly sentimental. In later sequences he would no more than imply a teleological scheme, and he would find a virtue in discontinuity. But even in the early years, in the midst of mythmaking, he was discovering a more directly autobiographical subject in the crises of love, and he seized upon a "crude" form (*Letters,* 1:108) to express these. In his love poems and in a last sequence of school poems, he replaced logically continuous narratives with a symbolic method, abrupt dreamlike shifts, and clashes in mood. Lawrence's urge to give form to change made brevity a characteristic feature of these poems. He never wrote a poem longer than Poe would have approved—only groups and sequences of short poems. The group that formed his first book is the final product of this early period. I deviate from what will be my usual practice by discussing poems in this section individually before looking at them in the context of *Love Poems and Others;* all the verse I will examine appeared there eventually.

Two crosscurrents of the contemporary art world stimulated Lawrence's self-definition: on one hand the international circle of Ford Madox Hueffer, Pound, and the symbolists; on the other, poets adhering to a regionalist British tradition (not necessarily native to England) like Hardy and Meredith, Synge and Burns. Commentators like to point out that Lawrence published in anthologies by both the Imagists and the Georgians. In August 1913 he sent along some "futuristic" verse to Harold Monro. He belonged to everyone and no one.[20]

Hueffer introduced him to many writers, including Pound, and to the doctrine of "impersonality." In 1910 Lawrence modeled himself after Flaubert, Maupassant, and Baudelaire, anxiously chiseling out an impersonal form for his novels: "those who belong to the accurate-impersonal school of Flaubert will flourish large shears over my head and comb my head very close: so I will not crow" (*Letters,* 1:169). Revising his poems for publication in *Love Poems and Others,* he cut his "long curls" to give them a spare dramatic shape. His "best" poems were "impersonal" (*Letters,* 1:340). Baudelaire is an unusual third party to the group of three "impersonal" writers listed above, his poetry notable less for chill, accurate observation than for the synesthetic rendering of illicit experience. Lawrence had been reading the symbolists long before he entered the art scene in London, and the symbolists, rather than the Imagists, were the shaping influence behind his verse, with Baudelaire rather than Verlaine the model. His was the impersonality, not of an unemotional objectivity or satiric distance, which Verlaine and T. S. Eliot practiced, but of impersonal passion. Lawrence's revisions of the poems from "Transformations" reveal this shift from communal sympathy to superpersonal passion. All the pieces become sparer in *Love Poems and Others,* none more so than "Michael Angelo." By cutting off the final five stanzas, Lawrence effectively eliminated Adam's male genealogy, to end instead with the kiss:

> *God, lonely, put down His mouth in a kiss of creation,*
> *He kissed thee, O Man, in a passion of love, and left*
> *The vivid life of His love in thy mouth and thy nostrils;*
> *Keep then the kiss from the adultress' theft.*

(*CP,* p. 919)

In an unsigned review of *Contemporary German Poetry* published by the *English Review* in November 1911, Lawrence chose the German poets as antagonists, teasing them for peering voyeuristically into corners Baudelaire had lit up for view. English poets should write frankly about "sex passion" as the symbolists had done. Some native writers, like John Synge, had already called for "brutalizing" poetry. Lawrence alludes here to the Preface of *Poems and Translations,* where Synge demands greater realism and less artifice in poetry.[21] Lawrence also considered Hardy and Meredith forerunners, roughening the texture of English poetry. The teasing tone of voice at the start of this essay escalates into a passionate, rough-hewn rhetoric when it reaches the heart of its argument, the proper subject for art. Nowhere is Lawrence's image of sex more "brutal":

> With Baudelaire, Verlaine, and Verhaeren, poetry seems to have broken out afresh, like a new crater. These men take life welling out hot and primitive. . . . Why do we set our faces against this tapping of elemental passion? It must, in its first issuing, be awful and perhaps, ugly. But what is more essentially awful and ugly than Oedipus? And why is sex passion unsuited for handling, if hate passion, and revenge passion, and horror passion are suitable, as in Agamemnon and Oedipus, and Medea. Hate passion, horror passion, revenge passion no longer move us so violently in life. Love passion, pitching along with it beauty and strange hate and suffering, remains the one living volcano of our souls.[22]

This is the first record of such a statement (its publication precedes Lawrence's meeting with Frieda by four months), and it is made with a fresh revolutionary fervor that would later be common in his pronouncements on art. Lawrence's mythic ideal is no longer painless encounter: the passionate concourse of man and woman is a catastrophic event that rives the self.

Lawrence's letters of 1910 reveal his growing need to define an aesthetic persona for himself that will not be pathetic or defeatist, and to justify himself—especially to the young women he cast in opposing roles. After a visit to an art exhibit, he wrote admonitory letters to several female correspondents, and from one letter to the next, these two terms, the "pathetic" and the "sardonic," reappear, peppering his remarks, identified respectively as old and new ways of seeing, until at last he uses them to point the difference between others and himself: "In the old pictures sorrow is beautiful; in the new it is awful—Bastien Lepage; the old is the divine sorrow of fruitfulness, the new is the cruel sorrow of destruction. Louisa, my dear, thou art a century or so behind—and I am at the tip of the years. So thou art very comfortable and charming and I am uncomfortable and a nuisance" (*Letters,* 1:124). As opposed to a resigned, sympathetic, and distant approach, as in *Pauvre Fauvette* by Lepage, Lawrence demands the bold, iconoclastic attitude he finds in Sargent. Pauvre Fauvette, like Louisa herself, is an example of pathos to be corrected and ultimately discarded.

In *Sons and Lovers* Lawrence staged the relationship between his fictional counterpart, Paul, and Jessie's alias, Miriam, as a conflict between aesthetic contraries, between Baudelaire and Wordsworth. Miriam is depicted as a broodingly spiritual personality (as always in this novel), whose preference for Wordsworth draws Paul's ire: "It was a beauteous evening, calm and pure, / And breathing holy quiet like a nun." In rebuke, Paul recites Baudelaire to her: "Tu te rappeleras la beauté des caresses" (p. 209). Since Paul has been teaching Miriam French, without much patience for the task, his character attack is peculiarly hurtful. The schoolmaster has little sympathy left for his pupil.

It was the struggle itself between antithetical personalities that was becoming the subject and passion of Lawrence's art. Like the passage from *Sons and Lovers,* many of the poems rehearse this clash of antinomies, though these are almost exclusively love poems. "Cherry Robbers" (known for its parallel to a scene in *Sons and Lovers*) shifts from one perspective to another to produce violent discord: from the apparition of a tree hung with cherries, to three dead birds spattered with blood, to a girl laughingly offering the narrator red fruit. In the swift move from the gory birds to the pastoral girl, it is as if one image had attacked the next:

> Under the glistening cherries, with folded wings
>> Three dead birds lie:
> Pale-breasted throstles and a blackbird, robberlings
>> Stained with red dye.
>
> Against the haystack a girl stands laughing at me,
>> Cherries hung round her ears.
> Offers me her scarlet fruit: I will see
>> If she has any tears.

(CP, pp. 36–37)

In the sardonic closing lines these contraries take on a human edge; with the narrator's intrusion, the impersonal attack on the girl becomes personal. The balladlike effects of the gratuitous conjunction of the bloody birds with a sentimental landscape were common enough in nineteenth-century verse, but the movement through these images is Lawrence's. The half-innocent, "robberling" girl is to be "stained" by tears.

Sandra Gilbert singles out "Cherry Robbers" as one of the best early poems because here "the mystery with which he invests things and happenings is no longer the flush of feeling, pure and simple, but the shadow of tensely conflicting impulses." Gilbert believes, however, that irony and complex plot-making are inessential, even distracting, to the early Lawrence who, when he obeyed what she calls a fundamentally lyric impulse, transmitted "the mystery in things and happenings." The "novelist" in

Lawrence intervenes effectively when he enables the "poet" to focus on a situation of "hidden mysteries," not on the dramatic twists of plot and without "deliberate irony."[23] But these are differences primarily in degree, not kind. Like his more ironical contemporaries, Eliot and Pound, Lawrence exercised his talents on brief verse narratives or monologues rather than on controlled verse forms, and though his sense of irony differed from Prufrock's, he exposed disjunctions in "things and happenings." Rather than focusing on the gap between an immediate emotional, or "subjective," perspective and a distanced, or "objective," stance, Lawrence pointed to the disjunction between two emotional moments. When we read Eliot or Hardy, we wince and become stoical. When we read Lawrence, we wince and wince again.

The poem "Renascence" is less widely known than "Cherry Robbers," yet is an effective example of his methods, and since an early version was enclosed in a letter where Lawrence argues for "crude" form, the poem may introduce his conscious aesthetic reformation (*Letters*, 1:110–11). "Renascence" coyly sets aside the Miltonic account of creation and Miltonic form—replacing the epic with a brief, emotional poem, which elides the fall of man and inscribes a paradise "wider" than Eden. Unlike "Raphael" and Lawrence's simpler mythic poems, "Renascence" shifts alogically and disorients time, setting, and emotional norms.

As in the versions that follow, the first casual line in this early version turns back history, countering the Christian version of man's original fall: "We have bit no forbidden apple." Having defied history, Lawrence narrates no new causal series of events, but suspends his narrative, telling us only that his "valley" is "no longer" the same, not saying how, when, or why it changed. The scene is timeless, though full of transformations:

> We have bit no forbidden apple—
> Eve and me—
> Yet the splashes of day and night
> Falling round us no longer dapple
> The same Eden with purple and white.
>
> This is our own still valley,
> My Eden, my home.
> But the day shows it vivid with feeling
> And the pallor of night does not tally
> With the dark sleep that once covered the ceiling.

Although the next two stanzas locate the narrative in a definite time, between them the poem jumps from "tonight" in a violent barnyard, "Take the lantern, and watch the sow, for fear she grab her new litter / With red snarling jaws," to "morning" and a pacific landscape, "And wake to the sound of the wood-pigeons" (*Letters*, 1 : 110–11). Lawrence has suppressed the implied movement through time and the causal connection between stanzas.

We learn in the last two stanzas the cause, but more crucially we receive a referent for the poem's contradicting images—the innocent kiss:

> *I didn't learn from her speech—*
> *Staggering words.*
> *I can't tell how it comes*
> *But I think her kisses reach*
> *Down where the live web hums.*
>
> (*Letters*, 1 : 110–11)

In the 1912 revision of this poem, there is no "kiss," but the penultimate stanza remains to provide an interpretive key: "I learned it all from my Eve." The poem's crisis—Adam encountering Eve—is a moment of fused feelings, which in the revised Whitmanesque version, "change and quiver: / And all things seem to tally." [24]

In the 1928 version Lawrence intensifies the "change" once again, so that the landscape "tallies" not just "with something in me," but with "the clash of a river":

> *So now I know the valley*
>   *Fleshed all like me*
> *With feelings that change and quiver*
> *And clash, and yet seem to tally,*
> *Like all the clash of a river*
>   *Moves on to the sea.*
>
> (*CP*, p. 38)

Lawrence's letters to Blanche Jennings show him conscious from the first of the effect he wanted and a method to gain it. In his first mention of poetry to her in July 1908, he contradicts nothing less than Verlaine's "L'art poétique":

> My verses are tolerable—rather pretty, but not suave; there is some blood in them. Poetry now a days seems to be a sort of plaster-cast craze, scraps sweetly moulded in easy Plaster of Paris sentiment. Nobody chips verses earnestly out of the living rock of his own feeling: You know Verlaine's famous verse . . . [here he quotes and translates "L'art poétique," lines 1–4]. Something undecided, vague, suggestive. I like it, but will not practise it. Before everything I like sincerity, and a quickening spontaneous emotion. I do not worship music or the "half said thing." (*Letters*, 1 : 63)

In "Art and the Individual," the rock of Lawrence's church was sympathetic, spontaneous emotion. Here he calls for harshly tangible art, "chipped" from feeling. One is reminded of Pound's kindred notions of what "the 'age demanded'" in "Hugh Selwyn Mauberley," "chiefly a mould in plaster, / Made with no loss of time," but whereas Mauberley asked for "alabaster," Lawrence answered with "blood" more often than with rock.[25] His love for blood had its roots, as we have seen, in nineteenth-century anatomical studies. Blood had also the appeal of mystery—unseen in the body—and this separated Lawrence sharply from Pound. In the letter (January 1909) that contained "Renascence," Lawrence directly linked "mystery" with the power of art. The gist is that poetry cannot express life through abstraction, but must somehow embody "mystery" in concrete things: "All mysteries and possibilities lie in things and happenings, so give us the things and happenings, and try just to show the flush of mystery in them, but don't begin with a mystery and end with a foolish concrete thing, like taking Death and making a figure with 'yellow topaz eyes—each a jewel.'" For his example of how to achieve the right effect, Lawrence describes the painting *Love and Death* by Watts: "its beauty lies in the aesthetic unknowable effect of line, poise, shadow, and then in the blurred idea that Death is shrouded, but a dark, embracing mother, who stoops over us, and frightens us because we are children" (*Letters*, 1:107). Watts's effect is not in fact unanalyzable in Lawrence's account: Watts places a woman in a fearful pose and manner—hovering over the onlooker, larger than he, darkly embracing. Her histrionic gesture, maternal and threatening, induces Gilbert's "tensely conflicting emotions." In "Renascence" when Lawrence juxtaposes clashing images of violence and passivity, the vicious sow "mysteriously" subsumed to a pacific landscape, he exposes the reader to the same invigorating clash of feelings that inform his unstable self-portraits: Lawrence's "commonplace me" shaken by the demon.

Lawrence later called this method intuitive. In a letter of 1914 disputing Harriet Monroe's criticism of "Ballad of Another Ophelia" (eventually collected in *Amores* and *Collected Poems*), he argued that "dream symbolism" moves "instinctively" rather than logically through changing mental states. (Carole Ferrier notes that Pound helped initiate the correspondence with Monroe, who published many poems by Lawrence, in *Poetry*, beginning in January 1914 with those to Frieda.)[26] "Why oh why do you want to cut off the tail of poor Ophelia's ballad. Don't you see the poor thing is cracked, and she used all those verses—apples and chickens and rat—according to true instinctive or *dream* symbolism. This poem—I am very proud of it— has got the quality of a troublesome dream that seems incoherent but is selected by another sort of consciousness. The latter part is the waking up part, yet never really awake, because she is mad" (*Letters*, 2:203). Today the stream of consciousness and madman narrator are clichés, but Lawrence's remarks catch him at a definitive point in his aesthetic, the moment at which he adopts symbolist methods and transposes the monologues of Tennyson and Browning. By no means did he discard narrative continuity altogether. Lyric and dramatic monologues prevented his poems from ever becoming "music or the 'half said thing'" and offered vehicles for the clash of man and woman. Lawrence clearly is unapologetic when he describes his poem as "a troublesome dream" and calls his protagonist mad. Like his predecessors, he had great sympathy for mad Ophelia—more, indeed, than he had for saner young ladies.

The difference is that Lawrence deflected attention from the moral crimes against Ophelia to her constraining morality. He represented the battle between woman and man as a timid, spiritualized morality fending off an aggressive, yearning, and spontaneous nature. Tennyson's monodrama *Maud* is a classic example to contrast with Lawrence's verse (*Maud* influenced T. S. Eliot's *The Waste Land* as well as Lawrence's *Look! We Have Come Through!*). Tennyson's speaker is mad with many emotions: with love for a woman socially above him, with hate for her condescending brother, and finally, with guilt after killing her brother in a duel. In Lawrence's dramatic monologues, such as "Ballad of Another Ophelia" and "Love on the Farm," his crazed speakers are barely able to leave their homes; barnyard violence seems to them larger than life. But if feeling terrifies them, that terror brings them to the verge of other passions and the sex conflict. The dialect poems—for example, "A Collier's Wife" and "Whether or Not"—focus on manipulative women, figures of morality and cold control. In his lyric monologues, however, Lawrence speaks in his own impassioned voice. The "kiss" that "hummed" in "Renascence," proves in "Lightning" to be fatal to a "good" woman:

> I leaned in the darkness to find her lips
>   And claim her utterly in a kiss,
> When the lightning flew across her face
> And I saw her for the flaring space
>   Of a second, like snow that slips
> From a roof, inert with death, weeping "Not this! Not this!"

(CP, p. 62)

Critics have often drawn an analogy between Lawrence's early monologues and Hardy's similarly "brutal" poems. In contrast, compare it with the less personal crisis of *Maud*, which occurs just after the murder:

And there rises ever a passionate cry
From underneath in the darkening land—
What is it, that has been done?
O dawn of Eden bright over earth and sky,
The fires of hell brake out of thy rising sun,
The fires of hell and of hate.[27]

Maud conceals its author behind a mask, to create a distanced form for rage, and when Tennyson's speaker goes mad, he fantasizes an exploding, vengeful cosmos. Lawrence's more controlled reaction in "Lightning" is edged as sharply against his lover and himself as against their world:

Almost I hated her, sacrificed;
Hated myself, and the place, and the iced
Rain that burnt on my rage.

(*CP*, p. 62)

In the version in *Love Poems and Others*, Lawrence had phrased his complaint even more distinctly, "Almost I hated her, she was so good" (*Love Poems*, p. 20). Stripping off masks, Lawrence presents his conflicts with others or within himself as a mode of passionate concourse.

Lawrence wrote one sequence composed entirely of internal monologues, entering seven poems under the title "The Schoolmaster." This sequence was less schematic, less doctrinaire, than its predecessors. It was sufficient to imply his doctrines in an account of himself, in a state of siege with his pupils. The sequence appeared serially in the *Saturday Westminster Gazette* (1912), and its appeal to the public obviously lay in its authenticity—the experiences of a schoolmaster at first hand. The sequence was never republished by Lawrence in its entirety (though it has been reprinted by Pinto in *The Complete Poems*, pp. 897–903). But the occasion of its first publication had special significance for Lawrence, and the sequence vividly reembodies his classroom trials. It was the last of his early sequences, finished and prepared for publication when he had decided to quit teaching and published just after he eloped with Frieda. Lawrence's alternative title for it, "Heart of a School-Teacher" (rejected by the *Gazette* editor), highlights his idea of the poems as a poetic diary, which, like his later books, presents "the story of my heart" (*Letters*, 1:382–84).

"The Schoolmaster" sequence is framed by a brief first poem, "To one of my boys," in which Lawrence is almost seduced by the disarming strength of "laddishness" in one of his pupils, and a lengthy last poem, "The Best of School," in which he emerges a triumphant schoolmaster who can leave the classroom behind. In both pieces the speaker links his own activity to the vitality of his pupils; the second poem records a moment in which he is strengthened by them and they by him. He enjoys these episodes, aware of their tentative nature, confident at the end that

> *it keeps*
> *Me comforted to feel the warmth that creeps*
> *Up dimly from their striving; it heartens my strife.*
>
> ("The Best of School," *CP*, p. 903)

Between these endposts, Lawrence entertains more painful recognitions:

> *three score*
> *Of several insults of blotted pages and scrawl*
> *Of slovenly work that they have offered me.*
>
> ("Afternoon: The Last Lesson," *CP*, p. 898)

The middle poems would seem unordered if it were not for their titles, which indicate that day is passing and that Lawrence's mood is not improving: "Morning: Scripture Lesson," "Afternoon: The Last Lesson," "Evening," "The Punisher," "A Snowy Day in School." The single piece conforming to a strict verse form, the rondeau "Evening," uses its rotund measures to mimic the teacher's boredom: "The hours have tumbled their lustreless, tarnished sands: . . . / I carry my anger sullenly 'cross these waste lands" (*CP*, p. 899).

"The Schoolmaster" records the genesis and struggles not only of the schoolmaster's authority but of his self-expression, a theme that makes this sequence something more than a diary. The sixth poem, for example, recreates a failing dialogue between the speaker and his students. He is dwarfed by cosmic circumstances; confronting, not his students, but silence; alternately tempted and threatened by its engulfing presence: "My God, I must break from this hoarse silence." Everything in the poem points toward that moment when the "mere man" will fall silent:

> *I must look*
> *Them an answer back. It is more than I can bear.*
>
> *The snow descends. . . .*
> *And all things are possessed by silence.*
>
> ("A Snowy Day in School," *CP*, p. 901).

The poet-teacher is seized by conflicting impulses to speak and to yield, to command and to surrender command, a trial that ceases only temporarily when the particular occasion ends. In the logic of this sequence, endings create new occasions for conflict and new poems.

Along with Lawrence's other classroom verse, the poems from "The Schoolmaster" traveled a complex route through his books. In addition to "A Still Afternoon" and "The Schoolmaster," Lawrence experimentally grouped four poems in his second college notebook under the title "School," but he abandoned all these groupings when he gathered them into his books. Three poems from "The Schoolmaster"—"A Snowy Day in School," "The Best of School," and "Afternoon in School" (nos. 6, 7, 3)—found their way into *Love Poems and Others*, where they form the last section, again titled "The Schoolmaster." "The Punisher" (no. 5) was reserved to be reprinted with those from "A Still Afternoon" in *Amores*. A fifth, "Evening" (no. 4), became, after slight rephrasings, a poem about the war, "Rondeau of a Conscientious Objector," collected in *Bay*. (The analogy was not entirely accidental, since Lawrence is a conscientious nonconformist in both settings.) "To one of my boys" (no. 1) and "Morning: Scripture Lesson" (no. 2) were not reprinted (perhaps because they overlapped with "Dreams . . . Old" and "Discipline"). In their final state in *Rhyming Poems*, volume 1 of *Collected Poems*, the pieces from *Love Poems and Others* and *Amores* became part of a classroom series, staggered in three phases, and measuring, not the progressive triumph of the schoolmaster, but his deepening sense of education's unruly, abundant battleground—a sequence that can be gleaned from the titles: *RP*, nos. 21–22, "The Best of School" and "Dreams . . . Old"; *RP*, nos. 46–48, "Last Lesson of the Afternoon," "School on the Outskirts," and "A Snowy Day in School"; and *RP*, nos. 57–59, "Prophet," "Discipline," and "The Punisher."

Lawrence did not select or organize the pieces in *Love Poems and Others*, and he had mixed reactions to the selection it offers, but the book gives a full-length portrait of the debutant poet. Two editors, Walter De la Mare and David Garnett, worked on the book; De la Mare passed it on to Edward Garnett of Duckworth's when Heinemann rejected the volume, and Garnett then gave it to his son David to edit. There is no indication of changes made by David Garnett in De la Mare's selection of poems beyond the inclusion of "Violets," "Lightning," and the school poems, though this is enough to indicate Garnett's interest in the more personal Lawrence. The arrangement by De la Mare initially pleased Lawrence, but he was still more pleased by David Garnett's choice, which made him think De la Mare's "a bit exquisite," designed "to convince the critics I was well brought up" (*Letters*, 1:455).[28] David, Frieda, and Lawrence joked even about the final version of the book, trying out farcical titles for it, "Asphodels," "Cabbage Roses," and "Asphodels in the Kitchen Garden" (*Letters*, 1:442). "Asphodel" was their pet name for the conventional literary man. But the volume contained, Lawrence also believed, some of his "best, impersonal" poems. The combination of "pretty" love poems and more vigorous poems, such as "Cherry Robbers," "Lightning," "Renascence," and "A Snowy Day at School" (there were, altogether, thirty-two poems in the book), lends an air of self-conscious, yet authentic artistry to this book—the beginnings of a distinctive, radically passionate art.

Beyond giving the young poet his debut, *Love Poems and Others* is a partial account of his loves. In retrospect, Lawrence saw in his book a potential cycle of love poems. In a comment revealing his real pride in the volume, he confessed that "I thought the book awfully nice—I loved it. F[rieda] refuses to have sufficient respect for it—but there, she *would*. There are in it too many heroines other than herself. Queer, there is one poem to her 'Bei Hennef'—I wish it had been the last in the book" (*Letters*, 1:462). When he collected his poems in 1928, he placed "Bei Hennef" among those of his later volume (those to Frieda) in *Look! We Have Come Through!* and explained in his Note that it represented the beginning of "the new cycle" (*CP*, p. 28). The threading of *Love Poems and Others* is tightened by internal groupings, both incidental and planned. Certain poems are so close in theme—"Wedding Morn," "Kisses in the Train," "Love on the Farm," "Cherry Robbers," "Lilies in the Fire," "Coldness in Love" (nos. 1–6)—that they form a natural cluster. Others were composed or gathered together deliberately, the triads "Aware," "A Pang of Reminiscence," and "A White Blossom" (nos. 12–14, composed for Jessie) and "Return," "The Appeal," and "Repulsed" (nos. 16–18, addressed to Helen Corke). His mother appears in only two poems, grouped together, "End of Another Home Holiday" and "Reminder" (nos. 7–8). In the last third of *Love Poems and Others* appear six pieces from "Transformations" (nos. 20–22, 25; the title "Transformations" was now employed at the head of three poems, "I. The Town," "II. The Earth," and "III. Men"), and, closing the selection, there are two sections headed "Dialect Poems" (nos. 26–29) and "The Schoolmaster" (nos. 30–32). Although out of their original sequences, the mythic and school poems blend smoothly into the book's many monologues. Altogether this verse gives an accurate measure of Lawrence's emerging skills, his own transformations from a struggling apprentice into the experimental and vigorous "new" author of 1913.

When *Love Poems and Others* is examined as a whole, certain poems take on an emblematic character, introducing issues to be explored later. "Wedding Morn," the headpiece for the volume, does this by inaugurating the book's treatment of power battles between men and women, and it is intriguing that the poem predicts "Pomegranate," the headpiece of *Birds, Beasts and Flowers*. The first two lines of "Wedding Morn," "The morning breaks like a pomegranate / In a shining crack of red" (*CP*, p. 58), reappear in essence in the last line of "Pomegranate": "It is so lovely, dawn-kaleidoscopic within the crack" (*CP*, p. 279). The remainder of these poems is a study in contrasts, for the new bride of "Wedding Morn" hungers after power over her husband, tyrannizing over him ("that spinning coin") in her aggressive fantasy, whereas in "Pomegranate" Lawrence boldly defies such women:

> *I am not wrong.*
>
> *In Syracuse, rock left bare by the viciousness of Greek women,*
> *No doubt you have forgotten the pomegranate-trees in flower,*
> *Oh so red.*
>
> (CP, p. 278)

But if the woman of "Wedding Morn" ignores the symbolism of the pomegranate, Persephone's fruit, the reader easily discerns her dawning battle: "He will lie negligent," she hopes,

> *resign*
> *His truth to me, and I*
> *Shall watch the dawn light up for me*
> *This fate of mine.*
>
> (CP, p. 59)

"Wedding Morn" sets the scene for the passionate contest between women and men that continues through *Love Poems and Others*. In the dialect poems, women commonly dominate conversations and their men, unconsciously glad when a man gets into trouble because it gives them an occasion to put things right: "What a traipse it is, if a man gets hurt! / I sh'd think 'e'll get right again" ("The Collier's Wife," *CP*, p. 46). (Lawrence gave some of his male speakers greater power when he revised these poems in 1928.) Other pieces cry out against cold, faint women. Read in context, the widely anthologized dramatic monologue "Love on the Farm" (titled "Cruelty and Love" in *Love Poems and Others*) becomes a particularly frank rendering of these power plays. The crux of the poem is the female speaker's dream vision, as in "Renascence," of a farm where the lovemaking of plant and animal is quietly violated by a hunter's "ominous tread," and "'Tis the wound of love goes home!" (*CP*, pp. 42–43). "Love on the Farm" goes beyond "Renascence" to realize the human passions behind such violence. When a man takes the female speaker in his arms, she succumbs to the brutality she has fantasized, thinking he throttles her:

> *I know not what fine wire is round my throat;*
> *I only know I let him finger there*
> *My pulse of life, and let him nose like a stoat*
> *Who sniffs with joy before he drinks the blood.*
>
> (CP, p. 43)

Like Lawrence's other dramatic monologues, this one tells against its speaker; she must awaken to the terror of violence before she will feel passion: "so I drown / Against him, die, and find death good."

Lawrence was angered by a five-month delay in publication of *Love Poems and Others* and by what he considered "faint" praise by the critics, though Pound called it "the most important book of poems of the season."[29] Lawrence thought so too, "I *know* I can write bigger stuff than any man in England" (*Letters*, 1:546). He planned to follow with a book, not of poems to Frieda (despite her impatience for one), but of elegies to his mother. His mother had been his first love, heroine of *Sons and Lovers*, and in *Amores* Lawrence would retell her story in his own voice. War broke out, however, within a year of publication of *Love Poems and Others*, and it brought Lawrence's poetic development temporarily to a halt. He turned his attention away from poetry to philosophy. In 1916 when he returned to give his elegies and the poems to Frieda their final shape, they meant still more than when he was first inspired with them. Belonging to the past, they steadied him against the less certain future.

CHAPTER THREE

—

Marriage

AMORES AND *LOOK! WE HAVE COME THROUGH!*

CHRONOLOGY:

The war	1914
"The Study of Thomas Hardy" written	1914
Amores collected, and published	1916
Look! We Have Come Through! collected, and published	1917

"Mr. Lawrence's last volume of poems, *Look! We Have Come Through!* is an amazing book. It is to my mind a greater novel even than *Sons and Lovers,* for all that it is written in a rather disconnected series of poems."[1] Amy Lowell's happy judgment turned *Look! We Have Come Through!* into something both more and less than it is, for although Lawrence's book is no more a novel than Meredith's *Modern Love* or Dante's *La vita nuova,* all three works challenge us to read them as something other than miscellaneous collections. Lawrence appended a Foreword and an Argument, instructing us to read it as a formal whole. The poems aspire to the condition, not of the novel, but of a long poem: "These poems should not be considered separately, as so many single pieces. They are intended as an essential story, or history, or confession, unfolding one from the other in organic development, the whole revealing the intrinsic experience of a man during the crisis of manhood, when he marries and comes into himself" (*CP*, p. 191). This chapter recreates the context in which Lawrence brought forward his first coherent poetic books, *Amores* and *Look! We Have Come Through!* to reveal the extent of his investment in poetry during the years of his great novels, and present a description of these poetic books that suggests how they may appeal to readers. *Amores* and *Look! We Have Come Through!* originally were companion volumes, where Lawrence transformed his private knowledge of death and marriage into public testaments of initiation: the treacherous and exultant passage into manhood.

To recover the sources of Lawrence's concept of the verse book, it is necessary to return to the early years when he composed the poems of *Amores* and *Look! We Have Come Through!* and when he was just beginning to develop a form for what critics have called his lyrical novels. He sought to design a spiritual autobiography, which could be recorded either in prose or poetry, and the design he found would later count among his most distinctive contributions to both genres: the confessional impulse of his novels, the story form for a book of poems. This idea of a secular story of the soul reemerged and was more elaborately defined in the war years, when Lawrence was writing the "Study of Thomas Hardy." He thought of that essay also as a spiritual autobiography, providing a metaphysic for his art. The war years are commonly viewed as the second major period in Lawrence's development as a novelist, and these years turned out to be equally crucial for the poetry. Shortly after completing *The Rainbow*, he began work on *Amores*, and after nearly completing *Women in Love*, he turned to *Look! We Have Come Through!* The timing of these verse books was in fact more deeply interwoven with the novels than this history suggests, since Lawrence wrote the original drafts for the poems in *Look! We Have Come Through!* before writing *The Rainbow*, while those in *Amores* predate *Sons and Lovers*. The verse authenticated the anecdotes of the novels, testifying to private realities behind his fiction; and it reached past the achievements of the novels, to tell the story of a man who finally had to do without an audience, his novels banned, his world at war. War distanced Lawrence from the events of his youth, promoting a retrospective attitude to his prewar poems, and because he saw the elegies and marriage poems already as products of an old life superseded by larger social concerns, he composed these books with a double vision of the earlier progress of his life: seeing both triumph and failure in his effort to survive "the crisis of manhood" or reach "some condition of blessedness" (*CP*, p. 191). *Look! We Have Come Through!* ended with a few of his most recent poems, written out of his anguish during the war.

Lawrence also wrote a small number of new poems during the war, most of which he placed in "Bits" and *Bay*. "Bits" was in fact composed before *Look! We Have Come Through!* though none of it was published until a selection appeared in the July 1919 issue of *Poetry*. But because these two books were composed in direct response to the war, they belong with *New Poems* and *Birds, Beasts and Flowers*, shaped, not around the poet's new manhood, but around the war and its aftermath.

Part I: The Story

In 1916 when Lawrence was collecting *Amores*, he explained that these poems "make a sort of inner history of my life, from 20 to 26" (*Letters*, 2:521); a year later he called *Look! We Have Come Through!* an "essential story" from the "sixth lustre of a man's life" (*CP*, p. 191). From then on he conceived of his poetic sequences as stories of the heart. In his Note to *Collected Poems* of 1928, he added few details to that description: "I have tried to establish a chronological order, because many of the poems are so personal that, in their fragmentary fashion, they make up a biography of an emotional and inner life" (*CP*, p. 27). With each successive book he rewrote his autobiography, deriving still another "new" story to accommodate his experiences. Lawrence was not alone in this ambition. W. B. Yeats in his autobiography bears witness to this desire for a "sacred book": "Is it true that our air is disturbed, as Mallarmé said, by 'the trembling of the veil of the temple,' or 'that our whole age is seeking to bring forth a sacred book'? Some of us thought that book near towards the end of last century, but the tide sank again."[2] Whether or not a newer testament was likely to emerge, writers like Yeats and Lawrence were sorely tempted by the possibility.

The roots of their hopes stretch back into the nineteenth century, with its explosively popular autobiographies. Autobiographers commonly patterned their works after the mysterious "phases of the soul." In this age of intense debate and social reformation, writers obeyed strong impulses to build epic poems out of their lives. Not only poets followed Wordsworth in this; a logician like John Stuart Mill could write that "in an age of transition in opinions, there may be somewhat both of interest and of benefit in noting the successive phases of any mind which was always pressing forward."[3]

Lawrence's particular interest in autobiography dates back to his earliest reading, when he encountered a popular philosophical autobiography by Richard Jefferies, *The Story of My Heart*. The young Lawrence deeply admired this book, and his "essential story" is probably indebted directly to it. Jefferies had undertaken an unusual experiment with the confessional mode, exploring his thoughts and allowing them to unfold until "new ideas" emerged. He called *The Story of My Heart* a "confession" in which "The Author describes the successive states of emotion and thought through which he passed, till he arrived at the conclusions which are set forth in the latter part of the volume. He claims to have erased from his mind the traditions and learning of the past ages, and to stand face to face with nature and with the unknown." Jefferies' experiment is not entirely or even primarily of the mind; physically he embarks on Wordsworthian excursions into nature to hold an "intense communion . . . with the earth, the sun and sky, the stars hidden by the light, with the ocean," to be filled "with a rapture, an ecstasy, an inflatus."[4]

For Lawrence as for Jefferies, it did not matter much whether this was a story or history or whether his subject was the heart or the soul. They used several terms and let vagueness creep into their phrasing, "a sort of . . . history," to keep their categories fluid. One problem was to replace the Christian *soul,* and no term seemed quite adequate: *heart* was equally conditioned by previous thought; *psyche,* too scientific; *intuition,* too superficial in its associations. The inner self must be as nebulous as the unknown future. They resorted most often to using *soul* in clearly non-Christian contexts. Eventually in 1928 Lawrence came up with *ghost* and *demon* (much like Yeats's "daimon") for this self; *demon* satisfied him more than any previous term because it defined the soul as an antiself, unattached to orthodox religion, unearthly and beyond knowing.

In a sense the elements of Jefferies' "new book" were old ones. The aspirations of his "soul, or psyche" and his encounter with the unknown are nearly indistinguishable from the Romantic imagination wondering at nature. His unknown is, however, more impersonal and vast, closer to infinitude, while his encounter with it is no less sexual than that of Shelley and Keats. The central terms of Jefferies' meditation are Lawrence's: so, Jefferies writes, "Now is eternity; now is the immortal life"; "I, who am here on the verge . . . am in the mystery itself." Yet, as for the Romantics, the "search" is also for self-expression: "search out a new and higher set of ideas in which the mind should work. The simile of a new book of the soul is the nearest to convey the meaning—a book drawn from the present and future, not the past," even though that book can be "only a fragment, and a fragment scarcely hewn."[5] In keeping with this idea of "a new book of the soul," *The Story of My Heart* progresses rhapsodically, not, he adds, in strict order, but phase by phase through its author's memories, reconstructing his soul journey. The aims and design of Jefferies' autobiography strikingly anticipate Lawrence's intention to supplant previous traditions in his poetic sequences and, by following instinct, to enter new territories of thought. But above all, what attracted Lawrence was this book's use of confession as a mode for facing and at length entering the unknown.

Lawrence's allusions to Jefferies appear in letters of 1911–12 concerning his second novel, *The Trespasser,* a work that emerged at a critical juncture in the novelist-poet's development. Lawrence sought Helen Corke's permission to use her diary for a long prose poem, which then became *The Trespasser.*[6] Whereas his first novel, *The White Peacock,* had an elaborate plot intentionally modeled on George Eliot's novels, *The Trespasser* reflected Wagnerian drama with its dreamlike progression of episodes and tragic love story. Less obvious, but equally influential, was spiritual autobiography; for the question of form—whether to write a novel or a poem, whether to emphasize plot or symbolic association—yielded place to a more fundamental issue for Lawrence, how to negotiate confessionalism with the distancing techniques of fictional narrative. He experienced considerable anxiety in writing *The Trespasser,* and in the heat of his project, compared his ambivalence about it to what he imagined Jefferies had felt: "I give myself away so much, and write what is my most palpitant, sensitive self, that I loathe the book, because it will betray me to a parcel of fools. Which is what any deeply personal or lyrical writer feels, I guess. I often think Stendhal must have writhed in torture every time he remembered *Le Rouge et le noir* was public property: and Jefferies at *The Story of my Heart.* I don't like the *Story of my Heart*" (*Letters,* 1:353).[7] Lawrence may have disliked himself, his book, and its models, but discomfort was rapidly becoming one of his aesthetic aims. The uneasiness that *The Story of My Heart* and *The Trespasser* arouse marked their success in getting at the "palpitant, sensitive self."

Lawrence's worries were in part those of any writer learning his craft, but the problem had special force for him because it involved the larger question of how to define himself in relation to others. Relationship was the central subject of his art, and it was now conditioning his search for an appropriately mixed confessional and narrational method. He believed egoism as great an evil in authorship as in daily interactions, whether or not one was writing autobiography. Here again he would have found confirmation in Jefferies' theories, but it is at this point that Lawrence also distanced himself from his model, for Jefferies' intense communion was with Nature, not woman. Jefferies was alone with his rapture. In Lawrence's view, man and woman set each other's borders: "the whole crux of life now lies in the relation between man and woman, between Adam and Eve" (*Letters,* 3:27).

In a letter of 1913 Lawrence devalued the "lyric" in favor of the "dramatic" author, classifying them respectively as the "egoist" and the "fertile" writer. The lyricist "has nothing that goes on, no passion, only a few intense moods, separate like odd stars, and when each has burned away, he must die. It is no accident that Shelley got drowned—he was always trying to drown himself—it was his last mood." In contrast to this, the "man with dramatic capabilities, needed fertilising by some love. . . . from a woman he wants himself re-born, re-constructed" (*Letters*, 2:115).[8] In practice, however, Lawrence applied this standard to all genres, as had Browning before him. Although what is asserted here resembles the common distinction between "intensity" in the lyric as opposed to the continuities and relational properties of narrative, it is probably no coincidence that Lawrence's criteria mirror the "subjective" and "objective" artists of Browning's famous essay on Shelley. Shelley stood for the "subjective" poet, looking inward for inspiration, while Shakespeare presented the type of "objectivity," directed outward, recreating the world. A still greater artist might combine these attitudes in nearly equal proportion.[9] Lawrence returned to these thoughts in the "Study of Thomas Hardy," this time contrasting Shakespeare as the fruitful "female" type against Shelley the isolated "male," the supreme artist balanced between these (*Phoenix*, p. 459). In theory as in practice, Lawrence meant to merge the different powers of different genres, reinvigorating every form in which he worked.

While Lawrence's novels have long been recognized for the power they lend his myth of relationship, the subject was obviously as suitable for expression in verse, and the story form may be traced further to models among previous poets. In one of the few studies on this subject, *The Heart's Events*, Patricia Ball has discussed the highly versatile uses of verse sequences by Victorian poets writing of domestic relationships. Not a mere imitation of the Victorian novel, the verse sequence sprang from impulses and aims of its own:

> Technical resource and themes of emotional involvement are aspects of a single poetic ambition, for Victorian poets set up new concepts of the long poem, or the lyric group, principally in order to accommodate two of their central notions: first, that change—whether of growth or decay—is integral to love and, secondly, that the inner life as it is affected by close relationships evolves with a logic of its own which is not merely that of temporal sequence. The technical energy is generated by the pursuit of psychological realities and out of the consequent need for poems longer than the single lyric unit. It is an energy which is hostile to narrative in the simple sense, even while it appropriates some story-telling characteristics by admitting the question, "and then?"[10]

Victorian sequences continued the tradition of the sonnet sequence, redirecting it to a fresh worldliness, embodying, not the transcendental sufferings of a solitary man, but all the vicissitudes, ironies, and mundane needs of a man coping with ordinary relationships. Such sequences could combine narrative and nonnarrative systems of connection, and they could contain a high degree of discontinuity. Lawrence learned the lessons of both the traditional sonnet cycle and the nonce forms, invented for the occasion, by Meredith, Tennyson, and Browning; he set aside the sonnet sequence to create his own more mobile form, while reinfusing his domestic dramas with an exalted value. Like the keenly ironic elegies of Hardy, *Amores* candidly rehearsed the personal history of Mrs. Lawrence's death, but with a greater optimism than Hardy ever felt. In *Look! We Have Come Through!* Lawrence expressly repudiated the defeatism immortalized in Tennyson's *Maud* and Meredith's *Modern Love,* poems of failed romance and broken marriage. *Amores* and *Look! We Have Come Through!* exalt the simple fact of life as Lawrence saw them: the spiritual marriage to his mother, his fleshly marriage to his wife. And both take shape with "an energy which is hostile to narrative," for even while "admitting the question, 'and then?'" his poems refuse an answer.

Lawrence's first books may be reviewed in the context of several poetic sequences, early and late—including Hardy's *Poems of 1912–1913,* Dante's *La vita nuova,* Whitman's *Children of Adam,* Tennyson's *Maud*—but like his idea of a spiritual autobiography, Lawrence's thoughts about verse sequences extended back to his early reading. His studious attention to the poetry of Rachel Annand Taylor, for instance, went far beyond concern with her symbolism. Taylor's books provided an example of poetic autobiography that he could easily appreciate and criticize and could eventually outpace. In his paper of 1910 on Taylor, he began his analysis by narrating her story: with a broken heart and "left to herself, she developed as a choice romanticist." Lawrence focused his criticism of Taylor on the contrast between her "crude" experience of a broken heart and her romanticization of that experience, until her "verses are transformed from the experience beyond recognition." He singled out for consideration poems that reveal the biography of the artist as well as her "creed," reserving his highest praise for her third volume, a sonnet sequence titled *The Hours of Fiammetta,* "which, upon close acquaintance, are as interesting, more interesting far to trace than a psychological novel" (*Phoenix II,* 217–20). Here again is Amy Lowell's comparison of the verse sequence to the novel, strangely anticipated in the young Lawrence's response to a woman's verse autobiography.

Taylor's Preface to the Fiammetta sequence reveals an even closer parallel to Lawrence's story. Fiammetta is Taylor's symbolic persona for the woman artist:

> No single sonnet expresses absolute truth from even [Fiammetta's] own point of view. The verses present the moods, misconceptions, extravagances,

revulsions, reveries—all the obscure crises whereby she reaches a state of illumination and reconciliation regarding the enigma of love as it is, making her transition from the purely romantic and ascetic ideal fostered by the exquisitely selective conspiracies of the art of the great love-poets, through a great darkness of disillusion, to a new vision infinitely stronger and sweeter, because unafraid of the whole truth.[11]

Progressing beyond an ascetic point of view to a "new vision," "unafraid of the whole truth," the story of Fiammetta's dilemma and "transition" foreshadows Lawrence's process of self-transformation in a book of unpredictable hours. Taylor's Preface also gave Lawrence, as M. C. Sharpe first noted,[12] his key terms for a symbolic typology of women in 1910–12: in Taylor's Preface, "There are two great traditions of womanhood. One presents the Madonna brooding over the mystery of motherhood; the other, more confusedly, tells of the acolyte, the priestess, the clairvoyante of the unknown gods."[13] Before titling his second novel *The Trespasser,* Lawrence had considered calling it *The Man and the Dreaming Woman* (*Letters,* 1:378); in poems among the juvenilia, the Madonna and the Dreaming Woman were principal antagonists, set against each other and himself, and this antagonism informed the making of *Amores.* But Taylor's Preface also indicates a sharp difference in their aims. Lawrence took exception to *The Hours of Fiammetta* because its poetic techniques remained, despite Taylor's claims to the contrary, those of a "romantic and ascetic" work of art.

What methods, then, did Lawrence initially apply to his poetry, comparable to the devices of a lyrical novel, which would embody the story not only of his own soul, but of a man reconstructed by a woman? The story of the heart exists in what is not told as often as in the telling—in the absence of a full circumstantial narrative, linking one episode to the next. Jefferies and Taylor spoke of their works as sequential forms, transacting, in Jefferies' terms, "successive stages of thought," while in Taylor's belief, "no single sonnet expresses absolute truth from even [Fiammetta's] own point of view." Lawrence adopted the psychological episodes of Jefferies and Taylor with their discontinuous logic and shifting perspectives. He had already settled, however, for more casual and changeable structures in his individual poems than that of Taylor's sonnets ("odd stars" [*Letters,* 2:115], easily disengaged from their cycle) and, as we have seen, his poems were becoming increasingly focused on conflict, dialogue, and argument:

You are the call and I am the answer,
You are the wish, and I the fulfillment,
You are the night, and I the day.
　　What else? it is perfect enough.

> *It is perfectly complete,*
> *You and I,*
> *What more———?*
>
> *Strange, how we suffer in spite of this!*

("Bei Hennef," CP, p. 203)

A lack of permanent closure and, as Lawrence hints, the sense of estrangement produced at the edge of a poem drive the reader forward to add one poetic piece to the next. Still, the major force of cohesion in a verse sequence is the frequent use of internal monologue and the illusion, which this can create, of an internal debate. No matter how brief or how philosophical, Lawrence's lyrics generally manage to imply dramatic engagement through the speaking voice, so that each poem articulates a temporary crisis. If at the end, as Taylor suggested, the speaker "reaches a state of illumination," it is because he has discovered certain new limits to what he has known, rather than infinite vision. So, in "Bei Hennef," the speaker twists and turns in his mind, internalizing his newfound partnership, until he reaches the extreme end of "perfectly complete" comradery, and his thought snaps, "What more———?"; in this fissure, he finds yet another point of contact, another point of divergence: "how we suffer in spite of this."

While there is clear evidence that Lawrence early interested himself in the ways and means of a "story of my heart," the phrase did not take hold in his thoughts until the war years, where it appeared in reference to his philosophy. Mark Kinkead-Weekes and Keith Cushman both stress the importance of the "Study of Thomas Hardy" as a step in a chain of writings from the *Prussian Officer* stories to *The Rainbow*. If the study of Hardy helped lead Lawrence, as Kinkead-Weekes first argued, to the "discovery of a 'structural skeleton'" for *The Rainbow*, it also led him to a parallel discovery for the book of poems: authorizing in broad outline an argument for his books.[14] Much as Yeats's *A Vision* had generated "metaphors" for Yeats's poetry, the "Study of Thomas Hardy" answered Lawrence's need to develop an ethical measure for experience: "Oh Lord, and if I don't 'subdue my art to a metaphysic,' as somebody very beautifully said of Hardy, I do write because I want folk—English folk—to alter, and have more sense" (*Letters*, 1:544).[15] Where Yeats was content with vision, imagining the world altered but not altering it, Hardy and Lawrence were driven to produce a reformative vision.

The idea of the story turns up suddenly in Lawrence's writings as a kind of touchstone, alerting us to an almost archetypal pattern that Lawrence had recognized and was attempting to describe. His study of Hardy's characters is a "*Story of My Heart:* or a Confessio Fidei," and the Book of Job,

which Lawrence contrasts to Hardy, revering it above any of Hardy's novels, is a "story of your own soul" (*Letters*, 2:243, 247). The "Study of
Thomas Hardy" interprets Hardy, in other words, according to Lawrence's life story.

In a letter to Gordon Campbell of 1914, he outlined the "whole history
of the Soul of Man." He begins by arguing for an organically continuous
use and interpretation of symbols, as opposed to a fragmented and egoistic
cooptation. His antagonist in this passage is the early Yeats:

> We are such egoistic fools. We see only the *symbol* as a *subjective expression:* as
> an expression of ourselves. That makes us so sickly when we deal with the
> old symbols: like Yeats.
>
> The old symbols were each a word in a great attempt at formulating the
> whole history of the Soul of Man. They are *unintelligible* except in their
> whole context. (*Letters*, 2:248)

Lawrence's mention of Yeats recalls his paper of 1910 on Rachel Annand
Taylor, where he was equally concerned with the symbolist tendency to
abstract symbols from their contexts, depriving them of effective significance. The egotistical sublime and its suffering should have been merely
one piece in the human puzzle, but "it is characteristic of us," Lawrence
says wryly, "that we have preserved of a trilogy which was really *Prometheus Unbound,* only the *Prometheus Bound* and terribly suffering on the
rock of his own egotism" (*Letters*, 2:248).

Much of this letter is devoted to rewriting the Christ story, emphasizing
the double nature of Christ, His relationship to others, the moments of
change in His history and the direction of His life toward "some condition
of blessedness." Even in an egoistic state, Christ is perceived in relation,
though set in hard resistance against the unknown God: "the Spirit of the
Father procreating the human flesh forms the *ego*. And the Ego would fain
absorb the position of the Eternal god. Therefore it must suffer crucifixion, so that it may rise again praising God, knowing with the Angels." The
changes in Christ—a fluctuating series of births and crucifixions—always
move past death toward a physical bliss: "after our Crucifixion, and the
darkness of the tomb, we shall rise again in the flesh, you, I, as we are today, resurrected in the bodies, and acknowledging the Father, and glory-
ing in his power, like Job" (*Letters*, 2:249). Lawrence draws much the
same analogy in the "Study of Thomas Hardy" (*Phoenix*, p. 481) and,
slighting Hardy's Jude, compares Arabella favorably with Job: "she felt
also strong and abundant, arrogant in her hold on life" (*Phoenix*, p. 490).
Lawrence's chief complaint with the moderns was the bleak devastation of
their tragedies, and it is here that Job could be a counterfoil. Lawrence
turned away from Christ to reforge Christian doctrine on the anvil of a fig-

ure with whom he could more readily identify—the earthy, self-righteous, and defiant Job.

In the "Study of Thomas Hardy," Lawrence propounded a single principle to explain all stories. Male (which he also calls Love) and female (which he also calls Law) coexist in opposition to each other. By the standard of this dualism, he evaluates the history of religion and art and criticizes Hardy's novels. Christianity is a phase in the fluctuation from female- to male-dominated systems of belief and eventually back again to a female-dominated system. Lawrence decides that religion can never attain a condition of equipoise, because it is in the nature of any moral outlook to exclude options: either one principle or another must dominate, without any possibility of balance between them. Although the history of art also fluctuates, here an ideal balance may be reached. In Botticelli, for example, the male principle becomes fully reconciled with the female, though after Botticelli, the arts again divide into two branches of expression, male or female, and modern art (like modern religion) suffers from an extreme male, mechanistic atomism (*Phoenix*, pp. 444–76). Works of art should embody the morality of their age, but if they are to be more than propaganda, they must also contain the criticism of that morality, must somehow counterbalance a male with a female system of thought. The great artist will ground his art in a metaphysical framework that goes beyond reconstituting the morality of his age to articulate a more comprehensive "theory of being and knowing" (*Phoenix*, pp. 476–79).

Lawrence could have lifted a preface for *Amores* or *Look! We Have Come Through!* directly from the prose of the "Study of Thomas Hardy." His poetic persona in these books moves from a relationship overshadowed by his mother's morality to the transcendence of her church, and from female- to male-dominated moments. Yet only one type of event occurs throughout. Man comes joyfully, painfully into discordant communion with woman. As Lawrence expressed it in his study of Hardy:

> It is as if life were a double cycle, of men and women, facing opposite ways, travelling opposite ways, revolving upon each other, man reaching forward with outstretched hand, woman reaching forward with outstretched hand, and neither able to move till their hands have grasped each other, when they draw towards each other from opposite directions, draw nearer and nearer, each travelling in his separate cycle, till the two are abreast, and side by side, until even they pass on again, away from each other, travelling their opposite ways to the same infinite goal. (*Phoenix*, p. 449)

In ideal moments they transcend moral obstacles and gender differences to touch one another, though briefly. There is no final beginning or end to this process of continuous relationship; it is a series of indeterminate revolutions.

Shaping the arguments of these first two books is the speaker's changing relation to a woman, imagined spatially as his separations from her and slow reapproaches. In the "Study of Thomas Hardy" Lawrence divided his "dance" into a "threefold utterance": "the declaring of the God seen approaching, the rapture of contact, the anguished joy of remembrance, when the meeting has passed into separation," and these three moments follow each other in endless succession, "as if this cycle dance where the female makes the chain with the male becomes ever wider, ever more extended" (*Phoenix,* 449–50). But whereas he ascribes only one "utterance" each to David, Solomon, and Job, his own songs appear to include all three, often within the same poem. The poems offer a more mixed experience than the dance Lawrence describes in his Hardy essay. In refusing the ethical belief that the reward of virtue is bliss in an afterlife, Lawrence replaced the central formula of Christianity with an existential logic. What integrates Lawrence's story is dynamic conflict and debate.

Part II: Companion Books

AMORES

The war rapidly became the backdrop for Lawrence's own troubles, as it kept him stalemated in England and obstructed from publishing his novels. Like Job, he was compelled to retrace the earlier episodes of his youth that led to, but did nothing to explain or justify, his present difficulties. Lawrence's poetry did not annex new territory in the way that Lawrence's philosophy, as Keith Cushman argues, annexed ground from past novels to prepare ground for new ones.[16] Rather, Lawrence revisited old territory in his poetry, returning to the personal matter that informed his fiction, to tell the story again, this time as his own history. Even so, he was not without optimism.

In the "Study of Thomas Hardy," he complained that Hardy ended his novels where Job began: "Job says in the end: 'Therefore have I uttered that I understood not; things too wonderful for me, which I knew not' . . . . But Jude ends where Job began, cursing the day and the services of his birth, and in so much cursing the act of the Lord, 'Who made him in the womb'" (*Phoenix,* p. 481). This might also be said of Hardy's elegies, which trace only the faintest progression through grief. Hardy learned to accept his ghosts—

And scan and trace
The forsaken place
Quite readily[17]

—but his sense of time, the burden of the past, did not change. In *Amores,* death shakes Lawrence out of boyhood to face the future. The unbearably recurrent sorrow of his mother's death remains as constant for him as for Hardy; but equally constant is his impulse to move forward, to make headway against grief and end where Job ended with the possibility of a plentiful life.

Lawrence probably read Hardy's elegies before publishing his own, because they appeared in print in 1914, two years before *Amores.* Even without definite evidence of this, we know that Lawrence had Hardy in mind when composing his poetry, for in a review of 1913, praising the first anthology of Georgian poetry (which included Lawrence's "Snap-Dragon," republished in *Amores*), he had this to say of Hardy: "The last years have been years of demolition. Because faith and belief were getting pot-bound, and the Temple was made a place to barter sacrifices, therefore faith and belief and the Temple must be broken. This time art fought the battle, rather than science or any new religious faction. And art has been demolishing for us: Nietzsche, the Christian religion as it stood; Hardy, our faith in our own endeavour; Flaubert, our belief in love. . . . And behold, out of the ruins leaps the whole sky" (*Phoenix,* p. 304). Out of the ruins emerged the new Georgian poetry: "This flesh and blood sitting here writing, the great impersonal flesh and blood, greater than me, which I am proud to belong to, contains all the future" (*Phoenix,* p. 306). In stressing the kinship between these novelist-poets, however, I do not mean to suggest that Lawrence's sequence was as great an achievement as Hardy's. Only a few of Lawrence's elegies stand out next to Hardy's powerfully compact sequence of twenty-one poems. Hardy's was the work of an old man, appearing in his fifth book of poems, whereas *Amores,* Lawrence's second volume, was the work of a new poet. Comparison of the two tells us a great deal about the aims of a writer who had just begun to work against the grain of his elders.

The single most traumatic event in life for Lawrence as for Hardy was the death of a woman, and for both men this event exposed a potentially devastating fact about themselves. The death of Hardy's wife, who had been estranged from him for twenty years, forced him to remember his first passionate love for her. The death of Lawrence's mother made him recognize that he adored her as a lover, not a son: "And so, my love, my mother, / I shall always be true to you" ("The Virgin Mother," *CP,* p. 102). Yet the differences between these elegists are as great as the affinities. With his wife's death, the present slid back into the past for Hardy. As if thrown down a hall of mirrors, he reexperienced every previous parting as vividly as if it had just occurred. He was desolated not only by the loss of his wife but by the loss of their love twenty years before:

> Woman much missed, how you call to me, call to me,
> Saying that now you are not as you were
> When you had changed from the one who was all to me,
> But as at first, when our day was fair.[18]

Lawrence felt all the irony of a memory vital enough to defy the actual absence of his mother. But he experienced this as a struggle in the present between his mother's absence and her haunting presence. From this conflict, as from a labor of rebirth, he had to reemerge a man. So while his poems, like Hardy's, hinge on the irony of discrepant facts, that irony is an event of the present moment and one that will admit an altered, open future for the poet.

Evidence of Lawrence's intentions for *Amores* exists in plenty. At the outset he told Amy Lowell, "I find I have such a lot of poems, now, and such nice ones. I can make a most beautiful book" (*Letters*, 2:513). He had finished the book by the first of February and mailed it to his friend and patroness, Ottoline Morrell, complete except for "Snap-Dragon," which he planned to send later and asked her to reinsert in its "right place, according to the index" (*Letters*, 2:521). The next day he mailed the poems to agent J. B. Pinker with this dictum: "Here is the complete MS. of the poems. I don't want it altered" (*Letters*, 2:522). Lawrence's pride in the book weathered even "impertinent" criticisms and rejection by the publishers Sidgwick and Constable (*Letters*, 2:558). In April he notified Dollie Radford that the book was at the printers to be published by Duckworth, and he added, "there is something peculiarly exciting and delightful about a book of verse" (*Letters*, 2:596).

With one exception, the final order of *Amores* bears no resemblance to the sequences in the juvenilia. The earliest drafts are interspersed with verse from every other volume in Lawrence's two college notebooks (Ferrier MSS 1 and 5; Vasey MSS E317 and E320.1). Even in the notebook where Lawrence drafted his elegies in 1916 (Ferrier MS 27; Vasey MS E320.2), the sequence bears no relation to *Amores*.[19] Only one group is reduplicated in MS 5, MS 27, and *Amores:* "The End," "The Bride," and "The Virgin Mother" (*RP*, nos. 66–68).

In contrast, the order of *Amores* is followed closely in *Rhyming Poems*, volume 1 of *Collected Poems*, proof that Lawrence still liked most of the published order of *Amores* in 1928. Whereas the poems from other early volumes—from *Love Poems and Others*, *Bay*, and *New Poems*—were thoroughly reshuffled for inclusion in *Rhyming Poems*, the verse in *Amores* was transferred in parallel groups. (See the contents table for *Rhyming Poems* in Appendix A.) Out of the sixty poems in *Amores*, thirty-eight elegies form strong core groups in *Collected Poems*. Lawrence's love poems to various sweethearts in *Amores* were subject to the greatest changes, suggesting that he felt less necessity to give these a final order and, late in his life, did not hesitate to reshape them. The central group of twenty-one elegies, from "Suspense" to "The Enkindled Spring," reappears in essentially the same order as in *Amores*, with three exceptions: "Suspense" and "Endless Anxiety" (*AM*, nos. 20, 24) were moved from slightly earlier positions to join the other elegies (*AM*, nos. 26–43), and one poem, "Reminder," was inserted from *Love Poems and Others* (*RP*, no. 70), to generate a final sequence of twenty-two elegies (*RP*, nos. 64–85). Immediately following these elegies in *Collected Poems* are two other groups, twenty-three poems altogether: from "Excursion Train" to "Under the Oak" (*RP*, nos. 86–99; *AM*, nos. 21, 44–50, 52, and 54; including one poem from *Love Poems and Others*, "Kisses in the Train," and three poems from *New Poems*, "Twofold," "Tarantella," and "Under the Oak") and from "Brother and Sister" to "A Passing-Bell" ("Birdcage Walk" of *NP* was the single insertion in *RP*, nos. 100–108; *AM*, nos. 51, 53, 55–60). In *Collected Poems*, both groups were reconstructed in the same general clusters as in *Amores*, though in different sequences.

Mandell has noted parts of these groups (reporting those that reappear in identical order in *Rhyming Poems*, nos. 66–69, 71–77, 81–85, and 103–7), yet does not believe that Lawrence took much care with *Amores*. She argues that this book spent much less time in the process of assemblage than the others, three or four weeks for *Amores* as compared with a year or more for *Bay* and *New Poems*.[20] In fact, Lawrence may have devoted less than three weeks to *Amores*, for he does not mention receiving his notebooks from Italy, where he had left them in storage, until 15 January 1916. He worked rapidly, however, on all three projects, as he characteristically did whether composing prose or verse. In 1917, while rewriting *Women in Love*, he worked for four weeks on and off preparing *Look! We Have Come Through!* After a year, in March and April 1918, he returned to his old notebooks to construct *Bay* and *New Poems*. Although he may have begun to write some poems in *Bay* in late 1917, as he claimed in his Note to *Collected Poems* (*CP*, p. 28), the evidence of the letters indicates that he did not begin to think seriously about the book until late March 1918 and had completed a booklet within three weeks. The exact timing of *New Poems*, which he began to compile after finishing *Bay*, is less clear; he worked sporadically on this, at times thinking he would make two books, but had *New Poems* ready by mid-June.[21] We know enough about Lawrence's calendar to determine that he rarely gave as much as a month to develop a book from poems previously composed. And in the spring of 1918 he was also developing *Studies in Classic American Literature* and *Aaron's Rod*, whereas he worked almost exclusively on *Amores* in January 1916.

Lawrence dismantled several early sequences and long poems to create the contents of *Amores*. The book begins with poems recording his early youth, proceeds to the elegies, and ends with groups of broken-love stories and mystical elegies, in which the poet grapples alone with nature. At the center of the book are "The End," "The Bride," and "The Virgin Mother" (*AM*, nos. 26–28). Lawrence gave drafts of these poems to Jessie Chambers shortly after Mrs. Lawrence's death in 1910 and told her how he had adored his mother. His three elegies present the fact for all to read. Jessie despaired when she saw him hand the laurels to his mother after Mrs. Lawrence's irrational demand (as Jessie saw it) for absolute devotion, and she finally ended the relationship with Lawrence after reading *Sons and Lovers* because it seemed to her a nearly libelous distortion of the facts.[22] In *Amores* Lawrence acted even more unscrupulously than in the novel to project an image of his mother as the central figure of his young life; all other women appear as lesser and usually anonymous adjuncts in a story of mother and son.

He revised several earlier manuscript verse groups to shift the focus from his young female friends to his mother. In all biographical accounts of Lawrence's adolescence, we see him preoccupied with typing women, testing one against another, and his manuscript poems often hinge on a contrast between two women, with, at most, oblique reference to Mrs. Lawrence. In *Sons and Lovers*—while giving a prime role to his mother, of course—he divided his youth between Miriam and Clara, whom he contrasted in exhaustive detail. In *Amores*, poems dealing with a contrast between two women are split apart, and any distinct characterization of these women becomes far less firm.[23] In a manuscript group of three letters— "An Epistle from Thelma," "An Epistle from Arthur," and "Epilogue from Thelma" (Ferrier MS 5)[24]—a woman pleads with her lover to be faithful, and when he demurs, she predicts that a "June-hot woman" such as he wants in preference to her "chill dusk" will stifle him. The second two pieces in this group appear in *Amores*, retitled "Disagreeable Advice" (*AM*, no. 9; not in *RP*) and "Epilogue" (*AM*, no. 13; *RP*, no. 56), and separated from each other, so that the individual personalities disappear. Similar revisions occurred in a manuscript set of "Blue" and "Red" (Ferrier MS 5).[25] These were joined in a symbolic diptych of contrasting loves, following the typology of Rachel Annand Taylor, her "Madonna" in "Blue" and "dreaming woman" in "Red." "Red" was never published in any form, but "Blue" was transformed into two mystical elegies, rededicated to the memory of his mother (*AM*, nos. 53, 60; *RP*, nos. 101, 107).

While reenforcing the story line, such revisions also fragmented the volume, suppressing any too obvious pattern. Among the best-known pieces in *Amores* are those in the first half that Lawrence took from his ambitious early sequences. Lawrence would revise most of these once again, making them among the most carefully considered verses in *Rhyming Poems*. All of the pieces published together as "A Still Afternoon" in the *English Review* reappear in *Rhyming Poems*, but none recur in juxtaposition except in *Amores*, where "Dreams Old and Nascent" remain as pendants (*AM*, nos. 10–11; *RP*, nos. 22, 144). "Discipline" was split into two, the second piece titled "Prophet" (*AM*, nos. 15, 17; *RP*, nos. 58, 57). "Movements," a manuscript sequence (Ferrier MS 1) that had also been a vehicle for "A Baby Running Barefoot" and "A Baby Asleep after Pain" in "A Still Afternoon," yields one further piece, "Virgin Youth" (*AM*, nos. 14, 23, 5; *RP*, nos. 32, 45, 8). From "A Life History" (Ferrier MS 5) Lawrence saved "Discord in Childhood" and from "The Schoolmaster" he reserved "The Punisher" (*AM*, nos. 4, 25; *RP*, nos. 4, 59). These selections are representative of the poems prior to the elegies in *Amores*, speaking more often for the difficulties of youth than its satisfactions.

Similarly, Lawrence broke down a number of long manuscript poems for the elegiac sequences in *Amores*. "Silence" and "Troth with the Dead" (Ferrier MS 5) each became the parent of two or three shorter poems, spawning antithetical points of view. "Silence" became a set of pendants: "Silence" and "Listening" (*AM*, nos. 34–35; *RP*, nos. 75–76). In a more complex evolution, "Troth with the Dead" was broken into three, "Troth with the Dead," "The Enkindled Spring," and "Dissolute" (retitled "At a Loose End" in *RP*), and their order was altered. In *Amores* and *Rhyming Poems*, "At a Loose End" follows "Troth with the Dead," and a fourth poem, "Submergence," intervenes between "Dissolute" and "The Enkindled Spring." Whereas the original long poem traced a smooth curve from a grief-stricken, torn state of mind to a sense of resignation, the revised order disrupts this into a more erratic sequence from grief to resignation to, in "Submergence," momentary obliviousness, and finally to chaotic turbulence in "The Enkindled Spring" (*AM*, nos. 40–43; *RP*, nos. 82–85).

Lawrence shuffled his early drafts for the closing sequence of *Amores* as thoroughly as a deck of cards. "Afterwards," "Grief," and "Twilight"[26] were dismantled and recombined as two mystical elegies, "Grey Evening" and "Firelight and Nightfall" in *Amores* (*AM*, nos. 58–59; *RP*, nos. 105–6).

Both "Afterwards" and "Grief" had been straightforward, personal accounts of Lawrence's mourning, much like the elegies in the middle of *Amores,* while "Twilight" was a city poem like those in the early bardic sequence, "Transformations." Lawrence reworked stanzas from each of these to create two poems far removed from their juvenile counterparts. The poet-persona of the revised pieces is stranded in a fiery Arthurian landscape of "queens" and "diapered" skies. Stanzas from "Blue" (Ferrier MS 5) contributed material both for a revised version, still titled "Blue," and for a second poem, "The Mystic Blue," which is the last poem in *Amores* (*AM,* nos. 53, 60; *RP,* nos. 101, 107). The latter repeats and elaborates upon "Blue" without adding any substantially new theme, acting as a harmonic variation. In *Rhyming Poems* these were again revised to eliminate seven stanzas from "Blue" (retitled "The Shadow of Death") that closely resembled "The Mystic Blue" (retitled "Blueness"). (In some ways that later revision is less satisfying, the effects too subdued, as I will indicate below.) Together "Blue" and "The Mystic Blue" suggest a conclusion to the poet's misery and bind together the closing elegies.

Revisions as extensive as these will reward closer attention than I can give them here. Beyond indicating how far this book is from being a spontaneous eruption of verse, these patterns of revision reveal Lawrence interesting himself deeply in the mythos of *Amores.* Jessie's belief that Lawrence had misrepresented her underlines the fact that his mother's death had acquired mythic proportions in his imagination. Despite the anguish it brought him, her death gave him a warrant to transvalue the relationship between male and female. Turning to the final version of *Amores,* we may be tempted to follow the scheme of the Hardy essay and call it a story of separation, while *Look! We Have Come Through!* is, of course, a marriage cycle; and both books set his mother's church in question. Neither volume, however, is quite that simple. Lawrence's enforced renunciation of his mother brings with it a more satisfactory rapprochement, for he eventually internalizes her shadowing memory to gain his "inheritance," the "gift of tongues" ("The Inheritance," *CP,* p. 108). In the meantime he hastens to replace her with a series of young women, who rebuff him or whom he proudly rebuffs, until he makes the empty unknown his companion. These elegies for Lawrence's first muse achieve for him an initiation into poetic power that resembles the initiation achieved by other poets in elegies for dead precursors or poetic rivals. But because *Amores* is not conventionally elegiac—lacking overt classical allusion, the memorial wreath of flowers, and the questioning speaker—the initiation it performs for Lawrence seems uncontrived. Its most remarkable characteristic is the frankness with which, like *Sons and Lovers, Amores* details the Oedipal bond between mother and son, brightened with a poet's romantic belief in the pristine nature of his love. The spare, local, personal stance of these elegies asks us to take them at face value, to believe that these events actually happened, to consider them every man's possible fate; the Oedipal theme appears all the bolder set before us as a common fact.

For his first poem, Lawrence chose a piece that introduces its themes from an odd angle. This was not "The Wild Common" which, as headpiece of *Rhyming Poems* and an energetic celebration of Lawrence's erotic nature, has become one of his most famous poems. "The Wild Common" was placed just after a slier piece titled "Tease." Written tongue-in-cheek, "Tease" (*RP*, no. 60) was in Lawrence's younger days one of his favorites. He wrote several versions of it and sent them to various lovers. But "Tease" is a satiric antechamber for this book of love and death. It inaugurates the mysteries of Eros, but does so through an ironic scene of courtly love, with the male speaker mocking his vain "châtelaine." Rather than bequeathing her the treasure of his soul, he laughs down her efforts to unlock its secrets:

> *Still you are not satisfied!*
>   *Still you tremble faint reproach!*
> *Challenge me I keep aside*
>   *Secrets that you may not broach.*
>
> *Maybe yes, and maybe no;*
>   *Maybe there* are *secret places,*
> *Altars barbarous below,*
>   *Elsewhere halls of high disgraces.*
>
> *Maybe yes, and maybe no,*
>   *You may have it as you please;*
> *Since you are so keen to know*
>   *Everything, Miss Ill-at-ease!*

(CP, pp. 95–96)

Punning on the figure of the "châtelaine," Lawrence exposes the vanity of a woman's attempt to pry out secrets which, after all, she wants to suppress. He teases out the facts about her: her futile scrambling after knowledge without touching the deeper, erotic truths.[27] "Tease" is as fine an opening as Lawrence could have wished for *Amores*. Like "Wedding Morn" before it in *Love Poems and Others* and "Pomegranate" after it in *Birds, Beasts and Flowers*, its subject is the secret of Lawrence's "other" life, which his books were designed both to uncover and to keep.

After "Tease" the organization of *Amores* does little to accent individual poems, even if they are intrinsically memorable. Bold and dexterously contrived poems like "The Wild Common," "Ballad of Another Ophelia," or

"Snap-Dragon" are not more noticeable than slighter poems like "Tease." But this means that the reader's attention is drawn to the gathering lines of its story. Events begin in the *Amores* version of "The Wild Common" with an excursion into nature, a domain of sexual possibility. After four stanzas, this eroticized nature becomes the backdrop for an allegory of body and soul:

> *If my veins and my breasts with love embossed*
> *Withered, my insolent soul would be gone like flowers that the hot wind took.*
>
> *So my soul like a passionate woman turns,*
> *Filled with remorseful terror to the man she scorned, and her love*
> *For myself in my own eyes' laughter burns.*
>
> (CP, p. 894)

The moral, and countermoral, could not be clearer: the soul requires its body, nature is her residence, and any woman who insists on soul over body will wither. Then with a jump in metaphor, Lawrence shifts to the sensation of two bodies, first "the soul of the wind and my blood compare," and later "Oh but the water loves me and folds me, . . . / Blood of a heaving woman who holds me" (*CP*, p. 895). Images jar against each other throughout *Amores*, usually more successfully than this (Lawrence revised the passage effectively for *Collected Poems*). Nonetheless, this poem sets forth the book's ethical aim: to wrestle down the Christian doctrine of the soul and give victory to the desired physical life. That "The Wild Common" also glances at the problem of Narcissus is not an irony directly contemplated, but neither is it easily avoided, shading without contradicting the overt allegory. The boyish speaker imagines his body returning to him, forgiven and blessed, in the guise of a woman. He will have to sacrifice this narcissistic fantasy in the poems that follow and acknowledge himself cut off, groping for himself among others instead.

Yearning for a woman is strong in these early poems and, complicating the Hardy scheme into something more psychologically accurate, he looks for her both in the future and in memory. In "Study" (*AM*, no. 3) the daydream of his sweetheart is more prominent than his present circumstances, which are thrust into parentheses at the end of each stanza. In "Virgin Youth" (*AM*, no. 5) the speaker yearns "clamorously," and desire becomes a physical power "knotting" his body with "wild strength," though without fulfillment: "the wild, strange tyranny of my body" exhausts itself on nothing (*CP*, p. 896). Between these, "Discord in Childhood" (*AM*, no. 4) replaces daydreaming with a glimpse of unmitigated strife, "two voices" raised in terrible battle, with the implication of physical battery, "a male thong booming and bruising, until it had drowned /

The other voice in a silence of blood" (*CP,* p. 36). Lawrence gives us this scene without comment. Although one might look for its explanation in Paul Morel's parents of *Sons and Lovers,* or in the biographical parents, *Amores* gives it a different, simpler frame. "Discord in Childhood" is the first of a number of pieces in which we see the "rapturous possession" of man touching woman of the Hardy essay as abusive, and love as an unsentimental contest for survival.

Why this is so becomes clear in the next poem, "Monologue of a Mother" (*AM,* no. 6), the only piece in which Mrs. Lawrence speaks. She cannot live outside her son. So she begins to mourn, first for her son,

> *Strange he is, my son, for whom I have waited like a lover;*
> *. . . as if his soul were chaunting*
> *A monotonous weird of departure away from me*

(CP, p. 47)

then for herself, "I must sit alone and wait, and never know / The loss of myself, till death comes" (*CP,* p. 48). Unwittingly, however, her creed intersects with her son's when her possession by death is figured in sexual terms: "the thought of the lipless voice of the Father shakes me / With dread, and fills my heart with the tears of desire" (*CP,* p. 48). The next two poems follow up this moment closely. The son tries to possess a young lady by challenging her God in "In a Boat" (*AM,* no. 7), "even / Stars are not safe in heaven" (*CP,* p. 49); and "Weeknight Service" (*AM,* no. 8) is an animated dialogue between the church and an indifferent sky. At length, cynically, "the five old bells" will cease and "the stars can chaff / The cool high moon at their ease" (*CP,* p. 54). The contrast of church and sky returns later in *Amores,* when the dead mother ceases to be associated with Christianity and is instead presented in the mutable and recurrent imagery of the moon.

The volume builds in groups of two, three, or at most four poems. "Disagreeable Advice" (*AM,* no. 9) follows from the previous three, though not closely (Lawrence later dropped it from his collected works; Pinto and Roberts added it to the end of *Rhyming Poems* in *CP*). Titled "Irony" in the American edition of *Amores,* it employs indented lineation to set off two pictures of springtime love that disagree with each other, a woman who "keep[s] the sunny-swift March-days waiting" and "A come and go of March-day loves" (*CP,* p. 179). Then follows a series of pendants, "Dreams Old and Nascent," "A Winter's Tale" and "Epilogue," "A Baby Running Barefoot" and "Discipline" (*AM,* nos. 10–15). In *Amores* "Dreams . . . Nascent" begins where the *English Review* version of "Dreams . . . Old" had ended, initiating "Dreams . . . Nascent" with a gesture of self-contempt that moves the poet to a more active stance and out of memory: the past that "compell[ed] my soul to conform" is "shaken and scattered" (*CP,* p. 911). This poet's story, however, is only in part self-propelled or self-motivated like Jefferies' pursuit of "new ideas." Lawrence searches among his pupils for "a glimpse of the shape of the coming dream" (*CP,* p. 912). The continuing friction with others, which Jefferies did not allow, sets boundaries to this pursuit. Construction of pendants in particular cuts across the pedantry in Lawrence's moral allegorizing to play out frictions. The poet anticipates a wintry farewell in "A Winter's Tale," though he looks forward to "One day a . . . June-hot woman" in "Epilogue" (*CP,* p. 91); while the titles attach a contrary set of suggestions, a romantic thaw in the former, a settled conclusion in the latter ("Epilogue" lost this inflexion when retitled "Forecast" in *Rhyming Poems*). "A Baby Running Barefoot" is a poet's dream of beneficent, sensuous nature embodied in the baby, "white flowers in the wind," "ripples lapping across the water," "a little robin's song," "two white butterflies," and so on (*CP,* p. 917). Among the schoolboys of "Discipline," however, "it is stormy, and raindrops cling like silver bees" (*CP,* p. 92). "Dreams" of the flesh work in strange ways, forcing him to conclude in the 1916 version, "We are not brothers, . . . we fight and we do not spare" (cf. *CP,* p. 92).[28]

Knowledge of pain and a more consciously reflecting speaker now take over, and a number of the next poems are written with hindsight. The following section (*AM,* nos. 16–25) is also the first to bear some correlation to the reworked arrangement of *Rhyming Poems* (*RP,* nos. 51–65), and since that reorganization often strengthened the sequence, I will mention variations from it in the following pages (see contents table for *Rhyming Poems* in Appendix A). All but one of the ten succeeding poems remained in this general section of the elegies, though they were reordered in *Rhyming Poems* to sort the love poems from the school verse and to group all the elegies together. In the *Amores* sequence, "Scent of Irises," "Prophet," "Last Words to Miriam," "Mystery," "Patience," "Ballad of Another Ophelia," "Restlessness," "A Baby Asleep after Pain," "Anxiety," and "The Punisher," we find a restless shifting of type-scenes and moods. "Prophet," "A Baby Asleep after Pain," and "The Punisher" (*RP,* nos. 57, 45, 59) were pushed forward to join groups of school verse; "Patience" (retitled "Suspense," *RP,* no. 64) and "Anxiety" ("Endless Anxiety," *RP,* no. 65) would precede the elegies; "Scent of Irises" and "Mystery" (*RP,* nos. 55, 61) were joined by other love poems. ("Last Words to Miriam" [*RP,* no. 78] and "Ballad of Another Ophelia" [*RP,* no. 89] were the only poems removed to later spots, and "Restlessness" was dropped from the collection.) In the group that stands in *Amores* the poet's energy mounts in the force of his impatient thoughts. In "Scent of Irises" he daydreams about his sweetheart and is glad her "sacrifice" is over, their love failed (*CP,* p. 90). In

"Last Words to Miriam" he regrets his failure to bring his lover to full sexual life and wonders what other man will manage "to plough / The shrieking cross" (*CP*, p. 112). Even the brief message of "Prophet"—"the shrouded mother of a new idea . . . / . . . seeks her procreant groom" (*CP*, p. 91)— is not merely a doctrinal statement. "Procreation," "crucifixion," and "sacrifice" were for Lawrence real events of love and death.

Then his mother is dead, and nearly all the following poems mourn her:

> the chart
> Of memory unrolls again to me
> The course of our journey here, here where we part.

> ("The End," *CP*, p. 100)

The "here" of parting is where this journey has taken place all along, but only now does the speaker acknowledge its results: in "The End" his grief-stricken regrets about her unconsummated past; in "The Bride" the amazing sight of her, keen as a bride; in "The Virgin Mother" the future, that "strange countrie" she grants him now twice from her womb (*AM*, nos. 26–28; *RP*, nos. 66–68). The metaphors of this third poem proclaim him indeed her husband: "You are a seed in the night-time, / I am a man, to plough" (*CP*, p. 102).

Sandra Gilbert argues that of these three poems, only "The Bride" has merit, while the two other "sentimental" poems were better omitted from the collected works.[29] But although the middle poem is a grippingly imagistic description of a dead bride, much would be lost from the collection without its less image-laden companions. Even individually, such poems should be judged, not by the wealth of imagery, but by the interest in the voice, its idiomatic and consciously nostalgic expression, its shifts in sentiment. Lawrence strikes up a dialogue with himself that takes on a different, complex tone with each poem, speaking first in "The End" with resentment,

> And oh, that you had never, never been
> Some of your selves, my love; that some
> Of your several faces I had never seen!

fraught with longing, "And still they come before me, and they go; / And I cry aloud in the moments that intervene" (*CP*, p. 100). In "The Bride" he adopts the unsettling neutrality of a ballad speaker, while seeing in his mother "his love": "My love looks like a girl to-night, / But she is old" (*CP*, p. 101). In "The Virgin Mother" he regains his cheer, dropping bits of dialect into his speech, then falls into dumb despair: "I must go, but my soul lies helpless / Beside your bed" (*CP*, p. 102). Without these poems we would lose Lawrence's first reactions to this death. To the graphic aspect of a dead bride, these voices add the sweet and the harsh emotions of her unacknowledged husband.

After this heightened vision of death, the more desolate grieving process begins. A "window" in previous poems functioned as the threshold for the poet's daydreams, much desired in "Dreams Old and Nascent," forsworn in "Scent of Irises," but now it is a mirror on emptiness, more distinctly in the 1916 version than in 1928: "two dark-filled eyes / That watch for ever earnestly from behind the window glass" ("At the Window": *AM*, no. 29, p. 67; cf. *CP*, p. 103; *RP*, no. 69). Instead of dreams, hallucinations of the future in "Drunk," the past in "Sorrow," and of the present in "Dolour of Autumn" possess him (*AM*, nos. 30–32; *RP*, nos. 71–73). His search for something starts up again in real earnest,

> Come then, my love, come as you will
>> Along this haunted road,
> Be whom you will, my darling, I shall
>> Keep with you the troth I trowed.[30]
>>>> ("Drunk," *AM*, p. 72; cf. *CP*, p. 106)

The mixed mess of images betrays utter confusion, his body "naked exposed on the bush," his spirit drawn "reeling," "prowling," "disseminated out" ("Dolour of Autumn," *CP*, p. 107). Entering, however, into this "dissolute" state, which he had only philosophized about in "The Wild Common," will take him to a different idea of integrity later in the volume, where loss of the maternal "soul" betokens his own leaner self.

First, a dialogue of sorts with his dead mother starts up. Language stands in for her

> You left me a gift
> Of tongues, so the shadows tell
> Me things

in "The Inheritance" (*CP*, p. 108; *AM*, no. 33; *RP*, no. 74), and in "Listening" he hears her in silence, "I feel your silence touch my words" (*CP*, p. 110; *AM*, no. 35; *RP*, no. 76).[31] Her words somehow reach him, though at first minimally in the form of "leaves" in "At the Window," and so the elegies keep coming. This should remind us how few poems there are about his mother when she was alive. There is no poem at all about her slow death, which Lawrence described in detail in *Sons and Lovers*—only the briefest foreshadowing in "Patience" and "Anxiety." Her death brings up his elegies in a rush of words, a long lyric sequence unlike any previous, deliberate effort.

"Brooding Grief" breaks the series of hallucinations; a "leaf" stops the words when it "hops like a frog before me" (*CP*, p. 110; *AM*, no. 36; *RP*, no. 77). Only that—reversing the nostalgic significance of some meager leaves in "At the Window" and the cigarette of "Sorrow"—is sufficient to tear him from "brooding" on unrealities. These epiphanic recognitions are more widely liked than their less "realistic" and imagistic companions, perhaps because even when nostalgic, they seem more representative of a bleak mourner's condition. The leaf or cigarette is more real when, like William Carlos Williams's wheelbarrow and plums, the frailty of their vehicle in language is exposed. But while these images occur only once or twice in *Amores* (and are the more eventful), other, less visual figures leap from one poem to the next to bind the sequence, working against and despite "disseminating" grief—"shadows," a burning "darkness," "silence," "ghosts," and "acrid scents" of the lingering world—all these carry on the poet's hallucinatory dialogue. Those terms also touch on a more profound problem, as Lawrence's effort to define himself in relation to "thou" merges with the more difficult task of confronting nothingness:

> *I move among a townfolk clad*
> *With words, but the night shows through*
> *Their words as they move.*

("The Inheritance," *CP*, p. 109)

That encounter is more raw, less explained, more groping in verse than it could ever be in Lawrence's novels. What is not told in the spaces within and between poems enlarges the emptiness that confronts the poet.

His mourning subsides briefly as two poems record further "hurts" in love and sickness, "Lotus Hurt by the Cold" (renamed "Lotus and Frost" in *RP*) and "Malade," and he pleads in "Liaison" ("The Yew-Tree on the Downs" in *RP*) for his lover to "draw the thorn from my discontent" (*CP*, p. 113; *AM*, nos. 37–39; *RP*, nos. 79, 80, 81). ("Last Words to Miriam," *AM*, no. 18, would later be placed at the head of this group at *RP*, no. 78.) But then in the tight sequence of four poems headed by "Troth with the Dead" (*AM*, nos. 40–43; *RP*, nos. 82–85), he reacknowledges his true bride, and his melancholy takes hold in images more thoroughly visualized than before. In "Troth with the Dead," a broken half-moon shifts in symbolism at least four times (the personal references were sharper in the 1916 version), standing first for his broken troth, then for his mother buried "like a moon in secret," then as a reestablished "sign / Of the troth with the dead that I am pledged to keep," finally for himself, "broken lover who turns to the dark of sleep" (*AM*, p. 90; cf. *CP*, pp. 114–15). Not only is his mother his betrothed, she is his other half. Identifying thus with her, he accepts her death, even if at first this means his own destruction. In "Dissolute" ("At a Loose End") he finds his "dream" in himself:

> I enclose
> Blue shadow within me . . .
> . . . inviolate,
> A darkness that dreams my dream for me.
>
> (*CP*, p. 115)

Surrounded by people "flickering" in "Submergence" (*CP*, p. 115), he forgets his "gap," but then again in the 1916 version of "The Enkindled Spring," he loses himself in the "conflagration" of spring, "a shadow that's gone astray" (*AM*, p. 94; cf. *CP*, p. 116).

Poems like these prompted Mandell to find the submerged mythic symbolism of Persephone in *Rhyming Poems,* with Mrs. Lawrence newly crowned queen of the underworld. Mandell points to mythic allusions revised out of the poems, for example, a line canceled in the Ferrier MS 27 draft of "The Bride," where Mrs. Lawrence explicitly called God her bridegroom.[32] But while Lawrence extended the symbolism of his narrative in *Collected Poems* to include overt references to Persephone (and other myths), this analogy is not hinted at in *Amores.* Lawrence probably rejected the experimental line in "The Bride" because it invites a Christian reading parallel to that of "Monologue of a Mother," and this would distract from narration of his own belated "troth." He settled in "The Bride" for an image that merges his mother with nature: "her dead mouth sings / By its shape, like thrushes in clear evenings" (*CP*, p. 101). His chosen theme supersedes religion, is bolder than myth, and stands firmly without external references.

Lost, he looks for himself among the women left in his life, longing to transfer his passion, though half-resenting the transfer in the single case where he is allowed to make it in "Reproach" (*AM*, no. 44; retitled, however, "Release" in *RP,* no. 87). This group—"Reproach," "The Hands of the Betrothed," "Excursion" ("Excursion Train"), "Perfidy" ("Turned Down"), "A Spiritual Woman" ("These Clever Women"), "Mating" ("Come Spring, Come Sorrow"), "A Love Song," "Brother and Sister," and "After Many Days" (*AM*, nos. 44–52)—was reshuffled and supplemented in *Rhyming Poems* by "Ballad of Another Ophelia," "Snap-Dragon" (both moved from other positions among the elegies), "Kisses in the Train," "Twofold," "Tarantella," and "Under the Oak" (*RP,* nos. 86–100). The reordering helped emphasize a distinctly separate stage of failed love, prior to the final elegies. In *Amores* this group is more focused on disappointment than the complex medley of *Rhyming Poems,* but in 1928 it is clearer that a search for substitutions must take place among these other women, and must partially succeed, before the poet is released from his mother. The insertion of "Reminder" between "At the Window" and "Drunk" (*AM,* nos. 29–30; *RP,* nos. 69, 71) is another example of this theme, for it describes Lawrence's first vain attempt, immediately after his mother's death, to escape despair by throwing himself upon another woman's love. In *Amores*—unable to reach the restless "hands" of his virtuous beloved in "The Hands of the Betrothed," suffocated by her unmoving nearness in "Excursion," betrayed for someone else in "Perfidy," watched and analyzed by "A Spiritual Woman," pleading for her to accept "increase" and "pain" in "Mating" and "A Love Song," worried for his sister in "Brother and Sister," and forced to accept a last dismissal in "After Many Days"—women all show him blank faces.

The reorganization of *Rhyming Poems* also appreciably strengthened the final elegies through a few minor changes. In *Amores,* nos. 53—60, this last sequence comprised "Blue" ("The Shadow of Death"), "Snap-Dragon," "A Passing-Bell," "In Trouble and Shame," "Elegy" ("Call into Death"), "Grey Evening," "Firelight and Nightfall," and "The Mystic Blue" ("Blueness"). The final sequence of these elegies (*RP,* nos. 101—8) would be "The Shadow of Death," "Birdcage Walk" (inserted from *LP*), "In Trouble and Shame," "Call into Death," "Grey Evening," "Firelight and Nightfall," "Blueness," and "A Passing-Bell." ("Snap-Dragon," a little epic of lovemaking, was placed earlier among the preceding love poems, and "A Passing-Bell" was placed at the end of the elegies, just ahead of "The Drained Cup" [*RP,* no. 109] from *Love Poems and Others.* Like "The Drained Cup," "A Passing-Bell" is a fictionalized study, proposing only an indirect analogy to Lawrence's personal mourning.) "Brother and Sister" was detached from its place above "After Many Days" to precede "The Shadow of Death," carrying with it the potent suggestion that the poet is catalyzed into the next phase by his sister, when he sees the "dead moon heaped within the new moon's arms" (*CP,* p. 132; *AM,* no. 51; *RP,* no. 100). Concern for her saves him from himself, somehow transforming his mother's doom from the static half-coin of "Troth with the Dead" into a covenant that impels him forward:

> let us take the sheer
> Unknown that lies before us, bearing the ark
> Of the covenant onwards where she cannot go!

(CP, p. 132; AM, no. 40)

To leave her like that is also to have possessed her. In "Blue" ("The Shadow of Death"), the most stunning of these last poems, he reaccomplishes this transition by way of a visionary, Whitmanesque sequence of thought. As the earth like a "ship steams out of the dark sea," he is "on the deck" to be "startled by this dawn confronting / Me." But because he is "substance of shadow," he feels himself "undawning," "wrongly" lost, buffeted by crowds of daylit things. He no longer cares: "what do I care though the very stones should cry me unreal." He holds his own, "darkling," in a scene that echoes the drift of Hardy's "The Darkling Thrush,"

> *though love is dead,*
> *I still am not homeless here, I've a tent by day*
> *Of darkness.*

> ("The Shadow of Death," *CP,* p. 133)

The 1928 version (*RP,* no. 101) ends at this bleak impasse, but in *Amores* (no. 53) he continued, "I know the Host . . . / Of living darkness" that, when "challenged" and "assaulted" by dawn, "bursts fretfully" ("Blue," *AM,* p. 120). This last conjunction is the start of something less static. The next six stanzas, indented and running in parallel tercets, play out the "confrontation" of dark with light:

> *Runs like a fretted arc-lamp into light,*
> *Stirred by conflict to shining, which else*
> *Were dark and whole with the night.*

> (*AM,* p. 120)

With every tercet new images of conflict and resistance ("a racing wheel," "the whole . . . chafed to anger," "a silent grasp") nudge the poet from his insistence on sleep, wholeness, and silence, into lengthening "leaps" of "blue sparks," "streams of bright blue drops,"

> *all the hosts of day,*
> *All lovely hosts of ripples caused by fretting*
> *The Darkness into play.*

> (*AM,* p. 121)

The "rapturous" conflict of self with nothingness, of loss against the ripening day, changes the poet where he stands—engendering in him revived motion and abundance:

> *Water and stones and stars, and myriads*
> *Of twin-blue eyes, and crops*
> *Of floury grain.*

Loss, instead of killing, jogs him into a brilliant labor.

Inserted in *Rhyming Poems* just after "The Shadow of Death," the short, enigmatic "Birdcage Walk" from *New Poems* (*RP*, no. 102) suggests a frightening uncertainty about who is caged and what is unveiled:

> *When the wind blows her veil*
> *From the woes I bewail*
>   *Of love and hereafter: . . .*
> *I cease, I turn pale.*   (*CP*, p. 133)

Is "she" a woman in mourning? His mother? Or the wind? The prospects are now as tantalizing as they are fearful. Instead of any definite revelation in the succeeding poems (identical in both collections), the poet makes a last stand against life, longing to discard his body in "In Trouble and Shame," to fall and rest in "Elegy" ("Call into Death" in *RP*), bemoaning the lost gay hours of his past in "Grey Evening" and "Firelight and Nightfall" (*AM*, nos. 56–59; *RP*, nos. 103–6).

All this makes "The Mystic Blue" (*AM*, no. 60; "Blueness" in *RP*, no. 107) seem especially confident, rebounding with "the dazzle of living" and transporting him toward the more deeply desired "fire" of the dark:

> *All these pure things come foam and spray of the sea*
> *Of Darkness abundant, which shaken mysteriously*
> *Breaks into dazzle of living, as dolphins leap from the sea*
> *Of midnight and shake it to fire, till the flame of the shadow we see.*
> ("Blueness," *CP*, p. 136)

In the equivalent scene closing *Sons and Lovers,* Paul Morel had to resist the night sky insurgent with his dead parent. The poet of 1916 can call her back, transform her in a visionary resurrection, an erotic, "dolphin-torn" sea change.

Set against the rhythms of Whitman in "Blue" and "The Mystic Blue," highly romantic effects of language—often evoking Arthurian legend— can be found in many of Lawrence's manuscript poems, but were mostly edited out when published. Only traces of grail imagery, for example, were left in "Discipline" and "Mystery" (*AM*, nos. 15, 19; *RP*, nos. 58, 61). As if making a deliberate exception of the mystic elegies, "Firelight and Nightfall" and "Grey Evening" (*AM*, nos. 58–59; *RP*, nos. 105–6), Lawrence added gilt touches in 1916 and retained these through heavy revisions for *Collected Poems:*

>   *queens in hyacinth and skies of gold,*
> *. . . woods are scrolled*
> *And diapered above the chaunting flowers.*
> ("Firelight and Nightfall," *CP*, p. 135)

Such language suggests that its speaker is in a hallucinatory state of mind, imagining himself his mother's shining knight. But Lawrence may also have wished to strike an aestheticized and archaic note near the end of this book. References in "Grey Evening" to the Book of Hours recall his interest in Taylor's romanticized work *The Hours of Fiammetta:*

> *When you went, how was it you carried with you*
> *My missal book of fine, flamboyant Hours?*
> *My book of turrets and of red-thorn bowers,*
> *And skies of gold, and ladies in bright tissue?*

(CP, p. 135)

Amores is the male counterpart to Taylor's book, the passion of the Madonna's son, and it coolly alters the Book of Hours with its traditional account either of Mary's life or of Christ's by narrating the passionate relationship between the two.

The latinate title *Amores,* which Lawrence suggested for the book after it was in proof, casts a decadent air over the finished volume. Months later he recalled the "unreal" mood that possessed him when compiling it: "I almost wept when I put together the *Amores* poems. It all seems so strange and far-off, unreal, and yet, in another mood, so near and *navrant*" (*Letters,* 3:61). *Navrant* possesses the ambiguous connotations of "grievous" and "annoying," indicating Lawrence's ambivalent attitudes about himself—his grief, yet his impatience with the past. He used the term *navrant* in other contexts to describe the old-fashioned: Bastien Lepage's Pauvre Fauvette "too is navrante. . . . It seems that the great sympathetic minds are all overwhelmed by the tragic waste, and pity, and suffering of it" (*Letters,* 1:120). He associated *Amores* at the last with the tragic world of Hardy, which he put off, not in a careless act of dismissal, but in mourning. In trial dedications of the book to Ottoline Morrell, he expressed this ambivalence with his usual wit:

> *To Ottoline Morrell*
> *my friend*
> *I dedicate these poems*
> *records*
> *Of the pain and of my hope*
> *now spent*
> *Into her safe-keeping*
> *That she may be free*
> *To forget them.*[33]

In the fall he wrote to Cynthia Asquith, "I send you a bit of the world that has passed away—my book of poems" (*Letters,* 2:649). The "records" of

his old efforts to thrust himself out of the past are themselves thrust behind. He advised his patrons to do so as well, to shed their hours of pain
with his books.

LOOK! WE HAVE COME THROUGH!

Look! We Have Come Through! cast what had seemed new in *Amores* even
further into the shadow of the past and completed the cycle of poetry that
remained from Lawrence's history as an unmarried man, bringing that
story up to 1917, when he prepared his verse for publication. The mystical
unknown heralded in *Amores* seemed incarnated in Frieda. He wrestled
fiercely to capture her loyalty, finding in her the woman he so desired in
the "Study of Thomas Hardy," his proper mate; and their union released
him to dare the public in pursuing his writing. Still, the freedoms he found
through her struck severe limits. In 1917 he was desperately anxious to ex-
tend his world beyond Frieda, to make new contacts in the sphere of
manly endeavor and to find larger public arenas for his influence. These
other plans remained in limbo. As he compiled his book, he had finished
the penultimate draft of *Women in Love* and was planning to leave England
as soon as possible. *Look! We Have Come Through!* was meant to be his
"last work for the old world" (*Letters*, 3:90). As it turned out, *Women in
Love* did not find a publisher, and *Look! We Have Come Through!* became
the only vehicle by which the experiences informing *Women in Love* could
reach the public. *Look! We Have Come Through!* rehearses the story of Ursula and Birkin, their marriage and Birkin's "struggle for verbal consciousness" (Foreword, *Women in Love,* p. viii). And though its protagonist is
stranded in England, unable to begin the wandering on which Ursula and
Birkin embarked, this book ends like *Women in Love* on a note, not of triumph, but of plaintive hope.

In *Look! We Have Come Through!* Lawrence succeeded in completing a
third and final phase in his initiation as a poet. His earliest publications
had done no more than announce his debut, though they aroused hopes of
powerful work to come. *Amores* had enabled him to confront a terrible
personal loss, but stopped short of his "new life" and did not compel readers to see it as much more than a miscellany. Only with *Look! We Have
Come Through!* did he create a design for his book that, no matter how
much they disliked it, readers could not ignore. One key to recognizing his
poetic powers was the acknowledgment of Whitman. Although only a few
poems owe a direct debt to Whitman's style, their affinities in purpose are
at last fully admitted, as Bernice Slote in *Start with the Sun* explained: "to
paraphrase a line from 'Song of Myself,' Lawrence seems to be stuccoed
with Whitmanese all over," and "most significantly in *Look! We Have Come*

Through! a book which is the equivalent of Whitman's 'Children of Adam,'" Lawrence celebrates "the mystery of the life force—the body, physical love, and sex—all the Adamic wonder in life incarnate."[34] He sought to correct Whitman's "Song of Myself" by emphasizing the fact that "myself" may not necessarily be loved—composing his "Song of a Man Who Is Not Loved" as well as "Song of a Man Who Is Loved"—but Whitman's precedent stands before all the poems, particularly its three "Songs" and its other didactic climaxes, "New Heaven and Earth" and "Manifesto." The titular poem, "Song of a Man Who Has Come Through," subdued Whitman's "Song of Myself" once and for all to Lawrence's theme: "Not I, not I, but the wind that blows through me! / A fine wind is blowing the new direction of Time" (*CP*, p. 250). After publication of *Look! We Have Come Through!* Lawrence wrote "Poetry of the Present" and wished it could have appeared as a preface to this book (which it now does in *The Complete Poems*). This essay, which proved to be the most famous statement of his poetics, is nothing less than a joyous confession of indebtedness to Whitman: "One realm we have never conquered: the pure present. One great mystery of time is terra incognita to us: the instant. The most superb mystery we have hardly recognized: the immediate, instant self. The quick of all time is the instant. The quick of all the universe, of all creation, is the incarnate, carnal self. Poetry gave us the clue: free verse: Whitman. Now we know" (*CP*, p. 185).

What did it amount to, this instant moment of Now? The concept is unhelpful if applied strictly to Lawrence's narrative and sequential, hence time-bound, verse. "Poetry of the Present" was in part polemic, meant to hustle readers out of any complacent formal expectations. When we consider how he actually framed time in his book, we discover that, as in *Amores*, he gave his story a dialectical orientation: by placing these poems in the order in which they originally occurred in the vital *present*, into which he had "come through" with Frieda from his Victorian past; yet by indicating in the closing poems (from "New Heaven and Earth" to "Craving for Spring") and in his introductory Argument to this volume that, nonetheless, all these poems belong to the *past*, from which once again he is trying to emerge. Only at the end may Frieda and Lawrence "transcend into some condition of blessedness" (Argument, *CP*, p. 191). The future New World always hovers just beyond grasp: so Lawrence cries out in the last two lines, "Ah, do not let me die on the brink of such anticipation! / Worse, let me not deceive myself" ("Craving for Spring," *CP*, p. 274). Still it would be a mistake to say that Lawrence failed to reimagine Whitman's Eden of instancy. Located on the mobile edge between the past and the future, between fate and fortune, this is Lawrence's Edenic:

Now, at the day's renascence
We approach the gate.

Now, from the darkened spaces
Of fear, and of frightened faces,
Death, in our awed embraces
Approached and passed by;

We near the flame-burnt porches
Where the brands of the angels, like torches,
Whirl, —in these perilous marches
Pausing to sigh;

We look back on the withering roses,
The stars, in their sun-dimmed closes,
Where 'twas given us to repose us
Sure on our sanctity.

("Paradise Re-entered," *CP*, p. 242)

Although there are no surviving notebooks to compare with the final version of *Look! We Have Come Through!* there are many signs of Lawrence's intentions: "I have gathered and shaped my last poems into a book" (*Letters*, 3:87). The drafts that remain indicate that the poems were extensively revised before inclusion in *Look! We Have Come Through!* but further revised only minimally in 1928 for volume 2, *Unrhyming Poems*, in *Collected Poems*. At least twenty-five of the sixty-five pieces in *Collected Poems* (sixty-six, with Pinto and Roberts's inclusion of "Meeting among the Mountains" in *CP*) were altered from their original versions, and—whether in 1917 or 1928—these tend to reflect the same concern that affected the larger organization of the book: moving away from the strictly personal nature of Lawrence's marriage to its broader symbolism. In "Song of a Man Who Is Loved," a busy and humble Lawrence—

All day long I am busy and happy at my work. . . .
. . . I need only come home each night to find the dear
Door on the latch. . . .

And what I have failed in . . .
Comes up unnamed from her body.

(*CP*, pp. 948–49)

—cedes to an elemental universe:

Rocks seem, and earth, and air uneasy, and waters still ebbing west.
All things on the move, going their own little ways.

. . . . .

So at last I touch
All that I am-not in softness, sweet softness, for she is such.

(*CP,* pp. 249–50)

So too in ordering these poems, Lawrence excluded a group recording his first meetings with Frieda at her husband's home in Nottingham, England, and at Edward Garnett's farmhouse, the Cearne, near Edenbridge, Kent. Garnett, who was Lawrence's editor and a man with progressive views, invited Frieda and Lawrence to his home before their elopement to Germany. It is unlikely that Lawrence had forgotten the poems he wrote about these English nights. Even if he destroyed the originals, Lawrence must also have had access to these manuscripts, since he sent copies to Garnett, who kept much material for him to recall at any time.[35] Had he included these poems, they would have preceded "Ballad of a Wilful Woman" and "First Morning" (and, in the 1928 sequence, "Bei Hennef"), poems set in Germany and describing his elopement with Frieda. But Lawrence had come to think of the journey as the beginning of his new life, endowing these events with symbolic priority over his meetings with Frieda in England. The flight to Europe conclusively broke their connections with the old world. In the Note to *Collected Poems* he explains: "Of this volume [*Look! We Have Come Through!*] the first few poems belong to England and the end of the death-experience, but 'Bei Hennef,' written in May 1912, by a river in the Rhineland, starts the new cycle" (*CP,* p. 28). Because it was previously published in *Love Poems and Others,* "Bei Hennef" was not returned to the "new cycle" until *Collected Poems.* Analysis of *Look! We Have Come Through!* is based here on its second version in *Collected Poems* because, while not widely different from its first published form (in comparison with the drastic changes wrought in *Amores* when it was incorporated into *Collected Poems*), the second version reflects Lawrence's fuller and, for the most part, original intentions.

Several key poems, missing from the first version, were added in 1928, including some previously published—"Bei Hennef," "Everlasting Flowers," "Coming Awake"—and one rejected by Lawrence's publishers in 1917, "Song of a Man Who Is Loved." Three of these register occasions when Lawrence felt himself entering the "condition of blessedness" mentioned in his Argument to the volume (*CP,* p. 191), while one, "Everlasting Flowers," revives old memories. A fifth poem, "Meeting among the Mountains," had also been rejected by Chatto and Windus, but Lawrence made no effort to restore it in *Collected Poems,* perhaps because even in 1917, he did not "feel strongly about" it (*Letters,* 3:145–46). Pinto and Roberts returned it to its original position in *The Complete Poems.* It is the single piece in which Lawrence encounters the phantom of an angry male rival, "the brown eyes black with misery and hate" (*CP*, p. 225). Although all five poems would seem to be unforgettable moments of emotional intensity in Lawrence's marriage story, they were eliminated without substantially altering the contours of the volume because, like all his collections, *Look! We Have Come Through!* is a book of crises. Three years later in May 1920, Lawrence mentioned yet another poem that was "to go with 'Craving for Spring' and 'Frost Flowers,' at the end of *Look*" (*Letters*, 3:513). This appears to be "Erinnyes," which belongs more comfortably with the war verse (see chapter 4) than with these poems, and Lawrence made no effort to retrieve it in 1928 for *Collected Poems*. In style and theme it jars with the 1917 conclusion, having nothing to do with marriage and going far beyond "Frost Flowers" to picture the war dead:

> *There are so many dead,*
> *Many have died unconsenting,*
> *Their ghosts are angry, unappeased.*

("Erinnyes," *CP*, p. 739)

The reason behind the publishers' censorship was, according to Lawrence in a first draft of his Note to *Collected Poems*, that they "objected to mixing love and religion" (*CP*, p. 852), but this mixture could not be removed with revision of a few poems. *Look! We Have Come Through!* offers its blasphemies as a version of the sacred: "But I hope I shall spend eternity / with my face down buried between her breasts" ("Song of a Man Who Is Loved," *CP*, p. 852). On the advice of Catherine Carswell, with whom he corresponded frequently about his publication problems with *Look! We Have Come Through!* Lawrence removed a love letter to Frieda and never replaced it (*Letters*, 3:94 n. 1). Its inclusion would have further authenticated the story, while highlighting its association with *La vita nuova*, its primary Christian subtext. For the heavenly Beatrice, there is the restive Frieda, whom Lawrence must subdue sufficiently to marry. Rewriting his own "history of the soul of man," he is reborn through Frieda: he engages in life's deadly conflicts with her, and is born again in marriage, reconstituting the sacrament from within. Near the end of the book, Lawrence's bout with marriage brings him a final blessing—the intuition of a worldly church, contracted between man and the still greater existence in and around him:

> *The unknown, strong current of life supreme*
> *drowns me and sweeps me away and holds me down*
> *to the sources of mystery.*

("New Heaven and Earth," *CP*, p. 261)

In praising marriage, Lawrence sought no sanction from society. Society must take its sanctions from personal lives such as his.

But how can the common reader perceive a significant form in this book, how can it appeal to his need for order, when Lawrence conceived of the "order of experience" as a series of crises with no moment more precious than the next? Imbedded in this conception is the paradox of an order ever-immanent in disorderly existence, and Lawrence built this paradox into every level of his book, from its framing devices to the least of its verse. The Foreword introduces the reader to his methods by explaining that while this is a coherent volume, its form is indefinable, not conforming to anything previously written, "an essential story, or history, or confession" (*CP*, p. 191). Lawrence omitted this Foreword in the 1928 *Collected Poems* (though it was restored by Pinto and Roberts), probably because he duplicated its message in his prefacing Note: "many of the poems are so personal that, in their fragmentary fashion, they make up a biography of an emotional and inner life. . . . Even the best poetry, when it is at all personal, needs the penumbra of its own time and place and circumstance to make it full and whole" (*CP*, pp. 27–28).

Lawrence appended an Argument also to his book, and this he kept even in the 1928 version: "After much struggling and loss in love and in the world of man, the protagonist throws in his lot with a woman who is already married. Together they go into another country, she perforce leaving her children behind. The conflict of love and hate goes on between the man and the woman, and between these two and the world around them, till it reaches some sort of conclusion, they transcend into some condition of blessedness" (*CP*, p. 191). Without this Argument, the plot of the book would be far more difficult to decipher; the particularities of "a woman who is already married" and her "children" left behind are mentioned directly in only two poems, "She Looks Back" and "Ballad of a Wilful Woman," the latter an allegorical fable of Mary, Joseph, and a beggar. The Argument articulates the ethical impulses behind Lawrence's book, his urge to create a parable of himself and an Arnoldian belief in the power of life to make itself whole. If by the end of the book the protagonist-Lawrence learns to see beyond himself into the nature of being, the poet-Lawrence (and the reader) discovers coherence in the poems by identifying their place and relevance in a phase of this man's life. But there is also a deep restlessness in this story that prevents the reader from finding any easy formula for experience or any possibility for everlasting peace. The Argument differs significantly from Lawrence's paradigm of the chain dance, delightfully closing and opening time and again in the "Study of Thomas Hardy," for here, summed up neatly in the last sentence, the central action is a perpetual conflict of love and hate. When the Argument was reprinted in his 1928 *Collected Poems* Lawrence eliminated the last seven words, "they transcend into some condition of blessedness," leaving the end of his Argument still more open than before. (Lawrence's editors replaced these words in *Complete Poems*.) *Look! We Have Come Through!* is the story of a lover's quarrel, writ large.

In the terms of the Hardy essay and in comparison with *Amores,* the story of *Look! We Have Come Through!* should, of course, be described as a rapturous possession, sung in the mood of Solomon rather than bewildered Job. Yet the problem of the elegies, the temptation of narcissistic merging and the necessity to split from the other, is the challenge also of this book of marriage, and as in an elegiac cycle, the man must give up the other before he can attain her. The consequent ethical concerns are more prominent and more complex than in *Amores,* for the lovers' contest not only rewrites "the history of the soul of man" of his letter to Gordon Campbell in 1914; it transacts a series of skirmishes against orthodox Christian values, against the Christian virtue of self-sacrifice, against motherhood reembodied in Frieda, and against her preordained marriage with Weekley. To redeem her is to reach the equipoise preached in *Women in Love,* within and between man and woman, the devil weighed in with the angel, selflessness countered by pride. Even their triumphs and doubts stand in balance. And at the end, true to the processive character of this sequence, final satisfaction is postponed for desire to go on.

Several structures organize the poems. In addition to the story outlined in the Argument, Lawrence locates his verse on a geographical map and a calendar, creates sets of framing poems, and segments its dramatic progression into more manageable verse clusters. The sequence itself is more tightly knit than in *Amores,* gathering into groups of as many as seven poems, linked by theme and mood, and within those groups, smaller clusters of two and three literally continue each other's thoughts. There is far more dialogue as well, both suggested and actual within and between poems: in one he may boldly assert, "the night was a failure / but why not—?" ("First Morning," no. 10, *CP,* p. 204), only to retreat upon himself in the next, "No, now I wish the sunshine would stop, / . . . / . . . and it would be thick black dark for ever" ("'And Oh—That the Man I Am Might Cease to Be—,'" no. 11, *CP,* p. 205); or he begs, "do not leave me" ("Humiliation," no. 17, *CP,* p. 215), and she replies, "The pain of loving you / Is almost more than I can bear" ("A Young Wife," no. 18, *CP,* p. 215); or they may proclaim their love, each in turn, first he in "Song of a Man Who Has Come Through" (no. 56, *CP,* p. 250), then she in "One Woman to All Women" (no. 57, *CP,* pp. 251–52). There is still plenty of air in the sequence, much that is not said; the causes and ends of particular quarrels are usually hinted in fictional poems rather than detailed in the first person. This flexible system of linkage at times replicates the "chain dance" of the Hardy essay, at other times the quarrels and conflicts of the Argument, but never does it imitate the circumstantial detailing and elaborate continuities of the novel.

Place-names appended to a third of the poems appear in the approximate order in which Frieda and Lawrence visited those spots, so that Keith Sagar in his *Calendar* of Lawrence's writings has been able to collate the "placed" poems with dates.[36] These geographical tags authenticate their narratives and endow them, as geographical naming often does, with the symbolic value of genii loci. But these tags also simplified Lawrence's actual journeys, not recording their return to Germany from Italy in April 1913 or a visit to England in June 1913. The first poems are set in England (nos. 2–7, "Elegy" to "Hymn to Priapus," *CP*, pp. 193–99); the early section of love verse in Germany (chiefly in the Isarthal near Munich, nos. 8–29, "Ballad of a Wilful Woman" to "A Doe at Evening," *CP*, pp. 200–22); the mountain poems in places along the lovers' route to Sterzing, Austria (nos. 30–33, "Song of a Man Who Is Not Loved" to "Meeting among the Mountains," *CP*, pp. 222–26); which in turn flow into the poems of Italy, the couple's home for some time after their mountain walk (no. 34, "Everlasting Flowers," *CP*, pp. 226–27, heads this group, which has no certain termination). Most of those after the mountain walk are not located geographically, and their emotional ascent is made without reference to actual places. The symbolic value of these spottings was best summed up by Lawrence when he called his walking tour of Europe "my sentimental journey," alluding, with a touch of irony, to Laurence Sterne's *A Sentimental Journey through France and Italy*, which Sterne described as "a quiet journey of the heart in pursuit of Nature, and those affections which arise out of her."[37] Lawrence's Nature is Frieda, and he keeps a record of their journey south as one would a spiritual diary. Finally, his geographical map alerts us to the disruptive ending of this "sentimental journey," for amid the marriage poems (nos. 50–57, "Paradise Re-entered" to "One Woman to All Women"), the place-names chart his return to England in June 1914 and leave him there (nos. 53–66, "Wedlock" to "Craving for Spring").

The calendrical system gives the book an equally mixed realistic and mythic character. The Foreword explains that, "the period covered is, roughly, the sixth lustre of a man's life" (*CP*, p. 191), but the "sixth lustre" refers to ages twenty-five to thirty, whereas Lawrence's book actually covers the history of six or seven years from ages twenty-five to thirty-two (1910–17). (*Lustre* denotes either a five-year period or a purification rite enacted by the Romans every five years.) Among many hints that Lawrence paid little heed to the order in which these poems were written, at least three—"Martyr à la Mode," "People," and "Street Lamps" (nos. 4, 58, 59)—derive from the earliest extant manuscripts. The greater part of these sixty-six poems (all but eighteen or nineteen) derive from two years, May 1912 to July 1914. Three more years pass rapidly in the last twelve poems: a year-long gap intervenes between Lawrence's return to the Cearne recorded in "History" (no. 54) and his marriage to Frieda, which inspired "Song of a Man Who Has Come Through" (no. 56); another year passes by in the next five poems (nos. 57–61); and a second gap of one year separates these from "Elysium" (no. 62). These three years were war years extending from 1914 to early 1917. But the calendar of *Look! We Have Come Through!* is not likely to be experienced by the reader as either a five-year or a seven-year cycle, nor would he notice its uneven distribution. Far more evident is the transcription of two seasonal cycles, two winters and springs, and a third rapid passage through winter, reflected in the titles of the last three poems, "Autumn Rain," "Frost Flowers," and "Craving for Spring" (nos. 64–66). Implicitly in the elegiac opening (explicitly in Christmas Day of "Hymn to Priapus," no. 7), winter is the first season of the book. From there it turns to spring in "Bei Hennef" (May 1912; no. 9) and to the summer of their "First Morning" (no. 10); plunges into winter as if prematurely in the mountains; returns to spring in England and summer, when the couple marries; and closes wintering again.

A frame for the book is produced in part by these structures of place and time, with England and winter ironically the source and the end of the story. Sets of framing poems are further highlighted by styles unlike the personal middle series. As scholars have often noted, Swinburne, Hardy, and Tennyson are all mimicked in the first six poems, predating the encounter with Frieda and devoted to the old world of Lawrence's youth, while Whitman oversees several poems near the end, dating from Lawrence's marriage and its aftermath. The headpiece, "Moonrise" (a poem that should be better known than it is), contains several allusive lyric elements. It is a compact sonnetlike poem in blank verse and consists of a single loftily rhetorical question:

> And who has seen the moon, who has not seen
> Her rise from out the chamber of the deep,
> Flushed and grand and naked.

> ("Moonrise," *CP*, p. 193)

The impersonal rhetoric and consistently high-toned diction set this poem apart from the first-person, starker speech of Lawrence's poems to Frieda, as in "Bei Hennef" and its successors: "You are near to me, and your naked feet in their sandals" ("On the Balcony," no. 13, *CP*, p. 208).

But as marked as this stylistic heightening is the way in which "Moonrise" predicts many other poems in the volume; the frame is not detachable from its more central urges. Its symbolism has been noted by previous scholars, transforming the maternal moon into a bridal figure, Frieda replacing Mrs. Lawrence as the poet's Persephone. "Moonrise" also appears to emerge out of an older style, strikingly like and unlike a sonnet, with thirteen lines in rough iambic pentameter. Its vocabulary is echoed throughout the volume, "deep, / Flushed and grand and naked." Moving away from a poem like Keats's "When I Have Fears That I May Cease to Be," Lawrence sees the moon as a bride, "rise and throw / Confession of delight upon the wave," not at all like amorphous "Huge cloudy symbols of a high romance"; and rather than deciding, like Keats, that "then on the shore / Of the wide world I stand alone, and think," Lawrence concludes that

> *time will dim the moon*
> *Sooner than our full consummation here*
> *In this odd life will tarnish or pass away.*[38]

Lawrence repeats, to reverse the direction of Keats's passionate thought and even of his imagery—sky and sea rising, not sinking, into numinous presences of "this odd life."

The first line alone suggests the ends Lawrence has in view: the questioning line that begins in mid-sentence, "And who has seen . . . , who has not seen," rhetorically anticipates the unspoken answer "no one." The negative, both stated and delayed, establishes the rhythm of Lawrence's thought and points to the philosophic resolution of the volume. He searches and will find his being in nonbeing, the I in the not-I, and will learn to see after learning not to see. "Moonrise" threads together some key, antiphonal themes of this book: of death and revival, the odd and the consummate, I and thou, and a visionary sense that surpasses actual sight.

Similarly, the last, didactic prothalamia of the volume emerge from, while framing, the more personal poems of the book's interior. "New Heaven and Earth" (no. 61), for example, has been widely read and recognized, for the simple reason that it shows off a new style indebted to Whitman. This poem takes us beyond the personal into more generalized discourse and the expansive, self-regenerating structure we associate with Whitman. Like "Moonrise," "New Heaven and Earth" begins in midstream, though now Lawrence addresses us in his own voice, aware of his experience as a rite of passage: "And so I cross into another world" (*CP*,

p. 256). Also like "Moonrise," this poem uses style to dramatize its passage into "another world"; it mimics (as did Whitman) the language of the Bible, but it replaces the third-person discourse with first-person and abruptly shifts (in mid-section, in parts 4, 6, and 7) from a biblical historical past—"When I saw the torn dead, I knew it was my own torn dead body" (CP, p. 257)—to Whitman's present tense: "When I am trodden quite out, quite, quite out, / every vestige gone, then I am here" (CP, p. 258).

Where "Moonrise" predicts the themes and direction of the book, "New Heaven and Earth" recapitulates the book's nearly completed progress and structure. "New Heaven and Earth" is more than a summary of themes, more even than, as Anaïs Nin described it, "an allegory of Lawrence's wide cycle of experience";[39] its tense changes, its extensive parallelism, repeating and unfolding Lawrence's history in eight long verse sections, enable this poem to reiterate the book's dialectical progress. Lawrence moves, defiant of any logic, from sea to shore to a further, "unknown" sea: as he reaches shore, "I touched her flank and knew I was carried by the current in death / over to the new world, and was climbing out on the shore," and then "the unknown, strong current of life supreme / drowns me" (CP, pp. 260–61).

Lawrence did not make "New Heaven and Earth" or any of the other overtly Whitmanesque poems the last piece of his volume, however. Instead, breaking the effect of his manifestos, he concluded with three poems that mourn the "acrid winter" of England. The final poem, "Craving for Spring" (no. 66), is mixed in nature, inviting comparison as much with Shelley's great poem of autumnal yearning, "Ode to the West Wind," as with anything by Whitman: "I wish it were spring / cunningly blowing on the fallen sparks, odds and ends of the old, scattered fire" (CP, p. 271). Yet Lawrence uses Whitman's devices of repetition and expansion to explode the tight terza rima of Shelley's ode, and he counters Shelley's wistful uncertainties with the aggressive self-assertion that he shared with Whitman:

> *Let it be spring!*
> *Come, bubbling, surging tide of sap!*
> *Come, rush of creation!*
> *Come, life! surge through this mass of mortification!*
>
> (CP, pp. 270–71)

The resemblance between Shelley and Lawrence can hardly be accidental, since in "Poetry of the Present" Lawrence established Shelley with Keats as poets of "perfection" to be contrasted with Whitman, great poet of "imperfection." His essay calls up unmistakable analogies between the poetry of Keats and Shelley and his own. He writes at first with apparent sympathy:

> It seems when we hear a skylark singing as if sound were running forward into the future, running so fast and utterly without consideration, straight on into futurity. And when we hear a nightingale, we hear the pause and the rich, piercing rhythm of recollection, the perfected past. . . . Perfected bygone moments, perfected moments in the glimmering futurity, these are the treasured gem-like lyrics of Shelley and Keats.
>   But there is another kind of poetry. (*CP*, pp. 181–82)

Lawrence sees that other kind, the poetry of the immediate present and of imperfection, as emerging at the wellspring between the future and the past: "Here, in this very instant moment, up bubbles the stream of time, out of the wells of futurity, flowing on to the oceans of the past" (*CP*, p. 183). The Keatsian "Moonrise" describes just such an ocean of the past, and the Shelleyan "Craving for Spring" describes just such wells of futurity: "bubbling, surging tide of sap" (*CP*, p. 270). Whether he fully intended it or not, Lawrence gave his volume a frame that succeeds—where more faithfully Whitmanesque verse and a definitive ending could not—in remaking the isolated, gemlike poetry of past and future into the wedded momentaneous poems of the present.

Between these framing poems, no core section forms the heart of the volume. Rather, several groups mark phases in the story: an initial elegiac section, a group of poems marking the couple's first love, five "Rose" poems, another group recording the Lawrences' walk south through the mountains, five "Night" pieces, a marriage section, and the closing manifestos and wintry odes. While these groups do not account for all the poems in the volume or for all its changes in mood, they roughly mark a double curve in its progress, parallel to the seasonal changes. The Rose and Night poems record periods of reconciliation; between these, the mountain-walk poems transact an anti-Wordsworthian descent from joy into the lovers' uneasy memories. Lawrence's death experience, in other words, is not confined to the first poems in the volume; he devolves into agony, "crucified" in the midst of his adventure with Frieda. His story climbs upward from its elegiac beginning into the Rose poems, down again into the moral and elegiac struggle of the mountain-walk poems, then steadily up into the climactic prothalamia, and takes a sudden, final, ambivalent drop.

The opening section (nos. 2–7) rehearses the problems of the elegies, the "grey days" and night, that "great dark glittery window" through which "I can almost touch you" ("Elegy," no. 2, *CP*, pp. 193–94), the solipsistic exhaustion with stars, wind, and grass "dabbling in me" as in a pool ("Nonentity," no. 3, *CP*, p. 194), and the sterility of a man without a woman, "celibate and single. . . / Sea, you shadow of all things, now mock us to death with your shadowing" ("The Sea," no. 6, *CP*, p. 197). Water, which had been the maternal temptation in the elegies and Swinburne (to whom "The Sea" alludes), is here the narcissistic male. But in "Martyr à la Mode" (no. 4), he rises from lethargy to accept a "dream of flesh" unlike his "old dreams," a "keen dream / Of sudden anguish" (*CP*, p. 196), and in "Don Juan" and "Hymn to Priapus" (nos. 5, 7), he looks to the gods of fertility for his resurrection, to Isis and Priapus. Among his most startling poems, "Hymn to Priapus" is also an elegy; barely mournful, his depression gone, grief itself has become fertile, "freeing" him to be both loyal and at large:

> Grief, grief, I suppose and sufficient
> Grief makes us free
> To be faithless and faithful together
> As we have to be.

(*CP*, p. 199)

"Ballad of a Wilful Woman" (no. 8) complements "Hymn to Priapus" with the female version, a will-less and willful woman. This allegorization of Frieda leaving her husband and children for several suitors and, finally, "the cruel journey" with a "beggar" (*CP*, pp. 202–3), introduces the next section of Lawrence's first love for Frieda (nos. 9–18). With "Bei Hennef" (no. 9), dialogue enters the poems, and the sequence becomes personal— "too personal" in the opinions of some readers: in the words of Auden, "I must confess that I find Lawrence's love poems embarrassing because of their lack of reticence; they make me feel a Peeping Tom."[40] Yet the details are translated into symbols of nature, shadows and light, mountains and rivers, squirrels and frogs, so that the personal must be something of an illusion, produced by the contrast of this iconoclastic, plainspoken sequence with previous verse cycles. Even in comparison with the *Sonnets from the Portuguese* of Elizabeth Barrett Browning, Lawrence's poems seem more intimate; her choice of the sonnet on the one hand and her pious sentiments on the other, have little in common with the style in which Lawrence brings his domestic disputes into the public. Some of those readers who have been most critical of the poems' private nature defend them, nonetheless, as a series: thus A. Alvarez points out that the sequence is better than its individual pieces, its impact "as direct and painful as anything since Clare. Yet if would be hard to localize this power in any one poem."[41] It was precisely because Lawrence could not see his experience as merely a personal one that his book could perform its rite of initiation, enabling him to realize himself as a man, a poet and visionary, with insight even into the nature of being. No less so for the reader, the "personal" poems cannot be severed from this series; the collection is greater than any of its members.

Even the rhythm of this cycle, its successive stages, goes against our expectations. Running contrary to anticipation almost from the start, the group of first love from "Bei Hennef" to "A Young Wife" (nos. 9–18) is about misery and struggle, the obstacles to "achieving" love: the "night a failure" ("First Morning," no. 10, p. 204), the woman dragged back by "motherhood" ("She Looks Back," no. 12, *CP*, p. 207), and afraid of his "darkness" ("In the Dark," no. 15, *CP*, p. 211). In "Mutilation" (no. 16), he has let her go and is again alone, and in "Humiliation" (no. 17) he begs her, "do not leave me" (*CP*, p. 215). In the consolatory verse, "still we have each other" ("On the Balcony," no. 13, *CP*, p. 209) and "we dance together," "in triumph" ("Frohnleichnam," no. 14, *CP*, p. 210): assurances that defy the roaring "thunder" and the fact that they have hurt others. Their sprightly dualistic love is wrenched out of a past that tends to turn her into a pillar of salt, to cripple him. Yet these initial obstructions also stave off the desire for perfect echoing, mirror reflection, in which individuality would be lost. Opposed to all the world and opposites of each other, conflict will become their way of being. By the end of the sequence, she has admitted his difference: in contrast to her sunny nature, "the darkness starts up where / You stand" ("A Young Wife," no. 18, *CP*, p. 215).

These first meetings and separations are then repeated in two closely knit groups, gathered around "Gloire de Dijon" (nos. 19–24) and around "Forsaken and Forlorn" (nos. 25–29). In "Green" and "Gloire de Dijon" (nos. 19, 21) Frieda is identified with nature, much like the child in "Baby Running Barefoot" and "A Baby Asleep after Pain." Through their interactions, the speaker may become a thing of nature also, like "mauve-red petals on the cloth" ("Roses on the Breakfast Table," no. 22, *CP*, pp. 217–18). When she calls him "beautiful," he sees himself "lovely" as roses. Yet he also realizes that his effort makes this possible:

> *I achieve*
> *My very self.*
>
> . . . . .
>
> *I to myself am brought.*
>
> ("I Am Like a Rose," no. 23, *CP*, p. 218)

He is born from himself—born from *his* effort to reach the other rather than from her maternity: "this heave of effort / At starting other life, fulfilled my own" ("Rose of All the World," no. 24, *CP,* p. 218). The closing piece of this group, "Rose of All the World," is the most curious. Alluding to Yeats, whom Frieda loved despite anything Lawrence could say, these poems are written as much in despite of Yeats's ethereal symbols as in response to actual roses ("He seems awfully queer stuff to me now—as if he wouldn't bear touching. But Frieda is fond of him" [*Letters,* 1:488]). "Rose of All the World" is the most philosophic of the group and contains much of Lawrence's distinctive imagery:

> *Rose-leaves that whirl in colour round a core*
> *Of seed-specks kindled lately and softly blown*
>
> *By all the blood of the rose-bush into being—* . . .
> *To bring together two strange sparks.*

> (*CP,* p. 218)

Although Yeats also had his roses stand for both source and end, this poem has little else in common with his. In addition to Lawrence's eventual conclusion, that roses stand for themselves and nothing else, his form of thought is mobile, no gemlike structure. He seems to be thinking aloud and, remarkably, when he gets no response from Frieda to his idea that roses are less consequential than seeds ("The seed is all in all. . . . / . . . Does it strike you so?"), he changes his opinion to claim that any moment in the cycle from rose to seed is equally vital ("The rose is all in all, / . . . unchidden and purposeless," *CP,* p. 219). This resolution is undercut, however, by an obvious problem: Lawrence has used the rose in this group to stand for a man's ability to achieve himself, for his ability to become blissfully one with nature, and for his desire to merge with Frieda, to merge her ideas with his, his being with hers. No such merger is allowed in the poems that follow.

The next group, linked by autumnal metaphors of mating—the cornfield, harvest, huntsman—begins with a fictional poem, "A Youth Mowing" (no. 25), which like "Ballad of a Wilful Woman" suggests by analogy a shift in their relationship. Just as a "young man mowing" does not want to hear his lover is pregnant, Lawrence may have become frightened by commitment, unable to give himself over entirely. In "Quite Forsaken" and "Forsaken and Forlorn" (nos. 26, 27), we do not know whether the woman or the man is responsible for their separation (we are given no causal event), but without her he shrivels up. When "*She speaks*" in "Fireflies in the Corn" (no. 28), she blames him for lacking pride, cringing after her. Forlorn-ness is itself at fault: her challenge to him, to be autonomous in love. "A Doe at Evening" (no. 29) closes this group as it began, with indirection, yet it suggests *his* final answer to her. Its speaker follows a doe that is flighty, aloof, yet "fled on the same wind" as he (*CP,* p. 222). For him to "follow" is to assert his connection. If he must be her upstanding "knight" among the corn, she must be his flighty companion—like the cat, Mino's lover in *Women in Love,* forced to acknowledge a bond with him.

But again our expectations are upset as, instead of a shift into a rosier mood, the sequence enters its long descent, beginning with "Song of a Man Who Is Not Loved" (no. 30) where he does not "count in the wind" (*CP,* p. 223). The series that follows (nos. 31–43) builds in groups of two or three and extends through Germany into Italy, the destination of the mountain walk. This journey south is more distinctly a battle against morality than between the two of them. The "sinners," companions of "bee," "squirrel," and "mountains," would be happy "in the gap" if "swarming" mankind did not exist ("Sinners," no. 31, *CP,* pp. 223–24). But there is "Misery" (no. 32) and loss of purpose, no point in going through the mountain passes to find more pines; and even in the mountains there is the hatred of other men like the angry man in the "bullock wagon," a symbol of Christ in His despair ("Meeting among the Mountains," no. 33, *CP,* p. 225). Closing this group is an elegy to his mother set in Italy, which serves to resolve him to the past: at first "my soul turns back" but then, as he knew her through the "lovely things" he gathered for her, he "know[s] you here. . . . at peace" among the "everlasting flowers," watching with him ("Everlasting Flowers: For a Dead Mother," no. 34, *CP,* pp. 226–27).

So he can return to the problems with Frieda (nos. 35–38), beginning with a "Sunday Afternoon in Italy" (no. 35). This is another distanced, fictional poem about two people whose awkwardnesses with each other and greater comfort with their own sex mark them "chosen for the fight" of marriage (*CP,* p. 228). With this poem, Lawrence has begun to set up alternative rituals and views of marriage in society, the sacred use of Sunday and the proper sentiments of a couple. In "Winter Dawn" (no. 36), he acknowledges for himself that his love is full of hate, and this in turn empties him of feeling, while in "A Bad Beginning" (no. 37), the two lovers accuse each other of cruelty, unable to "begin again." Clearly these two are "chosen for the fight." Meanwhile the "personal" (in Lawrencean terms)—the petty needs of intimacy and piety to dead hopes—is being burned out of both lovers. In "Why Does She Weep?" (no. 38), he assures her that no matter how much she cries for the "abomination of our past righteousness," God "won't come": "it is we who walk in the trees" and "it is he who hides" (*CP,* pp. 231–32).

In the third group (nos. 39–43) in this mountain-walk series, he moves still more deeply into his counterreligion. "Giorno dei Morti" (no. 39) and "All Souls" (no. 40) are pendants, one a description of the service to the dead under the "banner of death" (*CP*, p. 232), the second his alternative service: weeds may grow on "your grave, in England," but "The world is your grave" and "I am your naked candle" (*CP*, p. 233). This final elegy releases him once and for all to be, as in "Hymn to Priapus," "faithless and faithful" (*CP*, p. 199). He will return to his beloved, his pride brazened by misery. In "Lady Wife" (no. 41), he tells her he has no use for angels or queens:

> *Put ashes on your head. . . .*
> *Be common stuff. . . .*
> *Since I must serve and struggle.*

> (*CP*, p. 234)

In "Both Sides of the Medal" (no. 42), he offers her the counterplaint that *he* is obstinate, hateful though lovable, "But we will learn to submit" (*CP*, p. 236). "Loggerheads" (no. 43) closes this sequence, leaving them at cross-purposes, at the opposite point from that registered in the rose poems, in utter antagonism.

In the logic of this book, they may now begin again (nos. 44–48). In "December Night" (no. 44), the lectures are gone, and the speaker gently invites his lover to the fireside; in "New Year's Eve" (no. 45), he repeats his invitation to night and the fire and more explicitly to sex; on "New Year's Night" (no. 46), she is his "sacrifice"; on "Valentine's Night" (no. 47), awakening from her long "night," she is a "maid" and "woman," knowing "good, evil, both / In one blossom" (*CP*, p. 239); in "Birth Night" (no. 48), it is her turn to be reborn. This series of "nights" is a ritual made to follow a natural cycle and performed according to the new morality they create together.

Several of the internal groupings in *Look! We Have Come Through!* fall into complementary pairs, as in the framing poems: the struggles and uncertainty of the poems of first love are counteracted and balanced in the joyful marriage poems; the rose poems balance the night (the long sequence of the mountain walk stands asymmetrically outside these parallels). The rose and night poems require special comment because it is less obvious that they, like other sections, form nodal episodes in the action of the story. The rose poems narrate morning encounters with Frieda and are sentimentally personal in detail.[42] The night poems are brutal, self-styled rituals of love. The original titles of "Valentine's Night" and "Birth Night"—"Eve's Mass" and "Candlemass"—emphasize the sacramental nature of all these poems, as in "New Year's Night": "You're a dove I have bought for sacrifice, / And to-night I slay it" (no. 46, *CP*, p. 238). The rose group celebrates the spirit of fertile creativity, while the night exalts the counterbalancing force of destruction in fire and night. Together these sections reproduce the scheme of the "Study of Thomas Hardy": the woman dominates her lover in the rose poems, while in the night sequence the male governs their interaction, so that they may reach a balance in the marriage poems, law polarizing love.

That impulse toward complementarity is expressed also in the numerous companion pieces, even when widely separated in the volume, as in "Song of a Man Who Is Not Loved" (no. 30) and "Song of a Man Who Is Loved" (no. 55). The two nature poems, which stand out from the others as delicate imagistic studies not directly involving Frieda, are placed at balancing points in the volume. "A Doe at Evening" (no. 29) appears just before "Song of a Man Who Is Not Loved" (heading the desolate mountain-walk poems), and it expresses a last moment of half-blissful awakening, typical of the rose poems. Located at the opposite end of Lawrence's adventure, "Rabbit Snared in the Night" (no. 49) follows the final night, conjuring up the intense, violent passion of Lawrence's dark rituals. Parallels such as these become a fundamental device in structuring Lawrence's search for equipoise.

In the next section, the couple "comes through" time and again in eight marriage poems (nos. 50–57, "Paradise Re-entered" to "One Woman to All Women," including the two added in 1928, "Coming Awake," no. 51, and "Song of a Man Who Is Loved," no. 55). As if in their first awakening and first beginning, the two triumphantly enter into "star polarity," magnetizing without merging into each other. In the first "Song," he admits his beloved as the "not I" of his desires ("Song of a Man Who Is Loved," no. 55); in the second, he would be a "good well-head" by surrendering himself to "not I, but the wind," which so frightened him previously ("Song of a Man Who Has Come Through," no. 56, *CP,* p. 250); and in the last poem of this group, "she" has her turn to speak in praise of marriage ("One Woman to All Women," no. 57). Three or four of these poems, however, are retrospective accounts—"Paradise Re-entered," "Spring Morning," and "History" (nos. 50, 52, 54)—not permitting even this privileged moment to break free of its context. "Wedlock" (no. 53) treats history as a series of present moments. Like miniatures of the book, these poems repeat its path up to the "now" in which "we have come through" and suggest how to read the book as a whole—not, of course, as isolated events or moods, but as a struggle driven, ecstatically, out of the past into futurity.

"People" (no. 58) is the next pivot, as Lawrence turns his sights back to the world around him, and while prophetically hinting that "people" also may change, in this and its pendant, "Street Lamps" (no. 59), he mourns their sickening endlessness. He has a still harsher complaint to lodge, for though he has married Frieda, she thinks they are "one," not seeing in him the untouchable "adder" and "bull" ("'She Said as Well to Me,'" no. 60). Thanks to their conflicts, he has arrived fully only now at the hard-won philosophy of the Hardy study, but he must still preach it to his wife. In two further retrospectives, however, to reach her flank is to border the world ("New Heaven and Earth," no. 61), and he "waits" to be born from the "monstrous womb of time" ("Elysium," no. 62, *CP,* p. 262).

"Manifesto" (no. 63) is the clearest statement of his next mission and brings *Look! We Have Come Through!* past the "conclusion" of its Argument into direct confrontation with the problem of being. This too is accounted for in the Hardy study: "But the chain is not broken by the letting-go of hands. It is broken by the overbearing of one cycle by the other. . . . Solomon, when he lay with a woman, knew God and possessed Him and was possessed by Him" (*Phoenix,* p. 450). "Manifesto" enumerates the needs that have been satisfied in Lawrence, and one remains:

> *To be, or not to be, is still the question.*
> *This ache for being is the ultimate hunger.*
> *And for myself, I can say "almost, almost, oh, very nearly."*

(CP, p. 265)

This final hunger "to be" is served when he is touched as if he were "not-being":

> *It is the major part of being, this having surpassed oneself,*
> *this having touched the edge of the beyond, and perished, yet not perished.*
>
> . . . . .
>
> *I want her to touch me at last, ah, on the root and quick of my darkness*
> *and perish on me, as I have perished on her.*
>
> *Then, we shall be two and distinct, we shall have each our separate being.*
> *And that will be pure existence, real liberty.*

(CP, p. 266)

Without fully achieving the promised relationship with Frieda, Lawrence arrives at the struggle with being itself. Through and despite her, he finds that "to be" is to be "touched" by the other. Paul Delany believes that the dogma of "Manifesto" stems from a "vision of universal solipsistic vitalism":

> Here, as so often in Lawrence, metaphysics is grounded in biology: the poet embraces even the harshest implications of Darwinism and finds them good, in a complete inversion of Tennyson's Victorian fear of nature "red in tooth

and claw," at strife with both itself and God. . . . If this should seem like a paean to mere bloodthirstiness, one should recall that Lawrence was not one of those who, like Tennyson or Kipling, viewed war as a bracing purge for a society gone slack; wars, he believed, were caused by too much repression of instinct rather than too little.[43]

But it might be more accurate to say that Lawrence embraced this aspect of Tennyson's vision of nature at war with itself rather than inverted it, for it remains a fearful apparition. In doing so, he indulged, not in a "solipsistic" vitalism, but in an atomistic one, where beings are single, distinct from one another, though their violently live natures touch.

"Manifesto" is significant for yet another reason, for it specifies the shape of Lawrence's new poetics in terms similar to those of "Poetry of the Present." In the marriage poems, he celebrated his new status as a "good well-head" along with his marriage; in "Manifesto" he locates the origin of song in the friction between opposite states of being, and "sheer utterance," the spontaneous lyric cry, is "like" utterly original creation:

> *Every man himself, and therefore, a surpassing singleness of mankind.*
> *The blazing tiger will spring upon the deer, undimmed,*
> *the hen will nestle over her chickens,*
> *we shall love, we shall hate,*
> *but it will be like music, sheer utterance,*
> *issuing straight out of the unknown.*
>
> (*CP*, p. 268)

In setting down the "music" of love and hate, this book becomes a vessel of the "unknown." Creating it, Lawrence produced also its poetics: poetry is and should be the hymnal of man's "surpassing singleness." This description romanticizes to some degree what actually took place in its production; for even if at the end he has become a good fountain, a competitor to Whitman, he is still engaged in the struggle for verbal consciousness. The latter phrase from *Women in Love* describes far better than the spontaneous "well-head" the character of this verse, a poetry that does what it says, enacting conflict upon conflict with both Frieda and the world. In its poetics, this volume repeats the paradox of its larger framework: if at the end he is about to "come through" as man and poet, this is because he has been willing from the start to push himself to the edge.

Delany's reference to Tennyson is an especially appropriate one, since *Maud* was one of Lawrence's chief models, and antitype, for this sequence. Tennyson's "little Hamlet" echoes in the framework of this book, extending from allusions in the first poems (one title refers directly to *Maud*,

"'And Oh— / That the Man I Am Might Cease to Be—'") to the final glimpses of wartime England. In both works the protagonist pursues a lover in defiance of the dictates of society. Tennyson's hero goes mad and enters the Crimean War to save himself. In his own persona, Lawrence transforms the "mad" strife of emotions into an essential means of communication with Frieda, and that preserves him against society's wars.

Time and a retrospective position were necessary before Lawrence could shape this history, which did not come to completion until three years after it was consummated in marriage. He juggled three titles, one evoking yet again the message of his Hardy study, "Man and Woman," the other more daringly stressing his own achievement, "Poems of a Married Man." "Look! We Have Come Through!" declares the volume's split commitments, its exclamatory narrative of triumph in the mystic NOW ("Manifesto," *CP*, p. 268), and its context at the edge of the ever-renewing past. Writing to Catherine Carswell early in 1917, Lawrence expressed his sentiments about this book far more strongly than he had for his first two: "I feel more inclined to burst into tears than any thing. . . . I loathe it to go to a publisher. I feel for the moment most passionately and bitterly tender about it" (*Letters*, 3 : 94). But he also already saw it as a phase behind him, "a sort of final conclusion of the old life in me—'And now farewell' is really the motto" (*Letters*, 3 : 87). He swore that "the next must be for something new" (*Letters*, 3 : 90). At least one tearful poem, "Frost Flowers" (no. 65), may have been introduced after he wrote to Carswell, incorporating his "farewell" into the book literally after he had "finished" with it.[44] After "Manifesto," the book falls off anticlimactically: in "Autumn Rain" (no. 64) the rain is like "sheaves of dead," "slain" and "winnowed," "manna" of pain (*CP*, p. 269). In "Frost Flowers" (no. 65), as in *Women in Love*, he sees in people the "issue of acrid winter," its "corruption" and "dissolution" (*CP*, p. 270), and he yearns in "Craving for Spring" (no. 66) not to "die on this Pisgah," but to "live through" (*CP*, p. 273).

CHAPTER FOUR

War

"BITS," *BAY, NEW POEMS,* AND
BIRDS, BEASTS AND FLOWERS

CHRONOLOGY:

The war	1914–18
Collaboration with Bertrand Russell fails	1915
Suppression of *The Rainbow*	1915
Amores published	1916
"Bits," *Bay,* and *New Poems* composed	1916–18
Look! We Have Come Through! censored, and published	1917
Eviction from Cornwall	1917
New Poems published	1918
"War Films" (selected from "Bits") published in *Poetry*	1919
Bay published	1919
Italy	1919–22
Birds, Beasts and Flowers composed, and published	1920–23
Travel to America via India and Australia	1922–23

To be a hero was Lawrence's next impulsive goal after marriage to Frieda. The outbreak of war less than a month after his marriage deeply irritated him, but since he saw war as the idiocy of a society overripe for change, it only deepened his ambition to play a messianic role. The letters of the fall of 1914 in which he recorded his initial reactions have often been cited for signs of the enervating depression that would increase with the years. Written in anger, these letters also express Lawrence's urgent desire to explain the world. To his agent, J. B. Pinker, Lawrence complained, "What a miserable world. What colossal idiocy, this war. Out of sheer rage I've begun my book about Thomas Hardy" (*Letters,* 2:212). His study of Hardy was the first of a long sequence of visionary writings with which he meant to reform the English mind.

Lawrence's endeavors to be a hero are remembered chiefly for their failures—the failure of his collaboration with Bertrand Russell, the failure to gain an audience for his political views, his eviction from Cornwall as a suspected spy, his failure to establish the ideal society he dubbed "Rananim." Publication of *The Rainbow* and *Women in Love* should be added to this list, since *The Rainbow* was suppressed, and *Women in Love* could find no publisher in England. But none of this quenched Lawrence's ambitions. When the war ended he still believed, as he said in *Fantasia of the Unconscious,* that after marriage with a woman, a "new story" begins: "Men, being themselves made new after the action of coition, wish to make the world new" (*Fantasia,* p. 108). He had been married seven years by the time he wrote these words, all that time trying to remake the world; the priestly role had become an article of faith.

Lawrence himself would not have judged this a period of personal failure. True to the type of Carlyle's modern hero, whom he emulated from his earliest years, he fought his battles through the medium of print. The war was a period of enormous endeavor when, in addition to completing *The Rainbow* and *Women in Love,* he wrote the "Study of Thomas Hardy" and produced five books of poems: *Amores, Look! We Have Come Through! Bay,* "Bits," and *New Poems.* Immediately after the war, he became even more explosively productive. In three years, he finished three philosophical works (*Studies in Classic American Literature, Psychoanalysis and the Unconscious,* and *Fantasia of the Unconscious*), three "leadership" novels (*The Lost Girl, Aaron's Rod,* and *Kangaroo*), and most of *Birds, Beasts and Flowers.* These novels and poetic books not only recorded his vision of world conflict; they became the objects and the means of his personal struggle, as he was persecuted by, and in turn assaulted, his censorious public. During the war, his books were censored, altered, delayed, or refused publication, difficulties that intensified his effort to reform the public conscience. The printed book seemed to him a vital form, both vulnerable to its readers and capable of changing them. At no other point in Lawrence's life is it clearer that his career was no mere matter of finances; he cared deeply what effect he had on the public and continually elaborated new strategies aimed at an international readership.

Lawrence's spirit of enterprise is most evident in the writings after the war, when in 1919 he launched himself into action, traveling around the globe "to make the world new." Yet his spirit was also set hard against specific goals—driven by wanderlust, as in *Women in Love* he had predicted it might be: "Why bother! Why strive for a coherent, satisfied life? Why not drift on in a series of accidents—like a picaresque novel? Why not?" (*Women in Love*, p. 294). Whereas in the novels and poetic books of the war years he presented himself as an Arthurian type, around whom marriage and society might be reconstituted, after the war he became a picaro, questing eastward, staging mock battles among the birds and the beasts. The picaresque mode represented a radical departure from the techniques of his previous novels, but the "book of the soul" that Lawrence had created in *Amores* and *Look! We Have Come Through!* prepared a flexible mold for the dreamlike accidentalism of *Birds, Beasts and Flowers*—a poetic book of the world. This new book was conceived, moreover, not primarily as a narrative sequence, but as a more open, dynamic field of oppositions.

The departures of *Birds, Beasts and Flowers* had been prepared for also through several short books of war poems. At the same time that Lawrence was collecting his earliest poetry, he was writing new poems. These have suffered neglect because they are slighter works than Lawrence's others and because they fall short of the best poetry of the period. But they released him from the personal love lyric; in these poems he expresses a sense of cultural history for the first time. In the early months of 1915, he transformed his story of the heart into a history of war, a story of self-sacrifice and uncertain expectation of the end. Moreover, he turns from a poetry of human possibility to a poetry of stringent constraint. Yet the pastoral mode of the war poems and their elimination of a single, individualized narrator prepare us for the apocalyptic fables of *Birds, Beasts and Flowers*. At his best in the coolly enigmatic verse of *Bay*, Lawrence showed himself master of an ironic method that can bear much closer attention than it has received. I will narrate Lawrence's trials over publication during the war and examine his war books on their own, before evaluating what stands as his most original contribution to modern verse in *Birds, Beasts and Flowers*.

Part I: The War Finished Me

Lawrence claimed dramatically that the war changed and "finished" him forever—without saying quite how (*Letters*, 2:268). It depressed him, but it is impossible to know whether this was the effect of the war or of the sporadic bouts of illness he suffered. The double claim that the war finished and changed him was, however, typical of Lawrence. What was less typical was his experience of the war as a process of withering negation— of himself, his public endeavors, his friendships, and his poetry. He made no effort, of course, to envisage life in the trenches, which he had not seen, or to sing patriotic songs of military prowess in which he did not believe. Instead he translated war into another autobiographical story. In so doing, he emptied the story of events and of personal authority. The poetry was as much changed by desolation as Lawrence was.

Lawrence's ignorance of the war at firsthand and his tendency to refer events instead to his own beliefs account in part for neglect of the war poetry by his critics. The more personal meditations on war at the end of *Look! We Have Come Through!* have received much attention, while the war verse published in contemporary magazines and his books are judged by Tom Marshall a lessening of his powers or are left as a gap in the career by Vivian de Sola Pinto and Sandra Gilbert.[1] Lawrence's best writings about the war were not very different from those his fellow Georgians were producing. Paul Fussell is only half right about Lawrence when he says that

> The roster of major innovative talents who were not involved with the war is long and impressive. It includes Yeats, Woolf, Pound, Eliot, Lawrence, and Joyce—that is, the masters of the modern movement. It was left to lesser talents—always more traditional and technically prudent—to recall in literary form a war they had actually experienced. Sassoon, Graves, and Blunden are clearly writers of the second rank. But their compulsion to render the unprecedented actualities they had experienced brought them fully to grips with the modern theme which we now recognize as the essence of Frye's ironic mode.[2]

Lawrence saw wartime England existing in extreme unheroic, frustrated depletion, such as he later recorded in the famous "Nightmare" chapter of *Kangaroo*. He had a second sense for this aspect of wartime reality. And like his fellow poets, he composed poems in an ironic mode—expressing a condition of paralyzing bewilderment, nearly unspeakable. The Lawrence of the war poetry was as "traditional and technically prudent" as any others of his generation, as if lacking the means to cope with such a subject, and he occupied the position of a rivulet in the mainstream—one of the humblest positions he would ever hold as a writer. Like the wartime memoirs of which Fussell writes, Lawrence's poetry seems "delicately transitional, pointing at once in two opposite directions—back to the low mimetic, forward to the ironic and—most interestingly—to that richest kind of irony proposing, or at least recognizing, a renewed body of rituals and myths."[3] The difference is that Lawrence crossed through this transition to create that renewed body of rituals and myths. In the postwar poetry of *Birds, Beasts and Flowers,* there would be no central self or author, only a mobile voice narrating fables of worldwide transformation.

In the first year after the outbreak of war, Lawrence considered poetry and poets dead in England. The war number of *Poetry* annoyed him when he saw it in November 1914 and roused him to write his first war poem, an early version of "Eloi, Eloi, Lama Sabachthani?" (*Letters,* 2:232–33). In September 1915 he wrote to Harriet Monroe, "there is [no poetry] in England: the muse has gone, like the swallows in winter," though he also declared his intention, despite all this death, to "speak for life." Accordingly he offered her a copy, not of poems, but of a circular describing his publication *Signature,* in which he hoped to print his philosophical writings (*Letters,* 2:393–94). But a month later, after more than a year of inactivity, his letters reveal him writing poems again and searching for poets in England. In October he sent "Resurrection" to Harriet Monroe, and in November he began a letter to Cynthia Asquith with "The Turning Back" (an early version of "Erinnyes," *CP,* p. 739; *Letters,* 2:417, 421–23). He wrote that same month to Hugh Meredith to say he liked Meredith's war poems and to commend the themes they shared: "Like you in your poems, I believe an end is coming: the war, a plague, a fire, God knows what. . . . One must try to save the quick, to send up the new shoots of a new era" (*Letters,* 2:426). Later in November he wrote in what can only be taken as delight at his discovery of Robert Nichols: "I think you are a poet: take care, save yourself, above all, save yourself: there is such need of poets, that the world will all perish, without them. You have a mission, to be a living poet. For God's sake fulfil it— . . . I am so glad to have found you." Lawrence commented at length on Nichols's poems, reiterating, "you are a poet, my dear fellow! I am *so glad:* the first I have found: the future" (*Letters,* 2:443–44).

Lawrence was eager to admit these lesser poets to "the future," and his reaction to Rupert Brooke's death suggests by contrast the kind of ambition he harbored for them and for himself. Brooke's death he described irritably as "the real climax of his pose." Lawrence thought this death a futile, vainglorious suicide: "The death of Rupert Brooke fills me more and more with the sense of the fatuity of it all. He was slain by bright

Phoebus shaft—it was in keeping with his general sunniness—it was the real climax of his pose. I first heard of him as a Greek God under a Japanese Sunshade, reading poetry in his pyjamas, at Grantchester, at Grantchester, upon the lawns where the river goes. Bright Phoebus smote him down. It is all in the saga" (*Letters*, 2:330–31)—a saga Lawrence was determined to rewrite. He himself sentimentalized the war, of course, perhaps all the more because he could not participate, but he must have believed that his version of it was at any rate daring. The first change he made in the romantic legend suggested by Brooke's death was to represent war as profound self-martyrdom. There was nothing sunny and no pretense in such death. Glory could not be bought cheaply, if at all.

The story of the war, as Lawrence told it, is summed up in a letter of 31 January 1915 to Cynthia Asquith (*Letters*, 2:267–69), in which he described his first reactions to England's declaration of war. This narrative begins with an image of his own death: "We have no history, since we saw you last. I feel as if I had less than no history—as if I had spent those five months in the tomb. And now, I feel very sick and corpse-cold, too newly risen to share yet with anybody, having the smell of the grave in my nostrils, and a feel of grave clothes about me." Life in the present is at an end. The past is reduced to a pastoral memory of what was catastrophically lost: "The War finished me: it was the spear through the side of all sorrows and hopes. I had been walking in Westmoreland, rather happy, with water-lilies twisted round my hat—big, heavy, white and gold water-lilies that we found in a pool high up—and girls who had come out on a spree." Finally, there is the tentative future, the possibility for a new start: "now I don't feel so dead. . . . I couldn't tell you how fragile and tender the hope is—the new shoot of life." Lawrence sees his account as another Christ story: the war "was the spear through the side of all sorrows and hopes." Perhaps this crucifixion would mark a past and future life, but the past is a memory, the future a vague hope. It is an antistory of a Lawrencean kind: "We have no history."

This nonhistory of partial self-entombment set the scene for his letters and literary writings. War even stood behind the composition of his books of elegies and love poems. Writing in December 1916 to A. W. McLeod, he said of the "unreal" mood of *Amores*, "so near and *navrant*": "You are the only person who brings it near, really: the old Davidson Road past. . . . I feel we are all like drowning men, who remember the past vividly in a flash. . . . But out of the chaos we must rescue a future, that is all" (*Letters*, 3:61–62). *Amores* belongs to the estranged past, which resurfaced as in the "flash" of a dying man. In the closing poems of *Look! We Have Come Through!* Lawrence forcibly subordinated the war experience to his relationship to Frieda, as if through marriage he could transcend the personal past and move beyond the nation's limited destiny. Various commentators have noted the resemblance of the language and imagery in Lawrence's letter of 31 January 1915 to that of the poem "New Heaven and Earth," though the narrative is greatly expanded in this poem:[4]

> *When I heard the cannon of the war, I listened with my own ears to my own*
> *destruction.*
> *When I saw the torn dead, I knew it was my own torn dead body.*
> *It was all me, I had done it all in my own flesh.*
>
> (*CP*, p. 257)

War is absorbed into a narrative of self-immolation and miraculous resurrection, which occurs when he reaches the edge of "the future," in this poem "the unknown . . . flank of my wife."

The narrative of Lawrence's autobiographical war letter of 31 January 1915 also anticipated his war poems, especially those published only in journals (Lawrence did not retrieve these for *Collected Poems*, but they were included in *CP* by Pinto and Roberts).[5] The details of Lawrence's personal history with Frieda disappeared, leaving in their place morbid fantasies of war. In "Eloi, Eloi, Lama Sabachthani?" he arose a messiah, altering the plaint of Christ into a Bacchic shriek:

> *God, how glad I am to hear the shells*
> *Droning over, threatening me!*
> *It is their threat, their loud, jeering threat,*
> *Like screaming birds of Fate*
> *Wheeling to lacerate and rip up this my body,*
> *It is the loud cries of these birds of pain*
> *That gives me peace.*
>
> (*CP*, p. 741)

Murder and martyrdom lead in this poem to absolution and resurrection, with the crucifixion an occasion for sexual closure:

> *Like a bride he took my bayonet, wanting it,*
> *Like a virgin the blade of my bayonet, wanting it,*
> *And it sank to rest from me in him,*
> *And I, the lover, am consummate.*
>
> (*CP*, p. 742)

Not the suicide of a golden boy, this is praise rather for the sex act of a soldier. The theme of homoeroticism was common in poetry of this period, but Lawrence gave it his own twist when he used it to distinguish between desirable and undesirable murder: if men murdered others in "interdestructive" acts of aggression, they would annihilate themselves, but if they acted out procreative impulses by yielding themselves to death (and murder), then men could die and come through (*Letters,* 2:636).

To the modern reader, there seems small novelty in this anachronistically personal vision of the soldier's passionate death. In "Erinnyes," the narrative is even more fantastic, the war no longer between soldiers, but between men and their ghosts. Solemnly Lawrence blames the war on people for failing to accept death:

> For one year's space, attend on our angry dead,
> Soothe them with service and honour, and silence meet,
> Strengthen, prepare them for the journey hence,
> Then lead them to the gates of the unknown.

(*CP*, p. 740)

Lawrence saw only that a world was being demolished, giving way to something unimagined. Each of his poems represents at least an effort to imagine and, by imagining, to recover from what it would mean "not to be":

> To come at last to nothingness, and know
> Nothing and nothing any more, and so
> Not even dream, not even pass away
> Nor cease to be: dark on the darkness stay.
>
> And then within the night where nothing is,
> And I am only next to nothingness,
> Touch me, oh touch me, give me destinies
> By touch, and a new nakedness.

("Resurrection of the Flesh," *CP*, p. 738)

Lawrence appears more honest and more hauntingly persuasive when he faces "nothing" than subsequently when he imagines a "touch"; for he gives up one ideal—"not even [to] pass away"—only to assert another in terms equally doctrinaire—"a new nakedness." The "nothing" he imagines exceeds fantasy to evoke the mythic character of a war so large that it could never be quite real.

Lawrence's "discovery" in November 1916 of still another poet in the husband of his friend Cynthia Asquith may well have motivated his first book of war poems (*Letters,* 3:38). Cynthia Asquith acted as something like a patron saint for Lawrence at this time, and he wanted to thank her. By December he had prepared "Bits" (then called "All of Us") and requested permission to dedicate it to her. He held the poems back, however, because he thought them a "bit wicked," sending them only to his agent, Pinker (*Letters,* 3:51, 221). In the meantime he set to work on *Look! We Have Come Through!* hoping this would be his last work for the "old world" (*Letters,* 3:90). More than a year passed before he returned to "Bits" in March 1918, when Cyril Beaumont asked for a small book to publish. Beaumont rejected "Bits," so in late March Lawrence set to work on *Bay,* derived in part from juvenilia. Within three weeks of retrieving his notebooks from Ottoline Morrell, he completed *Bay* and dedicated it to Lady Asquith.

The poems in both books are shorter than Lawrence's magazine pieces and are offered, not as didactic histories, but as gently ironic parables. Each book represents fragmented, wartime relationships, which occur in bits of time with almost no hint of progression. Rather than stressing wartime killing, Lawrence emphasizes war's dreamlike nature, its endless moments of waiting, its preapocalyptic silences, and the suffering of passive anonymous spectators. He writes in a pastoral mode, picturing rural and communal scenes both off and on the battlefield or back in England. In this he flees the morbid facts of the time, yet also expresses the sense of limitation created by the war. Even the language of these poems has emptied out—becoming sparer, less densely imagistic than Lawrence's magazine poems. Like the poems of Sassoon, Thomas, or Owen, the slightness of this verse is eloquent, telling of the need to face and cope with severe limits—the sense of an ending too terrible and, for Lawrence, too wonderful to contain within a poem.

"BITS"

"Bits" is a collection of abbreviated folktales (usually no more than four to eight lines in length, never published in Lawrence's lifetime, but included in all editions of *CP,* pp. 749–59), which approach an aphoristic style, as in "The Last Minute": "When in the morning I rose to depart, my love came to say farewell. / She wept bitterly, hiding her face in her kerchief" (*CP,* p. 749). "Bits" contains twenty-nine such stories, tales of departure from a mother, lover, or father; unfaithfulness or loyalty between lovers; tales of nurses and priests, harem girls and prisoners. Lawrence derived at least eight from whimsical love lyrics he had written years ago and sent to Louie Burrows for her amusement. It seems likely that he composed the others during the war. Often a title change was sufficient to transform his sentimental whimsy into a war memoir: "Two-fold" became "Casualty," "Love Message" turned to "Message to a Perfidious Soldier," "Beloved" became "Land-Worker," and "Elixir" was retitled "The Jewess and the V. C."[6] In-

ternal changes were minor, but together with the altered titles, the trans-
ferrals gave these poems a sardonic edge. When a grey nurse appears in a
rose garden instead of a prophet, our thoughts shift from a pretty and obvious didacticism to a more realistic ministry, just a touch unpleasant.

After Lawrence's passionate love poems, however, these seem oddly
trivial. "Bits" has no special order. Although eighteen of the twenty-nine
poems appear in parallel sequences in two extant manuscripts, there are
only vague thematic links among these ("Mesopotamia," "Tales," and
"Foreign Sunset" are united, for example, by their foreign location).[7] With
few poems clustered even by theme, the arrangement is almost as various
as possible. But little poems like these might sink under the weight of a
proper sequence; left as they are, associations range freely among them.
Though Lawrence himself doubted that these poems were "tours de force,"
he only half doubted, thinking the "tiny book" "Might have a real popular
success. Give it the people as the 'war *literature*' they are looking for: they
will find themselves in it: good, a popular success. For myself, as I say, I
doubt the poems are tours de force, but for *people*, so much the better"
(*Letters*, 3:51). *Sleight of hand* would have been an apter phrase.

Lawrence's object in "Bits" is elucidated by comparison to *Pansies* (1929),
the last verse book to be published in his lifetime. Its introduction could as
easily describe "Bits": "This little bunch of fragments is offered as a bunch
of *pensées*, anglicé pansies; a handful of thoughts. Or, if you will have the
other derivation of pansy, from *panser*, to dress or soothe a wound; these
are my tender administrations to the mental and emotional wounds we
suffer from" (*CP*, p. 417). In 1916 Lawrence dressed "the mental and emotional wounds we suffer from" with sympathetic vignettes of wartime
society:

> The grey nurse entered a rose garden
> Where roses' shadows dappled her.
> Her apron was brown with blood. She prayed,
> And roses wondered at her prayer.

("The Grey Nurse," *CP*, p. 753)

The clashing emotional attitudes that we found in "Cherry Robbers" and
"Bei Hennef," we find here from a more impersonal perspective. Suffering
is imaged in the overlay of "roses' shadows" and "blood" on the nurse's
apron. The simple speech and quiescent scene, "She prayed, / And roses
wondered," cool the sense of irony. William Empson might have found in
this a function of pastoral, because a simple nun in a cloister garden is
made to represent the complex sufferings of the war beyond her. The
poem offers the reader a way to manage something larger than any indi-

vidual life can actually contain, by finding in this grey nurse a symbol.[8] Lawrence would have explained his effect as he had always done: for there to be life in a poem, there must also be "blood." To have a "whole" portrait of the self, one must admit its obverse, whatever it is that breaks and extends the self—whether that is the mystery of eros, male violence, or an unknown god. Every "bit" looks briefly into the cracked state of humanity in a war, yet thereby suggests and promotes the human faculty for healing and wholeness.

There is even less distance between "Bits" and *Pansies* than one would imagine at first glance. The most notorious *Pansies* are satiric curses against English society rather than the "tender administrations" Lawrence promised in his preface, but many pansies are no sharper than these bits. One poem, "Tales" (retitled "The Gazelle Calf"), eventually migrated from "Bits" into *Pansies,* and this is especially gentle in comparison with the other squibs of 1916: the gazelle calf "Goes behind his mother with bare, blithe foot / Wearing no boot" (*CP,* p. 757; cf. *CP,* p. 466). Lawrence described "Bits" to Cynthia Asquith as "bitterly ironical" (*Letters,* 3:221). In addition to the intrinsic irony of Lawrence's method in poems like "The Grey Nurse," irony emerges from without, in satiric reference to the war, and from within the collection, as the poems' morals rub against each other.

Wartime casualties are only occasionally a direct subject, as when one speaker cries out for rain to cool her "parched vision," but then reveals,

> My brother died in the heat
> And the jackal found his grave;
> Nibbled his fingers, the knave;
> No more would I let him eat.

("Dust in the East," CP, p. 754)

More often, war is a casual, unlikely backdrop for slices of life, when a young girl fears she may betray her passion to her beloved ("Sighs," *CP,* p. 752), or begs her lover's superior officer to let them meet ("The Girl in Cairo," *CP,* p. 754). "Wicked" ironies were accented more sharply in "All of Us," the first version of "Bits," where Lawrence added enormous titles to his bits. "The Girl in Cairo" (*CP,* p. 754) was called "A Powerful Ally: A young lady speaks to the colonel of her lover's regiment." Explaining and expounding are titles like "Foreign Sunset: Coloured labourers behind the fighting-line complain that they are done up" ("Foreign Sunset," *CP,* p. 757) and "Supplication: A young lieutenant who joined the Roman Catholic Church whilst at Oxford, prays on the battlefield" ("Pietà," *CP,* p. 753), or "Straying Thoughts: A girl goes to the cathedral church, to pray for her beloved" ("Maiden's Prayer," *CP*, p. 751)—titles more ironic than the poems. Even the original title of "The Gazelle Calf" (*CP*, p. 466) had an edge: "The Gazelle Calf: A blind soldier tells his children about Arabia."[9] Headings like these also suggest the kinds of friction that accumulate within the collection between love and war, religion and the simple lives of common people. There is never a simple moral; the tensions are too closely interwoven.

"The Last Minute" gives "Bits" an appropriate start, beginning with "last" things (the first and last poems are identical in "All of Us" and "Bits"), and this becomes the basis for densely woven irony:

> *When in the morning I rose to depart, my love came to say farewell.*
> *She wept bitterly, hiding her face in her kerchief. I said, "Why then?"*
> *She said to me, "Stay three hours, to comfort me." Such is a girl!*
> *Do not ask me, Almighty God, to part from her again.*

(CP, p. 749)

The parting of lovers is presented with a brevity and mundanity that masks and bandages the difficult fact that the speaker's prayer will be answered whether or not he returns. Their parting is the first of two possible deaths. Moreover, parting is protectively enveloped by two intimate encounters. The time of departure has already passed; we know of it only through the conversation of the lovers, and their conversation is in turn remembered and enveloped in the present moment as the speaker addresses "Almighty God." So too the difference between the lovers—one "a girl," the other a soldier; one staying, the other leaving; one weeping, the other rational—is smoothed over by what they share: their mutual desires for each other, for consolation, for more time. This "last minute" is more than a final moment; it is a prayer, like that of the grey nurse, to "stay" this moment—to prevent, contain, and survive it.

Love is the great thing in these poems, yet Lawrence's creed is otherwise remarkably subdued; his opinions emerge in passing glimpses. The volume could be enjoyed equally by the pious and patriotic, while Lawrence avoids choosing sides. Catholicism is the religion of "Pietà" and "Litany of Grey Nurses" (p. 753), but in "Casualty" a woman catches several doves at St. Paul's to "kill for Aphrodite" (*CP*, p. 750). There is something exotic about a war in the east, where war prisoners can be pitied by harem ladies ("Prisoner at Work in a Turkish Garden," *CP*, p. 758) or soldiers slake their thirst at a "well of Kilossa" ("The Well in Africa," *CP*, p. 759), and Lawrence never pictures the enemy. He shows his hand more clearly in "Zeppelin Nights," where the children refuse to obey their mother and go on playing under "the bright / Moon all ablaze" (*CP*, p. 755), or in "The Child and the Soldier" when the child tells his soldier-brother to handle him with care, "For God / Takes everything from you tomorrow, and gives me everything" (*CP*, p. 752). Still more distinct are the women, the feisty types who wish their men were real lovers, "'Tis strange what a shoddy / Lover you make, such a hero in front of the foe" ("The Jewess and the V. C.," *CP*, p. 755), and the deathly, "I wish I might kiss her fingers; but full / Of danger I find her, even worse than the fields where we die" ("Daughter of the Great Man," *CP*, p. 752). The courageous ones in "Bits" are unconcerned: they have no interest in the war, caught up in their own livelihoods.

When "Bits" ends with a coy poem about God—

God is forever, and only He.
Where, white maid, are the men you have loved?
They are dead, so God was between you

("Neither Moth nor Rust," CP, p. 759)

—we could read this in either of two ways: as a warning to believe in the traditional, absolute, and invulnerable God and to lay up treasures in heaven where "neither moth nor rust doth corrupt" (Matt. 6:20), or as an ironical comment on any such consoling beliefs. In the clause, "God was between you," the emphasis would then fall as much on the connecting, transient "between" as on God.

There is only the story of a time and a people in "Bits," arising from its twenty-nine narratives. Its method parallels that of another book that caught Lawrence's eye in 1916, the *Spoon River Anthology* by Edgar Lee Masters. Lawrence thought Masters had expressed the spirit of the age:

> The essence of poetry with us in this age of stark and unlovely actualities is a stark directness, without a shadow of a lie, or a shadow of deflection anywhere. Everything can go, but this stark, bare, rocky directness of statement, this alone makes poetry, today. . . .
>
> I send you the *Spoon River Anthology*. It is good, but too static, always stated, not really art. Yet that is the line poetry will take, a free, essential verse, that cuts to the centre of things, without any flourish. (*Letters*, 2:503)

In these remarks to Catherine Carswell, Lawrence seizes on *Spoon River* as an example of the American blunt and candid manner, which he also admired in Whitman. The analogy extends beyond style, however, to the selection and purpose of "Bits." *Spoon River Anthology* is a verse novel made of tombstone poems, in each of which a departed soul rehearses the story of his life and death, stressing its moral strictly from his own point of view. As the anthology unfolds, the voices reveal their relations to each other, and the book becomes the work of the entire Spoon River community, recording all its sententious views on human failure and achievement.[10] "Bits" cuts short this epic anthology and places itself, not in a graveyard, but among the thoughts of live men and women. It does not reproduce a particular community, and it avoids nationalism, to represent "all of us" in a war—the nation of the living. It is composed, not of sententiae, but of the minutiae of individual thoughts and feelings, acquiring a gnomic character that is as much of the flesh as of the mind. Together, these bits, like the more didactic *Pansies,* reflect Lawrence's attempt to perform an act of healing with poetry by reproducing the whole state of mind of his society, fragmented in wartime and craving for life.

BAY

In contrast to these cheerful folktales, the longer lyrics in *Bay* focus on horrific moments of inaction, when men or women are waiting for the end. Lawrence concentrates more directly on the sense of limitation that is experienced by individuals rather than as it affects a community, and he concerns himself with stark and unlovely actualities rather than with charming trivialities. At least seven of the eighteen poems in *Bay* derive from Lawrence's earlier manuscripts. He was able to turn nearly any theme into a question of war: transforming the fifth poem of "Movements" (Ferrier MS 1) into "Guards" and two vignettes about his hometown into "The Little Town at Evening" and "Last Hours"; creating "On the March" out of a love poem and "Bombardment" out of a city poem; and turning two school pieces into "Ruination" and "Rondeau of a Conscientious Objector."[11] These revisions rarely required much work to render the apprehensive scenes of war, but the transformations were significant: gone is the personal intimacy of *Love Poems and Others.*

  Lawrence compiled *Bay* at the request of publisher Cyril Beaumont, to supply some "Impeccable Poems" in place of those "doubtful little pills" in "Bits" (*Letters,* 3:234), but he thought several of the poems the "best of any I have done" and described them to Harriet Monroe (who agreed to publish some of them in *Poetry*) in terms identical to an earlier comment about *Look! We Have Come Through!* "I feel a bit tender about them—don't print them unless you feel them" (*Letters,* 3:305). To Cynthia Asquith, he called them "delicate, I think—in their own way the rarest things I've done" (*Letters,* 3:494). No complete dramatic actions occur in these poems. A woman may simply be left behind, or soldiers may not arrive where they are headed: "Inscrutable small lights glitter in rows. / They come no nearer" ("On the March," *CP,* p. 163). These moments transpire in and through the perceptions of anonymous war victims, in interior monologues in which the speakers are paying attention to whatever lies ahead. Occasionally this state of attention reaches a crisis, which in several poems Lawrence identifies as a dawning perception of Apocalypse:

> *the elms are loftily dimmed, and tall*
> *As if moving in air towards us, tall angels*
> *Of darkness advancing steadily over us all.*

("Ruination," *CP,* p. 164)

Images are understated, uncertainly prophetic—signs of something treacherous, which come to nothing:

> *A dark bird falls from the sun.*
> *It curves in a rush to the heart of the vast*
> *Flower: the day has begun.*

("Bombardment," *CP,* p. 166)

Even the title is deceptive, for it leads us to expect the laurels of war, but we find instead the specters of men perpetually held at bay.

There is greater doubt about Lawrence's intentions for the organization of *Bay* than for his other books because the manuscripts are lost or unreliable. Only sets of proofs have been located.[12] But since he normally included a numbered list of titles, either as a table of contents or an index, when submitting his work to publishers, it is likely that he did so also for *Bay* (he did this even for "All of Us"). He assiduously corrected the proofs, insisting, for example, that Beaumont fix the indentation of "Obsequial Ode" because "I want that slightly fantastic formation" (*Letters,* 3:390). He remained dissatisfied, however, with the final product, which omitted the dedication (eventually restored by Beaumont) and two poems and had a binding "rather like spring," not "sombre" enough (*Letters,* 3:465). The omitted poems, "Labour Battalion" and "No News," had previously appeared in an anthology, *New Paths,* also published by Beaumont. Each adds a touch of realism to the themes of *Bay,* the first picturing the labor force back in England and the second a soldier at the front hungering for mail (*CP,* pp. 746–49). Lawrence made no attempt to retrieve either of these for *Collected Poems.*

As in "Bits," there is no detailed evolution in *Bay* either of Lawrence's personal history or of the war. None of the poems refers to his actual circumstances, and though several were inspired by actual incidents, they are distanced from those events. "Guards," which carries the subtitles "A Review in Hyde Park 1913: The Crowd Watches," probably derives, for example, from a review Lawrence had witnessed as early as 1909 (not just before the war, as its title suggests), since the poem appears as a verse epistle in Lawrence's earliest notebook, dating from 1908–10, and Lawrence changed the dateline to 1910 for his 1928 collection. As for progress in the war, there was none: the war had "smashed the growing tip of European civilization." [13]

Bay establishes a dialogue, nonetheless, between "I" and the hazy future, "This and me" ("The Attack," *CP,* p. 165). Every difficult separation implies that further encounter. And although the theme of a dying morality is less insistent here than in *Look! We Have Come Through!* the theater of Western civilization quietly sinks back into a primeval or pagan "vegetable" town ("Last Hours," *CP,* p. 49). Moreover, a series of stages in this story are etched out both in *Bay* and in the reconstructed version in *Rhyming Poems* (*CP* follows the order of *RP* exactly). In *Bay* the first five poems present scenes of town and city on the eve of war. Five further pieces present its early stages, from a leave-taking to the climactic battle attack. Three elegiac poems and three more war stories push to the fringe of the war's destruction, its wasteland. The two last poems raise the question of final results and, as in Lawrence's previous books, are at once optimistic and nostalgic. The changes in *Collected Poems* in some ways simplified his organization of the war verse, to make it blend into *Rhyming Poems* (see the contents table for *Rhyming Poems,* Appendix A): removing four poems about Eastwood and London to earlier sections (*CP,* nos. 17, 19, 34, 42), regrouping the war stories together (*CP,* nos. 130–35), placing after them poems about survivors back in England (*CP,* nos. 136–41), and closing with "War-Baby" and "Nostalgia" (*CP,* nos. 142–43). In its details, however, the rearrangement of the *Bay* poems appears more arbitrary, weakening the sequence, as if in 1928 Lawrence paid more attention to titles than contents of poems. I will therefore consider the order of *Bay* as it appeared in 1919, referring to *Rhyming Poems* solely for the sake of comparison.

"Guards," the headpiece of *Bay,* is the only poem in which we see soldiers massing in parade. Rather than preach about its subject, as in the magazine verse, Lawrence narrates two fabulous encounters, between a general and his soldiers, then between the army and the watching crowd. Although the soldiers' coats are a British red, their parade represents no national cause, and though they present a violent picture, it is not the pacifist's mass of mindless killers. This army is a phenomenon of nature, like blood or the twilight, pulsing in a sexual rhythm: "emerging as blood emerges . . . / Encroaching towards a crisis" (*RP,* no. 34, *CP,* p. 66). We do not meet this sight again in *Bay,* but we are forewarned not to anticipate political debate, to expect instead a confrontation of the senses.

Lawrence assigns his speaker in "Guards" the passive position of an outsider watching with the crowd. The "outsider" is the insider of these narratives, and war is something that happens to him rather than anything governed and controlled: "darkened rencontre inhuman . . . / . . . passing above us, over the wreck of our bark" (*CP*, p. 66). The speaker of the other poems is always possibly a soldier, and though Lawrence later separated four pieces from the war verse in *Rhyming Poems* (*B*, nos. 1–3, 5; *RP*, nos. 17, 19, 34, 42), they are all enriched by that association and by the question of identity this raises. In "After the Opera," when the speaker leaves behind the weary "bar-man" of the city opera to "go back," the fact that this could refer either to a soldier or a nonsoldier underlines the insignificance of that distinction to Lawrence (*B*, no. 5; *RP*, no. 42, *CP*, pp. 71–72). War treats all alike.

It is rarely clear whether the unnamed speaker is falling away from or toward his doom. He finds his fate as much in the pain of loss as in expectation. In poems 2–5 (*RP*, nos. 17, 19, 140, 42), the speaker's equivocal relations to events are established in two sets of pendants, the first located in a country town, the second in London. In "The Little Town at Evening," he is unaccountably excluded from the town life he yearns toward, whereas in "Last Hours" he is dragged away from the "vegetable" town by a train call (*B*, nos. 2–3; *CP*, pp. 48–50). In "Town" ("Town in 1917" in *RP*) he glories in the primeval, "wolf-wrapped" state London has reverted to, but in "After the Opera" he willingly leaves behind its hollow men (*B*, nos. 4–5; *CP*, pp. 170–71, 71–72). These poems also hint at a moral, pointing the tension between the pomp of civilization and the cry of nature. If the mother church lords over him in "The Little Town at Evening," the vegetable town of "Last Hours" throbs with creaturely energy; by throwing off her "luminous garments," London returns to her "forest darkness" before the Romans; and in "After the Opera," it makes him "smile" to see the women's "tragic eyes" because "momentous emotion" is first at last. The appeal of these poems is in their apparent inadvertence, as if each image were merely the aptest one available, and what really mattered were the inexplicable occasion. Even in "The Little Town at Evening" something is happening: though the town at first leaves him out, in the end the church's shadow impinges on the speaker and his exclusion becomes, as in the elegies of *Amores,* an encounter with dark shadow. The events of all four poems occur without cause and, while short in the recounting, impose hugely on the speaker, a mere "insect" in his "Last Hours."

Poem 6, "Going Back" (*RP*, no. 138, *CP*, p. 169), could be spoken by a woman returning home from a leave-taking or a man leaving for the front. The complexities of "The Last Minute" of "Bits" are recaptured in a temporal sequence here. In "The Last Minute" a moment of departure was enveloped in two encounters; in "Going Back" the process of departing is resisted three times by a mental act of staying "at the pivot." Each time that the speaker resists parting, the apparent object of his thoughts shifts. At first when the train moves "outward bound," he is not "here, but there where the pivot is": presumably, this "pivot" is back at the junction where trains and people part. But then as he "sit[s] in tears / . . . torn with parting," still leaving, in his inner ear he hears "voices of men," "artillery," and a "dead-sure silence." In this case *here* includes parting as well as the train's movement, and both are insubstantial, as the speaker is transported to his final destination of "dead-sure silence." In the third round, the exchange of terms is completed and the opposite conditions—of pain and calm, then and now—merge:

> *There, at the axis*
> *Pain, or love, or grief*
> *Sleep. . . .*
>
> *Time sleeps again.*
> *No has-been, no hereafter; only the perfected*
> *Presence of men.*

In this striking poem, the voyage "outward bound" finds itself by stages a passage inward.

Poems 7–9 (*RP*, nos. 131, 135, 134) are less certain at the close. The "open road" in "On the March" is not Whitman's freewheeling route; it is a "wrong road" laid down in an alien land where everything fades or flees, the "final lull" indefinitely postponed (*B*, no. 7; *CP*, pp. 163–64). In "Bombardment" (*B*, no. 8; *CP*, p. 166) something happens, but without éclat. A town opens like a lily, and a dark bird falls out of the sun. This lily, a stepsister of Blake's sick rose, is no innocent—a "sinister flower"—but nothing moral comes of this one way or the other: "the day has begun." "Winter-Lull" takes up the negative sense of "lull" (opposite to that of "On the March") with the speaker nowhere, "crushed" in a void, his existence "belied" and "folded into nullity." Until now a stable concept, "silence" itself is unpleasant in this poem, and the prospect of waiting for something is deadening (*B*, no. 9; *CP*, pp. 165–66).

A fourth poem in this series breaks that "nullity." Like "On the March" and "Bombardment," "Winter-Lull" and "The Attack" (*B*, no. 10; *RP*, no. 133) are pendants. Unlike the inconclusive symbolism of "Bombardment," "The Attack" is all glory:

> *White-bodied and warm the night was,*
> *Sweet-scented to hold in the throat;*
> *White and alight the night was;*
> *A pale stroke smote*

The pulse through the whole bland being
Which was This and me.

(CP, p. 65)

Its "light" is heralded "fair" and "warm" like a woman; a "mighty," over-powering presence; a live "pulse" through the "bland" mass of soldiers; a dreamlike "wonder" uncannily emerging "in front of the terrible rage, the death"; a divine event, "transubstantiation" and "transfiguration" of man's sacrifice—ritual and real—into God. Such a poem could not have been much liked either by patriots or by objectors to the war. But it catches some of the grandeur we sense whenever a poet gives his incredible, or ghastly, version of the sublime. In *Rhyming Poems,* however, this middle sequence was reworked, so that "Ruination" (*B,* no. 14; *RP,* no. 132), a poem much like "Bombardment," succeeded "On the March" (*B,* no. 7; *RP,* no. 131) and was followed by "The Attack," "Winter-Lull," and "Bombardment" (*B,* nos. 10, 9, and 8; *RP,* nos. 133–35), an order dictated perhaps by the poems' titles.

After this war sequence, we return to scepticism and the mourning survivors. "Obsequial Ode" (*B,* no. 11; *RP,* no. 137, *CP,* pp. 167–68) is a long, moving piece—"obsequial" in its funereal mood and the speaker's submissive attitude. She does everything possible to think death good: "surely you've trod straight / To the very door!" As if reminding herself of her lover's creed, she acknowledges "it is evident you were right" that every man has a voyage. Above all, she imagines him glorious, his "boat" arriving, his treasures unloaded, his body and emotions changed into light and jewels. "Surely," she repeats to herself, this is an achieved fate. But then prayer bends back into question: "But what of us?" The pertinence of this poem to the larger sequence lies in this punning use of the question: the inverse of any prayer is question, and both are modes of speaking to the unknown. It is no surprise, then, when the answer returned in "Shades" (*B,* no. 12; *RP,* no. 139, *CP,* pp. 169–70) is not as "plain" as it claims to be. Speaking from the dead, the answerer lets her know that he still is with her, "there came a cloven gleam"; shadows of the dead descend into every living creature, no matter how small. To claim, he concludes, that the living do not contain the dead is mere pretense and delusion. "Shades" thus conforms to Lawrence's general doctrines of polarity, and it ends with the determined assertion that "I have told you plainly how it is." (Lawrence gave this poem the title "Pentecostal" when he published it in *Poetry* in 1919, but he retained the pagan "Shades" for *Bay* and *Collected Poems.*) But for all that, in "Bread upon the Waters" (*B,* no. 13; *RP,* no. 141, *CP,* pp. 171–72), his questioner has not heard, cannot be consoled, and continues where she left off: "So you are lost to me!" She imagines him an ear of corn thrown to hellish fowls, bread wasted on water, "untowards." Her last question tossed out—whether he will ever return to tell her something better—she decides that he is lost and gives him up: "Drift then, for the sightless birds / And the fish." In this final act of submission, she drops the "jewels" of her daydream for the blank alterity of the Lawrencean unknown in words closely anticipating *Birds, Beasts and Flowers*. When Lawrence reordered these poems, he set "Going Back" (*B*, no. 6; *RP*, no. 138) between "Obsequial Ode" and "Shades," and "Town" (*B*, no. 4; *RP*, no. 140) between "Shades" and "Bread upon the Waters," to expand upon the themes, respectively, of the voyage to death and the living darkness. Something is sacrificed in the translation—the dialogue was already sufficiently interrupted.

The next three poems chart the continuing war and its exhausted target. In "Ruination," "tall angels / Of darkness" advance upon unpeopled, grey streets and "the misty waste lands" (*B*, no. 14; *RP*, no. 132, *CP*, p. 164). In "Rondeau of a Conscientious Objector" a self-disgusted speaker watches his hourglass run out of sand for the evening (*B*, no. 15; *RP*, no. 136, *CP*, p. 167). The wartime title enlivens this poem, changing its simple anecdote about "nullity" into a glance at the pacifist. He is in no better shape than the soldier, equally bound by duty, his "soul compressed" and longing for a "little silence." "Tommies in the Train" (*B*, no. 16; *RP*, no. 130, *CP*, pp. 162–63) is a more intriguing poem than these and less easily defined. In *Rhyming Poems*, Lawrence placed it at the head of the poems from *Bay* (*RP*, nos. 130–43). Its speaker sees England as Danaë opening her lap to Jove's "cosmic gold," his "coins" of flowers, but no people are here; so he must ask, "What are we" who journey in fatigue "league after league / From our destiny?" There can be nothing in common between the cosmic marriage and the military train. But then the speaker plays a child's game with himself, creating an optical illusion that leads him to a very different line of thinking. Peeping through his fingers out the window, he speculates about the relationships between himself and what he watches, starting where he left off: Is it the train that falls? Or is that an "illusory world" that he imagines? Or, if he falls, is this train Jove's thunderbolt and not illusory, plunging directly into the world? The questions end with a fourth explanation that does not distinguish between the real and the imagined, or between what stays and leaves, or even decide which is found or "lost": "we fall apart / Endlessly," so "One or another / Is lost." One result of this indecision is that more possibilities are raised than are denied. The sexual and the mechanical, the illusory and the real, the world and its soldiers, become two sides of his flipping coins. Both and neither are delusions— "endlessly" they depart from each other.

One of the oldest beliefs about war, of course, is that men's deaths may fertilize their homeland. This is not quite Lawrence's belief, who thought that both a man and his home must fall before either would return. This more expected theme, less complex than that of "Tommies in the Train," is the point of the closing poems. In a letter of 1 June 1918 Lawrence told Catherine Carswell that "in the *English Review* today there'll be a little 'War Baby' poem, which I wrote for you— . . . I shall initial it to the infant" (*Letters*, 3:246). Lawrence never did append initials to "War-Baby," but then the poem he wrote was not personal. It is a simple allegory of war-time birth:

> *The child like mustard seed*
> *Rolls out of the husk of death*
> > *Into the woman's fertile, fathomless lap.*
> > > > (*B*, no. 17; *RP*, no. 142, *CP*, p. 172)

When in the version in *Bay*, Lawrence enjoins us finally to

> *Sing, it is all we need.*
> *Sing, for the little weed*
> > *Will flourish its branches in heaven when we slumber beneath*[14]

he rounded off an allusion to Matthew 13:31–32. A parallel allusion appears in the *Spoon River Anthology*: "Thus a tree sprang / From me, a mustard seed."[15] Lawrence's war allegory, however, reverses the valence of bomb as well as tomb:

> *As for our faith, it was there*
> *When we did not know, did not care;*
> > *It fell from our husk in a little hasty seed.*
> > > > > (*CP*, p. 172)

Revising the last stanza for his *Collected Poems*, Lawrence took pains to retain an equivocal note, resorting to a last rhetorical question,

> *Say, is it all we need?*
> *Is it true that the little weed*
> > *Will flourish its branches in heaven when we slumber beneath?*

Bay ends with not even that much hope, but with "Nostalgia" (*B*, no. 18; *RP*, no. 143, *CP*, pp. 172–73). A soldier returns home—"the place is palpable me"—to find himself outcast, his father dead, the family place sold. We are back to the problem of "The Little Town at Evening" and "Last Hours" with the soldier, or his ghost (only "ghosts" greet him), as unwanted as before. The poem closes, however, with a nearer prospect of violence. Reverting at last to the themes of the magazine poems, the ghostly speaker yearns to take his house in a Samson-like embrace:

I kiss the stones, I kiss the moss on the wall,
And wish I could pass impregnate into the place.
I wish I could take it all in a last embrace.
I wish with my breast I here could annihilate it all.

(*CP*, p. 173)

A murderous war will end in suicidal coition between the English home-stead and its ghosts. The previous poems pointed toward the alternative: man may surrender himself, giving himself over to the other with a changed sense of his limits. If "Nostalgia" does not describe that situation, neither does it replicate the sexual sword fights and ritual deaths of the magazine poems. Its scenario is more cautious. In *Studies in Classic American Litera-ture* Lawrence argued that the place to revive civilization is with its ghosts: "it is the souls of living men that subtly impregnate stones, houses, moun-tains, continents, and give these their subtlest form. People only become subject to stones after having lost their integral souls" (*Studies*, p. 84). "Nostalgia" is less clear even than this about a British Renaissance, but it pushes British souls over the verge into England's graveyard.

There are no heroes in *Bay* or "Bits," but these slight books are monu-ments to heroism of a different kind. Following Carlyle's prescription for modern heroism, Lawrence lived the active life through the medium of print. He read Carlyle religiously when young, and Carlyle is the first phi-losopher he mentions in his lecture of 1908, to justify his idea of art as he-roic feeling: "When Carlyle said that a hero could hardly express himself otherwise than through song, he meant that the vigorous emotion so moulded the speech of his hero—Mahomet, Dante, Burns—that this speech became Art" (*Phoenix II*, p. 224). These ideas derive primarily from *On Heroes, Hero-Worship and the Heroic in History*, where Carlyle argued that the modern hero could no longer be an active man—king, priest, or prophet—but as a result of the rise of the printing press, must be a "man of letters."[16] Lawrence applied himself to every mode of expression and their combinations—novel, poem, short story, drama, philosophical essay, travel sketch. Studying some of the stories, Keith Cushman has demon-strated how acutely aware Lawrence was of the literary marketplace, writ-ing to answer its needs as well as his own.[17] His livelihood depended on a continuous stream of publication, and he became increasingly involved in all phases of publication, not only in the editing and layout of his books but also in their marketing and distribution. At no time was the difficulty of this task more severe than during the war, when the marketplace be-came Lawrence's primary battleground. The immediate effect was to make life as hard as possible for him, but ultimately this struggle would shift the direction of his writing to make heroic action its primary function.

Rarely do critics consider what the physical production of books may mean to a writer, though nearly every writer must grapple with the problem of delivering a material, marketable work. In a study of Montaigne's autobiographical art, Barry Lydgate revealed Montaigne's sensitivity to the "lapidary" nature of books and of his public image, in distinct contrast to the fluidity of self: his history was one of successive conflict and reconciliation between fluid style and the intransigency of print.[18] Books, especially books of poems, took a less imposing shape in the twentieth century. Among Lawrence's chief delights when he was a young man just arrived in London was its stalls of "little" books: "I don't feel the need, of much food of new ideas, or of too new sensations. My books are enough. What I do love are little volumes of poetry, quite fresh acquaintances" (*Letters,* 1:106). Books for Lawrence would always be vital, pregnable forms, and his career a saga of battle and interpenetration of art with an intransigent marketplace.

Like his novels, his books of poems suffered rejections and censorship. *Look! We Have Come Through!* was the first volume of his poems to be censored. (*Pansies* was the only book of poems suppressed.) Reviews that appeared later in 1917 left Lawrence embittered: "As usual the critics fall on me: the *Times* says 'the Muse can only turn away her face in pained distaste.' Poor Muse, I feel as if I had affronted a white-haired old spinster with weak eyes. But I don't really care what critics say, so long as I myself could personally be left in peace" (*Letters,* 3:190). Lawrence *did* care about what his critics said, as well as about what they were doing to him. These last words, "so long as I myself could personally be left in peace," were uttered in complaint against police authorities in Cornwall who investigated the Lawrences, searched their papers, and eventually evicted them from Cornwall under suspicion of espionage. He was meanwhile at work on his war poems and hoped to "make other little books of poems like these," but again his pleasure was curtailed by publishers (*Letters,* 3:238). In 1918 he had three projects under way, including "Bits," *Bay,* and two books that he eventually combined into *New Poems.* Retitled "War Films," twelve "bits" were printed by Harriet Monroe in the July 1919 issue of *Poetry,*[19] but "Bits" never found its way into print as a book. In the meantime Beaumont had accepted *Bay,* and irritated Lawrence with a long delay in publication. In September of that year Lawrence had little progress to report of *Bay* to Cynthia Asquith: "that miserable little Beaumont is waiting for some opportunity or other" (*Letters,* 3:287). At first eager to see this volume, which was to be hand printed and illustrated with woodcuts, Lawrence's interest faded with the passage of time until he referred to *Bay* only with snarls. He finally received his copy in February 1920, when the war was over and he had departed England.

NEW POEMS

Lawrence's last production of the war years, *New Poems,* appeared nearly two years earlier than *Bay,* in October 1918. Its publication history and format epitomize his frustrations. He had gathered poems from his old college notebooks to revise for *Bay* and two other possible books, "Choir of Women" and "In London." In June 1918 he joined these under the title "Coming Awake." Secker accepted the book in August, but asked for a title change to *New Poems* (*Letters,* 3:244, 254–55, 277, 291). This title was grossly misapplied, since most of the poems were revisions of juvenilia. Despite his displeasure, Lawrence accepted the change, perhaps because he shared Secker's primary concern, which was to sell the poems. (*New Poems* would be remembered less for its poems than for its preface, "Poetry of the Present," which was added when Huebsch republished *New Poems* in America.) Since Lawrence had hoped in 1917 after composing *Look! We Have Come Through!* to begin "something new" (*Letters,* 3:90), this last return to his college notebooks was probably triggered by the pressure of circumstances. He needed the money and was failing to publish books of his "altogether new" concerns. His letters to Pinker about *New Poems* give abundant evidence of his anxiety to market the poems.

He had, nonetheless, intended *New Poems* to have a character of its own, suggested by the title "Coming Awake." Lawrence thoroughly revised many of its pieces, a process that was as responsible as his new compositions for the development of his technique, taking him farther past the achievement of *Look! We Have Come Through! Amores* would later set the framework for the sequence of *Rhyming Poems,* but *New Poems* would set the tone. As with *Bay* he revised poems of all kinds for *New Poems* and then left them almost untouched when it came time to collect his verse in the 1928 *Collected Poems*—love poems like "Under the Oak," city poems like the two titled "Embankment at Night," war verse such as "At the Front," and former elegies, including the headpiece and tailpiece of *New Poems,* "Apprehension" (formerly "The Inheritance," later retitled "Noise of Battle" in *RP*) and "On That Day" (retitled from "Her Birthday"). Perhaps the most curious cases are those where Lawrence revised mythic allusions, as Mandell has noticed, either to eliminate them or to incorporate direct references to them.[20] In the former case, Lawrence had, in his notebook, urged a young lover to join him in celebration of spring, to be his springtime Persephone: "You said you would be my Persephone—you would not / Persephone has passed through the town, fastening her girdle knot" ("Letter from Town: The Almond-Tree").[21] In another poem he invoked Persephone to rebuke his lover for her irreverent display of joy:

If out of the dreary halls of Dis Persephone had risen
To find the golden grainèd night aflower across the sky,
Would she have caught the last trail of her garment away from her prison
And run and tossed and swung in ecstasy

Across the meadows? She would have stood on the threshold
Lingering with her face to the stars, and spread
Her hands out to the night.

("Hyde Park at Night, before the War"²²)

These moral spankings were replaced with nonmythic images of love's threshold: "violets . . . pledge / Of our early love that hardly has opened yet" ("Letter from Town: The Almond-Tree," *CP,* p. 58), or "two streaming peacocks gone in a cloud" ("Hyde Park at Night, Before the War," *CP,* p. 70).

In "Autumn Sunshine," on the other hand, he cancelled the original ending—an intimate deathbed scene—to discover in the death of his mother an analogy to the hell queen. Persephone is no longer the spring maiden of the juvenilia; she is the demonic mistress of his later poems "Pomegranate" and "Bavarian Gentians," the bride of death:

The sun sets out the autumn crocuses
        And fills them up a pouring measure
        Of death-producing wine, till treasure
Runs waste down their chalices.

All, all Persephone's pale cups of mould
        Are on the board, are over-filled.

(*CP,* p. 177)

Together with "On That Day," which Lawrence revised similarly into a prophetic appeal, "Autumn Sunshine" closes the volume foreseeing a world *after* "terrible rage, the death" ("The Attack," *CP,* p. 165).

Although the manuscript evidence indicates that Lawrence had long given thought to a sequence of city poems, the final product is the most miscellaneous of his books. The college notebooks contain several pendants about the city, and the manuscript sequence of nine poems titled "Transformations" (Ferrier MS 5) includes three city poems. Already the theme of "coming awake" is present in symbolist cities that evaporate and metamorphose at twilight. As a young writer, Lawrence had before him several models for a verse book of the city. In addition to the Georgians' work, he read and was intrigued, for example, by *The City of the Soul* of Lord Alfred Douglas, which reproduced in English the French symbolist method of placing a city in slow-dissolve (*Letters,* 1:107). In a later manuscript notebook (Ferrier MS 27; Vasey MS E320.2), he collected and re-wrote many city poems—almost all of those that appear in *New Poems*.[23] Not only are most companion pieces joined in this notebook, but two sets are linked into five "London Nights."

In the final extant manuscript relevant to *New Poems* (Ferrier MS 43; Vasey MS E269.5), the verse appears in the same order in which it is now found in *New Poems*, with all previous sequences split apart and city poems mixed with love poems.[24] A table of contents enclosed with the manuscript confirms that this was the arrangement Lawrence wished. The list appears in nearly the identical order of the published contents and reveals some of Lawrence's last-minute decisions. He toyed with the order of a few poems. The triad, "Love Storm," "Sigh No More," and "Under the Oak," was re-worked to "Under the Oak," "Sigh No More," and "Love Storm" (*NP*, nos. 14–16). "Tarantella," "In Church," and "Piano" (*NP*, nos. 19–21) were exchanged for "Phantasmagoria" and "Next Morning" (*NP*, nos. 23–24), shifting the former group from below to above "Embankment at Night, Before the War: Charity" (*NP*, no. 22) and the latter from above to below. These final sequences (which did appear in the published *NP*) seem no more coherent after these changes than before, however, and in the second case he later reversed himself in 1928, returning "Phantasmagoria" (retitled "Late at Night" in *RP*) and "Next Morning" (*RP*, nos. 110–11) to above "In Church" and "Piano" (*RP*, nos. 117–18). Lawrence's construction of this manuscript list resulted in an order in which there are only two dis-crepancies from that of the published *New Poems*. One poem later omitted from *New Poems* at the request of the publisher (for reasons of space), "Late in Life," is included in the manuscript list (*Letters*, 3:278, 283). Set between "Bitterness of Death" ("A Man Who Died" in *RP*) and "Seven Seals" (*NP*, nos. 32–33), this poem announced the arrival of a satisfying love, a theme more appropriate perhaps to *Look! We Have Come Through!* The second discrepancy is more significant: "Apprehension" heads the published volume, but it is listed late in Lawrence's manuscript list be-tween "Reading a Letter" and "Twenty Years Ago" (*NP*, nos. 34–35), and there is no indication of any other intention. Lawrence meant at the time of compiling Ferrier MS 43 to enter the title "Coming Awake" for the vol-ume "after the first poem" (*Letters*, 3:254). He probably associated "Ap-prehension" with its original form as an elegy as much as with the apoc-alyptic tale of drowning London that it had become in revision, or with the war poem ("Noise of Battle") it would later become in *Collected Poems*. Since he had supervised the manuscript up to this point, however, it seems likely that this last decision was also his.

Despite all this attention, there are only pockets of sequentially ordered verse in *New Poems*. As usual among his revisions are several title changes; none of these are surprises, except perhaps one set of changes, where Lawrence decided the poems should not appear to be as old as they actually were. Below six titles (the two "Letters from Town," "Hyde Park at Night," "Piccadilly Circus at Night," and the two "Embankments at Night"), he had appended the words, "Year 1910," a phrase that lends a greater appearance of unity to the volume, but which he crossed out in every instance. As a result, the poems appear deliberately varied ("it is all different kinds of poems," he told Amy Lowell, to whom the book was dedicated—*Letters*, 3:254). "Apprehension" and "Coming Awake" form pendants at the head, heralding change: in "Apprehension" the destruction of "the great old city" (*RP*, no. 126, *CP*, p. 159), and in "Coming Awake," a new world of "lake-lights were quivering on the wall" (*UP*, no. 51, *CP*, p. 243). (Lawrence later removed "Coming Awake," however, to the climactic sequence of *Look! We Have Come Through!* in *Unrhyming Poems*.) The city verse in *New Poems* appears chiefly in pendants: "Letter from Town: The Almond-Tree" and "Flat Suburbs, S.W., in the Morning" (*NP*, nos. 6–7; *RP*, nos. 27, 20), "Suburbs on a Hazy Day" and "Hyde Park at Night—Clerks" (*NP*, nos. 10–11; *RP*, nos. 23, 40), "Parliament Hill in the Evening" and "Piccadilly Circus at Night" (*NP*, nos. 17–18; *RP*, nos. 113, 41), "Embankment at Night—Outcasts" and "Winter in the Boulevard" (*NP*, nos. 26–27; *RP*, nos. 115, 112). But of those he retained together for *Collected Poems*, none include these pendants. Obvious sets are divided in *New Poems*, but were reunited in 1928: two "Letters from Town" (*NP*, nos. 9, 6; *RP*, nos. 26–27), "Hyde Park" and "Piccadilly Circus" (*NP*, nos. 11, 18; *RP*, nos. 40–41), "Winter in the Boulevard" and "Parliament Hill" (*NP*, nos. 27, 17; *RP*, nos. 112–13), and the pair of "Embankment at Night" poems (*NP*, nos. 22, 26; *RP*, nos. 114–15).

Poems about women also fall into twos and threes in *New Poems*, and some of these groups remained intact in *Rhyming Poems*. "In Church" and "Piano," "Late at Night" and "Next Morning" (whose subject is in part women), were retained as pendants in 1928 (*RP*, nos. 117–18, 110–11). At the end of the book, five poems about women remained together, although this group was set in reverse order (with the exception of the final poem, the much-revised "Two Wives"): "Intime" (retitled "Passing Visit to Helen" in *RP*), "Twenty Years Ago," "Reading a Letter," "Seven Seals," and "Two Wives" (*NP*, nos. 36, 35, 34, 33, 37; *RP*, 121–25). Most significantly, in both volumes this fading choir of women precedes a final section of war verse. He retained together three war poems from near the end of

New Poems—"Heimweh" (retitled "At the Front" in *RP*), "Débâcle" (retitled "Reality of Peace, 1916" in *RP*), and "Narcissus" (*NP*, nos. 38–40)—then, heading them with "Apprehension" ("Noise of Battle"), he placed this group (*RP*, nos. 126–29) in front of those from *Bay*. Finally, he placed the closing pieces of *New Poems* (which had followed directly upon "Narcissus"), at the end of *Rhyming Poems* in reverse order, "On That Day," then "Autumn Sunshine" (*NP*, nos. 42, 41; *RP*, nos. 145–46)—suggesting that he meant them even in 1918 to be his last words on the condition of England.[25] The groups duplicated in both volumes should be considered whenever these poems are examined individually, but their contribution to the larger organization of *New Poems* is too small to justify close attention. The more significant contribution of this book would occur, not in 1918, but nine years later in *Collected Poems,* not only in the effect of its individual revisions, but in its organization. Lawrence drew from *New Poems* for connectives in the sequence throughout *Rhyming Poems,* for its ending, and, above all, for a long sequence to follow the elegies—from "Late at Night" to "Narcissus" (*RP*, nos. 110–29)—charting the "long haunting of death" (Note, *CP*, p. 28). Detailed interpretation of *New Poems* is therefore reserved for chapter 5 and *Rhyming Poems.*

Lawrence had motives for fragmenting *New Poems.* He may well have believed that the poems did not naturally form a single, strong sequence. There was no personal story to produce a background argument for the poems and, as we have seen, he was unable to represent the war as a period of real historical progression. Only when he wrote *Birds, Beasts and Flowers* did history begin again to unravel. Whether or not he intended it, however, *New Poems* is an expressive final product of the war. The shuffling together of love and city poems suggests both the achronicity and the disarray of apocalyptic experience: at any moment men, women, and their cities may "come awake."

Part II: Implicating the Reader

Lawrence's exodus from England in 1919 made just as great a difference as his marriage had in the circumstances of his life, in the management of his career, in his thoughts of heroism, even in his concept of a book. Like David in the wilderness now rather than like Job or Solomon, he was driven to wander. He traveled south to Italy and from there around the world to India, Australia, and America. Taking a decisive step in his career, he dismissed his literary agent Pinker in 1920 to oversee his own affairs more fully, asking his friend Robert Mountsier to act for him in America, but not looking for an agent in England until 1921, when Curtis Brown was recommended to him. He tracked his publications in a voluminous correspondence that had to travel around the world after him (*Letters,* 3:453–60, 504–5). And he imagined himself a different man with "a different story. Now there is new vision in the eyes, new hearing in the ears, new voice in the throat and speech on the lips. Now the new song rises, the brain tingles to new thought, the heart craves for new activity" (*Fantasia,* p. 108). Man's role in *Fantasia*'s new story was to play the "forerunner": "Primarily and supremely man is *always* the pioneer of life, adventuring onward into the unknown, alone with his own temerarious, dauntless soul" (*Fantasia,* p. 109). As he journeyed, he pictured himself a native of every region, projecting himself into the birds, beasts, and flowers of each place he saw. His heroic mission was not to attract a community of noble types to him so much as to advance social consciousness by running before it. He did this in and through books. In reaction to the marketplace, he had found a "new voice in the throat"—for the first time, he allowed himself a vivid public anger against his readers.

The end of the war presented Lawrence, however, with problems that complicated his personal and literary quest: what could happen next, what form would history take, what "new world" might emerge after war had "smashed the growing tip of European civilization" (*Movements,* p. 307)? The old question, how to begin again, must be asked of the world as well as of himself, and it became keenly perplexing in 1920, for it meant that he must turn his back on a great period in his own literary endeavor and on the answers it had produced: the idea of the autobiographical story, the notion of history unfolding in phases, the protagonist as a representative man, the centrality of marriage in society. In the theory of civilization developed in *Studies in Classic American Literature* (which he began during the war years, revised, and revised again until it appeared in its final form in 1923), we see Lawrence struggling with conflicting notions of history as regressive or progressive movement. Then too, he avoided any single theory by describing the works he examined, not as an epoch, but as one body on "the verge" of an indeterminable future (*Studies,* p. 4).

Lawrence did come up with a concept of history, eclectic though it was, that reconciled his divergent theses: "one cannot go back," he argued, and "God knows it looks like a *cul de sac* now. . . . [But] we have struggled on, and on we must still go. We may have to smash things. Then let us smash. And our road may have to take a great swerve, that seems a retrogression" (*Studies,* pp. 144–45). He replaced simpler models of a progressive, regressive, or even cyclical movement of history with a synthetic view: a manifold process, a kind of perpetuum mobile. History veers back into the past, to smash the present and emerge at some further point in the future; then it repeats itself. Any soul through whom history works its way would seem to the outsider to be directionless: "Meeting whatever comes down the open road. . . . Towards no goal. . . . Having no known direction even" (*Studies*, p. 181). This was the road Lawrence traveled as he headed around the world, eventually to reach America. To discover the western frontier he went south, then east, as if in deliberate retrograde to catch up with his forerunners.

Imagining a world after the war included thoughts of heroism, re-imagined by Lawrence as an aimless wandering between two worlds. Arnold's scholar-gypsy, torn between the intellectual and the natural man, is a prototype of the Lawrencean hero in *Birds, Beasts and Flowers*. To imagine such a being had been for Arnold an admission of defeat. In *Studies in Classic American Literature*, a man can be integrated only by acknowledging his disintegrated state, which Lawrence envisaged as Dionysian savagery and a crucifixion:

> The blood *hates* being KNOWN. Hence the profound instinct for privacy.
>
> And on the other hand, the mind and the spiritual consciousness of man simply *hates* the dark potency of blood-acts: hates the genuine dark sensual orgasms, which do, for the time being, actually obliterate the mind and the spiritual consciousness, plunge them in a suffocating flood of darkness.
>
> . . . That is our cross. (*Studies*, p. 91)

The dissociated hero appears as a paired set of heroes in the works of Carlyle. Carlyle allied himself in *Sartor Resartus* to Teufelsdröck and the Editor, and in *Past and Present* to a medieval hero, Abbot Samson, and his chronicler, the scribe Jocelin.[26] So too, in his "leadership" novels, in *David* (his ambitious last play, written at the end of this period), and in the poems, Lawrence turned to a divided heroism, a protagonist who travels toward a greater man, whom he must find, confront, and express. The poet-persona of *Birds, Beasts and Flowers* discovers, near the end of that book, an Indian, the red wolf, and meets his challenge.

Carlyle's double hero was, above all, the author himself. He acted through rhetoric, cutting into the ills of society, tempting us with mythic images of a world greater than any we know. Carlyle's subject in *Past and Present* was, more accurately, not Abbot Samson and his monastery, but his own mission as a man of letters: the reformation of his audience. Similarly, Lawrence defeats our expectations for a distanced narrative verse (to which we are accustomed by the earlier poetry); he now performs his poems, addressing them directly to us.

Vivian de Sola Pinto believed that Lawrence wrote his best poetry,

Birds, Beasts and Flowers, when he ceased to write about himself (*CP,* p. 11), but I would argue that these poems came only when he had fully developed his autobiographical strategies, the mode in which he knew himself, when he projected his experiences of crisis into a rhetoric of crisis, a verbal attack on his reader. Lawrence enters his poems as a lively commentator, alternately criticizing and admiring his beasts and vegetables, treating them at times as if they, like us, required his advice, at other times as if he and we required theirs. He implicates himself without making himself or "all of us" the entire subject of his poems. Eccentric though he seemed to a formalist like R. P. Blackmur, this realization of himself in 1923 as scholar, gypsy, and prophet brought Lawrence close to the center of modernism. We hear Whitman's voice echoing in "Who are you, who is anybody to tell me I am wrong?" ("Pomegranate," *CP,* p. 278), as in T. S. Eliot's "hypocrite lecteur" we hear Baudelaire. Eliot's disintegrated world in which a poet-priest, Tiresias, appears at the periphery, exiled, resembles that of Lawrence. In Eliot, however, we hear a more Arnoldean reverence for tradition—and greater despair. In Lawrence, the Carlylean vein flows with passionate rage.

The Foreword (1921) of *Fantasia of the Unconscious* suggests that Lawrence found his voice in direct response to his difficulties with the English marketplace. This foreword begins with a satiric jab at the reader: "The present book is a continuation from 'Psychoanalysis and the Unconscious.' The generality of readers had better just leave it alone." He follows up this attack with an assault on the marketplace: "I count it a mistake of our mistaken democracy that every man who can read print is allowed to believe that he can read all that is printed. I count it a misfortune that serious books are exposed in the public market, like slaves exposed naked for sale" (*Fantasia,* p. 11). So also Lawrence complained in the ditty "Traitors" (a poem that he did not collect in any of his books): if "they" could sell Shakespeare "to Crosse and Blackwells, to be jammed into jam," "everything in the world of culture and superiority" can be sold, including "whatever new comes along" (*CP,* p. 763).

Lawrence's rhetoric relies more than ever on overturning expectations, undermining complacency and passivity in reading, forcing us to acknowledge an active role in judging and being judged by the author. In the second chapter of *Fantasia of the Unconscious,* he delivers this mock apology: "Don't get alarmed if *I* say things. It isn't your sacred mouth which is opening and shutting. As for the profanation of your sacred ears, just apply a little theory of relativity, and realize that what I say is not what you hear, but something uttered in the midst of my isolation, and arriving strangely changed and travel-worn down the long curve of your own individual circumambient atmosphere. I may say Boh, but heaven alone knows what the goose hears" (*Fantasia*, p. 25). This jocular theory of noncommunication is founded on the assumption that the reader will misread and degrade Lawrence's words with his "sacred ears." Lawrence thus subjects his reader to a preemptive strike, and the angry terms of his attack, his impolitic and impolite name-calling, recondition the common meanings of the sacred and the profane.

In the concluding remarks of the Foreword, however, he issues an imperative that uncovers yet another motive at work. He means us to join his assault: "Rip the veil of the old vision across, and walk through the rent" (*Fantasia*, p. 16). The satirist, of course, rips through "the veil of the old vision" by attacking his reader. Yet Lawrence almost invariably expresses this as a counterattack, warding off the reader's criticisms in advance. While antagonizing his reader, he sets him up in opposition to himself, to move him to a position of equal power: "But remember, dear, reader, please, that there is not the slightest need for you to believe me, or even read me. Remember, it's just your own affair. Don't implicate me" (*Fantasia*, p. 33).

The first poem in *Birds, Beasts and Flowers* opens with a Whitmanesque bravado similarly intended to antagonize and upend its reader:

> *You tell me I am wrong.*
> *Who are you, who is anybody to tell me I am wrong?*
> *I am not wrong.*

("Pomegranate," *CP*, p. 278)

This battle cry should awaken us to difference, not merely a difference in opinion between Lawrence and ourselves, but a universe of difference. Like Blake (a strong presence behind these poems), Lawrence does not direct his ironies at his subjects (whether Tyger or Lamb), and he deploys his metaphors, not to describe, but to induce us to acknowledge and imagine the existence of two different worlds, one familiar, dead, and breaking apart under the thrust of another, revolutionary, mystical world:

> *The end cracks open with the beginning:*
> *Rosy, tender, glittering within the fissure.*
>
> *Do you mean to tell me there should be no fissure?*
> *No glittering, compact drops of dawn?*
> *Do you mean it is wrong, the gold-filmed skin, integument, shown ruptured?*
>
> *For my part, I prefer my heart to be broken.*
> *It is so lovely, dawn-kaleidoscopic within the crack.*

("Pomegranate," *CP*, pp. 278–79)

Lawrence's autobiographical strategy is fully at work, satirically rejecting an old self to project something new that is, however, an unstable, embattled, double self. His different world of the heart is "broken," changed, and exists in the midst of change: "dawn-kaleidoscopic within the crack." Somehow the problem—how to imagine a world after the war—had become its own solution: the gap produced Lawrence's brave new world.

Sandra Gilbert has argued in "Hell on Earth: *Birds, Beasts and Flowers* as Subversive Narrative" that the dominant pattern of this book derives from this revisionary impulse, and she develops a powerful argument for a central story of retrogression, "the overt story of a trip underground, a voyage of death and resurrection": "In the *Birds, Beasts and Flowers* narrative, perhaps more than anywhere else, this Blakeian poet makes it quite clear that in his version of the night-sea-journey the protagonist does not, like Beowulf, go down into the mere to slay the forces of darkness but rather to be strengthened and transformed by them."[27] As Gilbert argues, Lawrence also tells his story in a revisionary manner, replacing previous myths with his satanic versions and narrating the journeys of his creatures as retrograde movements into their dark underlife.

But while Lawrence does go underground in the book, this is not predominantly a process, as Gilbert suggests, of merging—of devouring and being devoured by the fruits of hell, of entering and reaching consummation with the diabolical. Gilbert emphasizes Lawrence's accommodations: "when he cracks open the pomegranate, therefore, we have to assume that this defiant speaker begins the revolutionary process of eating *and* entering the fruit— that is, eating and being eaten by it. . . . this poem/seed is a kernel of transformation," and again in the second poem, "Peach," he offers "the reader a peach stone to throw at him, showing that he at least *has* eaten the fruit."[28] Lawrence is, however, as much if not more concerned in this book to *separate* himself from the world, from familiar civilized states, to reach a further state of disintegration. This craving for separateness paradoxically "eats" corrosively at the reader; Lawrence refuses to satisfy our hunger. He unfleshes his images and shows us instead their fissures. In "Peach," he has eaten his fruit even before the poem begins: "Here, take all that's left of my peach" (l. 2). He refuses to give us a glimpse of anything we might recognize as a peach, showing us instead its pit, "Wrinkled with secrets / And hard with the intention to keep them" (*CP,* p. 279). By the end of this poem, we may be very willing to throw something at an author who insists on holding the pit of his peach at arm's length from us, while evidently gorging on its flesh himself in secret.

This paradox of merging into separateness controls the narratives of the book as well, so that while it is possible to reconstruct a "submerged" story

that retraces previous diabolical fictions, what actually happens in this sequence of poems (the "and then" of the story) is as difficult as possible to
follow. Its narrative threads, its fruitful, causal connections are all omitted.
While numerous connections do exist (such as those Gilbert recovers for
the first section of the volume, "Fruits"), the discontinuities must be considered with equal seriousness: the interrupted narratives and broken
structures of the book, all of which hinge on Lawrence's concern with a
dis-integrating integrity. He goes underground, but no Aeneas or Dante
could ever have imagined such a descent or entertained such a purpose for
it. He travels in a perpetual motion *down* the long road of the world, *back*
against its familiar rotation and *onward* to its farthest frontier. That skewed
sense of historical direction best describes the temporal design of this
strange new book of the world:

> *For we are on the brink of re-remembrance.*
> *Which, I suppose, is why America has gone dry.*
> *Our pale day is sinking into twilight,*
> *And if we sip the wine, we find dreams coming upon us*
> *Out of the imminent night.*
> *Nay, we find ourselves crossing the fern-scented frontiers*
> *Of the world before the floods.*
>
> ("Grapes," *CP*, p. 286)

Evidence of patterning in this book does not mean, then, that it is more
orderly or more overtly coherent than Lawrence's previous books; while
far more ambitious than *Amores* and *Look! We Have Come Through!* it appears far less like a verse novel. This problem emerges sharply in Gail Mandell's study, where, in the effort to trace a coherent, linear argument, she
fails to observe the book's fragmented nature—even when her own description betrays it: "the real subject of *Birds, Beasts and Flowers* is substan-
tiated by the prefaces that Lawrence wrote for the Cresset Press edition
. . . such as the fundamental nature of sexual opposition or the vitiation of
the white race and its gods. . . . a wide range of controversial topics, . . .
various political systems (democracy, socialism, and communism, in particular); female rights; industrialization; and organized religion." Mandell
also lists an equally wide range of mythic allusions.[29] Yet this multiplicity
of thought and the book's mixed texture—crossing social criticism with
myth—are large elements in its fascination for readers. Gilbert's theory of
a submerged story in *Birds, Beasts and Flowers* prompts her to conclude
boldly that this book is, like the "leadership" novels, a "fictional link between Lawrence's great middle-period novels of society" and "such late,
openly revisionary mythologies and romances" as *The Plumed Serpent* and
Lady Chatterley's Lover, and to claim that it is "a more successful and co-

herent work" than *Aaron's Rod* and *Kangaroo,* and hence "played a crucial part in his transformation from the romantic yet realistic novelist . . . to the mythic romancer."[30] To prove the truth of this shift that she sees, one has only to look at the generic character of this book in contrast with what precedes and follows it. But again, while generalized narratives can be discovered here, the most alert reader making his way from start to finish must confront something very unlike a verse novel. It is worth pausing to describe the generic character of *Birds, Beasts and Flowers* not only to understand what kind of "bridge" it is but also to establish a basis for analyzing its interrupted narratives.

Hovering between the miscellany and the verse novel, this book might be described (and more accurately so) as Lawrence described *Moby Dick:* a "phantasmagoric" voyage of the soul (*Studies,* p. 157). Lawrence interests himself persistently in questions of genre in *Studies in Classic American Literature* and at length suggests the curious crossbreed he produced in *Birds, Beasts and Flowers.* He had already begun to disdain the conventional, realistic narrative with its concatenation of cause and effect and to prefer to this even the romance where, though it never rains, some "myth-meaning" exists (*Studies,* pp. 64, 70). He prefers above this the "parable," which he characterizes as an "earthly story with a hellish meaning" (*Studies,* p. 89), or else something "picaresque, rascally, roving" (*Studies,* p. 148). Above all, he wants in literature a "dream-experience" (*Studies,* p. 165).

For his individual poems, he specifically chose the fable as a form that satisfied all these interests in the parable, the picaresque, and the dream-experience. The fable's character as fantasy made it a place where he could play his role as forerunner, exploring the world while leading his readers onward, and where he could enact still another rite of initiation, dreaming his way (and ours) out of one civilization and into another. The fable also would have appealed to Lawrence for its philosophic stance, down-to-earth while satirizing opposing views. In a renowned genre formulation of the eighteenth century, Le Bossu determined that the epic ("La Fable Epique") "est raisonnable & vrai-semblable; elle imite une action entière & importante; elle est longue & racontée en Vers: mais aucune de ces proprietez ne la fait changer de nature, & ne la rend moins Fable que toutes celles qui portent le nom d'Esope."[31] Lawrence probably interested himself in the fable because it was *not* always "vrai-semblable" and did not "imite une action entière." But with equally false humility, he took Aesop over Homer as the model for his most ambitious book of poems, because in it he could recover and reinvent a more primitive mode of heroic literature. "We like to think," he wrote at the beginning of *Studies in Classic American Literature,* "of the old-fashioned American classics as children's books. Just childishness on our part. . . . There is a new voice in the old

American classics. . . . a new experience," which the world needs and fears (*Studies*, p. 7). As commentators have often noted, the title for *Birds, Beasts and Flowers* derives from a childhood hymn by S. Baring-Gould:

> *Now the darkness gathers,*
> *Stars begin to peep.*
> *Birds and beasts and flowers,*
> *Soon will be asleep.*[32]

Recasting this allusion diabolically in his childlike hymns, Lawrence blacked out the stars of modern orthodoxy and conjured forth the ancient beasts of nightmare:

> *Rise, thou red thing,*
> *Unfold slowly upwards, blood-dark;*
> *Burst the night's membrane of tranquil stars.*

("Southern Night," CP, p. 302)

The "childish" fable of Lawrence speaks with "a new voice" to announce an unlooked-for set of heroes.

This book of fables should thus be understood (even more properly than *Fantasia of the Unconscious,* which digresses into farcical anecdotes less than it might) as a fantasia, a potpourri of fables in which Lawrence's fancy wanders unrestrained by strict narrative formulae or verisimilitude. There is no extrinsic scaffolding that unifies and organizes the book—only the lineaments of such patterns and an episodic movement from one poem to the next. Moreover, Lawrence had in mind a specific version of the fantasia, which gave it a comic shape: *Fantasia of the Unconscious,* he claimed whimsically, was a "Harlequinade of the Unconscious."[33] While characterizing *Birds, Beasts and Flowers* as a fantasia tells us the kind of experience this is, the harlequinade suggests an analogy to its rough, dreamlike plot.

Along with its medley of children's fables, farce, satire, music, and spectacle, the harlequinade possessed a stable set of four characters (in the late nineteenth century the harlequinade, originally the third section of the pantomime, was the only piece to be shown). Its hero appeared as Harlequin with a magic wand that doubled as a bat, his fiancée was Columbine, his rival Clown, and Pantaloon was the woman's guardian; all of them struggled with each other and with the audience in a sequence that had no obvious order. In the popular final transformation scene, these characters reappeared magically changed and reconciled to each other.[34] The specific characters of the harlequinade differ widely from those of *Birds, Beasts and Flowers,* with its scholar-gypsy-prophet and his animate kingdom; it was their interactions that interested and amused Lawrence. He compared the pantomime with *Fantasia of the Unconscious* to poke fun at his theory of the psyche, the answer to Freud that gained him richly earned notoriety: among the four dynamic centers of the psyche, two plexuses of the lower body polarize each other and are polarized in turn by two plexuses of the upper body, but when the upper body interferes with the lower, the lower body proves its superiority by subordinating and counterbalancing its other half. Whimsical though the analogy is, it should not blind us to its potential for elucidating Lawrence's methods: the story of psychic drama, as described in *Fantasia of the Unconscious* and reenacted in his poems, is a havoc-ridden comedy whose slightly absurd protagonists interact as in the relationships of star polarity of *Women in Love* (pp. 139–44).

Birds, Beasts and Flowers is an anthology of such tussles and acquires dimension as a harlequinade, with its restless ups and downs and final salvation. In "Pomegranate" Lawrence faces us with bat and wand to initiate us into his world of fissured, two-directional creatures. "Snake" appears at a critical juncture of the book, when the poet-persona himself falls into— and apart from—this differentiated world. Realizing his separateness and connectedness, he will learn what a polarized relationship with a snake must be like. The clownish speaker in his pajamas at the start of the poem draws attention to the contrastingly royal apparition of the snake; until his sudden muscular effort to throw a log at the snake emphasizes the opposite, degraded image of the retreating reptile. As I suggested in chapter 1, these contrasts play upon each other to enforce divided attitudes of revulsion and respect not only for the snake, but for that vulnerable and banal, fierce and unlikely, man who can admit at the end, "And so, I missed my chance with one of the lords / Of life" (*CP*, p. 351). The crisscrossed dualisms that so fascinated Lawrence become in this poem an experience for the reader of *discordia concors:* of fleshly beauty with ugliness and of both those qualities with the lordliness and pettiness of the mind. "Snake" is a pivotal poem in this fantasia because at this juncture a creature and a man, an instinctive man and his socialized second self, a speaker and his readers, must all reconsider each other.

In the course of the volume, Lawrence stages many comparable engagements with and among his beasts until he reaches a transformation scene where, in the last poem of "Animals" (the penultimate section of the book), his speaker encounters a ghostly Indian called a red wolf. Entering painfully and confidently into power play with his antagonist, he is at length transformed into a "red-dawn-wolf." The red wolf speaks first in this dialogue:

> We take no hungry stray from the pale-face . . .
>
> *Father, you are not asked.*
> *I am come. I am here. The red-dawn-wolf*
> *Sniffs round your place.*
>
> ("The Red Wolf," *CP*, p. 405)

After this, a confrontative reconciliation of the world's embattled races and of all men with women is, for the speaker, merely a matter of summoning their "ghosts" (the title of the last section of the book)—although that turns out to be a still-distant prospect at the end. Faint, but discernible, a narrative structure reveals itself in this book in the fragmentary, phantasmagoric comedy of a harlequinade.

Lawrence was not alone among modern writers in recreating this psychic drama. James Joyce, for one, used pantomime elements in the composition of "Circe," his Nighttown episode in *Ulysses,* where all the creatures of Leopold Bloom's unconscious are assigned roles and dramatically externalized. He must relive in an inverted style a middle-aged family comedy, his wife's affair with another man and his own yearning for a son. "Circe" ends with a transformation scene in which Bloom is granted a vision of his dead son, Rudy, resurrected before his eyes.[35] The dramatic format of "Circe" and the fabulist mode of Lawrence's poems turn the comic plot into such a fantastical form that it is at first unrecognizable. These freer, psychological forms reenact the ravages and rewards of the psyche; and they implicate us by exposing us more directly to the author's fantasies.

There is no such thing, of course, as a "pure" fantasia, nor is there anything pure about the generic character of *Birds, Beasts and Flowers.* It bears traces of several genres, including the travelogue, the romantic crisis-autobiography, the book of mythologies, and the missal book, each of which contributes a secondary narrative strand. Its sources are as rich as its world of beasts. These other structural patterns are broken or subverted, but they produce for the approaching reader a series of frameworks or paths through the book. I will use these secondary references to sort through its many poems and to provide local contexts likely to make individual poems more accessible. Some poems become more intriguing than others when considered as moments in a book: traditional anthology pieces like "Snake," "Medlars and Sorb-Apples," and "Tortoise Shout" are as interesting as ever, but other, lesser-known pieces rise in value: "Pomegranate," "Cypresses," "The Red Wolf," "Spirits Summoned West," and "The American Eagle." The proliferated narratives of this book suggest why so many of its poems possess a power and autonomy beyond those in any other book by Lawrence. The focus here, however, is not on individual poems, but rather on the way in which these structuring patterns bind and unbind the verse.

The multiple patterning of this book developed simultaneously with its growth. Lawrence gathered these poems, not at a later date, as he had done for *Look! We Have Come Through!* but concurrently with their composition. At times his design may even have dictated some stages in composition. *Birds, Beasts and Flowers* grew up as a book of books. As early as the spring of 1921, when he had written approximately two-thirds of the poems, he organized them into sections of birds, beasts, and flowers. In the fall he began to arrange small books, or "chapbooks," of separate groups to be published ("Tortoises" and "The Evangelistic Beasts"; *Letters*, 3 : 681; *Collected Letters*, 2 : 675–76). The reader perceives the structure of the finished volume as still more variable than this, for the notes that Lawrence added (apparently upon request) to the Cresset Press edition (1930) present, not one, but several arguments for each of the nine sections. These are often more enigmatic than elucidating, functioning like brief prose poems, meditations on the topics of each section.[36] The effect is that we must find our way among many paths and signposts from the start.

Lawrence's plan took on an evolutionary element like that of *Look! We Have Come Through!* early in the production of *Birds, Beasts and Flowers*. The title originally ended with an exclamation point, signaling a progress toward some triumph: *Birds, Beasts and Flowers!*. When he began compiling poems under this title, he had pieces for only the six earlier sections written in 1920–21, from "Fruits" to "Reptiles." The developmental scheme gained from poems written in 1922–23—three final sections created a structure suggestive of a chain of being: "Fruits," "Trees," "Flowers," "The Evangelistic Beasts," "Creatures," "Reptiles," "Birds," "Animals," and "Ghosts."[37] This scheme orients the creatures in a natural development preceding Darwinian evolution theories—a stable, hierarchical order of interdependent species rather than the monstrous growth of man out of monkey. In his Epilogue to *Movements in European History*, Lawrence articulated the anti-Darwinian sentiment of *Birds, Beasts and Flowers:* "Man and monkey look at one another across a great and silent gulf, never to be crossed. The savage shakes hands with me, and each of us knows we are of one ancient blood-stream. But if I attempt to shake hands with a monkey or an ape—it is a gesture only of mockery. We cannot really meet in touch" (*Movements*, p. 308). Lawrence lectures us on such separateness often in this book, by picturing the alternative as murder. Many beasts die (the mosquito, the fish, the mountain lion) or barely escape death (the bat, the snake, the dog) or—worst fate of all—sink into ignominious indistinction.

Lawrence's anti-Darwinian chain of being is not a regularly or closely linked chain. He originally placed six poems outside individual sections (a fact that has escaped most readers because no tables of contents are reprinted in *Complete Poems*). With the exception of "The American Eagle" (the closing piece),[38] these extrusive poems are not about birds, beasts, and flowers, but about landscapes, civilization, volcanos, and the like: "The

Revolutionary," "The Evening Land," "Peace," "Tropic," and "Southern Night." Making blatant what he argues elsewhere through indirection, the first three sections step, not from one kind of plant form to another, but from "Fruits" to exhortation ("The Revolutionary," "The Evening Land," and "Peace"), from "Trees" to sun and moon ("Tropic" and "Southern Night"), and back again to "Flowers." This oscillation is suggestive, but not of a chain of being; rather it expands the symbolic value of Lawrence's plant life, telescoping back and forth from microcosm to macrocosm. "The Evangelistic Beasts" stands out from the other poems as the single overtly religious category, separating the vegetable from the animal sections; positioned thus, it may represent a step beyond the vegetable universe toward creaturely life. As he hints in the notes in this section, "The Evangelistic Beasts" are cosmic seeds of the animal kingdom: "from the four quarters the four winds blow, and life has its changes" (*CP*, p. 319). The last section, "Ghosts," consists of a phase of being rather than a category: the "ghosts" are husks of the landscape, of beasts of prey, and of men. If there is a chain of being in this book, it is one that operates along two different axes, which at times clash with each other: the temporal, sequential pattern that we would expect is broken by metaphoric associations.

The book possesses also a geographical map of personal symbolism, as in *Look! We Have Come Through!* yet the apparent correspondence between Lawrence's life and his poems is deceptive. All the verse is located geographically, and its order roughly corresponds to his travels eastward to the New World. While nearly all poems in the first six sections were written before the spring of 1920 and January 1921, when Lawrence was in Italy, most in the last three sections were written in 1922–23, during his travels to and residence in America. But this is, at best, a sketchy outline of the chronological order. Few composition dates can be determined absolutely, and the exceptions to this rule suggest that the book is widely achronological. Keith Sagar argues, on manuscript evidence, that "Tropic," "Peace," and "Southern Night" were among the first pieces composed. Nor does Lawrence adhere absolutely to the order of geography. Three "Animals," for example, are located in Italy, though two of the preceding "Birds" have their sources in America. Sagar notes further that although "Humming-Bird" is located by Lawrence in Española, near Taos, it had its original source not in any country, but in a passage from Crèvecoeur.[39] The integrity of Lawrence's bestial kinds take precedence over geography. Here again Lawrence's soul journey demands that the semblance of natural processes gives way to the soul's more abstract fantasy.

Birds, Beasts and Flowers contains several cyclical narratives, which reinforce the fantasial narrative. First, there is the cycle of an autobiography, from birth to maturity to old age and from innocence to experience, in the sequence from fruits to animals to ghosts. The six "Tortoise" poems (succeeding "Snake" in the sixth section of "Reptiles") constitute the most obviously coherent section and encapsulate this growth pattern. After "Snake" (where Lawrence recognized the right of reptiles to exist), the "Tortoise" poems trace the process from turtle birth, to adolescent desire, to sexual death. This sequence might be taken as a miniature of the book and its climax: dividing into three parts, the first three sections ("Fruits," "Flowers," "Trees") urge upon us the sloughing off of an old world to be born again; the next three ("The Evangelistic Beasts," "Creatures," "Reptiles") trace the dual growth of identity and differentiation in the kingdom of creatures; the last three sections ("Birds," "Animals," "Ghosts") image domesticated, mostly male, creatures, overburdened by intimacy and aching to be pioneers. At the book's end we find Lawrence repeating the same announcement of a "new story" that he had expressed several years (and many poems) ago in *Fantasia of the Unconscious*. "The red-dawn-wolf" speaks for him here:

> Since I trotted at the tail of the sun as far as ever the creature went west,
> And lost him here,
> I'm going to sit down on my tail right here
> And wait for him to come back with a new story.
> I'm the red wolf, says the dark old father,
> All right, the red-dawn-wolf I am.

(CP, p. 405)

In the course of Lawrence's travels, the world has grown old, and the journey has taken him close to where he began, with "ghosts" of the past to confront and the New World's tired "eagle" to pursue.

Less obvious than this autobiographical progress from youth through age is a Christian paradigm, which provides one of the most likely models for the book's division into nine sections. As we know from Lawrence's composition of *Amores*, in its positive aspect the Book of Hours symbolized the fantastical, animate world that died with the death of his mother. When Lawrence began looking for illustrations for his poems in *Birds, Beasts and Flowers*, he asked friends to find engravings of "The Evangelistic Beasts" in Books of Hours and missal books (*Collected Letters*, 2:676). (*Birds, Beasts and Flowers* eventually was illustrated in the Cresset edition, though unfortunately without resemblance to a missal.) Lawrence's Book of Hours conforms in *Birds, Beasts and Flowers* to its hellish narrative.

Based on the life of Mary or Christ, the missal compiles biblical texts into nine sections, or "hours," that culminate with the assumption or the resurrection. In *Birds, Beasts and Flowers* Lawrence joins sacred man with sacred woman, leading them through the crucifixion of sex to resurrection as new men and women. The first note warns the modern "new woman" that although "fruits are all of them female, in them lies the seed," nonetheless, "the apples of life the dragon guards, and no woman gives them" (*CP*, p. 277). Her proper relationship to man becomes explicit in "Flowers:"

> *Hell rearing its husband-splendid, serpent heads,*
> *Hell-purple, to get at her—*
> Why did he let her go?
> *So he could track her down again, white victim.*
>
> ("Purple Anemones," *CP*, p. 308)

Then in "Lui et Elle" in the "Reptiles" section, where the tortoises have already found out their differences, we learn that males, too, take their turns as victims:

> *Alas, what a fool he looks in this scuffle. . . .*
> *Fore-runner.*
> *Now look at him!*
>
> (*CP*, p. 360)

The central lesson of *Birds, Beasts and Flowers* would seem to be that Woman with her Son has been superseded by man among the daughters and sons of man:

> *It was always an altar of burnt offering*
> *His own black blood poured out like a sheet of flame over his fecundating herd*
> *As he gave himself forth.*
>
> *But also it was a fiery fortress frowning shaggily on the world*
> *And announcing battle ready.*
>
> ("St. Luke," in "The Evangelistic Beasts," *CP*, pp. 326–27)

This theme announces itself most often in poems we are least likely to enjoy, but they are no less sprightly than the more cloaked, Edenic treatments of sex in "Medlars and Sorb-Apples" or "Grapes." "Spirits Summoned West," the last poem of the last section, "Ghosts" (and the penultimate poem of the book), is Lawrence's version of Judgment Day, calling the dead women of England—all "virgins"—to rise from their graves and enter his paradise in America. This poem in particular may seem to say more about Lawrence than about anything else, but it is staged at so late and crucial a moment of the book that its impetuous Shelleyan or Blakean appeal seems necessary and inevitable. Lawrence drops the fabulist mode to force confession upon us:

They are many, and I loved them, shall always love them,
And they know it,
The virgins.
And my heart is glad to have them at last.

Now that the wife and mother and mistress is buried in earth,
In English earth,
Come home to me, my love, my loves, my many loves,
Come west to me.

(*CP*, p. 412)

Both the romantic crisis-autobiography and the missal book, however, are obscured by the more prominent mythological cycles traced by Gilbert—the journey from ripeness into death to a tentative rebirth. *Birds, Beasts and Flowers* is a book of mythologies, an Ovidian set of metamorphoses, mythic transformations of plants:

Sorb-apples, medlars with dead crowns.
I say, wonderful are the hellish experiences,
Orphic, delicate
Dionysos of the Underworld.

("Medlars and Sorb-Apples," *CP*, p. 280)

Each creature has its totemic root in a distinct race, and each guides the speaker further along the path of disintegration. Carrying forward *The Golden Bough*,[40] the speaker first participates in the destruction of each race, then experiences increasing alienation from these others: from the peach he eats at the beginning, which reemerges with its secret, impenetrable pit intact, to the untouchable ghosts at the end, which he wishes he could revive. Midway through the book, the "Creatures" epitomize this pattern. The sequence begins with a nasty "mosquito," which Lawrence, posing as a greater mosquito, punitively crushes, only to discover in the bloodstain dwarfing the insect's remnants, the marked difference between the mosquito and himself. From "The Mosquito," he advances to the "Fish," which he admires at first, but then must examine out of water— dead, alien, though ever more gorgeous—as it withdraws its secret life from him. Only at the last, in two encounters with the "Bat," do another creature and he manage to escape each other, untouched and unlike each other.

Another model that accounts for as great a portion of the book (if not a greater), but that has previously been overlooked, is the travelogue. Like his journal, *Sea and Sardinia,* and his "leadership" novels, *Aaron's Rod* and *Kangaroo, Birds, Beasts and Flowers* reenacts Lawrence's quest for his own totemic roots. From the beginning, he sprinkles in references to this search for the dawn and "uncanny America," land of explorers and pioneers. His conception of such a quest was influenced by works read in his youth like *Lavengro* by George Borrow, a favorite autobiographical travel novel of the young Lawrence (not least because its title recalled his name).[41] The affinity between *Lavengro* and Lawrence's book leads us to the motives of this geographical-spiritual mission.

The eponymous Lavengro and Lawrence travel through language and society as well as across the countries of the earth; both seek to uncover the runes of an Ur-language, belonging to survivors of an original master race—existing on the distant frontiers of society. In *Lavengro* the Ur-language and the society is that of the gypsies, called "Romani" folk throughout this novel. Lavengro, which is a gypsy word in this novel for "word lover" (he is also called Sapengro, or "snake lover"), wanders along, picking up languages and scattered traces of the gypsies, until he himself devolves into a gypsy. So too in *Birds, Beasts and Flowers,* Lawrence dissects the familiar race of plants and creatures, to discover their totemic roots in a remnant, prehistoric underworld:

> *Folded in like a dark thought*
> *For which the language is lost,*
> *Tuscan cypresses,*
> *Is there a great secret?*
> *Are our words no good?*
>
> *The undeliverable secret,*
> *Dead with a dead race and a dead speech, and yet*
> *Darkly monumental in you,*
> *Etruscan cypresses.*

("Cypresses," *CP,* p. 296)

Like Lavengro, Lawrence digs through Roman ruins into Etruscan soil, tracing a master race until he becomes a member, under the totemic sign of the red wolf.

While the "Fruits" have established Lawrence's social, geographical, and spiritual aims, he waits for "Cypresses" (the first poem of the second section, "Trees") to unveil his philological quest. He mourns in this poem the burial of a language of evil:

> *What would I not give*
> *To bring back the rare and orchid-like*
> *Evil-yclept Etruscan?*
> *For as to the evil*
> *We have only Roman word for it,*

Which I, being a little weary of Roman virtue,
Don't hang much weight on.

For oh, I know, in the dust where we have buried
The silenced races and all their abominations,
We have buried so much of the delicate magic of life.

(*CP*, pp. 297–98)

Such a quest would eventually lead him to the ancient Anglo-Saxon four-letter words of *Lady Chatterley's Lover*. But in *Birds, Beasts and Flowers* he gropes for a buried language, teasing out an alien speech by hyphenating the current with the archaic, "evil-yclept." Named "evil" of old, its original "virtue" has faded with age and been silenced.

As Lawrence's search for language gathers strength, his own language metamorphoses; definitions are inverted ("weary of Roman virtue"); words multiply and are metonymically cracked on each other's backs; until in "Tortoise Shout" (when he records the sex act), he taps the enormous energies of primal song:

A far, was-it-audible scream,
Or did it sound on the plasm direct?

Worse than the cry of the new-born,
A scream,
A yell,
A shout,
A paean,
A death-agony,
A birth-cry,
A submission,
All tiny, tiny, far away, reptile under the first dawn.

(*CP*, p. 364)

This heroic song arises from a kind of linguistic crucifixion, yoking antithetical types, the "death-agony" and the "birth-cry," and stretching to represent many random utterances. All this returns us to Arnold's scholar-gypsy and past Arnold to the many other scholar-gypsies in nineteenth-century literature, who find themselves trapped, and aroused, by the gap they must bridge between the science of philology and the mythology of the Word.

Gilbert argues that Lawrence becomes increasingly articulate or, more precisely, increasingly conversant with the creatures he confronts as the book develops.[42] Although as usual there is no steady progress in his ability to talk with his animals, this journey ends (like the other paradigms) in

"The Red Wolf," when he enters actual dialogue with the Red Indian spirit, and in "Spirits Summoned West," with his discovery of a voice powerful enough to call up the dead. This quest also extends, however, beyond what the poet can acknowledge; so that a reader may unearth traces of an Ur-language, left in the poems without comment by Lawrence. In the closing poem, he confronts an eagle with a puzzle that, like a secret code we can now read, slyly reveals this bird's "true cross":

> So better make up your mind, American Eagle,
> Whether you're a sucking dove. . . .
>
> Or whether it actually is an eagle you are,
> With a Roman nose . . .
> And a Me-Almighty eye.

("The American Eagle," *CP*, p. 414)

The eagle must, like "St. Matthew" (a "traveller back and forth," *CP*, p. 323), be both hawk and dove, Roman and Judean.

These various cyclical and linear narratives do not merge into a symphonic swell, not only because they are discontinuous but also because they are undercut at many points by elegiac digressions, satiric endings, and an increasingly pessimistic mood. At key points, Lawrence steps back from his vision of the future to reminisce about the past. In "Tortoise Shout," for example, at the most pregnant moment in the tortoise's scream of triumph, he drops into a long meditation on his past: "I remember, when I was a boy, / I heard the scream of a frog" (*CP*, p. 365). This meditation spans the course of Lawrence's childhood until it returns to the tortoise shout, which is now a culmination of the past:

> And more than all these,
> And less than all these,
> This last.

(*CP*, p. 366)

Although the crucially located "Spirits Summoned West" functions as a Judgment Day and confession, it is composed in the spirit neither of judgment nor of ecstasy. It is an elegiac invocation to Lawrence's mother and young lovers: "So now I whisper: *Come away,* / *Come away from the place of graves, come west*" (*CP*, p. 411). Like "Nostalgia" at the end of *Bay*, "Spirits Summoned West" expresses as much sorrow as triumph in the effort to mate his soul with a ghost. In the notes to the last section he describes a still more painful mood among the ghosts. Harsher than the regrets of an Orpheus who looked back is the pain of a Eurydice: "For the journey is a far one, to sleep and a forgetting, and often the dead look back, and linger, for now they realise all that is lost. Then the living soul comes up with them, and great is the pain of greeting, and deadly the parting again. For oh, the dead are disconsolate, since even death can never make up for some mistakes" (*CP*, p. 406). This equivocal passage at first appears to mourn the loss of a more vital past (which Wordsworth had expressed in "Ode: Intimations of Immortality"—"Our birth is but a sleep and a forgetting"), but in fact mourns the pain experienced by the dead at their loss of consciousness in the sleep and forgetting of oblivion. The dead experience a double grief when they must reencounter a living soul and reexperience their "parting" from life: their terrible intimations of mortality. No new world makes its appearance at the end of *Birds, Beasts and Flowers*—just a man, the dead, man's persistent mistakes, and a possibility of rebirth that causes pain.

Any sense of a way forward or a ritual way out is shouted down by the satiric voice of these fables, which almost invariably accuses the creatures of having attained nothing. Lawrence strikes a harsh satiric note in anecdotes about the impotence of modern warlike figures in "Hibiscus and Salvia Flowers," "St. John," "Man and Bat," "The Blue Jay," the last poems respectively of "Flowers," "The Evangelistic Beasts," "Creatures," and "Birds." In the final three sections, the only virtue his creatures possess is obstinacy, the power to resist any response to the present. Lawrence directs our attention, not to any previous joy, but to the wasted present with its craven neediness:

> *Everybody so dear, and yourself so ultra-beloved*
> *That you have to run out at last and eat filth,*
> *Gobble up filth, you horror.*
>
> ("Bibbles," from "Animals," *CP*, p. 398)

In such poems he issues a strong reprimand or enforces upon us a choice. This obstinate note of the drill sergeant and its accompanying undertone of world-weariness are sounded with increasing frequency in the last sections—"Birds," "Animals," and "Ghosts." In the "Animal" poem "Mountain Lion," he faces none of the possibilities in his creature or its greater past—only its murdered body. He has sung the demise of the old world at the beginning of the book; he grieves for its death at the end.

But like most of Lawrence's books, this one ends neither in utter misery nor in joy. Even while appearing more preoccupied than ever with the death struggle, he offers the hope of remade men and remarriage, heralding the nuptials of an American chief with his virgins. Though there is something ridiculous in this, it recalls similar scenes in modern verse, like that in the penultimate stanza of Wallace Stevens's "Sunday Morning":

Supple and turbulent, a ring of men
Shall chant in orgy on a summer morn
Their boisterous devotion to the sun,
Not as a god, but as a god might be,
Naked among them, like a savage source.[43]

The savage, sensual man will dominate Lawrence's next work, *The Plumed Serpent*, where he developed the rituals, religion, and verse for a self-elected great man and his disciples. The protagonist of that novel acquires a posture of sardonic self-satisfaction much like that of "Turkey-Cock" (first in "Birds"):

Your sort of gorgeousness,
Dark and lustrous
And skinny repulsive
And poppy-glossy,
Is the gorgeousness that evokes my most puzzled admiration.

Your aboriginality
Deep, unexplained,
Like a Red Indian darkly unfinished and aloof,
Seems like the black and glossy seeds of countless centuries.

(*CP,* p. 369)

Lawrence does not, of course, give us the satisfaction of entry into this savage paradise. His grand master of fowls, the American Eagle of the last poem, remains "perplexed"—a word that also refers to the "unfinished" and novel complexity in Lawrence's creatures. The eagle stands at a crossroads wondering what he is, and Lawrence teases him to decide: "So better make up your mind, American Eagle" (*CP,* p. 414). It is up to the bird, passive and peaceable as yet, to assume his next shape as a "poppy-glossy" forerunner and strutting cock.

A book as unkempt as this, yet so obviously fashioned to suit a Lawrencean history, will defy most efforts to exhaust its meaning. Sandra Gilbert substituted her description of this book's revisionary structure for an earlier belief, stated in *Acts of Attention,* that the unifying method of the book is Lawrence's progress toward self-attainment.[44] Lawrence's method in this book, as I believe, lies both in and past these explanations. When he defined *evolution* as "attainment" in "Him with His Tail in His Mouth" (1925), he illustrated his meaning with a piece of nonsense verse and an anecdote about two more beasts: a bird and a cow shouting their "songs" at each other,

The bird gave a cluck, the cow gave a coo,
At the sight of each other the pair of them flew
Into tantrums, and started their hullabaloo.

They startled creation; and when they were through
Each said to the other: till I came across you
I wasn't aware of the things I could do!

> *Cuckoo!*
> *Moo!*
> *Cuckoo!*

And this, I hold, is the true history of evolution.

The Greeks made equilibrium their goal. Equilibrium is hardly a goal to travel towards. Yet it's something to attain. You travel in the fourth dimension, not in yards and miles, like the eternal serpent. ("Him with His Tail in His Mouth," *CP*, p. 761)

Such attainment of an "equilibrium" located in no normal time sequence is a story of barnyard squabble, something little short of chaos. But it is in this inner zone of rumble that *Birds, Beasts and Flowers* manages to remain, the antinomial poetry sweeping its readers forward.

CHAPTER FIVE
—
At Forty

THE PLUMED SERPENT AND COLLECTED POEMS

CHRONOLOGY:

Residence in America	1923–25
Illness in Mexico	1925
Return to Europe	1925
The Plumed Serpent published	1926
Collected Poems gathered and published	1927–28

Lawrence's heroic quest reached its inevitable end in America—the real and mythic destination of his journey through the world. With his arrival there came the long-awaited change he had expected in himself and predicted for the world in *Birds, Beasts and Flowers,* or so he claimed. Years in Sicily, months in Kandy, and long journeys to Australia, Tahiti, and California did nothing to shatter the "great psyche of materialism and idealism" or "essential Christianity on which my character was established": "But the moment I saw the brilliant, proud morning shine high up over the deserts of Sante Fé, something stood still in my soul, and I started to attend. . . . In the magnificent fierce morning of New Mexico one sprang awake, a new part of the soul woke up suddenly, and the old world gave way to a new" (*Phoenix*, p. 142). The forerunning Lawrence reached the end of his wanderings and stood ready for a magnificent transformation. In the last and greatest of his "leadership" novels, *The Plumed Serpent,* he enacts that transformation: the Mexican hero-gods return to power. But this culminating moment (in both his life and his work) soon gave way to another struggle with death. He endured extreme frustrations during his three years in America; on his third visit to Mexico he came close to dying, either from malaria or, as his doctors diagnosed, from tuberculosis. Like the war years, this was a period both of new endeavor and of stalemate. The American poems incorporated into *Birds, Beasts and Flowers* created an ending for that book that, like the war poetry at the end of *Look! We Have Come Through!* trails off into weariness and nostalgia. *The Plumed Serpent* envisages a world at war.

But when Lawrence returned to Europe in 1925, he experienced a resurgence in his powers equal to that of the immediate postwar years. He experienced his release from death, not as an escape (as he had in the postwar years), but as a return to youth and the world of his younger manhood. *Lady Chatterley's Lover* and *Collected Poems* celebrate the revitalization of "tender" relationships beyond what he called "the hero-follower business." If *The Plumed Serpent* represents the farthest extension of Lawrence's myth of a satanic, preternatural world exploding Western culture, *Lady Chatterley's Lover* returns to the more conventional form and subject of romance. A lesser known, but impressive, act of restoration appears in an introduction that he wrote for *Chariot of the Sun* by the poet Harry Crosby. Here Lawrence proposed the theory that every artist strives, as he did, to unsettle his reader. This essay articulated at last the rhetorical theory that had informed his poetry throughout his career.

The changes of mid-life form the thread of continuity between these otherwise disjunctive phases. In *The Plumed Serpent* he turned his frustrated efforts to become an elder hero-priest into the fictional account of a successful revolutionary. In *Lady Chatterley's Lover* and the *Collected Poems* he told equally fictional anecdotes of phallic restoration. And he refused despair. That perspective on the real continuity in Lawrence's life and work, as it emerged from one phase into another, from frustration into renewal, from death- to life-experience, closes the gap felt by previous commentators between the American and the European writings, and simplifies the task of tracing his career from one phase to the next. The heroic ideal that he brought to a final form in America became internalized in the phallic ideal of his final European writings, allowing the vision of a divinely inspired community to revert into a divinity within individual men.

In both phases Lawrence finalized his ideas of manhood in comprehensive, novelistic forms. *The Plumed Serpent* is one of his most original, and least understood, contributions to literature. In it he combined prose narrative with a verse sequence to create a form that would encompass the inner story of individual heroes within a social program: his hero a poet. *Collected Poems* appears to be Lawrence's closing statement on the shape of his career up to 1928. He reviewed all the verse he had written and re-ordered it to simplify his actual history: in this account, his career registered a single major crisis, marked textually by the shift from volume 1, *Rhyming Poems,* to volume 2, *Unrhyming Poems.* The rearrangement of poems produced a new narrative as well, wherein he portrayed himself drawn out of death and war into vital relationship with a woman and nature. This reconstruction of his career as a poet remains a vivid reminder to the reader, however, not to accept even the *Collected Poems* as the last word on his poems from 1906 to 1928. Lawrence himself warned the reader against an easy reading, just as he would have cautioned a lover: "'I can read him like a book,' said my first lover of me. The book is in several volumes, dear" (*Studies,* p. 103).

Part I: American Finale

America represented the farthest extension of dreams that Lawrence deeply wished to come true: "Since I trotted at the tail of the sun as far as ever the creature went west" ("The Red Wolf," *CP,* p. 405). If in *Birds, Beasts and Flowers* he endeavored to forge a new consciousness and a condition of "star polarity" in his race, in his American work he hoped to create a new civilization. He had come of age, with many masterpieces behind him in the novel, the short story, and the poetry; he was ready for a work of epic proportions. The masterwork of this period has few readers, however, and draws very mixed reactions from them. *The Plumed Serpent,* written in an alien climate and attempting to prophesy in the twentieth century, is often condemned without a full hearing. The book confronts the reader with the Lawrencean challenge redoubled, assaulting orthodox estimates of the known, the proper, and the necessary.

Lawrence's difficult relationship with Mabel Luhan generated some of the darker memories of this period. Harry T. Moore points out that Lawrence balked frequently at the willful persistence of his would-be hostess in Taos.[1] He may have delayed his journey to America not only for symbolic reasons, as he first headed east, but also to avoid the grasp of another devouring mother. Whatever his reasons, it is clear that he delayed in order to collect himself and to give America time to collect itself: "I feel it is my destiny to go east before coming west. Only to stay a short time: perhaps a year. But to get quite calm and sure and still and strong. I feel America is so *unreligious:* it's a bad word: and that it is on the brink of a change, but the change isn't quite ready yet, so I daren't come. And I feel you yourself are *harried* out there."[2] Once the Lawrences were in America, the cross fire between Mabel and Frieda became a constant irritant. Mexico itself was repugnant to him. Its impoverished conditions repelled and frightened him, and in 1925 he nearly died there.

What is missing from such an account is Lawrence's ceaseless, optimistic efforts to establish a community in America, propagating new myths. Moore, for example, emphasizes Lawrence's personal difficulties in Taos and his obvious failure as a hero. Moore sees these as the conditioning background for the "failure" of *The Plumed Serpent,* with its unnovelistic attempt to combine verse with prose and its religion of blood-consciousness.[3] These opinions ignore both the complexity of Lawrence's American experience and the claims on our interest of his boldly experimental production.

Despite reservations about coming to America, Lawrence hinted to Mabel that he saw himself a potential hero, who could provoke a change among the Indians: "I too believe in Taos, without having seen it. I also believe in Indians. But they must do *half* the believing: in me as well as in the sun." He worried that the Indians might fail to give what "this wearily external white world can't give, and which the east is just betraying all the time."[4] His failure in 1915 to establish a revolutionary movement with Bertrand Russell had dampened but not quenched his desire to create an ideal community like that of Rananim, a small anarchic community of his friends. As it turned out, he stayed with Mabel Luhan for less than half of his three-year sojourn in America—profound annoyance drove him from her side. Yet a year and a half in proximity to a nearly indomitable woman was a long time for the energetic and impatient Lawrence who, as Mabel put it, was always doing things. Mabel managed to appeal to him (despite Frieda's repeated, eventually successful, efforts to destroy her influence) and won his esteem, at least temporarily. Another close friend of Lawrence, Dorothy Brett, also established and maintained a companionable relationship with him until Frieda sent her off. Throughout this period, he was hard at work advising friends of both sexes, writing ceaselessly, and struggling for leadership in his small domain of vying companions.

The trials Lawrence endured had a still more personal dimension, which has gone almost unremarked by scholars of this period in his work. Middle life came to him as an unexpected test and proof of his commitment to change. Irritated with the trivialities of modern manners, which had invaded even Mexico ("the foreigners seem to make the Mexicans worse than they are. . . . And Mexico, or something in it, certainly makes the foreigners worse than they are"⁵), laboring to undertake a mission in America, while craving as ever for youth, Lawrence's mental trials must have had much to do with his physical breakdown. It is curious to observe this experience refracted by Bernard Malamud's *Dubin's Lives,* written in response to Lawrence's American experience. The protagonist, Dubin, undergoes the crisis of middle life while writing his magnum opus, a biography of Lawrence: with the boredom of his settled life and the burden of its responsibilities, he plunges into an affair with a woman half his age, in consequence enduring purgatorial uncertainties and a writer's block. In placing his biographer at this juncture, Malamud grasped the elusive, unlovely character of the same period in Lawrence's life. Dubin broke his writer's block only after he internalized a hard fact, which he knew Lawrence had also faced: that irritation, impatience, and neediness concealed, but could also compel a man to rediscover, his creativity and self-mastery.⁶

These experiences were less significant, however, as proof of his personal resilience, than for the opportunity they provided him to write his American myth. Unlike other self-made culture heroes such as Eldridge Cleaver or Norman Mailer, Lawrence lacked an effectual public arena for his activities (as well as the practical ability needed even for antithetical public life) and could become a public figure only by writing himself into mythology. He held himself to be a prophet, whose spontaneous confessions were heroic. "Open confession" was not alone sufficient, of course, for prophecy. In a review of *A Second Contemporary Verse Anthology* (1923), he criticized American versifiers for reducing the "fruits of sensation" to a "'composition salad'" or "word-games [played] around the camp fire." Even the thought that confession "is good for the soul" becomes formulaic in lines quoted, for example, from Robert Roe's "Recuperation":

> *Oh, ho! Now I am masterful!*
> *Now I am filled with power.*
> *Now I am brutally myself again.*⁷

There must be "an element of danger in all new utterance" for Lawrence to approve: "we prick our ears like an animal in a wood at a strange sound. . . . Man is always, all the time and for ever on the brink of the unknown" (*Phoenix,* pp. 322–26). When he saw New Mexico for the first time and spoke of it in terms of an instinctive "wonder," he fulfilled his own part as poet: "the moment I saw the brilliant, proud morning shine high up over the deserts of Sante Fé, something stood still in my soul" (*Phoenix,* p. 142).

A "dangerous" confession is good not only for the poet but for any one who can hear, prick up his ears, and wonder. Lawrence recognized, of course, how difficult it could be to obtain such hearers. In the poem "O! Americans" (a jeremiad that he did not see published), he argues for a world that would arise from a few beleaguered individuals: "to be faithful to something that has not yet come to pass, that does not yet exist, save as a subtle, struggling germ in individual hearts, / . . . That is a difficult thing to be faithful to" (*CP*, p. 775). Neither a long tradition nor the backing of a large constituency is the hero's source of power, but an innate "quickness" may leap from him to others.

Lawrence's personal experience of America, his struggle to become an elder statesman, formed the basis of his myth of social alteration, and, more profoundly, his experience of mid-life informed his vision of an aging society. It was this that took him beyond Carlylean confession to a more involved theory of societal needs: one must "live through to win through," he told Mabel Luhan. Change occurs like the changes in a serpent, which sheds dead skin to reemerge in brighter flesh (*Collected Letters*, 2:764). Lawrence studied the mid-life crisis in the women around him and in himself as they approached the age of forty. Another letter to Luhan begins by arguing with her to change, but ends in a more universal vein: "perhaps the only thing that will really help one through a great change is discipline, one's own deep, self-discovered discipline, the first 'angel with a sword'" (*Collected Letters*, 2:809). *Discipline* became the catchword. To win through this crisis, a man or woman must achieve discipline, forcibly resisting impatience and restlessness by subordinating the self to some deeper purpose.

What was new in this idea of change was a protofascist element, the emphasis on collective self-subjugation to a shared leader and a shared ideal. Lawrence turned his perception of the paradoxes of mid-life into too strait a dogma. Mabel complained that Lawrence repeatedly advised her to subdue herself, that he demanded that all women subjugate themselves to men, and in particular to him. Meanwhile, a man harnessed himself and others with rage. If angry enough, he could burn away his personal past and subject himself to his mission. Echoing and reaffirming the concerns of *Birds, Beasts and Flowers*, the prophetic hero of *The Plumed Serpent* moves an entire nation with "volcanic violence": "in the Songs and the Hymns of Quetzalcoatl, there spoke a new voice, the voice of a master and authority" (*Serpent*, p. 286). The volcano, which in *Birds, Beasts and Flowers* still symbolized the devouring power of a woman, now was assimilated into the increasingly dominant symbolism of masculinity. Like an inner god, anger disciplines and empowers. The hero-god is no stable ego; he is "shaken" by quick temper:

The snake has kissed my heel.
Like a volcano my hips are moving
With fire, and my throat is full.

("Welcome to Quetzalcoatl," no. 12, *Serpent,* p. 384)

Nor is this powerful male—the prophetic poet—self-sufficient. The demon within is "more than a man," as he says in *The Plumed Serpent,* capable of moving himself and others, but not omnivorous or omnipotent. The hero was to be a powerful fragment of an elite, and this in turn the fragment of a "new world." So Whitman, greatest of American poets to Lawrence, was "heroic" in his expression of the "quick" of experience, but failed when he attempted to be "all."[8] Lawrence called for self-discipline in men, self-subjugation in women, and self-sacrifice to a "greater" world—sacrifice to the state—in both.

The political implications of these opinions may seem oppressive, but when viewed in the context in which Lawrence subscribed to them, they are less dark than they appear to us after World War II. In a book where he is primarily concerned to develop a defense of Robinson Jeffers, the poet William Everson (himself a conscientious objector in World War II and a self-confessed follower of Lawrence) suggests what motivated Lawrence, and places both poets among the modernists: "The bolshevist triumph in Russia during the First World War had been so sudden and so total that it stunned Europe. Professing to be sacrally liberated, in fact it implemented the residual sacral elements in the culture by utopianism, projecting them into the future. The writers of whom we are speaking saw that this transfer was a delusion. Their attempt was to formalize those sacral values in their art, in a conscious endeavor to contain them against that threatening eventuality, so that a more realizable future might be secured." Everson includes the "pre-capitalist fiscal policy" of Pound, the "retention of hierarchical aristocracy" of Yeats and Eliot, and the "preservation of instinctual life" of Lawrence in his catalog of values, which these artists saw as the "key to the wholeness of man": "a wholeness which the triumph of humanistic atheism, with its establishment in industrial society had threatened, and which bolshevist revolution hoped to make permanent by preempting the future."[9] There is no question that Lawrence saw these as threats: in his Epilogue (1925) to *Movements in European History,* he described himself as hedged in on the one hand by the "Force of Finance," whereby "Nations are slowly strangling one another in 'competition,'" and on the other hand by the "bullying" and "worship of mere Force," or the *"Malice Oblige"* of Russia (*Movements,* pp. 318–23). The answer was for all nations to realize themselves, as Mexico does in *The Plumed Serpent* by returning to its native religion (with bloodshed, though ostensibly without holocaust). Once each nation knew its true self, the world might become a community of nations "polarizing" each other.

Lawrence's application of this dogma to his fictional writings was almost programmatic. Middle-aged protagonists sacrifice their personal pasts and then discipline themselves, to solidify their power as elders. His first American project was a novel (planned but not written) based on Mabel Luhan's life: narrating her journey to Taos, the breakup of her previous marriage, and her developing relationship to her fourth husband, the Indian Tony Luhan—a story that bore some resemblance, of course, to Frieda's. Redefining relationships to respond to the exigencies of his new myth, he told Mabel: "I believe what you say—one must somehow bring together the two ends of humanity, our own thin end, and the last dark strand from the previous, pre-white era."[10] The results were even more violent than in his war poetry. In the well-known short story "The Woman Who Rode Away" (which Mabel believes was intended by Lawrence to "finish her up"),[11] a forty-year-old woman, who has wearied of her life in the white world, rides away into an Indian camp where, after ritualistic preparation, she is sacrificed to their god at sunrise. Lawrence's image of the dawn recurs here as a symbol for renewal of the world *and* blood sacrifice, which he held to be a necessary catalyst for any racial transference.[12]

Lawrence recorded this myth in poetry as well. After endeavoring to become more submissive, as he had taught her, Mabel wrote a poem entitled "Change" in which she narrated her change of heart. Lawrence was sufficiently intrigued to rewrite her poem in an expanded version called "Change of Life."[13] This version ritualistically unfolds seven stages in a woman's life, as she faces loss and sacrifice and adopts a nonaggressive attitude. Her life is "Not bleeding away, to leave me with whitened gums," but "Only breaking camp, and entering / Slowly, insidiously, into new places." Lawrence probably intended this macabre portrait to evoke the realities of self-sacrifice, but it clashes sharply with the formalized diction of ritual ("life" in the following passage is masculine):

> *Where life looks me in the eyes*
> *And goes his way silently, unasserting.*
> *Where the meadow-lark wears his collar of submission*
> *On his throat below his song.*

(CP, p. 768)

The hero, whose emblem is the meadowlark, "wears his collar of submission" even while he sings. Such thoughts will recur more effectively in the poetry of *The Plumed Serpent*, where Lawrence took pains to generate a set of legends dissociated from any personal pathos, but instead directly registering the theme of transcendence.

A paraphrase of the action of *The Plumed Serpent* demonstrates how neatly it too falls into the pattern constructed by Lawrence. Three main characters "make a new world" by evicting Christianity from Mexico and establishing a program for communal existence. Stories of maturation of woman, man, and state are all combined. A forty-year-old Irishwoman faces the "second half of her life" like a "tomb" (Lawrence makes a great point of her age, devoting a chapter to her birthday), then slowly falls under the power of a Mexican man, Cipriano, to whom she sacrifices her personal life. She is compelled by this man beyond her personal desires to accept him as a "man who is more than a man." Cipriano, in turn, disciplines himself to follow the leadership of Don Ramón, whom one might identify as Lawrence's spokesman. In the central action of the novel, Don Ramón also surrenders his individual personality to be installed as the elect priest, or "First Man," of the Aztec god Quetzalcoatl (the "Plumed Serpent"). Shortly afterwards he is attacked by "peons," mercenary instruments of Mexico's Catholic priests. But the attempted assassination fails, confirming Don Ramón's mission and his charismatic power among native Mexicans. Rising from his wounds phoenixlike, he sets aside once and for all personal interests and hesitations. To complete the gods' installation, Cipriano undertakes a complementary trial and, under the Aztec name Huitzilopochtli, executes the peons who attempted to assassinate Don Ramón. While the guilt of the would-be assassins justifies their punishment, its chief purpose is to refresh the state.

The consistency with which Lawrence's paradigm for adult life shows up in his writings, widely different as it is from what he himself lived, suggests how much he worried over what this phase could mean or produce. "Discipline," Lawrence chanted—not realizing that he, the great proponent of blood-consciousness, had revived a key word of his mother's evangelical faith. The fiction suffers when it follows Lawrence's plan too strictly. Yet in "The Woman Who Rode Away" and *The Plumed Serpent,* he also dramatized the difficult emotions of such an experience: the tyranny of oppression, the attraction of symbols of authority, above all the *necessity* of anxiety, not as something to be resisted (as he had advised Mabel), but as a goad to greater manhood. It is to this art, an art of anger and authority, that we should turn next, to consider the narrative texture of *The Plumed Serpent.*

L. D. Clark's still stands as the best discussion of this novel and provides the point of departure for my analysis. Although a close reading of the novel lies beyond the range of the present study, a sketch of its narrative methods is necessary to appreciate its subject and the impact of its poetry. As Clark explains, Lawrence gives two access routes to, or perspectives on, his subject, and both are managed through conventional features of the novel: a realistic narrative and mythic symbolism.[14] Through the novel's protagonist, Kate Leslie, the reader encounters varied responses to Mexico and its heroes, so that the religion they establish seems possible if improbable, fearful rather than destructive, and responsive to Mexican needs. Through the symbolic texture, Lawrence reenforces these responses by compelling his reader—just as Kate is put upon—to experience the alien and sensual paradise of Quetzalcoatl. We encounter in *The Plumed Serpent* a fresh application of Lawrence's technique: to confront the reader with something alien (repellently alien), yet to make this vision a sympathetic one.

Lawrence is more willing than ever to alienate us, taking his audience through a trial of nerves. In the opening scene, he stages a bull fight as unlike Hemingway's as possible, ignoble and grotesque. Kate is a reluctant spectator from the beginning, irritated by the crowd, disillusioned by the spectacle ("there was no glamour, no charm," *Serpent,* p. 11), then disgusted when the bull gores two blindfolded nags. Lawrence repeats his description of the goring ("all its bowels slipping onto the ground," *Serpent,* p. 18) a third time, to ensure that when Kate abruptly departs, we go with her. Yet at this moment of extreme nausea she meets the general of the Mexican army, Cipriano. She soon wants to get away from him too, deferential though he is, but now to feel repulsed has begun to seem an exotic immersion:

> There was that heavy, black Mexican fatality about him, that put a burden on her. His quietness, and his peculiar assurance, almost aggressive; and at the same time, a nervousness, an uncertainty. His heavy sort of gloom, and yet his quick, naive, childish smile. . . .
>
> She felt again, as she felt before, that Mexico lay in her destiny almost as a doom. Something so heavy, so oppressive, like the folds of some huge serpent that seemed as if it could hardly raise itself. (*Serpent,* p. 22)

She will never experience Mexico otherwise, but she will eventually feel exhilarated by its power, as she plunges into the second half of her life.

By the time we reach the end of the novel, we have become accustomed to participating with Kate in her shock and pleasure. Language now acts out the devious, clownishly primitive and free gestures of a "plumed" serpent: "'*Yo! Yo!*'—his eyebrows lifted with queer mock surprise, and a little convulsion went through his body again. '*Te quiero mucho! Mucho te quiero! Mucho! Mucho!* I like you very much! Very much!' It sounded so soft, so soft-tongued, of the soft, wet, hot blood, that she shivered a little" (*Serpent,* p. 487). Such language does not remove us from rational consciousness; it provokes reaction, rousing the reader to withstand such savage discourse, but with a "shiver" allowing its strange effects, its tenderness. The next words are the last in the novel, as Kate responds, "You won't let me go." Her assertion is syntactically ambiguous, more intensely equivocal than Birkin's closing remark in *Women in Love* ("I don't believe that"). Angry resistance is enmeshed with imperious desire, "Don't let me go."

The Plumed Serpent has much in common with the work it succeeds. Like *Birds, Beasts and Flowers* it is a fable with satiric and mythic dimensions. It is a sacred book, performing an elaborate rite of initiation, carrying the reader half reluctantly along. Unlike *Birds, Beasts and Flowers, The Plumed Serpent* is not episodic or picaresque; it does not focus on Kate's wanderings so much as on her gradual subduction. She must learn to take a comparatively small place in a growing national scheme that is larger than any individual character, even than Don Ramón. *The Plumed Serpent* creates a world large enough to contain a prophetic poet, and verse reacquires its primitive function, to express the spontaneous utterances of heroic men.

But the question of poetry in this novel poses a special problem because in this context, prophetic verse breaks faith with the conventions of realism. *The Plumed Serpent* represents real lives in their social structures, but then stretches and disrupts the bounds of mimesis, first by expanding into prose poetry, then by erupting in lineated verse. In further violation of our expectations, this poetry arises from and merges into the narrative action, rather than occurring in isolated private moments in a character's thoughts. *The Plumed Serpent* acts out a revolution in the conventions of reading that makes palpable the revolution it records.

Lawrence asks his novel, first, to record the possibilities for surviving modern society's destruction, and then to operate as the means by which modern culture is replaced. He set at nought almost the whole of Western tradition in his American work, retaining only the Bible and ancient mythologies, such as that of the Aztecs. So while discarding one set of conventions, he set about reviving the ancient functions of literature as a medium for epic storytelling and for communal song. In his essay "The Novel" (1925), he speaks of the books of the Bible as novels: "greater novels, to my mind, are the books of the Old Testament," than any modern novels or than the "novels" of the New Testament (*Phoenix II,* p. 418). In *The Boy in the Bush* (1924), he further expounds his belief that the whole of Western culture produced nothing but falsified interpretations of the Bible—an opinion anticipating his later reconstruction of the Book of Revelation in *Apocalypse*. The Bible is to be translated, not as an exercise in spirituality, but as an expression of the savage underside of the world. Although *The Boy in the Bush* was originally the work of the Australian writer M. L. Skinner, and her name appears with Lawrence's in dual authorship of his novel, Lawrence left his imprint on every page. (Note that Easu is the name of the antagonist.)

> He had always *known* that the Old Testament never meant any of this Shelley stuff, this Hindu Nirvana business. . . .
>
> And when the flame came up in him, tearing from his bowels, in the sudden new desire for Monica, this was his spiritual body, the body transfigured with fire. And that steady dark vibration which made him want to kill Easu—Easu seemed to him like the Antichrist—that was his own spiritual body.[15]

The Plumed Serpent is Lawrence's grand satanic revision of the *New* Testament, narrating the passion of Quetzalcoatl, casting the figures of the Madonna and Child out of the Mexican churches to make room for live men, and inventing the services and hymns for their church.

Lawrence's ambition for *The Plumed Serpent* is only partly achieved: far from unfolding a biblical epic, *The Plumed Serpent* remains a novel with poetry in it. It is a novelist's fantasy of what might produce material for an epic—the traditional two couples of the novel transformed into gods. As Sandra Gilbert points out, "because gods and humans have a simultaneous rather than a causal relationship in *The Plumed Serpent,* Lawrence is often obliged to sacrifice the human impulses of his characters, out of which he would ordinarily build his novel, to the exigencies of the gods." But I cannot agree with her that, because poems are a suitable vehicle for expressing the transcendental, where the novel is necessarily ironic, "rather than the poems being irrelevant to the novel, it is the novel that is in a sense irrelevant to the poems." Her judgment simply reverses Graham Hough's earlier assessment that the book performs better as a novel than as verse.[16] Gilbert and Hough agree in finding the combination of poetry and prose unsettling. The novel cannot, however, be absolved from collaboration with its poetry; they are too closely interwoven. L. D. Clark more accurately estimates their interaction: "the prose creates a context of religion and art in which the poetry can function. . . . It is inseparable from the novel and has little meaning in the exterior world. . . . an extreme solution to the problem expressed by many poets in our time, that of re-establishing the bond between poetry and religion."[17] To this, I would add only that rather than a record of divine action, the novel follows the process by which characters and readers may acquire a transcendental second sense. This task might be better handled in a long verse poem—but not with wide effect, Lawrence believed, in the twentieth century; so his work seems still in transition, pointing to another art, attempting to dismantle the novel from within.

Beyond disrupting novelistic conventions, the poetry assumes a life of its own, functioning in varied ways and always in realistic contexts. Lawrence probably hoped we would forget its experimental character as we move into the thick of the plot. The poetry ranges in format from prose poems to lineated verse, yet there is little range in form; almost all of it is free verse, imitating or, occasionally, incorporating translations of Indian religious songs that Lawrence knew through Lewis Spence.[18] Neither is there a real diversity of rhetorical styles. Lawrence employs mythic symbols and biblical effects to evoke a smooth, ritualistic flow of song. L. D. Clark enumerates the variety of purposes accumulated by the poetry: "The poetry relates mythical matters, . . . chants of love human and divine and of mindless communion with darkness and stars. It performs marriage, welcomes the ceremonial hours of the day, defines in its own way the economic and social structure of Mexico, outlines a code of conduct; it invokes the gods and the deified elements, offers valedictions to Jesus and Mary, delivers anathemas, sings maranathas, and foretells the fate of the damned."[19] Clark's dense synopsis indicates the type of detailed study that this poetry might repay. He thus suggests, however, that the poetic effects are more mysterious than they are. Each function he lists has an inevitable place within the narrative, and the verse operates together in its own order, like a subplot, except that it "transcends" the main story line.

The gradual emergence of the verse from its enclosing narrative thus should be outlined while unraveling the "inner story" it tells. This inner account announces the main events in the changing of the gods, the departure of Jesus and the return of Aztec divinities. The sequence of twenty-six lineated poems (see also *CP*, pp. 786–813) reflects the typical shape of Lawrence's poetic books: witnessing at the retreating heels of an old regime the advancement of another; marching through episodes of struggle in Quetzalcoatl's rising power, each struggle motivated equally by the strength of resistance and yearning; all this enacted, moreover, chiefly through utterances in the I-voice with Quetzalcoatl and his companions facing off their antagonists in direct address; finally retreating with a prayer for a new world still distant. Every stage is closely woven into the prose narrative and has its impact in a local arena.

Kate discovers for us the first poem (on her fortieth birthday); glancing at a Mexican pamphlet, she reads "a sort of ballad" (*Serpent,* p. 129). This deliberately vague classification is the first of several such evasions. Don

Ramón will later call some of his poems "hymns," but two of these are written as prose poetry rather than lineated. At other times he calls them "songs" or "prayers." Often they go unnamed. The poem Kate first reads, "'In the place of the west,'" is in no technical sense a ballad. It is, like all the poems, a psalmlike narrative in the I-voice, and it tells of the coming of Quetzalcoatl when Jesus departs: "I rose again, to see a star falling, and feel a breath on my face" (*Serpent*, p. 130). The result of this process of unnaming, is to plunge us into a world in which poetry seems natural, "a breath on my face," in need of no name, performing common functions in men's lives.

We next encounter a series of manifestos intended to rouse the people: psalmlike prayers and prose invocations, alternating with one or two line-ated songs, chanted by Don Ramón or his men, then followed by the first two "hymns," widely published and propagated in prose poetry. The lineated verse of *The Plumed Serpent* is excerpted and anthologized by the editors of *The Complete Poems* (nos. 1–26), so that it is possible to examine the poems without being distracted by the narrative. But in the process much is lost, especially the graduated changes, from prose to prose poetry to psalm to song, and back again. Ramón may, for example, ease his thirsty listeners (and Lawrence mesmerize his more distant audience) with a purple prose passage describing an Adamic paradise: "The cup of my flowering is unfolded, in its middle the stars float balanced with array. My stem is in the air, my roots are in all the dark, the sun is no more than a cupful within me" (*Serpent*, p. 249). Attempts such as this at poetic persuasion (its magnetically linked oppositions governed by the symbolism of the plumed serpent) appear during indoctrination episodes, intoned ceremoniously by Don Ramón in the public eye of his village, or read surreptitiously by the people, clustering in their sheds.

With the third hymn, the first official hymn to be lineated and titled ("Quetzalcoatl Looks Down on Mexico," no. 5), the more personal circumstances of the poems become explicit. As if to counterbalance the increased formality of the verse, the plot surrounding the poems thickens. We are told that Don Ramón wrote a third hymn in anger and that some Mexicans have burlesqued it. As he meditates his situation, Kate starts up her own mockery. He leaves her in rage, to write his fourth hymn. We witness its entire evolution: Ramón's hasty composition, his trip to the printers, and his enactment of a scheme to circulate the poem throughout the nation. The rapid action of the narrative generates a momentum calculated to put us in a receptive mood for the equally packed invective of his hymn:

But lo! you inert ones, I will set the dragons upon you.
They shall crunch your bones.
And even then they shall spit you out, as broken-haunched dogs,
You shall have nowhere to die into.

Lo! in the back streets of the air, dead ones are crawling like curs!

("What Quetzalcoatl Saw in Mexico," no. 6, *Serpent*, p. 284)

These judgment-day poems do double duty, much like "Spirits Summoned West" in *Birds, Beasts and Flowers,* crying out against and *to* the dead.

After the assassination attempt against Ramón, the poetry acquires a more nearly autonomous life. The failure of the murder and Ramón's resurrection-like recovery spurs him and his Mexicans to rebuild their religion. In the first ceremony, Ramón will enter the Catholic church, throw out its saints, and reinstate the Mexican gods:

Mary and Jesus have left you, and gone to the place of renewal.
And Quetzalcoatl has come. He is here.
He is your lord.

(no. 9, *Serpent*, p. 370)

Thereafter, song enters the daily life of the citizens, who pray at dawn, midday and sunset. At length a bit of verse appears, spoken by the unseen narrator rather than a character, allowing poetry into the deepest element of the narrative:

The world was different, different. The drums seemed to leave the air soft and vulnerable, as if it were alive. Above all, no clang of metal, during the moments of change.

Metal for resistance.
Drums for the beating heart.
The heart ceases not.

(no. 16, *Serpent*, p. 393)

The narrator instantly attributes this as "one of Ramón's little verses," but with the effect of suggesting that, for the moment, the narrator himself is one of Ramón's messengers, with no more distance than a fellow initiate. Several paragraphs later, without skipping a beat in rhythmic description of his world of metal, he slips again into verse without comment: "Metal for resistance. / Drums for the beating heart" (*Serpent*, p. 394). The narrator says nothing, but to the intent reader, these two lines express the systole and diastole of the book: the force of resistance and the counterforce of desire.

The last, largest group of poems occurs in the final ceremony of the hero-gods, in a brief story of its own: Cipriano is elected priest; the execution of the peons is performed; and, once more triggering rebirth, Ramón ends the ceremony by announcing a goddess of nature, Malintzi. All these moments occur in lineated verse not far from the book's end, and together they form the climactic episode in this novel's inner history. We are asked to participate in the transcendent second world of the Aztec religion. This sequence constitutes, moreover, a divine and male counterpart of the poem "Change of Life." The state "matures" when men have lived and died for it, when they have disciplined themselves to the great, impersonal gods:

Man that is man is more than a man.
No more is man till he is more than a man.
Till the power is in him
Which is not his own.

The power is in me from behind the sun,
And from middle earth.
("'Man that is man is more than a man,'" no. 19, *Serpent,* p. 412)

All the poems are sung by men, and these heroes are renewed by what is repeatedly characterized as a male power, the power of rage. Its myth recalls the war poetry with its bloodletting and homoerotic consummations: "Huitzilopochtli gives the black blade of death. / Take it bravely" (no. 22, *Serpent,* p. 415). In the war poetry, however, there were no heroes; no garden emerged from the ashes; and no female Malintzi was finally admitted at the end. The inner history told by this verse is fantastically optimistic, far past the prose narrative.

The final poem of the book, appearing two pages from the end and in no melodramatic context, releases us back into daily life. Ramón relates it companionably to one of his men who wants to learn the song:

Be there along with me, oh men!
Reach across the hearth,
And laugh with me, while the woman rests,
For all we are worth.
("'My way is not thy way, and thine is not mine,'" no. 26, *Serpent,* p. 484)

It is a poem that Lawrence probably hoped the reader would take away with him, whimsical and fresh: "let the flame wrap round us." Yet it remains closely linked with the long sequence that it ends—a poem belonging entirely to Lawrence's imaginary religion of the serpent god: "And be there in the house of the cloven flame."

Unlike most of Lawrence's other sequences, this is not the story of one man's soul. We cannot even be sure that Don Ramón wrote all the poems, since we are not told; in some cases it is hinted that he collaborates with others in their composition. Ramón is a prophet who creates songs as much for the use of the outside world as for self-expression. Many characters read and sing the songs: as manifestos heralding the coming order, as gospels and lessons marking the closing and reopening of the church, as simple prayers and hymns to changes in the natural world. But while the songs belong to all Mexicans, each song takes the form of heroic, open confession. The individual Mexican, in reading one of these poems, momentarily surpasses himself, leaves himself behind to take on vicariously the person of a god:

> *I bound the bright fangs of the Sun*
> *And held him while Jesus passed*
> *Into the lidless shade,*
> *Into the eye of the Father,*
> *Into the womb of refreshment.*

("'In the place of the west,'" *Serpent,* p. 130)

Verse thus becomes the ground of intersection between the lesser and the greater men of Lawrence's new church, the story of the nation's souls; and it serves as the medium through which this whole dark, satanic race rises.

Never merely decorative, the purpose of the poetry recalls early views Lawrence held on lyricism in his "Study of Thomas Hardy," where he wrote that in Euripides, "the moments of pure satisfaction come in the choruses, in the pure lyrics, when Love is put into true relations with the Law, apart from knowledge, transcending knowledge, transcending the metaphysic, where the aspiration to Love meets the acknowledgment of the Law in a consummate marriage, for the moment" (*Phoenix,* p. 477). Poems break the narrative discourse at moments when heaven is "put into true relations" with earth, their marriage consummated:

> *So I took the sandals of the Saviour*
> *And started down the long slope*
> *Past the mount of the sun.*
> *Till I saw beneath me*
> *White breast-tips of my Mexico*
> *My bride.*

("'In the place of the west,'" *Serpent,* p. 130)

Lyricism, in other words, expresses the most complete moments in this history, when the Above intersects with the Below, or when a man encounters, in Kate's words, "a strange sort of categorical imperative. . . .

which he acknowledged in his own soul, and which really was like a messenger from the beyond" (*Serpent,* pp. 347–48).

That mystic paradox suggests too what in the language of these poems can provoke interest. Gilbert says briefly that the poetry is "simple, apparently naive verse that has some of the visionary quality of a *Douanier* Rousseau primitive."[20] Its style is almost as spare as that of the war poems, but it can be described. Lawrence has adopted a simplified version of standard formal English, colored with the vocabulary of Mexican legend and a repetitive use of ritualistic emblems ("circle of rest," "snake of my left-hand"). The primitive anthropomorphism of his images ("lidless shade") is consistently unironic. Lawrence achieves a union of high and low diction that reminds us of the first-generation Romantics. As Josephine Miles made clear, the apparently novel poetry of the Romantics revived eighteenth-century landscape symbolism by juxtaposing traditionally honorific terms with low (though never improper) earthy terms.[21] Lawrence in *The Plumed Serpent* may seem very distant from "the untrodden ways / Beside the springs of Dove."[22] This is because the vocabularies he unites are those of English sexuality and Mexican mysticism. Rather than bringing a Wordsworthian "Maid" to rest "among untrodden ways," Lawrence brings his "eye of the Father" to bear on "the womb of refreshment" (*Serpent,* p. 130). "Knees," "legs," "loins," "belly," "womb," are brought into contact with the Fatherhood of Quetzalcoatl:

> The snake of my left-hand out of the darkness is kissing your feet with his mouth
>   of caressive fire,
> And putting his strength in your heels and ankles, his flame in your knees and
>   your legs and your loins, his circle of rest in your belly.
> For I am Quetzalcoatl, the feathered snake,
> And I am not with you till my serpent has coiled his circle of rest in your belly.
>   ("'I am the Living Quetzalcoatl,'" no. 11, *Serpent,* p. 378)

The "untrodden ways" become flesh, a "Maid" would quail before the alien Quetzalcoatl. On both levels, high and low, Lawrence has changed the terms of the marriage, bringing the low terms of the sexual and reptilian to merge with the high terms of an exotic religion.

Lawrence had proposed to throw away the conventional methods of the novel with its dramatic tricks. Neither the novel nor the world was a "stage," so he said: "I can't bear art that you can walk around and admire. A book should be either a bandit or a rebel or a man in a crowd. . . . An author should be among the crowd, kicking their shins or cheering on to some mischief or merriment. That rather cheap seat in the gods where one sits with fellows like Anatole France and benignly looks down on the foibles, follies, and frenzies of so-called fellow-men, just annoys me. After all, the world is *not* a stage—not to me" (*Collected Letters,* 2 : 827). His is a graphic picture of the book as a live man, not framed by a stage or between covers, a picture that wars against the common experience of the novel with its fictional action, its characters, its dust jacket. It wars also against the apparition of *The Plumed Serpent* with its melodramatic plot and hymnal, its costumes and ceremonies, its sexual romanticism, its superhuman characters. Despite anything Lawrence said, *The Plumed Serpent* possesses a strong stage presence, and it is this that lets it play the rogue, attacking the conventional beliefs and behavior, envisaging a religion of underworld characters. More than any other aspect of the book, his poems create this histrionic effect, wedged into the narrative, hedging its expected progress, and lifting it to a mystical plane. Though it has failed to move many readers to see it as more than an arrogant charade, this novel is book *and* stage, something to be watched and watched warily. The bandit has struck the pose of a prophetic priest.

Part II: Re-Collecting the Poems

After his close escape from death, Lawrence wrote his most notorious, most-widely read and gossiped-over book, *Lady Chatterley's Lover.* Fewer readers know that in these years he also collected his poems. *Lady Chatterley's Lover* is a colorful backdrop for the *Collected Poems:* the erotic fantasy in *Lady Chatterley's Lover* of two individuals who rediscover themselves in mid-life found its complement in Lawrence's image of himself as a revived and fertile prophetic poet. *Collected Poems* was intended as the summation of his career.

Lawrence was no longer attracted to heroic self-sacrifices after 1925. He clung to the possibility of an inward resurrection. Many references to the "change of life" appear in his letters, and these now pertain to pressing anxieties about his personal life rather than to his more abstract mythology of the "serpent." If, as Frieda has claimed, he was impotent after his return from Mexico, the mid-life crisis had taken a fresh, brutal form.[23] By contrast, the serene tenor of his European writings is the more remarkable. In a letter to E. H. Brewster he describes aging as a patient and bold readiness to break repressions:

> You and I are at the *âge dangereuse* for men: when the whole rhythm of the psyche changes: when one no longer has an easy flow outwards: and when one rebels at a good many things. It is as well to know the thing is physiological: though that doesn't nullify the psychological reality. One resents

bitterly a certain swindle about modern life, and especially a sex swindle. One is swindled out of one's proper sex life, a great deal. But it is nobody's individual fault: fault of the age: our own fault as well. The only thing is to wait; and to take the next wave as it rises. *Pazienza!* . . . I stick to what I told you, and put a phallus, a lingam you call it, in each of my pictures somewhere. And I paint no picture that won't shock people's castrated social spirituality. I do this out of positive belief, that the phallus is a great sacred image: it represents a deep, deep life which has been denied in us, and still is denied. (*Collected Letters*, 2:967)

Not only does he confess to the noisome irritability accompanying middle life, he recognizes its necessity and "let[s] it go at that." It is indeed a changed Lawrence who admits that his anger may be a personal business, not to be massively imposed. According to his altered sense of things, a man at mid-life, compromised by the interminable "sex-swindle," can evade its thievery by faith in the "deep life which has been denied."

In March 1928 in a letter to Witter Bynner, he had this to say "about *The Plumed Serpent* and the 'hero'": "The hero is obsolete, and the leader of men is a back number. . . . We're sort of sick of all forms of militarism and militantism, and *Miles* is a name no more, for a man. On the whole I agree with you, the leader-cum-follower relationship is a bore. And the new relationship will be some sort of tenderness, sensitive, between men and men and men and women." Denunciation of that "cold egg," "the militant ideal," is as adamant as, eight years previously, his disgust had been at wartime England (*Collected Letters*, 2:1045). Lawrence even relocated the inspiration for prophetic song: no longer springing from the triumphant utterances of the *miles*, "the root of poetry, lived or sung" was (he informed Harriet Monroe) "phallic consciousness" (*Collected Letters*, 2:1047).

Yet this change of heart also reflects an internalization of his heroic ideals, an inward pride, which he could achieve only after pursuing his ambition for heroic activity as far as it would lead him. He acknowledged as much when, later in his letter to Bynner, he added that still "one has to fight" and "so I wrote my novel, which I want to call *John Thomas and Lady Jane*." The story of Mellors in *Lady Chatterley's Lover* begins with his return to England where he had lived and loved in his youth, *after* experience as a military man and world traveler. Lawrence described another work written after 1925, *The Escaped Cock* (1929; republished in 1931 as *The Man Who Died*), as the story of a resurrected former hero, that is, Jesus, whose life is a replica of Lawrence's own: "as he heals up, he begins to find what an astonishing place the phenomenal world is, far more marvellous than any salvation or heaven—and thanks his stars he needn't have a mission any more" (*Collected Letters*, 2:975).

In *Collected Poems* as in *Lady Chatterley's Lover,* Lawrence built a sanctuary for his demon to have "its full say" despite any and all repressive social situations. Boldly, patiently, Mellors ignores English conventions to receive Connie; Lawrence did the same for himself when he revised his poems to shock people's "castrated social spirituality." Aside from the obvious "chronology" developed for *Rhyming Poems* and several revisions of individual poems, few of the significant changes he made are widely known or cited, and those few attracted notice because he drew attention to them in his Note: "some of the earliest poems, like 'The Wild Common' and 'Virgin Youth,' are a good deal rewritten. They were struggling to say something which it takes a man twenty years to be able to say" (*CP,* p. 28). Mandell has been the first to consider changes beyond these, making *Collected Poems* almost her exclusive object, but she regards all the poems as established by—or in the case of *Look! We Have Come Through!* and *Birds, Beasts and Flowers* "pointed" toward—*Collected Poems,* while *Collected Poems* is "nearly simultaneous" with *Last Poems* (*Collected Poems* was gathered, however, in November to February 1927–28, *Pansies* a year later in November to February 1928–29, and *Last Poems* two years later in October to January 1929–30). The informing doctrine of the collection, according to this argument, is the primarily religious thought of *Last Poems.* It is useful to describe Lawrence's demon, as she does, as a type of "Holy Ghost," an unworldly manifestation;[24] in an early version of the Note, Lawrence referred to his demon as "the ghost" (*CP,* p. 849). But the ghostly demon is primarily an erotic creature in the revisions of 1928. Lawrence did everything he could to loosen its tongue, reliving what it was like to be young, then redesigning the course of his career.

To cite just one of the notorious revisions, the *Amores* version of "Virgin Youth" had alluded vaguely to the phallus, but explicitly addressed the frustration of hugging empty air, a frustration every nice young man experiences:

> *And my soft, slumbering belly*
> *Quivering awake with one impulse of desire,*
> *Gathers itself fiercely together;*
> *And my docile, fluent arms*
> *Knotting themselves with wild strength*
> *To clasp—what they have never clasped.*

(CP, p. 896)

In the 1928 revision, he does not consider whether or not he has an external object. His object is himself:

My soft, slumbering belly,
Quivering awake with one impulse and one will,
Then willy nilly
A lower me gets up and greets me;
Homunculus stirs from his roots, and strives until,
Risen up, he beats me.

(*CP,* p. 39)

The heroic poet of 1928 surrenders to Homunculus.

The most striking feature of the collection itself was Lawrence's deci-sion to reconstruct his career, fictionalizing his development. In its Note, he claimed that the poems were placed in "chronological order," so that "What was uttered in the cruel spring of 1917 should not be dislocated and heard as if sounding out of the void" (*CP,* p. 28). Yet he deliberately broke the chronological sequence, most significantly by placing much of the verse written "in the cruel spring of 1917" before the poems written to Frieda in 1912–14. He does not attempt to hide this alteration. On the contrary he states clearly where war poems appear in *Rhyming Poems:*

> The crisis of Volume I is the death of the mother, with the long haunting of death in life, which continues to the end, through all the last poems, which come from *Bay,* and which belong to the war. *Bay* appeared in 1919, but the poems were written mostly in 1917 and 1918, after I left Cornwall perforce.
>
> A big break in scene, however, had happened before then, in 1912, when I left England for the first time. In 1912 begins the new cycle of *Look! We Have Come Through!* Of this volume the first few poems belong to England and the end of the death-experience, but "Bei Hennef," written in May 1912, by a river in the Rhineland, starts the new cycle, which ends with "Frost Flowers," written in Cornwall at the end of the bitter winter of 1916–17.
>
> (*CP,* p. 28)

The chronological and symbolic dimensions of these poems were prac-tically indistinguishable to Lawrence, to whom what was "real" was never quite literal, nor ever entirely supernal. Volume 1, *Rhyming Poems,* reached its crisis in his mother's death, and the death-experience is the central focus of that volume "which continues to the end, through all the last poems, which come from *Bay,* and which belong to the war." *Look! We Have Come Through!* "begins the new cycle" which, though concluding with poems written "at the end of the bitter winter of 1916–17," belongs to what could be called the life-experience of volume 2. Lawrence shaped these two volumes so that he appeared to leave behind the death-experience and England forever upon the arrival of Frieda.

Lawrence's heroic reconstructions also brought back the first principles of his art. Just after finishing *Collected Poems,* he wrote an introduction to *Chariot of the Sun* by Harry Crosby, a younger poet he championed. Despite its obscure context, this exposition is the most complete statement Lawrence devised of his poetics and so deserves separate discussion before we proceed to the organization of *Collected Poems.* The Bible and ancient mythologies no longer provided his exclusive model for poetic achievement. He drew upon all his early influences in this introduction, from the classics to Romantics, seeing in Homer, Shakespeare, Wordsworth, and Keats the roots of his own cherished desires.

INTRODUCTION TO *CHARIOT OF THE SUN*

Sandra Gilbert derived from this brief introduction a theory to apply to all the poetry—the poetic act Lawrence described as an "act of attention": "The essential quality of poetry is that it makes a new effort of attention, and 'discovers' a new world within the known world" (*Phoenix,* p. 255). Explicating this, "a perceptual process through which the poet relates himself to the cosmos" and, more specifically, a "passive" act in which "his whole being is concentrated in awareness of the thing in itself," Gilbert redefines the "act of attention" as an epistemological gesture of discovery.[25] For Gilbert, that idea belongs to Romanticism, and she adduces Lawrence's example of Wordsworth: before Wordsworth "men had only seen a primrose dimly, in the shadow of the umbrella. They saw it through Wordsworth in the full gleam of chaos" (*Phoenix,* p. 256). The act of attention takes effect in Wordsworthian spots of time, when the growth of the poet's mind collaborates with his sense of an external scene. It is, according to Gilbert, "an act of absolute surrender to the visionary image," "passive," "intense," and "naive."[26]

But by abstracting this definition and this example, Gilbert overlooks its paradoxes. This passivity of the poet occurs in an *act* of attention; it requires a kind of bold vulnerability. Lawrence's ideas of sincerity and an open, naive state of mind have their roots both in the Keatsian chameleon poet and in Carlyle's heroic confessionalist. In another late essay, "Hymns in a Man's Life" (1928), where Lawrence elaborated his idea of "attention" or, as he calls it there, the "sense of wonder," he illustrates his meaning by comparison to the *miles* (proving his militance not, after all, defunct): "the battle-cry of a stout soul, and a fine thing too. 'Stand up, stand up for

Jesus / Ye soldiers of the Lord'" (*Phoenix II*, p. 601). This pun on "attention" is much like Birkin's "volonté de pouvoir" in *Women in Love*, which Birkin translates as a "will to ability," rather than "will to power" (*Women in Love*, p. 142). His punning redefinition of *pouvoir* is exactly what Lawrence means by *attention*: a willful receptivity. The act of attention is a faculty primarily *not* for empathy, but for "fertility," reciprocal interchange with the world. When the poet performs his "battle-cry," stale habits of vision crumble, he finds himself directly mixed with others, and he confronts the "new world within the known world" of his Crosby introduction. In opposition to the "intense" and "purely lyric poet" is, as we have seen, Browning's "man with dramatic capabilities," who only "needed fertilising by some love" (*Letters*, 2:115).

From a more sceptical point of view than Lawrence's, his "fertility" may seem no less a trap than Shelley's "odd stars" of the 1913 letter (*Letters*, 2:115), or than "the veil" he wants to tear (e.g., *Fantasia*, p. 16). In the latter metaphor, he mingles with orthodox images of marriage. But Lawrence ascribed a prior, more potent role even than fertility to the poet when he directed the would-be artist to "rip" through the veil. Underlying Lawrence's discussion is his radical adherence, not to epistemology, but to an apocalyptic theory of perception. It is "radical" in relying on a more primitive motive of the mind. To "fertilize" man's vision, he plunges his senses into chaos. *Chaos* is a recurrent term in this introduction, signifying the illimitable, unknown, vital psyche: "The unspeakable inner chaos of which we are composed we call consciousness, and mind, and even civilization. But it is, ultimately, chaos, lit up by visions, or not lit up by visions. Just as the rainbow may or may not light up the storm" (*Phoenix*, p. 255). Man fears and desires chaos and, according to Lawrence, is compelled by the poet to face his fear, to discover the "inward desire of mankind." Lawrence's poem is not a privileged place or a protected spot of time, from which either author or reader derives a consoling insight. The visionary poet forces the reader to see chaos—and lose his civilized mind.

Thus far, Lawrence's figure of the poet as a visionary revolutionist of the imagination, inseminating and impregnated by the world, fits the Romantic type, while from his Victorian antecedents he derives a bias for the dramatic and didactic. But Lawrence's poetics also has affinities with his modern contemporaries, the formalist's preoccupation with language conventions, Yeats's concern with the poet as "maker," and, in Gilbert's words, Eliot's "flippant ironist." [27] When speaking of tradition, for example, Lawrence unwittingly allies himself with a formalist model of literary history. Each poet makes innovative changes in his inherited conventions or, as

Victor Shklovsky termed it, "defamiliarizes" language, making it "strange" to force the reader to new awareness:[28] "Then comes a poet, enemy of convention, and makes a slit in the umbrella; and lo! the glimpse of chaos is a vision, a window to the sun" (*Phoenix*, p. 255). Wordsworth joined a throng of visionary poets when he made a "slit in the umbrella" and looked closely at a primrose. Shakespeare was the greater visionary because he showed us man: "And the greater joy when Shakespeare made a big rent and saw emotional, wistful man outside in the chaos, beyond the conventional idea and painted umbrella of moral images and iron-bound paladins, which had been put up in the Middle Ages" (*Phoenix*, p. 256).

For Lawrence as for the formalist, even a poetry of "chaos" must be managed through language. Disruptive "incongruity, in sound and sense" forces upon us the illogical, "a glimpse of chaos." To drive his point home, Lawrence praises Crosby's most nonsensical lines, quoting "sthhe fous on ssu eod" among examples of verse whose effect lies in "a dim suggestion of that which refuses to be said" (*Phoenix*, p. 258). Nonsensical language play was characteristic of Crosby and other, more reputable writers connected with the quarterly review *transition*. Founded by Eugene Jolas in 1924 to publish experimental work, such as that of James Joyce and Gertrude Stein, *transition* also promoted Jolas's religion of language.[29] Although Lawrence did not become much engrossed in the language revolution, he willingly sabotaged conventions of reading.

But how serious, one might ask, is Lawrence with his coy remarks about "parasols" and "painted patches," "annotated and glossed"? He may seem too "flippant" to be in earnest. While Lawrence took no "naive" pleasure in the visionary gleam, he disliked modern scepticism, its ennui, and the stiffened poetic forms of modernism, and he resorted to its own devices to undermine it. In his hands, the device of irony became satiric silliness. The very term *naïveté* he adopted to poke a hole in the more fashionable attitude of "sophistication." He was "sufficiently sophisticated to wring the neck of sophistication" (*Phoenix*, p. 262). Even as he introduces us to this unknown poet, he begs us to understand that Crosby does nothing that a "good" poet should do:

> There is no obvious incantation of sweet noise; only too often the music of one line deliberately kills the next, breathlessly staccato. There is no particular jewellery of epithet. And no handsome handling of images. Where deliberate imagery is used, it is perhaps a little clumsy. There is no coloured thread of an idea; and no subtle ebbing of a theme into consciousness, no recognizable vision, new gleam of chaos let in to a world of order. There is only a repetition of sun, sun, sun, not really as a glowing symbol, more as a bewilderment and a narcotic. (*Phoenix*, p. 257)

If there is no rhyme scheme, imagery, theme, symbolism—not even what Lawrence himself has espoused, a "new gleam of chaos"—what is there? But he anticipates us: "What is there, then, in this poetry, where there seems to be nothing?" And he answers, somewhat contradictorily, "It is a tissue of incongruity, in sound and sense. It means nothing, and it says nothing. And yet it has something to say. . . . And therein lies the charm. It is a glimpse of chaos not reduced to order" (*Phoenix*, p. 258). He wrings the neck of sophistication by offering us a minor poet and an account of his poetry that makes of it "nothing."

Then he makes something of it, imagining for himself Crosby's vision: "To me there is a breath of poetry, like an uneasy waft of fresh air at dawn, before it is light. There is an acceptance of the limitations of consciousness, and a leaning-up against the sun-imbued world of chaos. . . . It is poetry of suns which are the core of chaos, suns which are fountains of shadow and pools of light and centres of thought and lions of passion" (*Phoenix*, p. 259). This mysticism in Lawrence, the eagerness to perceive unnameable qualities in minimal objects and nonsense creates the closest tie of all to the prosaic, yet mythmaking, modern temper, to Yeats's occultism and Eliot's conglomerated myths. In Lawrence's hands, Crosby's poetry becomes a rhapsodically metaphoric rebirth, occurring in the instant when he touches "the core of chaos."

Lawrence took his theory of lyricism so seriously that he used it in the plot of *Lady Chatterley's Lover*. The central conflict between the paralytic, repressed Clifford and his energetic, unsatisfied bride is acted out in their opposite responses to poetry:

> "'Thou still unravished bride of quietness,'" he quoted. "It seems to fit flowers so much better than Greek vases."
>
> "Ravished is such a horrid word!" she said. "It's only people who ravish things."
>
> . . . . .
>
> She was angry with him, turning everything into words. Violets were Juno's eyelids, and windflowers were unravished brides. How she hated words, always coming between her and life: they did the ravishing, if anything did: ready-made words and phrases, sucking all the life-sap out of living things.[30]

Whereas Clifford applies a nearly proverbial verse line to the flowers, unthinkingly, his wife dimly responds to the actual sense of the line. She is sensitive to the fact that Keats committed the pathetic fallacy ("only people ravish things"), but worse than that, his reader, Clifford, *deanimates* the flowers with words ("ready-made words and phrases, sucking all the life-sap out of living things"). Connie has a muted awareness too that something brutal lurks behind Keats's lines, twisted and disguised in Clifford's application. But the incongruities of conventional poetic epithets merely irritate her, not rousing her emotions, "always coming between her and life: they did the ravishing."

But when eventually Connie revolts from her husband in thought and deed, the incongruities and extravagant phrases are then felt as rhetorical effects to "burn out false shames and smelt out the heaviest ore of the body": "She had often wondered what Abélard meant, when he said that in their year of love he and Heloïse has passed through all the stages and refinements of passion. The same thing, a thousand years ago: ten thousand years ago! The same on the Greek vases, everywhere! The refinements of passion, the extravagances of sensuality! And necessary, forever necessary, to burn out false shames and smelt out the heaviest ore of the body into purity. With the fire of sheer sensuality" (*Lady Chatterley's Lover*, p. 312). Connie was right in thinking Keats "ravished" his Greek vases, violating their silent forms with words, but in doing so he refired them in the heat of "sheer sensuality." In Connie's changed vocabulary, *ravish* ceases to be an English euphemism for rape and regains its punning force: to devastate and delight. The novel *Lady Chatterley's Lover* thereby enters tradition, ripping the veils of previous poetry to expose its chaotic body.

COLLECTED POEMS

If the novelist could be something of a poet, the poet could also be a novelist, creating a narrative framework for his *Collected Poems,* which could have carried the subtitle "The Life of a Poet." Lawrence revised and re-ordered his poems into an exemplary anecdote of the "change of life"—the effort of the poet to break from the dead hand of time. He made extensive alterations to create his collection. In letters of November and December 1927 he referred frequently to his work, proudly "sweating" over the poems.[31] He worked on them periodically for three months, and on 3 February 1928 he announced that volume 1 was nearly ready.[32] Completion of *Rhyming Poems* would mean that he had practically completed the whole, since he made far fewer changes in the poems of volume 2, *Unrhyming Poems.* Since the format of the books in volume 2, *Look! We Have Come Through!* and *Birds, Beasts and Flowers,* was left essentially intact, I will focus attention on the much more extensive rearrangement for volume 1 (for *Look! We Have Come Through!* see chapter 3; for *Birds, Beasts and Flowers,* chapter 4), while considering the revised poems there solely with reference to Lawrence's reorganization of the poetry.[33] Before examining volume 1 closely, I will discuss the general format of *Collected Poems,* for Lawrence created a rhetorically effective frame for his collection. *Collected*

Poems stands in stark contrast to the perpetual, lifelong editions of *Leaves of Grass*. Lawrence gathered his poems into a comparatively humble two-volume set and left it at that. Less humbly, these volumes deflected the Whitmanesque pattern by speaking of the urgency for poets to review their histories and engage against old selves.

His choice of titles for the two volumes, *Rhyming Poems* and *Unrhyming Poems,* loaded the perceived difference between the two. The opposition suggests a radical break in the career, as if at a single juncture he dispensed with formal verse. In fact, Lawrence never opposed rhyme altogether. Nor do the titles *Rhyming Poems* and *Unrhyming Poems* refer to actual rhyming procedures in those volumes. In many "rhyming poems" he uses rhyme inconsistently, while in volume 2 he often adopts a rhyme scheme. Nor can the relationship between the two volumes be one of irreconcilable opposition—why then would he have spent so much effort rewriting *Rhyming Poems?* The titles are rhetorical tags. At first Lawrence had referred to volume 1 as "Lyrical Poems," an epithet that recalls his aspersions against the "lyrical" as opposed to the "dramatic" writer.[34] Perhaps because this title does not carry similar associations for the reader, he chose instead a phrase connected with more common debates about free verse. His notions of rhyming had as long a history as his ideas about the lyrical. In 1913 he argued for "disjointed" rhythm and sound, explaining to Edward Marsh that "the ear gets a habit, and becomes master, when the ebbing and lifting emotion should be master, and the ear the transmitter." He was equally persistent in the matter of rhyming: "I *never* put them in because they are rhymes." He loathed the "habits" of verse: "This is the constant war, I reckon, between new expression and the habituated, mechanical transmitters and receivers of the human constitution" (*Letters*, 2:104).

Lawrence's famous apology for free verse, "Poetry of the Present," (1919), extended these early statements into an argument against "poetry of perfection" in favor of "poetry of imperfection." (Lawrence did not republish this essay in *Collected Poems,* though he suggested in its closing lines that it should have been placed as an introduction to *Look! We Have Come Through!* rather than to *New Poems;* the editors of *Complete Poems,* Pinto and Roberts, placed it just before *Unrhyming Poems.*) In contrast to an earlier title for this essay, "Verse Unfree and Free,"[35] *Rhyming Poems* and *Unrhyming Poems* have the more Lawrencean effect of expressing the undoing of the old, a poetry of *im*perfection. Like the verse of Harry Crosby, Lawrence's volume 2 is labeled, not by what it "recognizably" is, but by what it isn't: "no particular jewellery of epithet." In place of the "parade of forms and techniques," Crosby and Lawrence write *un*formed and *un*technical verse, to let in the "breath" of chaos. When Lawrence first began to collect his poems, he was less sure that he could so neatly undo the past. He wrote to Mabel Luhan with some dismay at his memories: "I am busy getting my poems in order, to go into one vol.—all the poems. My word, what ghosts come rising up! But I just tidy their clothes for them and refuse to be drawn."[36] By the time he wrote a foreword for *Collected Poems* (the preliminary version of his Note) in May 1928, he had succeeded in incarnating his "ghosts" in one "body of feeling": "Instead of bewailing a lost youth, a man nowadays begins to wonder, when he reaches my ripe age of forty-two, if ever his past will subside and be comfortably by-gone. Doing over these poems makes me realise that my teens and my twenties are just as much me, here and now and present, as ever they were, and the pastness is only an abstraction. The actuality, the body of feeling, is essentially alive and here" (*CP,* p. 849). The challenge to the mature poet is not to "tidy" the clothes of his ghost, but to allow their shaggy existence, "just as much me . . . as ever they were." In this mood he had a better chance of writing a persuasive preface. The terms of this foreword became confused, however, at the end, when Lawrence added this apology: "Perhaps it may seem bad taste to write this so personal foreword. But since the poems are so often personal themselves, and hang together in a life, it is perhaps only fair to give the demon his body of mere man, as far as possible" (*CP,* p. 852). Is this "body of mere man" different from or less "alive and here" than the "body of emotion," which he previously discovered in his poems? And did he expect us to approve this apologetic explanation for providing a biography? If so, it betrays a worrisome ambivalence about the bodies of both past and present.

The second version of the Note simplifies the detailed history of Lawrence's experiences as a young poet (in particular, eliminating discussions of his earliest patrons and publishers) and transforms the ambivalent apology into an energetic defense. He later described the second Note as a shortened rendition of the same thing and advised his publisher to make his own choice between them, but the thesis is significantly reshaped from one version to the next.[37] No mention is made of his "haunting" experience as he rereads his poems. Briefly, he abstracts a portrait of himself as a young poet, outlines the basic argument of *Rhyming Poems,* and ends up with a rhetorically potent apologia for confessionalism.

His introductory self-portrait of the conventional young man boxing with his demon, which gave us a key to Lawrence's autobiographical methods, is a clue also to *Rhyming Poems.* While his volume 1 is a "cycle of purely English experience, and death experience" (*CP,* p. 851), within this repressive condition we will find the turbulent, iconoclastic emotional spirit of a young man. The Note then gives more particularized instructions to reading volume 1, referring us to events and characters we would easily overlook otherwise—the major changes of scene, the three women of his love life (there could be many women here or only two), even the crisis of the volume, which passes rapidly in "The End," "The Bride," and "The Virgin Mother." Lawrence tells us almost nothing, meanwhile, about the poems in the second volume, beyond noting their chronological arrangement. This difference in what he says, and doesn't say, is one more headshake at the shift in his career. In the Foreword to *Collected Poems,* he explained simply that he wrote *Look! We Have Come Through!* when he "left teaching, and left England, and left many other things, and the demon had a new run for his money" (*CP,* p. 851), while the poems in *Birds, Beasts and Flowers* "are what they are" (*CP,* p. 852). He obviously felt that these spoke for themselves, that the demon had been liberated in them to "say his say" without interference from a "young man" (*CP,* p. 28)—certainly not to be molested by the elder. The mature man returned mainly to his juvenilia, to recapture his younger, demonic soul and to give this demon its biography.

The "story" of *Rhyming Poems* is not only the account of the young poet described at the head of his Note; his story takes place underneath the activity of the elder poet who, like his younger self, is unsettled by passion, shaken by the ghost of that youth, yet is able to find energy or wholeness in his past. The elder's story emerges not only from his coherent narrative of events but from the cracks in the sequence: from the collection of four books, too much verse to mold smoothly into one body, from disjunction between revised and unrevised poems, from the incongruities between former books and new superimposed patterns, and from tensions deliberately worked into the volume in 1928. The Note ends with an apology that acknowledges that fragmentation, then transfers the problem to the reader with an eloquent plea for biographical glossing:

> It seems to me that no poetry, not even the best, should be judged as if it existed in the absolute, in the vacuum of the absolute. Even the best poetry, when it is at all personal, needs the penumbra of its own time and place and circumstance to make it full and whole. If we knew a little more of Shakespeare's self and circumstance how much more complete the Sonnets would be to us, how their strange, torn edges would be softened and merged into a whole body! So one would like to ask the reader of *Look! We Have Come Through!* to fill in the background of the poems, as far as possible, with the place, the time, the circumstance. What was uttered in the cruel spring of 1917 should not be dislocated and heard as if sounding out of the void. (*CP,* p. 28).

In asking the reader to sort out his history, Lawrence is not also helping the reader to forget himself, or forget the effects of fragmentation. He directs attention as much to the "strange, torn edges" as to the "whole body." Like Lawrence's past life, his history is "dislocated" and lacks an inward sense of direction, such as was eventually found in *Look! We Have Come Through!* and *Birds, Beasts and Flowers.* The reader must reperform Lawrence's reading, suffer his ghosts, and restore their history.

This passage is as irritating to a reader as it is inviting, if only because it plays upon the anxiety readers often feel when construing poems. Other readers are bothered, however, by its very assumptions, its insistence on biography. Blackmur replied to Lawrence: "As for Shakespeare's Sonnets, if we did know more about Shakespeare's self, we should only know a little more clearly where he failed as a poet; the Sonnets themselves would be not a whit improved."[38] Lawrence's comments were meant for just such a reader as Blackmur, whose vision of poetry ended at the point where Lawrence's began—at the intersection of life with art. Yet like Blackmur, he was striving to revise the role of biography in criticism. The following passage by the critic Andrew Lang suggests the notion of biography he had targeted. These comments derive from Lang's introduction to the *Selected Poems of Robert Burns,* a book that fueled many of the Lawrences' debates. Burns's controversial life provided a model for Lawrence, but Lang believed: "His character, his career, are themes from which one is tempted to shrink in terror, so perilous are they. Once I ventured to say—Principal Shairp had said it before—that I wished we knew no more of Burns's life than of Shakespeare's. It was a vain thing to wish; we cannot keep his poetry, with its frequent confessions, and be ignorant of his life. But I meant no more than a natural desire to be spared sermons, scandal, tattle about a poet."[39] Lang's opinion as to how much should be "known" about Shakespeare and Burns reflects a comfortably orthodox view. Lawrence recalled such comments to upset them (as he would also have managed Blackmur's if the opportunity had arisen), turning Lang's "terror" and "desire" into a description of what poetry should arouse. Lawrence too wished to be "spared sermons, scandal, tattle about a poet," which he saw as cheap and shallow responses, attempts to fend off the real power of poetry. He confronted "scandal" and weakheartedness by scandalizing the critics, exposing the nether parts of poetry, its "strange, torn edges." And he conscientiously retained in "his poetry, with its frequent confessions" an outline of the circumstances of his life: not, as Blackmur believed, to "improve" upon the craft of the poet, but to assure himself that the confessions of his poems would be heard.

RHYMING POEMS

Lawrence's instructions are necessary guidelines to volume 1. Without them we might not look for order of any kind. His four early books generated a bulky, highly fragmented volume of 146 poems. But hitherto unknown manuscript evidence confirms that he gave much care to their order. On the opening pages of his personal copy of *Love Poems and Others,* he wrote, erased and rewrote, numbered and renumbered his table in penciled columns (see transcription of holograph list in Appendix B). So many decisions entered into the development of this table of contents (much of which is retrievable, since in many cases words can still be read through the erasures), that to sort all its details is laborious, but because many of his choices follow a consistent pattern, the significant decisions are relatively few in number. His manipulation of the poems produced an essentially ambiguous result: he made it possible to discover a coherent mythology in his young life, but it remained difficult.

The original order in which he wrote his poems cannot be known, since he assigned no dates to the early poems and did not record them chronologically in his manuscripts. The evidence of the Buffalo holograph indicates, rather, that what governed the apparent chronology of *Rhyming Poems* was the story he wished to tell, and to construct this he depended on, but also altered, the previous organizations of his published books.[40] He made no effort (as he had for other volumes) to retrieve poems published only in journals. The order of volume 1 roughly records the following sequence of books: the contents of *Love Poems and Others* appear chiefly in the first long section prior to the elegies of *Amores,* which yield the central sequence (nos. 64–109); *New Poems* affords the next sizable bunch, followed by a smaller section from *Bay* (see the contents table for *Rhyming Poems* in Appendix A). "Bits" was excluded once again from publication. When we recall the original sequence of publication in which *Look! We Have Come Through!* intervened between *Amores* and *New Poems,* Lawrence's drastic revision of the career becomes apparent. His career began, as we have seen, with a miscellaneous collection marking his debut as a poet of conflict. He then published two important companion volumes, his elegies in *Amores* and prothalamia in *Look! We Have Come Through!* After preparing these, he wrote and collected "Bits" and *Bay,* whose war poems marked the end of Lawrence's "new cycle" of love poems for Frieda. Finally, his frustration with the war and his firm belief that something must "come awake" (*Letters,* 3:254) were reflected in *New Poems.* The sequence of *Rhyming Poems* transformed this history of repeated, spiraling struggles, first with personal circumstances and then with the world, into the continuous agonies of a British son, whose personal conflicts come to represent the larger death struggle of his nation.

The construction of this story also altered the character of his original volumes. The passionate dramatic lyrics of *Love Poems and Others* are dispersed among landscape, childhood, and city poems, to reenforce the changing scenes in Lawrence's biography. His reshuffling of *New Poems* had the opposite effect. From this most miscellaneous of his collections, he restored a number of pendants, and these in turn became the basis for larger clusters. Returning to some of his original intentions, he gathered *New Poems* into separate bunches of city lyrics (e.g., nos. 40–41, 112–15) and love poems (e.g., nos. 26–27, 120–25) and united its war poems with those from *Bay* (nos. 126–43). The construction particularly of a lengthy sequence, nos. 110–29, following the elegies, helped determine the mythic significance of *Rhyming Poems*.[41] He tampered least with *Bay:* relocating only four poems from its opening section (nos. 17, 19, 34, 42), he then substituted four others from *New Poems* (nos. 126–29). He reordered *Bay* to sharpen the distinction, as registered in the titles, between war and its British survivors, from "Tommies in the Train" to "Nostalgia" (nos. 130–43). The rearrangements of these books could not have reconstructed "the order in which they were written." The poems from *Bay* are a convenient example of Lawrence's practice in this regard, for while three of the poems he relocated derived from early manuscripts ("Guards," "The Little Town at Evening," and "Last Hours"—nos. 34, 17, 19), at least four others retained with the war verse were also revisions of juvenilia ("Ruination," "Rondeau of a Conscientious Objector," "Bombardment," and "On the March").

Lawrence was clearly concerned, on the other hand, with groups of two to four poems (far simpler to arrange than a close knit of 146 pieces), often arranging these in antitheses, which contributed both to discontinuity and to continuity in *Rhyming Poems*. The heroic "Virgin Youth" is accompanied by "Study" (nos. 8–9), an exercise in frustrated daydreams. Triadic and dyadic sets bring many subplots into focus, but their parallel situations frequently undercut each other. The town rapidly shifts its aspect from "Letter from Town: On a Grey Morning in March" to a bright spring morning in "Letter from Town: The Almond-Tree" (nos. 26–27). Inter-ironic links are as frequent in love as in the city: from pendants that take a turn for the better, "Tease" and "Mystery" (nos. 60–61), to those that descend, "Kisses in the Train" and "Turned Down" (nos. 90–91). These couplings are so extensive that any individual poem should be evaluated in tandem with its neighbors; and they lend themselves to an antinomial reading of this volume.

More than any other book, *Amores* dictated the order of *Rhyming Poems*.

In the Buffalo holograph, the long sequences Lawrence preserved contrast sharply with the other sections of the list; while the rest were extensively reworked, there are few erasures, insertions, or alterations of any kind in the elegies (see transcription of holograph list in Appendix B). As the core group, *Amores* determined the narrative outline of volume 1, issuing from the poet's early childhood, charting the vigil at his mother's side, and falling off with her into the "long haunting of death in life" (*CP*, p. 28). But even *Amores* lost its individual identity. The passion of *Amores,* the death of Mrs. Lawrence, is deflected by the new passion for the poet's demon. The headpiece, "Tease," which introduced the book's secondary theme of an anticourtly love, was removed to a later section (no. 60), where it easily escapes notice. When "The Wild Common," the second piece in *Amores,* became instead the headpiece of *Rhyming Poems,* it was revised to eliminate its references to woman. Rather than encountering maternal shadows in the landscape, the poet now stands against his own shadows; and where before he had vicariously sunk himself into the womb, the 1928 immersion is strictly his own affair: "Oh but the water loves me and folds me, / Plays with me, sways me, lifts me and sinks me, murmurs: Oh marvellous stuff!" (*CP*, p. 34). Revisions such as these generally had a divisive effect on the final sequence of *Rhyming Poems.* The unrevised central elegies are far less prominent in a volume that contains the revised "Virgin Youth" and "The Wild Common." Like the "Rose" poems of *Look! We Have Come Through!* these elegies were brief, quiet consummations. It is left to the reader to notice when, midway through *Rhyming Poems,* the elegiac sequence finally begins.

Revised poems brilliantly illumine, however, the shape of Lawrence's desires in 1928. He cited "The Wild Common," "Virgin Youth," "Dreams Nascent," and "Whether or Not" (*CP*, pp. 850–52) as examples of his revisions. These and others that he altered to heighten a sexual encounter—including some poems altered years before, from 1912 to 1918 (for example, "Love on the Farm," "Snap-Dragon," "Narcissus," "Piano"—nos. 11, 93, 129, 118)—stand out abruptly from their less vivid neighbors. Several are well known because of more highly wrought language or because they are longer than usual. Others should be better known.

"Narcissus" (no. 129—revised for *New Poems*), for example, stands out sharply between the verse from *New Poems* and *Bay.* (See also the discussion of its earliest version in chapter 2). The revised version of "Narcissus" is an erotic fantasy, its language remarkably playful. It is far more appropriate in *Rhyming Poems* than in *New Poems.* Entirely unironic, the allusive, punning language and undulating rhythm, nevertheless, prevent any possibility of sentimentality:

Narcissus
Ventured so long ago in the deeps of reflection.
Illysus
Broke the bounds and beyond!—Dim recollection
Of fishes
Soundlessly moving in heaven's other direction!

(*CP*, p. 161)

As Carole Ferrier suggests, La Motte Fouqué's romance of a water nymph probably inspired "Narcissus,"[42] but its form here is original. Lawrence takes on the role of Narcissus *and* the river god Illysus (perhaps that too of Boreas, who abducted the mother of Cleopatra when he discovered her by the bank of the Illysus). In an earlier version, the poem was titled "Neckar," a soulless water sprite. "In the deeps of reflection," he moves toward and through himself, adventuring by reverting into another, "recollected" element. This narrative then cuts to invocation—addressing himself? or the other? Subject and object blur in the next lines:

Be
Undine towards the waters, moving back;
For me
A pool! Put off the soul you've got, oh, lack
Your human self immortal; take the watery track!

(*CP*, p. 161)

Noun crosses into adjective, and states of being into actions: while standing in place, everything seems at once to change. The water nymph, an "undine," becomes a condition "toward," which "you" can reach by "moving back," the converse of her illicit lover who "broke the bounds and beyond." Undying, he (and she) must "lack" the "soul" for the "watery track" and a second mortality. This poem does what it says, with its harsh end rhymes and disrupted syntactical forms. Language cracks and refleshes itself, more eloquent for its "torn edges." "Narcissus" obtrudes from the war verse like a dislocated dream, in which the poet *speaks* forth his inward quest.

The most significant use of revised poems is the volume's frame. "The Wild Common" is a poet's visionary set piece. He imagines a Romanticist, mystical transfusion of sun and earth like that, for example, of Coleridge in "This Lime-Tree Bower, My Prison," and then experiences that consummation in the flesh. All history "wheels" around in the present, takes substance in the mystic Now, defying the logic of cause and effect:

Sun, but in substance, yellow water-blobs!
Wings and feathers on the crying, mysterious ages, peewits wheeling!
All that is right, all that is good, all that is God takes substance!

(*CP*, p. 34)

"The Wild Common" was not, however, Lawrence's first choice to head *Rhyming Poems*. In the Buffalo holograph, he originally placed "Dog-Tired" at the beginning, then erased this title to substitute "The Wild Common." Had "Dog-Tired" begun the book, our entry would have been markedly different, since, true to its title, this is a poem of fatigue and defeat. "Dog-Tired" is not inappropriate to the themes of the volume. Its speaker wishes himself transposed from the fields in which he has worked all day into the fertile lap of his sweetheart. But the poem reaches forward, not to the miraculous grace of phallic renewal, but rather to puritan restraint between the two lovers and dissolution:

I should like to lie still
As if I was dead; but feeling
Her hand go stealing
Over my face and my head, until
This ache was shed.

(no. 2, *CP*, p. 35)

Even its rhymes are calculated to deaden sensation—"feeling"/"stealing," "still"/"until," "head"/"shed"—as opposed to the contrast of graphically odd nouns with resonantly traditional verbs in the last stanza of "The Wild Common": "water-blobs"/"lobs," "wheeling"/"peeling." "Dog-Tired" establishes the theme of the "death-experience," but Lawrence instead alerts us first to the demon life within.

Placed near the end of the volume before two closing elegies, the revised "Dreams . . . Nascent" parallels "Manifesto" in *Look! We Have Come Through!* which follows the climactic poems and precedes three final pieces of nostalgia. In the Buffalo holograph, Lawrence at first had "Dreams . . . Nascent" in an early section (corresponding to its relatively early placement in *Amores*), but he subsequently removed it from beside "Dreams . . . Old" (no. 22) to a position (no. 144) after the war poems from *Bay* and ahead of the two final poems, "On That Day" and "Autumn Sunshine." Like "Manifesto," it is a homiletic summation of the volume, calling for revolution for all men, not just for the individual. Men must rise out of their repressive cells to be mystically transfused—as in "The Wild Common"—in one "live world":

And our bodies molten drops of dream-blood that swirl and swell
In a tissue, as all the molten cells in the living mesh
Of a rose-tree move to roses and thorns and a delicate smell.

(*CP*, p. 176)

Previously a poem about the schoolroom, the revised "Dreams . . . Nascent" dreams of male resurgency, completing and moving away from the more personal vision of "The Wild Common." The phallic finds its best communion in male blood-being. Water, a metaphor in "The Wild Common" for fleshy substance, is dropped in "Dreams . . . Nascent" for "dream-blood" and "tissue," a "dream" of the thing itself. The simile of the "rose-tree" interrupts this picture, however, to remind us that "blood" is something like and unlike familiar concepts of it; to the official mind, for whom a rose is a rose, "molten drops of dream-blood" must be altogether unlike "roses and thorns and a delicate smell," even though the associations between body and tree, blood and roses, are age-old.

The memorable situations of revised poems repeat and vary each other, as in "The Wild Common" and "Dreams . . . Nascent," to create a pattern of echoing returns. This pattern is probably not a deliberate manufacture of 1928. It occurs coincidentally, as a result of Lawrence's frequent returns to the juvenilia, rehearsing similar scenes in different poems. Echoes bounce from one to the next unplanned, but these refractions help knot together *Rhyming Poems*. "Narcissus" (no. 129) advances from the situation of "The Wild Common," the narcissism of that earlier poem surfacing in the more explicit sequel; between these two the theme is picked up in "Tarantella" (no. 98—revised for *New Poems*), whose female persona keens by the waterside for her "neckar." Between "The Wild Common" and "Dreams . . . Nascent" is, of course, "Guards" (no. 34—revised for *Bay*), in which a rising troop of soldiers is compared to both water and blood. The musical dissonance of "Discord in Childhood" (no. 4—revised for *Amores*), a scene of parental violence, recurs in the despair of the bereaved poet in "Piano" (no. 118—revised for *New Poems*). In "From a College Window" (no. 3—revised for *New Poems*), the boy speaker holds aloof from charity, but drops into tears and gives a beggar his coin in "Embankment at Night, Before the War: Charity" (no. 114—revised for *New Poems* and again for *Collected Poems*). As significant as watery love and blood-being are the gestures of invocation, prophecy, and appeal: in "Prophet" (no. 57—revised for *New Poems*), the oppressed son and "procreant groom" invokes a ghostly queen, and "War-Baby" (no. 142—revised for *Bay*) becomes the child Lawrence, who agonizes with an emotional power that will mature when—as he prognosticates in the penultimate poem, "On That Day" (re-vised for *New Poems*)—"Dawns my insurgent day" (*CP*, p. 176).

Turning from an examination of the ways in which Lawrence reordered his books and revised poems to a closer look at the final order, it should be possible with a table of contents and Lawrence's instructions to trace the mythos of *Rhyming Poems*. Note that in the original editions of *Collected Poems*, a table of contents was printed at the back of each volume, and each poem appeared on a separate page or pages. Lawrence urged his pub-lishers to print his poems in this way, and with the exception of *Pansies*, a book of "doggerel," all his books conformed to this rule. *Rhyming Poems* particularly benefited from a format in which these short poems do not run into each other, while at the same time they can be pieced into the rest of the volume. (See Appendix A for the order of the poems in *Rhyming Poems*.) Together with poems left unchanged, the 1928 revisions add up to more than a single myth of human experience. Working his way back and forth between the poles of "death-experience" and "one live world," Law-rence drew upon a large body of mythic ideas: the mystic Now, phallic reno-vation, the Bacchic mysteries, the Grail quest, the myths of the Golden Bough, blood brotherhood, the maternal Persephone with her child bridegroom.

Phases in the assembled volume of *Rhyming Poems* are not very definite either in the poetry or in the prefaces. As the volume unfolds, the prose becomes increasingly vague. A reader must work for its argument, half create its progress. The terminal point of the first group, however, is indi-cated clearly in both prefaces: the "first change in scene comes when for the first time I left Nottinghamshire . . . to teach in a new school on the fringes of South London" (Note, *CP*, p. 27). "Flat Suburbs, S.W., in the Morning" (no. 20) marks that change. The sequence from "The Wild Com-mon" to "Last Hours" (nos. 1–19) charts Lawrence's youth, alone (the "subjective" poems, "The Wild Common" and "Virgin Youth") or with Miriam, a pseudonym for Jessie Chambers (Lawrence's examples: "Dog-Tired," "Cherry Robbers," and "Renascence"), and these "run into" (Fore-word, *CP*, p. 851) poems about his mother ("Monologue of a Mother" and "The Little Town at Evening"). This first group is one of the most care-fully worked over in the Buffalo holograph and creates an initial illusion of a chronology (see transcription of holograph list in Appendix B).[43] Within this sequence, six of the first seven poems in *Amores* are merged with poems from every other volume—about his college life ("From a College Window" and "Study"), his childhood ("Discord in Childhood"), and the countryside ("Twilight" and "Last Hours")—while "fictional" poems provide local color ("Love on the Farm," "Gipsy," and "The Collier's Wife"). But more compelling than any event in these poems are the emotional swings they register, between fierce energy and despondency. The Beulah-like laddishness of Lawrence's younger self is torn by discord, confusion, and fatigue. Less obvious revisions of 1928 emphasized those elements: in the "clash" of the river in "Renascence," which had previously only "tallied" (*CP*, pp. 37–38), or in his night in "Dream-Confused," which ends not in "rest," but in the awakened memory that "we misunderstood" (*CP*, p. 37). So it was in conflict as well as in visionary moments such as that of "The Wild Common," that the elder poet discovered the younger's "demon," ending his innocence. These are the "Last Hours" of youth. Though the times and seasons are mixed—set both in summer and autumn, at day and night—twilight dominates, here and throughout the volume.

Both prefaces express an unmixed nostalgia for the scene of the next stage in this volume (nos. 20–49): "From the playground we could look north at the blue bubble of the Crystal Palace, fairy-like to me" (Note, *CP*, pp. 27–28), and "to me, who saw it then for the first time, in lovely autumn weather, beautiful. . . . the country was still only just being built over, and the elms of Surrey stood tall and noble" (Foreword, *CP*, p. 851). This is the setting and mood of "The Best of School" and "Dreams . . . Old" (nos. 21–22). But the indications of the prose have already begun to break down, telling a different tale from that of the verse. In "Flat Suburbs" (no. 20), the "suburbs" are simply bleak: the street lamps like "desolate twigs . . . testify to a blight" (*CP*, p. 51). In other pieces, nostalgia itself is hateful, in "Weeknight Service," "End of Another Home Holiday," and "Sigh No More" (nos. 24, 31, 33). The recurrent fantasy of the "fictional" poems has a man dead or nearly so, brooded over by women in "A Man Who Died," "Wedding Morn," and "Violets" (nos. 25, 28, 29). In all these poems, we see the young man, "who saw it then for the first time," disabused of his "old dreams" (*CP*, pp. 52–53).

The third stage of *Rhyming Poems* is less clearly delineated than the first and appears to overlap with the second. According to the Foreword, the third stage starts when "then begin the poems to Helen, and all that trouble of *Lilies in the Fire:* and London, and school, a whole new world. Then starts the rupture with home, with Miriam, away there in Nottingham-shire" (*CP*, p. 851). All these events ("then" and "then") overlap, occurring almost simultaneously, as in fact they do in the poems. The "poems to Helen" would seem to refer to those from "Return" to "Coldness in Love" (nos. 51–63), which include "Lilies in the Fire" (no. 53) and occasionally name Helen. But the rupture with Miriam may be recorded just ahead of these in "A Winter's Tale" (no. 50), and the break with his mother is not recorded in nos. 51–63, though it is hinted at in as early a poem as "Mono-logue of a Mother" (no. 16). The "ruptures" had already begun; the differ-ence is that after "A Winter's Tale," he will demand such conflict, for the sake of a passionate life. Meanwhile, a new world has opened its doors to the poet despite the suburban blight. The continuing story of "London, and school, a whole new world" refers, again, more accurately to a prior group, "Corot" through "A Snowy Day in School" (nos. 38–48): in these eleven (derived from sequences among the juvenilia), earth is godly, God is man, man is multiform, and even in the city man may find an "innermost ocean" and "Paradise" (CP, p. 71).[44] Yet there is no reason why Lawrence should refer precisely in his prose to the events of his poems. The prefaces perform an oblique function of narrative, more like choruses echoing events in another key, suggestive of the elder man who sees things whole rather than of his uncertain youth.

The love poems (including those to "Helen") from "A Winter's Tale" to "Coldness in Love" derive from either *Love Poems and Others* or *Amores*, and Lawrence revised half of these extensively, so that, nonetheless, they form a tight third series in the volume. A transitional fictional poem just before these, "Whether or Not" (no. 49—also from *Love Poems and Others*), sets the tone for this group: in the long ending added in 1928, its hero is transformed from a trapped and passive victim of the woman he has cheated to a proud, verbal young man who throws her off in very explicit terms, not satisfied with the sex he has gotten from her (CP, pp. 83–85). This "broken" love theme gains intensity in the "Helen" poems, and so does Lawrence's philosophy of love. The "moon," formerly cool and haughty, is the most visible register of the change, appearing in a highly unmoonlike image of a red-hot womb in "Red Moon-Rise" (no. 54—CP, pp. 88–89). When Lawrence is not exhorting his lover to be his bacchante ("The Appeal"—no. 52, CP, p. 86) or to drink his "bowl of kisses" ("Mys-tery"—no. 61, CP, p. 96), he is criticizing her failures in love ("Lilies in the Fire," "Scent of Irises," "Repulsed"—nos. 53, 55, 62). The two school poems in this section, "Discipline" and "The Punisher" (nos. 58–59), are equally unflinching in the face of battle with his schoolboys. At the heart of the section, in "Forecast" (no. 56), his lover warns him of the "heavy-breasted" woman who will one day devour him (CP, p. 91). The response in "Prophet" (no. 57) is that men could do better than "hide" and "deny" the embraces of "the shrouded mother of a new idea" (CP, p. 91).

Much of the narrative of the central stage in this volume—in its ele-gies—was already present in the story of love and death of *Amores* dis-cussed in chapter 3, and I will not duplicate that analysis here, but I should indicate the force of the elegies (nos. 64–85) in this context. The "poems to Helen" condition our first approach to the elegies, so that we arrive amidst very explicit instructions about love. The revisions of love poems often produce long homilies on sex, and even though there are far fewer changes among the elegies, this makes them more difficult than ever to read piously. "The Virgin Mother" had in 1916 looked to the future "for God to endow" (*Amores*, p. 64); in 1928, it is "for seed to endow" (no. 68—*CP*, p. 102). Heated references are picked up shortly after the mother's death in "Reminder" (no. 70—added from *Love Poems and Others*), then again in "Last Words to Miriam" (no. 78—lifted from no. 18 in *Amores*), where he regrets his failure to possess her, "Body to body" (a phrase of 1928, *CP*, p. 111). In "The Yew-Tree on the Downs" (no. 81), "kisses" are not the issue; instead he asks her, in an earthy version of "Narcissus," to "be penetrate, like the tree" (*CP*, p. 114).

Between "The Enkindled Spring" and "Brother and Sister" (nos. 85, 100) is another group of love lyrics, from "Excursion Train" to "Under the Oak" (nos. 86–99). These are more eventful than the former group, as the speaker starts and as rapidly gives up on his affairs, on train rides, calling on women, waiting for them empty-handed. These love lyrics begin with an appeal to Helen in "Excursion Train" and his satisfaction with her in "Release" (no. 87). In the poems that follow, his annoyance rises, more stridently in revision ("These Clever Women," "Turned Down," "After Many Days," "The Hands of the Betrothed"—nos. 88, 91, 92, 95): "prudery" rather than "modesty" is, for example, the sin in "The Hands of the Betrothed" (*CP*, p. 127). Two pieces from *New Poems*, "Tarantella" and "Under the Oak," close this group in proud disdain. Yet it is one grace of this sequence, when reassembled in *Rhyming Poems*, that these poems hold neither sex, and no single person, altogether responsible for failures in love, and the power is shared with the blame. In "Tarantella," a woman "dances" in "mockery" at an "earnest" man (*CP*, p. 130), and in "Under the Oak," a man mocks back:

> *What have you to do with the mysteries*
> *. . . of my ancient curse?*
> *What place have you in my histories?*

(CP, p. 131)

Those lines hint at the next change in the volume—as its pitch rises into the mystical elegies (nos. 100–109). After "Under the Oak," only three further love scenes will appear, and these are detached, retrospective ("A Passing Visit to Helen," "Reading a Letter," and "Seven Seals," nos. 121, 123–24). The poet must nearly die himself and become quite alone before he can repossess his parent and himself, a process ripe for mythology, and so, as in *Amores,* myth begins to take over the volume, this time—thanks to the addition of *New Poems* and *Bay*—with longer and more dramatic results.

The story of Mrs. Lawrence's death traced thus far by the Foreword is a rhapsody of losses:

> And gradually the long illness, and then the death of my mother; and in the sick year after, the collapse for me of Miriam, of Helen, and of the other woman, the woman of *Kisses in the Train* and *Hands of the Betrothed.*
>
> Then, in that year, for me, everything collapsed, save the mystery of death, and the haunting of death in life. I was twenty-five, and from the death of my mother, the world began to dissolve around me, beautiful, iridescent, but passing away substanceless. Till I almost dissolved away myself, and was very ill: when I was twenty-six. (*CP,* p. 851)

When translated to the sequence in *Rhyming Poems,* the "long illness" was reduced to the space of two pieces, "Suspense" and "Endless Anxiety" (nos. 64–65). As in *Amores,* the elegiac narrative begins with "The End" (no. 66). The mourning "in the sick year after" flows directly into the collapse "then" of his three lovers and "everything . . . save the mystery of death." Lawrence put all this more simply in the Note; after "The End," death takes over, "the crisis of Volume I is the death of the mother, with the long haunting of death in life, which continues to the end, through all the last poems, which come from *Bay,* and which belong to the war" (*CP,* p. 28).

The concluding, mystic group of elegies, "Brother and Sister" to "The Drained Cup" (nos. 100–109), combine in *Rhyming Poems* with the long sequence developed from *New Poems*—nos. 110–29 (whose individual pieces were barely altered by Lawrence in 1928)—to record the "beautiful, iridescent" and "substanceless" "haunting of death in life." Cinching the two sections from *Amores* and *New Poems,* the fictional poems "A Passing-Bell" and "The Drained Cup" (nos. 108–9) sound the twofold moods of elegy and sexual energy that dominate *Rhyming Poems:* "A Passing-Bell" is a balladic elegy for a lost boy (*CP,* pp. 136–37), and, in a heavily revised version, the dialect poem "The Drained Cup" is a sermon delivered in winter by a June-hot woman, whose nervous young man cannot quite leave her for a more docile fiancée (*CP,* pp. 137–40). At the other end of the *New Poems* group, closing and framing it, is another set of pendants, which predict the final outcome of this struggle: the spiritual woman is defeated by her passionate reincarnation. Spoken by a chilly antithesis of "The Drained Cup," the woman of "Seven Seals" (no. 124, *CP,* pp. 153–54) would "seal" her lover with spiritual kisses, possessively enchaining him, protectively hemming in his passion. The fictional "Two Wives" (no. 125,

CP, pp. 154–58) narrates the confrontation between these two sorts, as they quarrel over their man's deathbed; its revised version leaves the fleshly wife undoubted master over the spiritual—the story to be continued in *Look! We Have Come Through!*

Between "The Drained Cup" and "Seven Seals," poems with many mythic values are gathered, and references that were dropped randomly in previous sections are enlarged in the *New Poems* group (nos. 110–23). The bowl, cup, or grail of passion, for example, comes into sharp relief in "The Drained Cup," recurring nearly as often as the "blue" shadow of the elegies, though more sporadically, in "Discipline," "Mystery," "Snap-Dragon," "In Church," and "Autumn Sunshine" (nos. 58, 61, 93, 117, 146). The "haunting" of death takes hold in earnest in "Late at Night" (no. 110), whose speaker fears that, contrary to the remarks of "Under the Oak," he has profaned "some female mystery" of the Bacchae (*CP,* pp. 140–41). In fact he is at this moment enduring those mysteries. In "Next Morning" (no. 111), he despairs at the dreary "hell," where he has arrived in the "house of life," frightened by his own "ghost" reflected in the mirror (*CP,* p. 141). The leaves on the trees (a typical metaphor for Lawrence's "utterances") have been stripped in "Winter in the Boulevard" (no. 112), their "summery wordage" silenced like "Romantic stories," and awaiting winter's "sentence" (*CP,* pp. 141–42). The city's corpse "corrodes," "ghastly" in "Parliament Hill in the Evening" (no. 113, *CP,* p. 142). But in "Embankment at Night . . . : Charity" (no. 114, *CP,* p. 143), the speaker ventures out into the city, and in "Embankment at Night . . . : Outcasts" (no. 115), despite the foulness of the scene before him, a long visionary panorama reveals "eloquent limbs," "thighs," "shins," "knees," "intertwined plasm," and, above all, "two faces"—a "little, bearded man" side-by-side a "heavy woman" (*CP,* pp. 144–46). In "Sickness" (no. 116), he explores the silence, still fearful—"What if unwitting I set the door of eternity wide"—but then, for the first time anticipating a key poem of *Look! We Have Come Through!,* "Song of a Man Who Is Loved," he backs off from death to call "to you": "Catch my hands, my darling, between your breasts" (*CP,* p. 147).

Mandell reads "Sickness" as concluding the sequence when "I . . . was very ill"; after which "slowly the world came back: or I myself returned: but to another world" (Foreword, *CP,* p. 851) in poems 117–29, "In Church" to "Narcissus." [45] This is, however, another of those vague passages in the Foreword, clarified in the Note where Lawrence explains that "the long haunting of death . . . continues to the end" of volume 1. It is in *Look! We Have Come Through!* which begins still in "England and the end of the death-experience" (*CP,* p. 28), that the world slowly "came back." "Sickness," as I read it, is one of several intenser moments as the poet's visionary mood rises in the unbroken sequence of verse from *New Poems* (nos. 110–29). The poet's "haunting" continues uninterrupted in the eight poems (nos. 117–24) that follow "Sickness," worried by memories and premonitions, the symbolism now becoming archetypal and extending to the condition of England. The relevance of the next poem, "In Church" (no. 117)—the "boys" singing "hymns" and the black blot of a "crow" suffusing Sabbath's "grail" (*CP*, pp. 147–48)—would go unnoticed without its companions, "Piano," "The North Country," and "Love Storm" (nos. 118–20). In "Piano," nostalgia for his hymn-singing childhood overcomes his older self, and he "falls" into second childhood (*CP*, p. 148). In "The North Country," however, the entire condition of industrial England, the country of Lawrence's birth, is condemned—"the man-life north imprisoned . . . asleep in the rule / Of the strong machine." The poet prophesies that this "convulsive" people will soon "burst" its prison (*CP*, pp. 148–49). The quieter fable of "Love Storm" in which roses are torn away, splashing red into the air as a hawk descends, plays upon the symbolism of its three predecessors to suggest that a "fall" is necessary for revolution and is not to be feared:

> *cease apprehending! . . .*
> *What, then, if a scarlet rose goes flapping*
> *Down the bright grey ruin of things!*

> (*CP*, p. 150)

In three final reminiscences, the failures of the past are at last stoically accepted. The speaker scorns to join or even criticize aloud Helen's old "game" in "Passing Visit to Helen" (no. 121)—she a "love-adept" who cultivates emotion to ward off passion (*CP*, pp. 150–51). In "Twenty Years Ago" (no. 122) he sees his childhood home in swift panorama—flowers, berries, woods, rabbit traps, the harvest stubble—and his "trouble lost" at a "mother's knees," and he wonders "what good beginnings" led to "this sad end" (*CP*, p. 152). But perhaps, as for the woman of the next poem, these good beginnings are also "sad," and he must eventually hold a balanced or dualistic stance toward both past and present. "Reading a Letter" (no. 123), a woman is lifted high above her surroundings and can see only desert and mechanical activity (*CP*, pp. 152–53), a scene obviously generated by a letter from Lawrence about "the north country." "Twenty Years Ago" reminds us of the entire scale of memory replayed in this volume: the educated young man, who according to the Foreword must now be twenty-six, looks back twenty years to his childhood in the "country of my heart," while his elder half also watches, nearly twenty years later, retrieving all his pasts—in country and city, in satisfaction and in sorrow, whether with mother or Miriam. It was the task of 1928 to make these things of the past "whole"; the task of the young man was to do something about the present—an argument not with his past so much as with all his mother still represented, his country's dying civilization.

Dying civilization is, of course, the final subject of this volume. The mythic *New Poems* (nos. 110–29) created a new context for the verse from *Bay* (nos. 130–43), so that its delicate story carries more symbolic freight. The Buffalo holograph reveals that prior to positioning the poems from *Bay*, Lawrence had copied out the last titles from *New Poems* in identical order: "Heimweh," "Débâcle," "Narcissus," "Autumn Sunshine," and "On That Day." He then began to play with them: bringing "Apprehension" and "Two Wives" (no. 125) to positions just ahead of "Heimweh"; changing the titles of "Apprehension," "Heimweh," and "Débâcle" to "Noise of Battle," "At the Front," and "Reality of Peace, 1916"; and shifting "On That Day" and "Autumn Sunshine" (in that order) to below the poems from the end of *Bay* (nos. 145–46). It might have made more sense to place "Narcissus" with *Look! We Have Come Through!* (as Mandell points out, its earlier title, "Neckar," also refers to a river in the Black Forest, which Frieda and he visited in 1912); its odd position (no. 129) suggests that Lawrence did not worry over every ligature of these poems.[46] Yet its symbolism is not altogether at odds with the war verse (nos. 126–28, 130–43). In "Noise of Battle" (*CP*, p. 159), the "flood" is "unsealed" by an "invisible woe," and London drowns like a beast (as also in "Town in 1917"—no. 140), the waters passing "beyond all bounds." Even after the title change from "Heimweh" to "At the Front," these poems clearly indicate that the war front is at home. Anticipating "Nostalgia," the speaker of "At the Front" calls his homestead to "fall with me . . . in one hurt" when the walls burst (*CP*, pp. 159–60). In "Reality of Peace, 1916," as in the 1917 essay of that title (*Phoenix*, pp. 669–94), "peace" is an enslaving, decadent condition, in which it is impossible to pass into any other state, "bitter" to "wait . . . only forbidden to expire" (*CP*, pp. 160–61). "Narcissus," of course, suggests the threshold to that other world. As in "Noise of Battle," man may break "bounds and beyond" by sinking back (*CP*, p. 161). This alternative theme of fertile remission is taken up again with the myth of Jove and Danaë in "Tommies in the Train" (no. 130, *CP*, pp. 162–63), with which Lawrence chose to open the poems from *Bay*. The revolutionary picture produced by this war poetry in nos. 126–43 is far less equivocal than in the original volume. Although the body of *Bay*, barely touched by revision, records the same attentive equipoise of a civilization at the brink that Lawrence had originally perceived in 1917–18, in their new context, these poems begin and end with anecdotes of revolution, joined and provoked

by the young speaker himself. After the last war poem from *Bay*, "Dreams
. . . Nascent" (no. 144—from *Amores*) blares the poet's cry for revolution
in a homily more detailed than any other in *Rhyming Poems*. The problem
of a dead nation is thus undertaken not merely in theory but in gesture and
act. Together with the war poems from *Bay* and *New Poems*, "Dreams . . .
Nascent" performs for Lawrence a second birth, of a very real kind as far as
he was concerned: his younger self dies with his homestead, with the death
of his mother and of the England he had known, to become a war-baby
and prophet.

To close the volume, Lawrence added one more elegy and one more appeal linked, at the last, by the single symbol of Persephone, and here the
elder poet was of one mind with the younger, who in 1918 revised these for
the ending of *New Poems*. (The editors of *Complete Poems* added three more
pieces to the end, but the Buffalo holograph removes any doubt of Lawrence's intentions.) The appeal for male power in "Dreams . . . Nascent"
quiets down in "On That Day" (no. 145) into the longing to wed his powers with the woman who had dominated him (and how separate had she
ever been from his motherland?):

> *A queen, they'll say,*
> *Has slept unnoticed on a forgotten hill.*
> *Sleeps on unknown, unnoticed there, until*
> *Dawns my insurgent day.*

> (*CP*, p. 176)

Through him, she will rise again. In a sense she does arise in "Autumn
Sunshine" (no. 146) as a spirit of change. Writing now in urgent invocation, Lawrence charges "all mortal men" to "drink" from the hell queen's
cup, "over-filled" with its "death-producing wine," and

> *Swear, in the pale wine poured from the cups of the queen*
> *Of hell, to wake and be free*
> *From this nightmare we writhe in,*
> *Break out of this foul has-been.*

> (*CP*, p. 177)

The "ancient curse" mentioned in "Under the Oak" (or the "invisible woe"
in "Noise of Battle") of desire or impotence, discord or inertia, may take
many forms; but like "Adam's Curse" for Yeats, it is satisfied in the expression, when permission is taken to feel its anguish, and an oath vowed
("swear") to act anyway, to "break" from the nightmare of history. In the
imagery of the Golden Bough (which appeared earlier in *Rhyming Poems*
in at least two poems, "The Appeal" and "Under The Oak"), the priest lies

wounded underneath a "powerful tree" as at a "sacrifice" by "the knife of a Druid" and above him "springs the blood-born mistletoe" ("Under the Oak," *CP,* p. 131).

Through all its revisions and rearrangements, among the many themes collected in *Rhyming Poems,* there emerges a highly consistent pattern in Lawrence's verse monologues, a rite of passage, or variation on the Romantic lyric, whose speaker must reinvestigate the past to achieve a future position.[47] When Lawrence's speakers break through inertia, they do so by breaking down. Whether or not a poem ends in illumination or in decline, the paths are remarkably alike: moving by way of the devouring past, desire for the mother, or childlike pathos. His persona relapses in the middle of a kiss or in any simple activity, gazing at water, lying in a field, listening to a piano. He sees himself again a child in "Piano" or falls into despondency in "Dog-Tired," submerges himself in his reflection in "The Wild Common" or responds as his lover quails in "Lightning." His sense of sight, hearing, touch, even smell, are disrupted, and he gives way to a demonic or pathetic experience:

> *The acrid scents of autumn,*
> *Reminiscent of slinking beasts, make me fear*
> *Everything.*

> ("Dolour of Autumn," *CP,* p. 107)

Such poems graphically enact the ideas he would later urge in his introduction to Crosby's verse: they drop into the "chaos" of the uncivilized imagination. But the speaker in these poems also learns that passion felt at these moments is matter for new power, that he should take his ghostly lover through fire in "Last Words to Miriam," or move through weariness and grief into rekindled life in "The Shadow of Death" and "Blueness," to be transformed by feeling, the "demon" unveiled.

"Piano" (no. 118) is one of the most resonant examples of this process (*CP,* p. 148). Its male narrator, listening to a woman sing "in the dusk," is "mastered" by song until he sinks back into a scene from his childhood: a Sunday evening in a cozy parlor. The poem ironically reverses the self-portrait of the Note, so that, rather than a conventional young man "shaken" by his greater demon, we are shown an adult man "cast down" by "the glamour of childish days." The redoubled irony of this scene returns in the ambiguous, value-laden terms of the poem—"Betrays" for example: "In spite of myself, the insidious mastery of song / Betrays me back." The problem confronting the speaker is not, as we might expect, that he betrays passion for the woman; rather, the passion of her song betrays his childhood emotion. He is a boy shaken into feeling and a man with a profound measure of sentiment, doubly revealed, doubly trapped:

> *The glamour*
> *Of childish days is upon me, my manhood is cast*
> *Down in the flood of remembrance, I weep like a child for the past.*

Once seized by "glamour," he is "cast down." But the "flood" and "weeping" are also unironically his salvation. If he "falls" this far, he has yet to achieve "manhood"; only by relapsing can he eventually know himself and, in the process, redefine manhood for himself. The rest of *Rhyming Poems* more than confirms the necessity of his descent. Besides, although "like" a child at the end, he has not altogether lost his older self; "remembrance" weds these two halves. I. A. Richards featured "Piano" in *Practical Criticism* to reveal the unskilled practices of his students, who were alternately touched and annoyed by its "sentimentality." "Sentimentality," he pointed out, arises in poems like this from the excessive response of readers, not solely from authors, and "Piano" is a study, not an indulgence, of such emotion.[48] Reread in context, late in a volume that reenacts the poet's "change of life," this poem also shows us ("song / Betrays me") that Lawrence's power as a poet arose from the antagonistic, yet generative, conflict between the maturing narrator and the eternal child.

CHAPTER SIX

—

Last Words

PANSIES, NETTLES, AND LAST POEMS

CHRONOLOGY:

Confiscation of "Pansies" manuscript	January 1929
Pansies published	July 1929
Confiscation of Paintings	July 1929
Nettles written	Summer 1929
Illness in Bandol	September 1929
Last Poems written	Fall 1929
Nettles prepared for publication	December 1929
Apocalypse written	December 1929
Death of D. H. Lawrence	March 1930

The end was hectic for Lawrence, as he was tossed by a fresh round of censorship. But in his last one and a half years he brought three further works of poetry to a finished state, *Pansies, Nettles,* and *Last Poems,* and demonstrated again his ability to alter the manner of verse and book to match the occasion. These works almost dance in the face of death. He had always thought that death was a necessary precondition for life; so when it came for him to die, he serenaded oblivion.

He started to write "pansies"—his punning anglicization of *pensées*—in November 1928, soon after finishing the expurgated edition of *Lady Chatterly's Lover*. Rhys Davies recalls Lawrence as a visitor at this time in Bandol, Var, France: "For all his furies and rages, he got immense fun out of writing *Pansies*. He would write them in bed in the mornings, cheerful and chirpy, the meek sea air blowing in from the enchanting little bay outside his window. He sat up in bed, a little African straw cap on the back of his head—"[1] In January 1929 (still in Bandol) he sent two manuscript copies of *Pansies* to his agent, and the package was seized in the mail. Once again he faced the task of expurgating his work. Meanwhile, he arranged for an unexpurgated edition to sell privately to fight off pirates (as he had done with *Lady Chatterley's Lover*), and he meditated these events in new "pansies." When in July an exhibition of his paintings was seized, he answered with a series of "stinging" pansies—calling these "nettles." He intended to follow with small bombs in a fortnightly magazine that he would edit and publish, called *Squib,* but succeeded in producing only one issue of "squibs" before he fell seriously ill in September. Tuberculosis staggered him, but as he recuperated, he readied *Nettles* for publication (completing it in December) and, as his friend Achsah Brewster reported, wrote the verse for a volume of *Dead Nettles:* "One afternoon we were with him and Frieda at Villa Beau Soleil, he began selecting some of his 'Nettles' for a small volume. There were to be others called 'Dead Nettles,' because they were to have no sting in them. He turned the pages of his notebook, adding that he had been writing some verses about death and would read them; then, shaking his head wistfully, he closed the book, saying: 'I can't read them now.'"[2] The poems with "no sting in them" undoubtedly included the first verses in *Last Poems,* composed throughout the fall and winter. Lawrence died in March of the new year, 1930.

Early studies divided this poetry unnaturally into two sharply distinct phases. The initial phase consists of almost five hundred poems from *Pansies, Nettles,* and a bulky, bound manuscript book—published under the title *More Pansies* (MS B) by its editor Richard Aldington. The sixty-seven pieces in a second manuscript book published and titled by Aldington as *Last Poems* (MS A), have been read separately as a second phase. When Aldington published the first editions of *More Pansies* and *Last Poems,* he argued that the two manuscript books were used for different purposes: one as a "continuation" of the pansies, the other holding "more serious poems." The former includes a group headed "Pensées" (published in *Pansies*), most of the verse in *Nettles,* many satiric poems never published by

Lawrence, and a final group of death poems. The second manuscript book contains some satiric verse among a large number of death poems. The manuscripts differ significantly in format: in contrast to the much worked over poetry in the MS B (*More Pansies*), MS A (*Last Poems*) contains chiefly fair copies. Aldington believed that *More Pansies* was used as a catch-all notebook primarily for drafts of pansies, while *Last Poems* was a nearly finished work in itself, the trial run perhaps for a long poem. But in Aldington's judgment—as well as that of Vivian de Sola Pinto, Sandra Gilbert, and Tom Marshall—what chiefly justified a division are changes in theme and style, from caustic verse addressing topical social problems to mythic poems seeking a private religion.[3]

More recently scholars, among them T. A. Smailes, Gail Mandell, and Ross Murfin, have softened the "phase" divisions.[4] Both manuscripts fluctuate between satiric and mythic verse. The stylistic break between them is far less disjunctive than Aldington suggests, and since *More Pansies* contains early versions (notably "Bavarian Gentians" and "The Ship of Death") for *Last Poems,* it makes more sense to recognize their affinities; Lawrence's experiments with "doggerel" led into the masterful technique of his death poems. The phases that these notebooks would seem to represent—a vision obsessed with its frustrations, succeeded by its creative resurrection—are in fact more inextricably connected in Lawrence's last works than in any previous period. The poems dissolve into each other in the vision of intertwined social and personal death.

More Pansies does not, however, merit the attention *Last Poems* has received as a cohesive sequence. *More Pansies* contains much fine verse that has drawn critical attention as frequently as the verse from *Pansies*. The *Norton Shorter Anthology of Poetry,* for example, includes three pieces from *More Pansies* and only two from *Pansies*. But *More Pansies* lacks an integrity separate from Lawrence's other works. Had he lived long enough, Lawrence would probably have used *More Pansies* to add to a book based on *Last Poems,* and it seems likely that he would have drawn on it for a third book of pansies, though this possibility is entirely a matter of conjecture. *More Pansies* may be considered a miscellany of drafts in the background of Lawrence's more finished works. *Pansies, Nettles,* and *Last Poems* all require and reward separate exegesis as sequences, with one caveat: that Lawrence probably would have revised *Last Poems* if he had lived to present it as a book. Any argument for internal coherence of that sequence should leave room for speculation about subsequent reshaping. But then Lawrence gave his reader much freedom for speculation about his intentions. In "Pornography and Obscenity" (1929), addressing this question, he seems to postdate Wimsatt and Beardsley: "It is the old vexed question of intention, become so dull today, when we know how strong and influential our unconscious intentions are. And why a man should be held guilty of his conscious intentions, and innocent of his unconscious intentions, I don't know, since every man is more made up of unconscious intentions than of conscious ones" (*Phoenix*, p. 173).

Informing Aldington's classification of the last poems was a harsh judgment of the satiric verse, the nadir in Lawrence's career as Aldington saw it, in contrast to the death poems, which he thought one of its pinnacles. The satiric poems in *Last Poems* also reflect, in his opinion, a brief lapse in strength. Since that appraisal, there have been several creative appreciations of the pansies, even when severed from *Last Poems*. One style differs from the other in its primary function, to attack rather than to charm the reader into new life, but the two tactics were, as always, interdependent.[5] And no matter how offensive this verse was, Lawrence conceived of it as love poetry. In "Pornography and Obscenity," composed soon after censorship of *Pansies*, he explained himself in familiar terms, pitting the masturbating egoist of pure lyricism against the marriageable man:

> One of my most sympathetic critics wrote: "If Mr. Lawrence's attitude to sex were adopted, then two things would disappear, the love lyric and the smoking-room story." And this, I think, is true. But it depends on which love lyric he means. If it is the: *Who is Sylvia, what is she?*—then it may just as well disappear. All that pure and noble and heaven-blessed stuff is only the counterpart to the smoking-room story. *Du bist wie eine Blume!* Jawohl! One can see the elderly gentleman laying his hands on the head of the pure maiden and praying God to keep her for ever so pure, so clean and beautiful. Very nice for him! Just pornography! . . .
>
> But if it is a question of the sound love lyric, *My Love is like a red, red rose*—! then we are on other ground. My love is like a red, red rose only when she's *not* like a pure, pure lily. And nowadays the pure, pure lilies are mostly festering, anyhow. (*Phoenix*, pp. 180–81)

Lawrence makes the argument of Shakespeare's sonnet no. 94 both a target and a model for his own. Clashing with the spiritual icon of a man "unmoved, cold, and to temptation slow" and upholding the "summer's flow'r. . . , / Though to itself it only live and die," he nonetheless reasserts Shakespeare's ends, exalting those who "husband nature's riches from expense" against "Lilies that fester."[6] Lawrence teases out a reinterpretation of Shakespeare's symbols, opposing the lily as a term for sentimental lyricism to the summer's flower, figure for an earthy poesy such as he described in the Introduction to *Pansies*: "the fairest thing in nature, a flower, still has its roots in earth and manure" (*CP*, pp. 417–18).

Lawrence's concern in these poems was not primarily, however, the sexual aim of *Collected Poems*—a restored virility. The last works emphasize sanity of body and mind. Deprived of physical well being, he had become preoccuped with his mental state. Redefining mind, he described the modern, cerebral consciousness as an "insanity" (Introduction to *Pansies, CP,* p. 420), then located man's metaphysical nature in his midriff. In contrast to discussions of the psyche in such works as *Psychoanalysis and the Unconscious* and *Fantasia of the Unconscious,* his 1929 prefaces for *Pansies* and the essay *Apocalypse* are explicitly concerned with the anatomy of thought and imagination, not self. Words also worried him more than they had done— the thriving mental activity of language. Perhaps that is why we find Lawrence referring in "Pornography and Obscenity" and in many of his later poems to Shakespeare, the most metaphysical of his influences. The "To be or not to be" soliloquy is the most frequent of these allusions. Hamlet brooded on death; Lawrence brooded on Hamlet's mistaken reasoning. To think properly was to live properly; avoid the expense of spirit with a husbandry of nature. As he had always chosen, Lawrence chose at the end to live forever.

The vision of death in the last poems was also more explicitly religious than in anything preceding them. Lawrence was as concerned with the progress of mankind as with his personal fate, and his religious quest began, as in his prior works, by turning back church history to capture in *Pansies* a "sense of wonder" and to sketch in *Last Poems* an eschatology grounded in flesh. But even here, mind—or (as Lawrence redefined it) the sensual faculty of understanding—predominated over body. Surprising though it may be, Lawrence returned to a Romantic notion he had once scorned: the belief that visionary poetic imagination was itself a thing divine, man's ship of death.

If Lawrence has shifted his thought to the dimmer realm of imagination, his writing never paled. Relying primarily on parallelism, repeated imagery and phrasing, he created clustered sequences; for the first time the poems seem to cling organically to each other. At one glance *Pansies* appears the most fragmented of his books, but is, in fact, deeply and pliably ordered. Lawrence designed it to reflect the modern mind in both its chaotic and its regenerative aspects. The much briefer *Nettles* was aimed as a counterblow at Lawrence's public, but it too was created by design. In *Last Poems,* as in *Etruscan Places* and *Apocalpyse,* Lawrence performed a third and final archaeological dig into civilization's tomb, to uncover there a private book of revelation.

Part I: Stinging Poems

PANSIES

Near the completion of *Collected Poems*, Lawrence grew impatient: "I'll sort of feel I've got everything behind me, when they are done,—and the novel. Then what next? Some sort of new start?" (*Collected Letters*, 2:1036). The introduction to *Chariot of the Sun*, which he wrote next, formulating his own poetics more than Crosby's, might as well have been a preface to his "new start": "Whims, and fumblings, and effort, and nonsense, and echoes from other poets, these all go to make up the living chaos of a little book of real poetry, as well as pure little poems like 'Sun-Ghost,' 'To Those Who Return,' 'Torse de Jeune Femme au Soleil,' 'Poem for the Feet of Polia.' Through it all runs the intrinsic naïveté without which no poetry can exist, not even the most sophisticated" (*Phoenix*, p. 261). Lawrence produced in *Pansies* a poetry of whims, nonsense, echoes, and pure poems with names like "Sun-Men," "At Last," "The Jeune Fille," and "Willy Wet-Legs." He assigned nonsense verse the difficult task of clearing man's congested senses, to make him "Stand Up!" (*CP*, p. 560) and assuredly *Pansies* commanded public attention: of its censors, its pirates, the private man on the street.

After his exertions with *Lady Chatterley's Lover* and *Collected Poems*, Lawrence had relaxed into a playfully antagonistic mood, using the pansies as purgatives. Sanity was not, in his view, equivalent to rationality; the Lawrencean man must be a creature of contradictions. One problem fascinating him in these poems was the investigation of a dissociation of sensibility. He complained bitterly about modern fragmentation, yet his solution to it placed him among the first writers to accept an answer indistinguishable from the problem: contrarious sensibility. The integrated mind, as imaged by the pansy, was "merely the breath of the moment, and one eternal moment easily contradicting the next eternal moment" (Foreword to *Pansies*, *CP*, p. 424).

Contrariety was a fact of his own nature. As Frieda remarked, he identified with both Mellors and Clifford in *Lady Chatterley's Lover*, in other words with the satiric figure of a debilitated intellectual as well as the more robust outdoorsman-lover.[7] In a revealing passage in "A Propos of *Lady Chatterley's Lover*," he saw an inevitable split between body and mind: "All the emotions belong to the body, and are only recognized by the mind. We may hear the most sorrowful piece of news, and only feel a mental excitement. Then, hours after, perhaps in sleep, the awareness may reach the bodily centres, and true grief wrings the heart" (Phoenix II, p. 493). This admits to a gap in sensibility that is negotiated by fluctuation from mind to heart and, though not confessed here, back again to mind.

Lest Lawrence appear more eccentric than he was, however, his case bears comparison with that of other modern poets. At the end of his life, Hart Crane, for example, was beset by troubles—money problems, unfavorable responses to his writing, alcoholism, his sexuality—until in despair he drowned himself at sea. Crane fits Lawrence's description of the "festering" lily: the homosexual who broods within himself until driven to suicide. How different was he from Lawrence? Yvor Winters sees in Crane the victim of an extreme romanticism, where reason is evil and impulse good. Whitman, who in Winters's view is a source for modern romanticism, "tells us that whatever happens to exist is perfect, but that any change is necessarily toward a 'higher' order of perfection. The practical effect of these notions is merely to deify change: change becomes good of necessity."[8] Winters thought that a life unconstrained by moral norms was by its very nature suicidal. By Winters's logic, Lawrence's views on "sanity" gave the measure of his insanity.

But Lawrence did not see himself as unconstrained or infinitely "impulsive"; to struggle for life was to face real constraints. In a remarkable passage from his Foreword to *Pansies,* he wrote of the flower, as of himself: "A flower passes, and that perhaps is the best of it. If we can take it in its transience, its breath, its maybe mephistophelian, maybe palely ophelian face, the look it gives, the gesture of its full bloom, and the way it turns upon us to depart—that was the flower, we have had it, and no *immortelle* can give us anything in comparison" (*CP,* p. 424). Lawrence's list balances in fine tension qualities split between limitation and possibility: the flower's transience, its spirit, "mephistophelian" evil and good, "ophelian" virtue maddened by knowledge, preening itself, gesturing, dying away. His language allows enormous scope for translation, but it contains no license for an egotistical sublime. Lawrence may seem, like Crane, to have rushed after death, and Winters would have thought him prey to his own temperament, but death was not a romantic fiction for Lawrence. Death was always near, and since it ended life, they took part in each other. He would have to yield, as to sex, to death:

> As the current
> thrusts warm through the loins, so the little one
> wildly floats, swirls,
> and the flood strikes the belly, and we are gone.
>
> ("Hark in the Dusk!" *CP,* p. 425)

Lawrence developed his philosophy of body and mind in "Pornography and Obscenity" and in two prefaces, the Introduction to the unexpurgated *Pansies* and the Foreword to the expurgated edition, both reprinted in *Complete Poems* (pp. 417–21; pp. 423–24). Delightedly he announced to correspondents and readers his "bunch of *pensées,* anglicé pansies; a handful of thoughts" (*CP,* p. 417). He anatomized mind with "veins" (not nerves) of "emotion": "a thought, with its own blood of emotion and instinct running in it like the fire in a fire-opal, if I may be so bold" (*CP,* p. 417). In a reverse move from Eliot, he blamed the disharmony of body and mind on emotional and sensual deprivation: "For by pretending to have no roots, we have trodden the earth so hard over them they are starving and stifling below the soil. We have roots, and our roots are in the sensual, instinctive and intuitive body, and it is here we need fresh air of open consciousness" (*CP,* p. 418). Lawrence's pansy had linguistic roots as well, in Pan: "a true thought . . . comes as much from the heart and the genitals as from the head" (*CP,* p. 417).

But while merging the divided self, Lawrence effectively enlarged its mephistophelian character. He often warned readers that they should be offended by his poems, as in a letter of 1929 to Marianne Moore, "some part of life must offend you too, and even beauty has its thorns and its nettle-stings and its poppy-poison. Nothing is without offense, and nothing should be: if it is part of life, and not merely abstraction" (*Collected Letters* 2:1142). Further etymologizing *pansy*—relating it to *panser,* "to dress or soothe a wound," he assures us that the pansies are meant for a medicinal purpose: "these are my tender administrations to the mental and emotional wounds we suffer from." Yet he also meant his lyrics to be light-hearted. In contrast to the moralism of Pascal and La Bruyère (both of whom he cites), "solid blocks of mental pabulum packed like bales," Lawrence invites us to "let every pensée trot on its own little paws" (*CP,* p. 417). The obscenities and ravings ("dung" and "nettle-stings") succeeded in thoroughly antagonizing the censors, but Lawrence seems to have hoped that his readers would experience more conflicting feelings.

Along with mind, language became a key issue of these prefaces. Lawrence explains that cutting language "off at the waist" is a sure sign of insanity: "the same with the Word which is God. If the Word is God—which in the sense of the human mind it is—then you can't suddenly say that all the words which belong below the navel are obscene. The word arse is as much god as the word face. It must be so, otherwise you cut off your god at the waist" (*CP,* p. 418).

Advocating views that would content a structural linguist if he had not been so contentious and coy, Lawrence assumes that "the Word is God" in respect to the human mind, then debunks orthodox notions of the Logos. If the Word is God and God is man, then language is made in his image, and will refer as often to parts below as above the waist. But thanks to its profane readers, language has "fallen": "When did the Word 'fall'? When did the Word become unclean 'below the navel'? Because today, if you suggest that the word arse was in the beginning and was God and was with God, you will just be put in prison at once" (*CP*, p. 418).

Lawrence adds, in passing, that "no one knows what obscene means." In "Pornography and Obscenity" he will define it for us, but first (having revamped the Logos) he attacks the status of words in rational discourse when conceived as "pure" (empty) abstractions or as possessing a single utilitarian value: "Take even the word *bread*. The mob-meaning is merely: stuff made with white flour into loaves that you eat. But take the individual meaning of the word bread: the white, the brown, the corn-pone, the home-made, the smell of bread just out of the oven, the crust, the crumb, the unleavened bread, the shew-bread, the staff of life, sour-dough bread, cottage loaves, French bread, Viennese . . .—there is no end to it all, and the word bread will take you to the ends of time and space, and far-off down avenues of memory" (*Phoenix,* p. 171). Lawrence's attack would include any theory of referential meaning that was too naive about the uses of language. "Mob-meaning" he calls it. Gone is the monochromatic, ordinary word *bread* after he breaks and distributes it into a large, potentially endless language family. All meaning is produced by individuals and is subject to personal acts of interpretation; meaning is relative: "The same with the word *obscene:* . . . Hamlet shocked all the Cromwellian Puritans, and shocks nobody today, and some of Aristophanes shocks everybody today, and didn't galvanize the later Greeks at all, apparently. Man is a changeable beast, and words change their meanings with him" (*Phoenix,* p. 170).

In *Pansies* and *More Pansies,* Lawrence's theories of mind translated into theatrical images conducted along the lines of *The Tempest.* To reach the sensual faculty of understanding, normal surface consciousness had to drown: "And those that do descend have got to suffer a sense-change / into something new and strange" ("Climbing Down," in *More Pansies, CP,* p. 667). In this satirical version of *The Tempest,* the poet shows the way to drown, and his conversion is distinctly un-Christian, a conversion out of Christianity.

Pansies begins with this anecdote of the drowning mind, narrating the loss of consciousness and implicitly defying traditional spirituality. Its first poem, "Our Day Is Over," revises a hymn from Lawrence's childhood to turn its sky-borne spiritualism into a tale of physical baptism:

Our day is over, night comes up
shadows steal out of the earth.

. . . .

we wade, we wade, we stagger, darkness rushes between our stones,
we shall drown.

Our day is over
night comes up.

(*CP*, p. 425)

Whereas in the hymn, "Shadows of the evening / Steal across the sky," in the poem, "Shadows steal out of the earth"; and where the Christian hymnist prays to "Guard the sailors tossing / On the deep blue sea," Lawrence calmly allows that "we shall drown." The hymn ends with the hope that

When morning awakens,
Then may I arise
Pure, and fresh, and sinless
*In thy holy eyes.*⁹

The poem closes still in the present moment, unworried as "Night comes up."

In "Hymns in a Man's Life" (1928), he wrote that the hymns of his childhood had imbued him with a "*natural* religious sense" uncorrupted by dogma: "They live and glisten in the depths of the man's consciousness in undimmed wonder, because they have not been subjected to any criticism or analysis" (*Phoenix II*, p. 599). The hymns stimulated a "sense of wonder" that (like the "glimpse of chaos" of his Crosby introduction) enlivened his mind to "sheer delight" in phenomena. But when Lawrence recalled a hymn in *Pansies*, as in its first poem, he inevitably altered it, stripping away Christian dogma, to get at the "sheer delight" of the verse. Many poems in *Pansies* are hymns in this sense, something like the "Hymns of Quetzalcoatl," simple folk songs about an earthy divinity rising from the decay of Christianity. Unlike those other Lawrencean hymns, these do not explicitly displace Jesus, because His displacement is forcefully implied in the form of the verse. Nor are the hymns uttered by fictional heroes, but directly by Lawrence, as he half recovers the voice of his childhood. They are poems that probably could not have been written before *Collected Poems*, where his boyhood came back, and they prepared for the writing of the powerfully religious *Last Poems*.

The anecdote of drowning told in *Pansies* as a whole does not develop as neatly as in "Our Day Is Over." There is a battle to be fought, and in this book the central agon is Lawrence's struggle for life or death. This is not a struggle for life "or else" death. Lawrence is caught up in a different version of Hamlet's question, whether to be or not to be: the question is, not how to choose between two kinds of living death, but how to decide between two ways of life, as in "To Let Go or to Hold on—?" (originally titled "To Be or Thus to Be"):

> *Must we hold on?*
>
> *Or can we now let go?*
>
> *Or is it even possible we must do both?*
>
> (*CP*, p. 429)

"To hold on" is to continue the battles of life. "To let go" is to yield the battle. In a coup de force, Lawrence chooses both. The paradox, lightly stated here, is familiar: to hold on, he lets himself go.

The mind that is sanely engaged in this question will be dual in nature, as it is in Lawrence's prose theories. In his pansies, he calls this an "alternating consciousness":

> *Come down now, from your pre-eminence, O mind, O lofty spirit!*
>
> *Your hour has struck*
>
> *your unique day is over.*
>
> *Absolutism is finished, in the human consciousness too.*
>
> *A man is many things, he is not only a mind.*
>
> *But in his consciousness, he is two-fold at least:*
>
> *he is cerebral, intellectual, mental, spiritual,*
>
> *but also he is instinctive, intuitive, and in touch.*
>
> ("Climb Down, O Lordly Mind," *CP*, p. 473)

Consciousness fluctuates between its two halves in a manner that will lead Lawrence to an amusing, but nonetheless serious, correction of Descartes. He accepts Descartes's conclusion, then adds to it a second conclusion, its opposite:

> *Only that exists which exists in my own consciousness.*
>
> *Cogito, ergo sum.*
>
> *Only that exists which exists dynamically and unmentalised, in my blood.*
>
> *Non cogito, ergo sum.*
>
> *I am, I do not think I am.*
>
> (*CP*, p. 474)

As *Pansies* unfolds, this thought-story reappears in many versions. There is no parallel, however, to the extended anecdotes of previous books, no complex narrative. *Pansies* can be said to "progress" only in an emotional extension. The book moves from mildly contemplative lyrics (in groups headed by "Our Day Is Over," "Swan," "Moon Memory," and "The Gazelle Calf") into severe attacks on personal and social issues, the mechanization of the modern mind and deadening individuality (in groups introduced by "Climb Down, O Lordly Mind," "The Root of Our Evil," "Nottingham's New University," "Salt of the Earth," and "Elderly Discontented Women"), to become even more pugnacious as Lawrence confronts the reader with final alternatives, whether to die a mechanical death or to revolt (in groups headed by "Always This Paying," "As For Me, I'm a Patriot," "Energetic Women," and "Ships in Bottles"). The intensely satiric character of this volume deepens into an obstinate anger, then ends with anticlimatically *cheerful* pieces of advice:

> *Stand up, but not for Jesus!*
> *It's a little late for that.*
> *Stand up for justice and a jolly life.*
> *I'll hold your hat.*
>
> ("Stand Up!" *CP*, p. 560)

In its casual way, *Pansies* moves down and out and up again.

The last poem in the book is "Trust," misplaced in *Complete Poems*, where it appears before three poems that had been expurgated in 1929. Neither the expurgated nor the original, unexpurgated edition[10] ended with "The Jeune Fille," a poem in which Lawrence blithely tells young women how to conduct their lives. ("The Jeune Fille" was deleted by censors of the expurgated *Pansies*; it was positioned last in *Complete Poems* by Pinto and Roberts.) "Trust" gives the book an unsatiric, wistfully optimistic ending, detached from the disasters witnessed thus far:

> *Oh we've got to trust*
> *one another again*
> *in some essentials.*
>
> (*CP*, p. 561)

"Trust" marks the inverse of the point where *Pansies* began: waiting for something to emerge but—as if it had gotten somewhere—now awaiting the sun, not night:

> *a sun that shines*
> *and goes dark, but shines*
> *again.*
>
> (*CP*, p. 562)

While making his way down this emotional course, the poet tacks between opposite moods (as he warned us, "one moment easily contradicting the next"). The book's beginning and end points mirror the character of the whole: a book of changes between a mood for destruction and a mood for renewal. There are no external time structures, no journey or calendar, and no novelistic life. Nor is there a logical development of its thoughts. His prefaces hint at something at once more fragmented and more naturalistic than any structure he had yet devised: "It suits the modern temper better to have its state of mind made up of apparently irrelevant thoughts that scurry in different directions, yet belong to the same nest" (*CP*, p. 417). Whereas in the Note to *Collected Poems*, the condition of "strange, torn" poems could be adjusted by a reader willing to fill in the circumstances, here he is invited to find in a deeply fragmented book an organic image of mind. We are asked neither, as in *The Waste Land*, to piece the fragments together nor, as in *Four Quartets*, to find a transcendent Word eliminating contradictions. Instead, Lawrence would have us allow this book its wild and free diversity.

The book has, however, more method than its disingenuous prefaces declare, suggested in these words: "this little bunch of fragments is offered as a bunch of *pensées*, anglicé pansies; a handful of thoughts" (introduction, *CP*, p. 417). *Pansies* is far more than a handful, containing more than two hundred poems. But it separates into "fragments," "bunches" or core groups, knit closely by repeated phrases and images within and among these groups. Each poem is a *mot*, and each is grouped with related *mots*. Not all the poems merge into obvious groupings, neither are there closed contours to groups of poems, but roughly twenty bunches give this book its inward shape. *Pansies* manages to be both more open and more tightly woven than Lawrence's previous books, a perky new demonstration of what he could do with the "expressive form" of a book. It is a closely linked, lengthy series that finds completion as it changes, one poem merging into the next, and it is the method also of verse clearly serious in nature in *Last Poems*, where mood and circumstance are equally liable to change.

The design for *Pansies* developed in several stages of selection, revision, *and* grouping. The verse in the single substantial notebook that exists was drastically revised and shuffled. Included at the back of this notebook is a list of titles that is closer to, though still distant from, the final published book. Lawrence further altered the poems and index in typescript.[11] Many poems in the notebook were omitted (to be published by Roberts and Pinto as "Additional Pansies" in *Complete Poems*), while a central group was added from the first seven pages of the "More Pansies" manuscript. The *Pansies* manuscript corresponds to the printed text in one important respect: Lawrence's "bunches" already existed there. He shifted, rearranged, and supplemented its clusters, so that their internal groupings and their order differ from that of the printed books, but approximately fourteen groups were derived from the notebook to form the basis for *Pansies*.[12]

Lawrence negotiated his tapestry effect by repeating words, phrases, and images, threading like to like to form a mnemonic poem, binding one poem to the next, finally stringing these "bunches" into a whole. Gilbert notes that different groups may develop in varying ways; one sequence may be "subtly progressive" (her example is a string headed by "Desire Is Dead"), another may "produce a logical argument" (like the series introduced by "Things Men Have Made"), while others gather into a "variorum" of anecdotes centered on one theme (she mentions groups from *More Pansies* and *Nettles*). But Gilbert clouds the nature of *Pansies* by mixing with it examples from *Nettles* and *More Pansies*. In *Pansies* these distinctions are barely noticeable, and all the groups might be described as "subtly progressive."[13] What rules their organization is the device of repetition, which Lawrence explained in his introduction to *Chariot of the Sun*.

This introduction is so relevant to the pansies that, while it articulates assumptions he had always had about verse, it clearly reflects a specific transitional stage in his poetics, preparing for *Pansies* and *Last Poems*. Repetition, he asserts, can undermine conventional word usage, and elaborate variation within a stable framework induces the reader to imagine unthought-of possibilities, and to revive faded idioms and metaphors. There should be no "sense" in poetry in the "common" meaning of that word: "Only a repetition of sun, sun, sun, not really as a glowing symbol, more as a bewilderment and a narcotic" (*Phoenix*, p. 257). The poet's "narcotic" reconditions its reader:

> The sun is very much in evidence, certainly, but it is a bubble reality that always explodes before you can really look at it. And it upsets all the rest of the things with its disappearing.
>
> Hence the touch of true poetry in this sun. It bursts all the bubbles and umbrellas of reality, and gives us a breath of the live chaos. (*Phoenix*, p. 259).

The "sun" will "upset all the rest of things" by "disappearing" into the mundane. When, due to monotony, the reader can no longer even imagine the sun, he catches a "glimpse of chaos." Nonsense and incongruity work similarly: doggerel "means nothing, and it says nothing. . . . [it] carries a dim suggestion of that which refuses to be said" (*Phoenix*, p. 258).

The principle of repetition begins within the individual poem, as in the single pansy "Nullus," a moment of misery in this sequence. Repetition mimes the poet's despair:

> *I am aware that I feel nothing, even at dawn.*
> *The dawn comes up with a glitter and a blueness, and I say: How lovely!*
> *But I am a liar, I feel no loveliness, it is a mental remark, a cliché.*

My whole consciousness is cliché
and I am null;
I exist as an organism
and a nullus.

("Nullus," *CP*, pp. 509–10)

He repeats not only the key terms, *dawn*, *cliché*, and *null* but also the central thought, "I feel nothing," "I am null," driving into our minds the nullity of self-conscious thinking. It was not unusual for Lawrence to identify himself with the evils he saw in society, since he felt that his fate was intimately bound up with a larger fate. At times he even lost his sense of difference, as in the Whitmanesque "We Die Together":

and I am "il Signore" and they love me here,
yet I am a mill-hand in Leeds
and the death of the Black Country is upon me.

(*More Pansies, CP*, p. 630)

By identifying himself in "Nullus" with the very mode of consciousness he sought to attack, he destroys himself. Bleakly introverted though he appears in consequence, he thus unleashes the power in redundancy. A self-conscious approach to the theme of self-consciousness wears away at that attitude from within.

One poem might not be enough, Lawrence thought, to subdue his calloused readers. By repeating his tale in one poem after another, he slowly forced the reader under with him:

I cannot help but be alone
for desire has died in me, silence has grown.

("Man Reaches a Point," *CP*, p. 507)

Desire has failed, desire has failed.

("Grasshopper Is a Burden," *CP*, p. 507)

When a man can love no more
and feel no more
and desire has failed. . . .

("Basta!" *CP*, p. 508)

Tragedy seems to me a loud noise
louder than is seemly.

("Tragedy," *CP*, p. 508)

After all the tragedies are over and worn out
and a man can no longer feel heroic about being a Hamlet—

("After All the Tragedies Are Over," *CP*, p. 508)

I know I am nothing.
Life has gone away, below my low-water mark.
I am aware I feel nothing.

("Nullus," CP, p. 509)

Even in these "null" poems, he allows the possibility for change, beginning with "Basta!" and enlarging with each poem until "Nullus": "This is a
pause"; "my shabby little defeat would do neither me any good / nor anybody else"; "Yet, when the time has come to be nothing, how good it is to
be nothing!"; "And in these awful pauses the evolutionary change takes
place." While piecing language and thought into redundant bits, Lawrence varies his verse; within repeated words and statements, he multiplies
distinctions. With diversity enough, he achieves the opposite effect from
that of redundancy, and these are "the best" moments: "the suffused fragments are the best, those that are only comprehensible with the senses,
with visions passing into touch and to sound, then again touch, and the
bursting of the bubble of an image. There is always sun, but there is also
water, most palpably water. Even some of the suns are wetly so, wet pools
that wet us with their touch" (*Phoenix*, p. 260).

Five poems pass between "Nullus" and one in which he recovers everything he had lost. In "Sun in Me" he performs an act of discovery, no
longer effacing himself, breeding "suns" beyond:

A sun in me.
And a sun in heaven.
And beyond that, the immense sun behind the sun,
the sun of immense distances, that fold themselves together
within the genitals of living space.
And further, the sun within the atom
which is god in the atom.

(CP, p. 513)

The poet completes his sun-rise when, at the farthest reaches of the "suns"
that appear to him, he conceives a cosmic man, "sun of immense distances,
that fold themselves together / within the genitals of living space." There
is nothing logical about this discovery. He blissfully finds his chaos, with
many suns viewed contemporaneously and nonsensically from dilating
double perspectives: in the "immensity" of "heaven" and "further" in "the
atom" (*CP*, p. 513). The self-chaotic exists kaleidoscopically in the farthest
distances of space and in the innermost element of matter.

Excerpted from the collection, a poem like "Sun in Me" may seem too
slight to bear its burden of new physics (which Lawrence seized upon as if
it were his idea, once and for all defeating social Darwinism). But Law-

rence knew his poems would be "true while they are true and irrelevant when the mood and circumstance changes" (Foreword, *CP*, p. 423). Having built into the poems a type of relativism, his pansies shift and grow in meaning among themselves, outlasting individual themes. Many of the poems stand poorly alone; certainly none is as memorable as "Snake" or "Bavarian Gentians." And the best are better when read among their relatives, simply because the bunches leave blank room for readers' minds to fill.

While related ideas are repeated among poems to generate a bunch, the boundaries of these groups blur, leaving it to readers to cut paths through the book. Lawrence dictates nothing. What we understand on the way through *Pansies* gathers from many intersections between his thoughts and ours. The character of any individual thought depends on what cluster of words happens to strike a reader from one poem to the next; that thought then changes as he perceives these words varied by cognates. For example, the first group in the book (from "Our Day Is Over" to "Destiny") may form around images in "Our Day Is Over" of "Shadows" that "splash between our thighs" (*CP*, p. 425). This image-cluster changes into "the flood strikes the belly" ("Hark in the Dusk!" *CP*, p. 425); then into "[they] show vast bellies" ("Elephants in the Circus," *CP*, p. 425); then into "the worn arches of their spines support" ("Elephants Plodding," *CP*, p. 426). But at this point the initial impression has (without our conscious realization) utterly changed. The thought of "aging time"—initially embodied in "shadows," "thighs," and "water"—radiates outward in several directions into "darkness," "elephants," and "bowls," embodiments of youth or agelessness.

A shift from one group to the next is signalled by a different, though still related, image cluster; for example, the first group of tender diluvian fables shifts to a group of satiric and philosophic tales, headed by "How Beastly the Bourgeois Is," but they are linked by the "beastly" burdens of man and elephant. We then shift back to another set of nature lyrics, in which the beast may take the offensive in images of a death-dealing swan. The shift in mode from fable to satire and back again reenforces the moodiness of *Pansies* as we stagger and night comes up. Every poem is a multiple *mot* qualified and expanded by the next poem, together collecting into "chaotic" groups of associated thoughts. Both within individual groups and among groups, the reader must lose his place as often as he rediscovers it, and when this happens, Lawrence has achieved as much as he hoped.

Lawrence created his first mock-up for the pansy in quite a different figure, the leopard, when in the introduction to *Chariot of the Sun* he pictured thought "trotting" through its changes: moving "the other way, back to the sun, the faith in the speckled leopard of the mixed self. What is more chaotic than a dappled leopard trotting through dappled shade? And that is our life, really" (*Phoenix,* p. 262). The metaphysical poet Andrew Marvell suffers modification here, the "green thought in a green shade" of "The Garden" startled into a "dappled leopard trotting through dappled shade." Lawrence's garden is a changeable, "mixed" mental paradise. Trotting through this garden, mediating its questions, giving passion to its lessons, is the seemingly sincere "me." As Gilbert argued, against scholars' dislike of these poems, "what critics object to most in Lawrence's *Pansies* and *Nettles* [is] . . . the polemical or confessional directness that gives the poems their power. . . . Yet directly stated, hortatory verse is, after all, as old or older than Horace's 'Integer vitae scelerisque purus' and as new as Blake's 'Jerusalem.'"[14] By the time these poems were written, this polemic was an old story, but the problem acquired special force from verse that makes fun out of mood and circumstance. When Lawrence chose as a frontispiece for his book a pen-and-ink drawing of himself, giving himself the look of an innocent satyr, this was not just another whim. The figure in this carpet is "I."

NETTLES

Nettles had its advent in Lawrence's battles over his paintings in July 1929. One of Lawrence's most unwelcome critics was Jack Squire: "I feel too bored and irritated by this last business to write anything serious against the Squirearchies and Noahsarkies. I can only let off a few *Pansies—Nettles,* rather—against them—and I do that—but I can't take them prosily" (*Collected Letters,* 2:1169). Lawrence had by this time nearly emerged from his struggles over *Pansies,* which appeared in its expurgated trade edition in July, then in the private uncut edition in August. He had fought hard for a complete trade issue, accusing his publisher Martin Secker of "outjixing Jix," the government's censor: "I can look for another publisher, without being in the least offended. But make the *Pansies* into a good, 'innocuous,' bourgeois little book I will not, and you shall not." In intense irritation and fatigue he began *Nettles:* "I will do another volume, of *Nettles,* this time . . . and get a bit more of my own back."[15] *Nettles* was ready by December for publication with Faber and Faber, who had printed "Pornography and Obscenity" that fall and now billed *Nettles* as a "continuation" of Lawrence's critique of modern society. In the wake of *Lady Chatterley's Lover, Pansies* had been a feisty joust with the reader; *Nettles* was created in a spirit of spite.

Nettles is generally disliked—disregarded and rarely considered apart from the other pansies. To Aldington *Nettles* was "about the worst and most trivial thing [Lawrence] ever published" (*CP,* p. 595). Smailes thinks that "Lawrence himself did not take *Nettles* very seriously; his own expression 'let off' suggests that he was being deliberately, shall we way, farcical."[16] But farce can be intended seriously. This book was a reprisal for attacks on Lawrence by his reading public, his censors, journalists, any and all reactionary elements that set the public standard of taste. That motive governed its selection of political satire, topical pieces, and poems on the suppression of Lawrence's works. *Nettles* is like *Bay* in characterizing a constricted state of society. It was meant to sting the public mind into consciousness of social repression, and *Nettles* does almost nothing but sting.

The documents behind *Nettles* indicate that Lawrence took some thought over its final shape. Most of the poems were selected in groups of two or more (as many as seven in a bunch) from the compendious "More Pansies" manuscript and then placed in essentially the opposite order.[17] (See the Table "*Nettles* and the 'More Pansies' Manuscript Book," below.) Organized roughly into three sections, the books opens with poems characterizing English patriotism as a determined spinsterhood. At the book's center is a group headed by three "Songs I Learnt at School," which satirize Britain's schoolmarmish treatment of her citizens and, more importantly, of their art. The third section sketches an effeminate journalism and the no-man's-land of industrial society. The tone in this last group steadily darkens until, in two closing poems, Lawrence offers an alternative to democracy:

> *Oh, I am a democrat*
> *of the grass in blossom*
> *a blooming aristocrat all round.*
>
> ("Magnificent Democracy," *CP,* p. 587)

Only Lawrence laughs at the end of this book, at Britannia's expense.

Lawrence's energies were not restricted, however, to a narrow vein of sarcasm. *Nettles* pinpoints a subject dear to every poet's heart. The headpiece, "A Rose Is Not a Cabbage," introduces the book's central conflict, the failed relationship between the individual imagination and the public mind, of which Lawrence had complained in "Pornography and Obscenity": "The public, which is feeble-minded like an idiot, will never be able to preserve its individual reactions from the tricks of the exploiter" (*Phoenix,* p. 172). In "A Rose Is Not a Cabbage," feebleminded "cabbages" overgrow the "roses" of England. Lawrence first adopted the cabbage for satire when he published *Love Poems and Others,* which Frieda and he considered a schoolboyish effort, facetiously nicknaming it *Cabbages and Asphodels.*

Nettles and the "More Pansies" Manuscript Book

Nettles (London: Faber & Faber, 1930): table of contents, with notes on discrepancies from *Complete Poems* (*CP*, pp. 569–87) and from the original typescript (Vasey MS E266c)

"A Rose Is Not a Cabbage"
"The Man in the Street" (not in MS E266c)
"Britannia's Baby"
"Change of Goverment"
"The British Workman and the Government"
"Clydesider"
"Flapper Vote"
"Songs I Learnt at School"
   I.   "Neptune's Little Affair with Freedom"
   II. "My Native Land"
   III. "The British Boy"
"13,000 People"
"Innocent England"
"Give Me a Sponge"
"Puss-Puss!"
"London Mercury"
"My Little Critics"
["Daddy-Do-Nothing": in *CP*, p. 582, and MS E266c; not in Faber]
["Question": in *CP*, p. 582, and MS E266c; not in Faber]
"Editorial Office"
["British Sincerity": in MS E266c; not in *CP* or Faber]
"The Great Newspaper Editor to His Subordinate"
"Modern Prayer"
"Cry of the Masses"
"What Have They Done to You—?"
"The People"
"The Factory Cities"
"Leaves of Grass, Flowers of Grass"
"Magnificent Democracy"

Drafts behind *Nettles,* in order and in groups in which they appear
in the "More Pansies" manuscript book (MS E192a) *

"Modern Prayer"

  *Where more than two poems intervene between the verse that duplicates *Nettles* in the

. . . . .

"Leaves of Grass, Flowers of Grass" ("Leaves of Grass, Flowers of Grass"
    and "Magnificent Democracy")

. . . . .

"What Have They Done to You—?" (*CP*, p. 630)
[one poem intervenes]
"City-Life" (*CP*, p. 632; "The People")
"The Factory Cities"
"Cry of the Masses"
[two poems intervene]
"Give Me a Sponge"
[one poem intervenes]
"Rose and Cabbage" (*CP*, p. 634; "A Rose Is Not a Cabbage")

. . . . .

"Puss-Puss!"
"London Mercury"
"My Little Critics"
"Emasculation" (*CP*, p. 658; "Daddy-Do-Nothing" and "Question")
"Editorial Office"
"British Sincerity"

. . . . .

"The Member of the British Public" ("The Man in the Street")
"Lucky Little Britisher" (*CP*, p. 670; "Britannia's Baby")
"Innocent England"
"13,000 People"
"Change of Government"
"The British Public and the Government" ("The British Workman and
    the Government")
"The Working Man" (*CP*, p. 670; "Clydesider")
"The Great Newspaper Editor to His Subordinate"
"Flapper Vote"

. . . . .

"Songs I Was Taught at School" ("Neptune's Little Affair with
    Freedom")
"Another Song / The British Boy"
"Another Song I Learned at School" ("My Native Land")

"More Pansies" manuscript, this is marked with ellipses. Titles are included in parentheses to
refer to their final published form in *Nettles* when the altered titles are difficult to recognize.
Pinto and Roberts did not reprint poems in the "More Pansies" manuscript book that reduplicated *Nettles* too closely, but when a poem does appear in the *More Pansies* section of *CP*,
this is also indicated in parentheses.

The title "A Rose Is Not a Cabbage" alludes, of course, to the nearly proverbial line by Robert Burns, Lawrence's model of the neglected, maverick
poet: "if only Robert Burns had been accepted for what he is, then love
might still have been like a red, red rose" ("Pornography and Obscenity,"
Phoenix, p. 181). Lawrence's poem is not about such a rose. Its subject is
public cabbages and their discontents:

> *Now that the winter of our discontent*
> *is settled on the land, roses are scarce in England, very scarce, there are none*
>   *any more.*
> *But look at the cabbages, Oh count them by the score!*
>
> (CP, p. 569)

In the public state, valued images fall to conventionalism: cabbages "fold /
nothingness, pale nothingness in their hearts."

At the heart of *Nettles* are anecdotes about the censorship he endured:
"Songs I Learnt at School," "13,000 People," "Innocent England," and
"Give Me a Sponge." Beyond his personal victimization, he mourns the
general loss of spirit in England as his own: "And still, in spite of all they
do, I love the rose of England, / but the cabbages of England leave me
cold." And with the satirist's mock-humility, he makes himself an example
of the condition of England: its self-destruction. In "Britannia's Baby," for
example, he speaks as the self-victimized "we":

> *It's called the British Public, the Public, the Public*
> *It's called the British Public, including you and I.*
>
> *It's such a bonny baby, a baby, a baby*
> *It's such a bonny baby, we daren't let it cry.*
>
> ("Britannia's Baby," CP, p. 570)

He engages "us" still more effectively by deploying language conventions and colloquialisms against us, stinging us awake to limitations in
modern manners. It was this that Auden admired enough to make the concluding point of his essay on the poetry:

> If formal verse can be likened to carving, free verse to modeling, then one
> might say that doggerel verse is like *objets trouvés*—the piece of driftwood
> that looks like a witch, the stone that has a profile. The writer of doggerel, as
> it were, takes any old words, rhythms and rhymes that come into his head,
> gives them a good shake and then throws them onto the page like dice
> where, lo and behold, contrary to all probability they make sense, not by law
> but by chance. Since the words appear to have no will of their own, but to be
> the puppets of chance, so will the things or persons too which they refer;
> hence the value of doggerel for a certain kind of satire.

—satire, that is, of "the anarchist rebel, who refuses to accept conventional laws and pieties."[18] Although Auden makes Lawrence out to be more an outsider than he was and his verse more *trouvé*, he catches both its character and its aim when he calls it puppetry. Lawrence faces us with repressively predictable mock-ups. Predictable social phrases and symbols, meters and rhymes exaggerate the social trap:

> *Mr Smith, Mr Smith*
> *if you stay in my office, you've got to be kith*
> *and kin with Miss Jupson, whose guts are narrow*
> *and can't pass such things as substance and marrow.*
>
>   ("The Great Newspaper Editor to His Subordinate," *CP*, p. 583)

What is unpredictable in these lines are the unmentionable "guts" and "marrow." A sarcastic inner voice hints darkly at what the no-choice philosophy of the great editor has suppressed: passing "such things as substance and marrow."

Lawrence stages the relationship between authority and the individual as a failed dialogue. The most poignant "nettles" use their exaggerated nonsense to make his pseudo-dialogues noisome. To return to the effective "Britannia's Baby," as it makes less and less sense, its verse is increasingly insinuating:

> *Drop of whiskey in its minky? well it shall, yet it shall*
> *if it's good, if it's going to be good little man.*
>
> *Want to go a little tattah? so it shall, of course it shall*
> *go a banging little tattah with its Auntie*
> *if it's good!*
> *If it's good today, and tomorrow-day as well*
> *then when Sunday comes, it shall go tattah with its Auntie*
> *in a motor, in a pap-pap pap-pap motor, little man!*
>
>   (*CP*, pp. 570–71)

The baby talk of "Auntie" gradually consumes every phrase of the poem until it sounds obscene. This is what Lawrence called real "pornography" when he redefined that term in "Pornography and Obscenity," covert self-tickling. In the oppressive coupling of the "lily" Auntie and her "little man," there is no such thing as an individual man or woman, let alone an original thought.

In the poems, "Songs I Learnt at School," Lawrence inserts into familiar, 'innocent' schoolboy's songs the hypocritical, adult chatter that underwrites them:

Father Neptune one day to Freedom did say:
If ever I lived upon dry—y land,
The spot I should hit on would be little Britain—
Said Freedom: Why that's my own I—sland!—

"Oh what a bright little I—sland!
A right little, tight little I—sland!
Seek all the world round there's none can be found
So happy as our little I—sland!"

So Father Neptune walked up the shore
bright and naked aft and fore
as he's always been, since the Flood and before.

And instantly rose a great uproar
of Freedom shrieking till her throat was sore:
Arrest him, he's indecent, he's obscene what's more!—

(CP, p. 574)

Seemingly innocent Freedom changes her tune when Father Neptune misreads her song—when he hears it as an invitation to freedom rather than a metrically nice act of repression.

Toward the end of *Nettles*, in a cluster about the plight of industrial society—"Cry of the Masses," "What Have They Done to You—?," "The People," and "The Factory Cities"—the speaker takes on a more lordly, prophetic voice and cries out against the common doom: "Ah the people, the people! / surely they are flesh of my flesh!" ("The People," *CP*, p. 585). The language is more brutal than ever, using exaggerated repetition to trivialize both authority and its subjects, the masses:

Trot, trot, trot, corpse-body, to work.
Chew, chew, chew, corpse-body, at the meal.
Sit, sit, sit, corpse-body, in the car.
Stare, stare, stare, corpse-body, at the film.
Listen, listen, listen, corpse-body, to the wireless.
Talk, talk, talk, corpse-body, newspaper talk.
Sleep, sleep, sleep, corpse-body, factory-hand sleep.
Die, die, die, corpse-body, doesn't matter!

("Cry of the Masses," CP, p. 584)

The shape of mass-produced command, prerecorded and overused, makes a dumb show of modernity.

Lawrence's triumph in the last two poems is the sound of voice recovered after long submission to empty talk: "Only the best matters, even the cow knows it" ("Leaves of Grass, Flowers of Grass," *CP*, p. 587). Mandell examines an earlier, unpublished version of this poem, but lets a curious allusion go unremarked. In the "More Pansies" manuscript this poem's mild parody of Whitman was spiked by the contention that even "poor impotent Ruskin knew it / better than you, Walt!"[19] It is difficult to tell how ironic Lawrence meant this to be. He probably thought that Ruskin's belief in labor was redeemed or at least undermined by an aristocratic sensibility. Lawrence was knowingly influenced by Ruskin, and in 1929 he shared both Ruskin's impotence and his contradictions. This ambiguous personal touch is gone in the *Nettles* version, but after all the satiric barbs of the rest of the book, his final affirmation comes as a relief. We may not be persuaded that "Only the best matters." But the fact that the cow "knows it" when the cabbage could not, is a sign that Lawrence's humor has lost its sting, that he has regained his affection for the ordinary.

In *Lady Chatterly's Lover*, Connie Chatterley recalls a biblical image of the nettle the moment she begins to break from her oppressive husband. The line runs through her mind, "Touch not the nettle . . . for the bonds of love are ill to loose" (*Lady Chatterley's Lover*, p. 126). This double-edged allusion expresses the misery she suffers from losing the bond with her husband and the potential risks in rebelling against a nettle. Life with Clifford has been filled with his prickly irritability. But there is yet another implication suggested by the word *loosen*. The nettle's sting "loosens," may release, the bonds of a deep love, such as Connie feels for Mellors. Lawrence's biting *Nettles* also serves a triple purpose: expressing an anxious irritability, mimicking the social ills that beset him, attacking the self-enchained, puritanical Britannia from within.

Part II: The Apocalyptic Sequence

Convalescing in the autumn of 1929, Lawrence began to write his "dead nettles"—dead because they had lost their sting, but also because these were flowers of death. One of the central questions readers have asked of *Last Poems* concerns its theme of reincarnation: Did this poet of the flesh believe he must be reborn in the flesh, or did he in the end embrace a Romantic belief, once scorned, in the vitality of the imagination? Yet questions and criticisms alike tend to be silenced by the unusual certainty expressed in the poems. Nothing in the earlier books of poetry compares with the serene, seemingly unproblematic nature of this one. The elements of Lawrence's faith had been so long established and are here so firmly in place that to die appears under the extraordinary guise of a wedding with the unknown. At the same time he invested himself in powers of mind that he had freshly discovered in his pensées. Not only did he conceive of a mind made flesh; in the end, the sensual consciousness reaches for the godly: "Prayer, or thought, or studying the stars, or watching the flight of birds, or studying the entrails of the sacrifice, it is all the same process, ultimately: of divination" (*Etruscan Places*, pp. 152–53).

Most readers agree that the quietly confident *Last Poems* is a cohesive sequence, even when they question the beliefs that uphold Lawrence's confidence. I establish in this section that, in its manuscript form, *Last Poems* details a sophisticated argument, organized in part as a naturalistic sequence in which he relives the Etruscan mysteries, and in part as a revisionary history of the end of things, a poetic apocalypse. This is of course to claim, as I have above, that Lawrence's poetry takes up the arguments of his contemporary prose, in this case those of *Etruscan Places* and of *Apocalypse*. More than twenty years ago Christopher Hassall noticed the close connection between Lawrence's last poems and his last travelogue, *Etruscan Places* (begun in 1926 and left unfinished at his death), and few scholars have missed the equally relevant thematic correlation with *Apocalypse*, Lawrence's last metaphysical essay (written in December and January 1929–30).[20] Scholars have stopped short of describing *Last Poems* as narrative, however, and this reservation has much to recommend it because the book contains so much thought:

> They say that reality exists only in the spirit
> that corporal existence is a kind of death
> that pure being is bodiless
> that the idea of the form precedes the form substantial.
>
> But what nonsense it is!

("Demiurge," CP, p. 689)

This was Lawrence's last word on Plato: "Before Plato told the great lie of ideals / men slimly went like fishes, and didn't care" ("For the Heroes Are Dipped in Scarlet," *CP*, p. 688). As in *Pansies*, he *thinks* his way through *Last Poems*. But though there is no extended story in *Pansies*, there is one, admittedly of an unorthodox sort, in *Last Poems*. The sequence should not be judged primarily as a theological tract. Like *Look! We Have Come Through! Last Poems* details a man's "rapturous possession" by oblivion, and like the earlier sequences, this one works its way toward darkness by severing itself insistently from its pasts. What is so different about *Last Poems* is that its dialogue takes place entirely within the poet's mind; he thinks and speaks largely to himself. Farther away than ever from orthodox narrative, the story of *Last Poems* is that of a poet thinking aloud about last things.

Lawrence argued often enough at the end of his life for the notion of "symbolic thought" and against further storytelling. In *Etruscan Places* he wrote, aggressively interpreting history, "when scepticism came over all the civilized world, as it did after Socrates, the Etruscan religion began to die, Greeks and Greek rationalism flooded in, and Greek stories more or less took the place of the old Etruscan symbolic thought" (p. 150). In *Apocalypse* he complained about centuries of Christian scribes who censored, edited, and obscured the original text of Revelation, "who wanted to smear over the pagan vision" (pp. 34–36). In both passages Lawrence attempts to reinstate the old "symbolic thought," and this includes, as in every other book, faith in the cyclic mysteries: "one radical thing the Etruscan people never forgot, because it was in their blood as well as in the blood of their masters: and that was the mystery of the journey out of life, and into death; the death-journey, and the sojourn in the afterlife: (*Etruscan Places*, p. 150). In *Apocalypse* he found "down at the bottom" underneath scribal additions, "some sort of book of a pagan Mystery," "probably the description of the 'secret' ritual of initiation into one of the pagan Mysteries, Artemis, Cybele, even Orphic" (p. 39). The "book" Lawrence reconstructed from its scribal ruins unfolds in two cycles, narrating the death and rebirth of the initiate, then the death and resurgence of the world.[21] As was so often the case in the move from philosophy to poetry, the order of his cycles is reversed in *Last Poems*. Whereas in *Apocalypse* he reconstructed the original sequence of the pagan mysteries, in *Last Poems* he was concerned with his present history: first he imagined the reemergence of a pagan world and argued at length against modern "ideas," then he prepared his own journey into death.

In all these last works Lawrence was preoccupied with his own religious preparation for death. Little separates this religion from humanism, conceived in the Lawrencean style as belief in a noble and fleshly humanity, or from a modern religion of imagination. Taking a second look at the last works, one finds in *Etruscan Places* and *Apocalypse* a final poetics and, in *Last Poems,* Lawrence's most complete verse discussion of poetic creativity. Michael Kirkham believed that it signaled a "shift" in philosophic attitude from his prior thought:

> The last house [in "Invocation to the Moon"], it emerges, is the house of memory redeemed by tenderness of imagination, a gift to those who are ready for death, a gift to the poet in return for his acquiescence in the loss of his physical powers and bequest of his body back to the universe. . . . This

seems to me, when set in context with the rest of Lawrence's thought, in which formerly there was no room for ideal sexuality, the reversal of a central tenet (one proclaimed, too, with no less vehemence elsewhere in this sequence)—at the very least a modification that reveals the earnestness of his struggle to reconcile a faith established on a belief in the sacredness of the body with the facts of dying.[22]

This shift is less sudden and less "startling" than Kirkham says. Lawrence's admission of faith in memory and imagination, where thought is sensual pansy-flesh, had deep roots in his belief that the body possesses mystical force beyond the "sex-swindle" (*Collected Letters*, 2:967) and in doctrines articulated years before of the sensual psyche of plexuses and ganglions. *Pansies* and *Last Poems* made the final readjustment to a faith already readjusted many times, the faith that he could regenerate himself in both body and mind. In *Apocalypse* he looked for recovery of an ancient, pagan consciousness: "the Apocalypse is still, in its movement, one of the works of the old pagan civilization, and in it we have, not the modern process of progressive thought, but the old pagan process of rotary image-thought. . . . the old human conscious process has to *see something happen*." In contrast to the fragmented, deathly modern mind, this visionary imagination animates all it sees: "Today, it is almost impossible for us to realize what the old Greeks meant by god, or *theos*. Everything was *theos*." More simply, "pagan thinkers were necessarily poets" (*Apocalypse*, pp. 52–54). *Last Poems* is the story of such a poet, wrestling for vision.

With the first poem, he "sees something happen":

> *Little islands out at sea, on the horizon*
> *keep suddenly showing a whiteness, a flash and a furl, a hail*
> *of something coming, ships a-sail from over the rim of the sea.*
>
> ("The Greeks Are Coming!," CP, p. 687)

In the next three poems, he trumpets his increasing joy: "They are not dead, they are not dead! . . . / Now the sea is the Argonauts' sea" ("The Argonauts," no. 2, *CP*, p. 687);

> *And now that the moon who gives men glistening bodies*
> *is in her exaltation, and can look down on the sun*
> *I see descending from the ships at dawn*
> *slim naked men from Cnossos*
>
> ("Middle of the World," no. 3, CP, p. 688)

"So now they come back! Hark! . . . / They are dancing!" ("For the Heroes Are Dipped in Scarlet," no. 4, *CP*, p. 689). Although he sometimes meditates philosophically, "This sea will never die," such thoughts occur in the context of his *seeing* "the Minoan Gods, and the Gods of Tiryns," who "without fail come back again" ("Middle of the World," *CP,* p. 688). He does not pause to distinguish gods from men. As in *Etruscan Places,* they converge: "man, by vivid attention and subtlety and exerting all his strength, could draw more life into himself, more life, more and more glistening vitality, till he became shining like the morning, blazing like a god" (*Etruscan Places,* p. 148).

In the next group, headed by "Demiurge" (nos. 5–14), Lawrence unfolds his theory of creation. Meditation now predominates over event. The few events narrated occur in the past tense as memories or legends, in "Maximus" (no. 11) and "The Man of Tyre" (no. 12). His method in the other poems is to reason away from traditional Western views to his anti-philosophy that existence precedes thought:

> *They say that reality exists only in the spirit.* . . .
>
> *But what nonsense it is!* . . .
>
> *Even the mind of God can only imagine*
> *those things that have become themselves:*
> *bodies and presences, here and now.*
>
> ("Demiurge," *CP,* p. 689)

In the second poem of this group, "The Work of Creation" (no. 6), he ponders the nature of God and, comparing Him to the artist, determines that God is nothing other than the "urge" of procreative desire. God is sensual consciousness:

> *The mystery of creation is the divine urge of creation,*
> *but it is a great, strange urge, it is not a Mind.*
> *Even an artist knows that his work was never in his mind,*
> *he could never have* thought *it before it happened.*
>
> . . . . .
>
> *His urge takes shape in the flesh, and lo!*
> *it is creation! God looks himself on it in wonder, for the first time.*
> *Lo! there is a creature, formed! How strange!*
> *Let me think about it! Let me form an idea!*
>
> (*CP,* p. 690)

The closing two lines may seem ironic, couched as they are in a thoughtful poem about creation; surely Lawrence develops "ideas" not only after writing this but in the very act of writing. Lawrence would have countered, however, that these poems do not contain "ideas" in any Platonic sense. They are emotional thoughts, expressed in wonder and conviction, not disinterested: "Lo! there is a creature. . . . / Let me think about it!"

The lines omitted above show Lawrence meditating on the process of composition, something he rarely does. They offer an account of the writing process in all his verse cycles:

A strange ache possessed him, and he entered the struggle,
and out of the struggle with his material, in the spell of the urge
his work took place, it came to pass, it stood up and saluted his mind.

Translated out of his prior self by "a strange ache," he enters into conflict with his material as with himself; in this process his work "comes to pass," until he moves beyond it, and the work, left behind as the embodiment of the heroic poet, "stands up and salutes his mind." While these few lines recapitulate Lawrence's fundamenal poetic, they are specifically relevant to the sequence of *Last Poems*, where he acts out, without indirection, the struggle for physically grounded consciousness. Another poem from the group, "They Say the Sea Is Loveless" (no. 13), is sufficient to illustrate the way he battles against the finished "idea" to sustain creative urgency:

They say the sea is loveless, that in the sea
love cannot live, but only bare, salt splinters
of loveless life.

But from the sea
the dolphins leap round Dionysos' ship

. . . . .

and the sea is making love to Dionysos
in the bouncing of these small and happy whales.

(*CP*, p. 693)

What "they say"—that "the sea is loveless" and that "love cannot live"—with their reduced imagination of things, "salt splinters," gives way in the second verse paragraph to a narrative of rich fleshly love: "dolphins leap," "masts have purple vines," and there are "the purple dark of rainbows," and "the nose-dive of sheer delight."

With the third group (nos. 15–20), such battles of thought are superseded by invocational narratives, introduced by "Invocation to the Moon" (no. 15), a verse form in which Lawrence calls upon ethereal muses and, in invoking them, imagines their guidance into an animate arcadia: "Lady, lady of the last house down the long, long street of the stars / be good to me now" (*CP*, p. 696). His desire is partially fulfilled in the third poem of this group, the well-known "Bavarian Gentians" (no. 17). Its place in the sequence deserves discussion.

In the poem just preceding "Bavarian Gentians"—the companion piece, "Butterfly" (no. 16)—Lawrence almost forgets his immediate surroundings, "Here in the garden, with red geraniums, it is warm," to imagine the butterfly flying

as up an invisible rainbow, an arch
till the wind slides you sheer from the arch-crest
and in a strange level fluttering you go out to sea-ward, white speck!

(*CP,* p. 696)

That is all—a "sheer" slide down the wind, "fluttering," vanished to a "speck." Unlike his Romantic predecessors, he does not follow the butterfly beyond its vanishing point into the cosmic harmonies of the sea and sky. But he concludes, "it is enough! I saw you vanish into air"—enough to have seen the butterfly vanish, a sight by nature unseen. He has witnessed oblivion. The discovery occurs with far less overt philosophizing than in the greater Romantic lyrics. Nonetheless Lawrence has reached a recognition like Wordsworth in the Immortality Ode, finding knowledge of the butterfly not by vision but by loss, "Fallings from us, vanishings."[23] The perception of the butterfly's absence brings the sharp recognition of its other life. With that recognition, he turns to the narrative of "Bavarian Gentians" and imagines his descent into the unseen underground.

"Bavarian Gentians" occurs in September rather than the October of "Butterfly," and the step back in time is jarring. Lawrence might have altered this for publication. Months are rarely mentioned in *Last Poems,* and in these two pieces, which Lawrence obviously designed as pendants (altering previous versions recorded in *More Pansies* and placing them side by side), he gives their months special emphasis. But even with a change in date, the reader would nonetheless be asked to think about the seasons in the symbolic way the uncorrected achronology enforces. The two opening lines of "Bavarian Gentians" play upon that ambiguity in the status of September: "Not every man has gentians in his house / in soft September, at slow, sad Michaelmas" (*CP,* p. 697). We presume that a man is lucky to have gentians this late in the season. But despite this idiomatic suggestion, we are reminded (the negative form provoking thoughts of what is "not") that it is unnatural to have flowers in September and in the house; they must sometime die, and they have reached a season for dying. As it will turn out, a man is lucky, not when he materially possesses flowers, but when he possesses an imagination for gentians even in winter.

This opening should recall the equally nonchalant "Snake":

A snake came to my water-trough
On a hot, hot day, and I in pyjamas for the heat,
To drink there.

(*CP,* p. 349)

We find the same juncture between the unceremonious ("I in pyjamas")
and the dangerous event ("A Snake came to my water-trough") through a
shared imperative (men and snakes must drink; men and gentians must
die). But the Lawrence of "Bavarian Gentians" acts upon the lesson learned
in "Snake," following the voices of imagination rather than those of education to find pleasure in the descent into a black hole. Whereas he must do
penance in "Snake" (recalling the Mariner's penance for the murder of an
albatross), in "Bavarian Gentians" he becomes the Mariner's docile, yearning wedding guest:

> *Reach me a gentian, give me a torch!*
> *let me guide myself with the blue, forked torch of this flower*
>
> . . . . .
>
> *among the splendor of torches of darkness, shedding darkness on the lost bride and*
>   *her groom.*

Lawrence first imagines, then demands, a torch for his journey, spinning
an elaborate conceit in which "darkness" becomes a metaphor for "light":

> *ribbed and torch-like, with their blaze of darkness spread blue . . .*
> *torch-flower of the blue-smoking darkness, Pluto's dark-blue daze,*
>
> . . . . .
>
> *. . . the sightless realm where darkness is awake upon the dark.*

There is little further detailing of what "falls away" and "vanishes." Without comment, Lawrence has remade the myth of Persephone's marriage
into his own myth of wedded opposites: "splendour of torches of darkness." This elaboration of images, moreover, creates the illusion of a journey that simply "comes to pass" as Lawrence described "The Work of Creation"; imagination in this poem is an urge in the flesh.

In the poem that follows, Lawrence nonetheless made certain that his
point about falling would be understood, glossing his great poem with the
brief "Lucifer" (no. 18). The very mention of Lucifer should remind us, if
we had forgotten it, that "Bavarian Gentians" takes place specifically "at
slow, sad Michaelmas," and that there is nothing sad in its determined neglect of the Christian archangel for the sake of Dis, pagan god of hell.
Lawrence revises Shakespeare also, taking the first line of "Lucifer" from
Macbeth:

> *Angels are bright still, though the brightest fell.*
> *But tell me, tell me, how do you know*
> *he lost any of his brightness in the falling?*   (*CP,* p. 697)

Malcolm's doubt of the loyal Macduff is shrugged off by Lawrence's doubt
about Malcolm's Christian values.

This poem's new myth of the fall ends in a curious shift of perspective from "Bavarian Gentians." Where in "Bavarian Gentians," Lawrence falls downward, in "Lucifer" he sees the fallen angel "coming like the ruby in the invisible dark, glowing / with his own annunciation, towards us." This shift "towards us" brings the triad of poems to a neat close, suggesting that no matter where it is positioned, imagination may spring with vanishings "into air," "down the darker and darker stairs," "towards us." In "Lucifer," we stand as if in hell, the lost bride and her groom watching the angel join us from above in a diabolical ascension. Satan descends into heaven.

"Lucifer" may be less imaginative than "Bavarian Gentians," even when imagination is defined in Lawrence's terms as the power to "see things happen," but it is a passionate thought, and its enlargement of "Bavarian Gentians" resembles the effect of Coleridge's glosses on the *Rime of the Ancient Mariner*. Omitting "Lucifer" and "Butterfly" as aspects of "Bavarian Gentians" would diminish the central poem. And the triad offers an example of the way poems work together throughout the sequence.

More of these poems—both those that present themselves as centrally "imaginative" and those that seem "thoughtful" or polemical—deserve the detailed critical attention a few have already received. In addition to the poems that attract commentary by standing in key positions like "The Greeks Are Coming!" (no. 1), "Demiurge" (no. 5), "Invocation to the Moon" (no. 15), "The Ship of Death" (no. 50), "Shadows" (no. 65), and "Phoenix" (no. 67), others reward the sort of scrutiny Sandra Gilbert gives to "Whales Weep Not!" (no. 14), and Michael Kirkham to "The Man of Tyre" (no. 12).[24] Such poems acted as the vehicle for Lawrence's strange urge to wrestle through his thoughts in a journey larger than any single poem could encompass.

Even the device of clustering poems into groups is employed here to imitate pagan consciousness. Although derived in part from his earlier experiments in *Pansies,* Lawrence's cluster effect in *Last Poems* reflects a process of cyclical thought that he describes in *Apocalypse.* He argues there that the sensual consciousness expresses itself in repetitive strands of imagery, not densely allegorical as in later Christian modifications, but a simple, lucid unraveling in a "rotational" movement: "every image fulfills its own little circle of action and meaning, then is superseded by another image" (*Apocalypse,* p. 52). To think as a pagan was to think in line and verse. This method differs from its counterpart in *Pansies* in being smoother, more expansive, more contemplative than the choppy, often cluttered repetitions of the earlier book. Lawrence's vision of gods, existence, evil, and death emerges in clearly pronounced stages and in a ritualistic progress that easily absorbs us—not scattering our attention:

The oracles . . . were supposed to deliver a set of images or symbols of the real dynamic value, which should set the emotional consciousness of the enquirer, as he pondered them, revolving more and more rapidly, till out of a state of intense emotional absorption the resolve at last formed; or, as we say, the decision was arrived at. As a matter of fact, we do very much the same in a crisis. When anything very important is to be decided we withdraw and ponder and ponder until the deep emotions are set working and revolving together, revolving, revolving, till a centre is formed and we "know what to do." (*Apocalypse*, pp. 50–51).

As opposed to the cerebral consciousness which insists upon an "on-and-on-and-on" logical chain, he creates a kinetic, associative form for the "emotional consciousness" (p. 54). The "crisis" of *Last Poems* is, of course, death. Its resolution is found by setting "the deep emotions . . . working and revolving together, revolving, revolving." In the crisis of dying, no "center" can quite be reached, and Lawrence will leave his sequence in mid-revolution, still preparing the way. In a sense this has been the case throughout his life and writing: the center vanished the moment it was reached, and a new cycle was begun. *Last Poems*, however, marks a special achievement. Having set aside most of the distancing techniques of narrative and the external structures of his more bookish designs, the device of rotational imagery permits him to move by the gesture of his own successive thoughts through

> *doors,*
> *in the great hush of going from this into that,*
> *in the suspension of wholeness, in the moment of division within the whole!*
> ("Silence," *CP*, p. 699)

As in *Pansies*, the process of revolution in *Last Poems* operates at every level, within the individual poem, knitting poems into groups, moving among groups. There are nine such groups, each linked by a narrative element or theological question, each blurring at its boundaries into the next. Groups develop in various ways and contain different numbers of poems. They may progressively enlarge an initial thought as in the first group, where a glimpse of Greek ships on the horizon unfolds into the vision of a host of gods disembarking. Or they may shift among closely related themes in subgroups, as in the second section (nos. 5–14), which begins in "Demiurge" with the idea of God as an "urge," shifts to the "body" of God in "Bodiless God" (no. 8), shifts again to two anecdotes of gods appearing to men ("Maximus" and "The Man of Tyre," nos. 11–12), and ends with two evocations of the "loveless," godly sea ("They Say the Sea Is Loveless" and "Whales Weep Not!" nos. 13–14). There is also oscillation in and among groups. The closing boundary of the third group merges with "The Breath of Life" and "Silence" (nos. 19, 20) into group four (from "The Hands of God" to "Lord's Prayer," nos. 21–28). "The Hands of God" is a demonic replica of "Bavarian Gentians":

> Did Lucifer fall through knowledge?
> oh then, pity him, pity him that plunge!
>
> Save me, O God, from falling into the ungodly knowledge.
>
>   . . . . .
>   sinking still, in depth after depth of disintegrative consciousness
> sinking.
>
> (CP, p. 699)

The group it represents alternates first between discussions of godly silence ("The Breath of Life," "Silence," "Pax," nos. 19–20, 22) and detachment from God in "abysmal" self-analysis ("The Hands of God," "Abysmal Immortality," "Only Man," nos. 21, 23–24), then between poems of the godly ("Return of Returns" and "Stoic," nos. 25–26) and the ungodly dead ("In the Cities," no. 27), to end with a revision of the Lord's Prayer:

> Give me, Oh give me
> besides my daily bread
> my kingdom, my power, and my glory.
>
> ("Lord's Prayer," no. 28, CP, p. 704)

Like the move from myth to gloss, from thought to seeing, this restlessness in theme and tone is part of the general motion of the sequence. At times it suggests the intimate connection Lawrence perceived between simple things and sublime knowledge (as in the disparities between "Butterfly" and "Bavarian Gentians"); at times it reflects his wrestle against everything "they say" (as in the shift from "Bavarian Gentians" to "Lucifer").

With the next group (nos. 29–32) we learn that this oscillation may be itself a divine operation of mind. Though structurally unlike the other poems of this group, "Mana of the Sea" (no. 29) stands at their head. Its rhetoric of reason is transformed into a rhetoric of wonder and then exaltation, until the poet sees in himself the sea.

> Do you see the sea, breaking . . .
> yet remaining unbroken . . . ?
>
> Have I caught from it
> the tide in my arms . . . ?
>
> Do the rollers of the sea
> roll down my thighs . . . ?

And is my body ocean, ocean . . . ?

I am the sea, I am the sea!

(CP, p. 705)

With "Salt" (no. 30), the poems become short, spare generalizations about the dualities embedded in the universe and mankind: "the two great and moving Ones, Fire and the yielding Wet" ("The Boundary Stone," no. 32, *CP*, p. 706), "the angels and the Sunderers," "the daimons and the demons" ("Kissing and Horrid Strife," no. 37, *CP*, p. 709). This group adds another premise to the major assertion of the second group, where Lawrence defined creation as a divine "urge." Consciousness is dual:

> *Life is for kissing and for horrid strife.*
> *Life is for the angels and the Sunderers.*
> *Life is for the daimons and the demons,*
> *those that put honey on our lips, and those that put salt.*

("Kissing and Horrid Strife," CP, p. 709)

The "twice godly" consciousness of *Last Poems* is for practical purposes indistinguishable from the "alternating consciousness" of *Pansies*. Creation is a god of mutations, changing back and forth between opposite versions of himself, one who reconciles and one who antagonizes. Lawrence's autobiographical portraiture, his typical method of portraying himself in agonistic strife, reveals itself in these poems for what it is: the creative self, both demon and man.

The caustic element in *Last Poems* more clearly resembles *Pansies* when the sequence nears its center. Acting as a pivot to the next group, "When Satan Fell" (no. 38) assures us that "Satan only fell to keep a balance." "But evil," he explains in the following piece, is "a third thing" (*CP*, p. 710). Eleven poems (nos. 39–49, "Doors" to "Departure") press into the nature of evil, strife, and murder. Like pithy manifestos, these poems redefine evil as belonging nowhere, without physical housing, centered in the soul of man, in his self-involvement and anxiety to be absolute, "sinless and stainless," and in his love of machines. When "Strife" (no. 45) is only a "thing of one," not two, it is evil (*CP*, p. 714), and—in "The Late War," "Murder," and "Murderous Weapons" (nos. 46–48)—results in murder. In "The Late War" (no. 46) men murder other, unfamiliar men, using guns and poison gas to level their victims unseen (*CP*, p. 715). Punctuating this group, only a few poems still urge otherwise: the heavens are not "a wheel"— rather, they wander, with "a footstep onwards" ("The Wandering Cosmos," no. 43, *CP*, p. 713); Lawrence asks the reader gently to "know thyself, and that thou art mortal" ("Death Is Not Evil, Evil Is Mechanical," no. 44, *CP,* p. 714); and he issues an imperative, "Now some men must get up and depart / from evil, or all is lost" ("Departure," no. 49, *CP,* p. 715). Lawrence does not directly condemn civilization, but the cumulative effect of his generalizations is a parting curse against modernity.

Then abruptly his criticism breaks, and he places "The Ship of Death" (no. 50) at the head of a mythological group of death poems (nos. 51–56). Had he lived longer, he might have plumped out this juncture with poems from *More Pansies.* As it stands, it is equally effective as a pause. The poet has fully met evil, writing in "Departure," the poem before "Ship of Death," that "Evil is upon us and has got hold of us" (*CP,* p. 716). With this he "departs," and in "The Ship of Death" he begins again to imagine. "The Ship of Death" and "The End, the Beginning" (no. 57) introduce the last two groups, foreseeing the journey into death and oblivion. The original version of "The Ship of Death" in *More Pansies,* as Elizabeth Cipolla and Gail Mandell have stressed, generated a number of poems that follow, creating its cluster. Mandell writes, "the manuscript B 'Ship of Death' becomes in its turn a protopoem for a cluster of related poems in manuscript A: 'Difficult Death,' 'All Souls' Day,' 'The Houseless Dead,' 'Beware the Unhappy Dead!' and 'After All Saints' Day,' poems that immediately follow 'The Ship of Death' in manuscript A."[25] In its final version "The Ship of Death" is itself a poem of poems, ten sections in length. Its ten sections tend to join into pairs, so that the poem develops symphonically in four or five movements.

This poem was the last, most monumental example of the way Lawrence built poems upon his own banalities and those of his predecessors. He makes the familiar slightly unpredictable, uncontrolled, to give what otherwise could be one more diatribe the quality of a search. Consider how the poem begins: "Now it is autumn and the falling fruit / and the long journey towards oblivion" (*CP,* p. 716). Nothing out of the ordinary in these ideas, the season named, the patent biblical allusion made, the Lawrencean theme stated. But when the naming of the season is followed, asyntactically, by a participial phrase modifying nothing but itself, its language seems unforeseen. The "falling fruit" silently drops its association with evil to become the metaphor for every man's "long journey towards oblivion," where man is as moldly as fruit. These two lines are almost unobtrusively enlarged by repetition of season, metaphor, and theme, in the lines that follow:

> *The apples falling like great drops of dew*
> *to bruise themselves an exit from themselves.*
>
> *And it is time to go, to bid farewell*

to one's own self, and find an exit
from the fallen self.

(*CP*, p. 716)

This "fallen self" has no more than the faintest connection with Christian ideas of wrongdoing; it is our decaying flesh.

Moving us then, expectantly, through the first two sections, Lawrence refreshes his unbiblical themes, familiar to anyone who read them in "New Heaven and Earth"; in section II, "The grim frost is at hand, when the apples will fall / thick, almost thundrous, on the hardened earth" (*CP*, p. 717). In sections III and IV he confronts Shakespeare, again choosing Hamlet's soliloquy as the overexposed piece he will wrestle with. Two lines that have become truisms to us, become assimilated into Lawrencean truisms through repetition:

III

And can a man his own quietus make
with a bare bodkin?

With daggers, bodkins, bullets, man can make
a bruise or break of exit for his life;
but is that a quietus, O tell me, is it quietus?

Surely not so! for how could murder, even self-murder
ever a quietus make?

IV

O let us talk of quiet that we know,
that we can know, the deep and lovely quiet
of a strong heart at peace!

How can we this, our own quietus, make?

This little killing of Shakespeare's famous words calls back to life Shakespeare's question, which Lawrence wishes to imagine his own, "How can we this, our own quietus, make?" Lawrence elides "quietus," "dagger," "bodkin," from their context in Hamlet's anxiety and transposes them into his; a speech that led to partial resolution for Hamlet, enters into Lawrence's. Little of substance has changed from one speech to the next, other than tone, from fearful worry to prayerful readiness. But this confrontation of parallel cases makes the difference all the greater. Lawrence will imagine a journey uncluttered by personalities, a lonely venture into death.

Here four sections pass with hardly a break as the poem approaches its climax, the moment of oblivion, "Nowhere!" (*CP*, p. 719). Lawrence makes the journey as lifelike as possible by drawing unimposing, coyly diminutive symbols from Etruscan culture, yet thoroughly ritualizing the mimesis of death: "Piecemeal the body dies. . . . We are dying, we are dying. . . . We are dying. . . . Now launch the small ship, now as the body dies" (*CP,* pp. 718–19). His Whitmanesque narrative and image are heightened against the sparest background to generate the impression of a life determinedly dropping away. These same techniques soften surprise, making it easy to imagine an apparition created entirely within the poem, the returning ship:

> *Wait, wait, the little ship*
> *drifting. . . .*
> *. . . the little ship wings home.*

> (*CP,* p. 720)

What fell away, returns.

Resorting to a Christian vocabulary even at the end, Lawrence jars again with Christianity, this time with the conception of the afterlife:

> *The flood subsides, and the body, like a worn sea-shell*
> *emerges strange and lovely.*
> *And the little ship wings home, faltering and lapsing*
> *on the pink flood,*
> *and the frail soul steps out, into her house again*
> *filling the heart with peace.*

> (*CP,* p. 720)

This passage describes both a sick man regaining consciousness and a vitalist dying and being reborn. Lawrence has avoided the Christian dichotomies—both body and soul are somehow flesh, and are equal agents. He imagines himself reincarnated, all his senses restored. If anything is added to his usual criticism of Christianity here, it is the revelation that the poet alone (he who thinks in images) may recreate himself.

The poems that follow (nos. 51–56) continue the "journey" of "The Ship of Death," extending it at first from the poet to others, "Be careful, then. . . . / For it is hard to die" ("All Souls' Day," no. 52, *CP,* p. 721). But because it is difficult for others, it is still more troublesome for him. Men do not help their dead die, "Beware the unhappy dead!" (no. 54). What begins in reassurance quickly changes into a pleading appeal, "Oh pity the dead" ("The Houseless Dead," no. 53, *CP,* p. 722), and the threat that, if we cannot feel pity, as in the war poems, the dead may breach our walls. This group closes with two slightly more optimistic poems, the first imagining the "slender soul" embarking ("After All Saints' Day," no. 55, *CP,* p. 723), the second urging us to "sing" with him the "Song of Death" (no. 56, *CP,* p. 723). Song will console the dead, if it first moves the living.

As if consoled, Lawrence shifts subject in the final group from the living dead to the "places" of oblivion on earth (nos. 57–65), and this more peaceful idea is explained in a series of shorter, more thoughtful pieces. One may forget everything and reawaken, as in sleep; to meet oblivion one must simply yield to God and to "not-knowing," blasphemous even to describe; one must build temples as well as ships, create places for oblivion on earth. The poem that closes the penultimate section, "Shadows" (no. 65), takes a second journey to oblivion. As in "The Ship of Death," Lawrence exploits his repetitions to imagine himself vanishing:

> *and then the softness of deep shadows folding, folding*
> *around my soul and spirit, around my lips*
> *so sweet, like a swoon, or more like the drowse of a low, sad song*
> *singing darker than the nightingale, on, on to the solstice.*
>
> (*CP*, p. 727)

But Lawrence still did not let himself or us go with this Keatsian dream. A set of pendants stands at the end of the *Last Poems* notebook, "Change" and "Phoenix," and these revive what is most difficult in the thought of death. Faintly echoing the provocative first lines of "Pomegranate" in *Birds, Beasts and Flowers*, the punchy three-line "Change" asks:

> *Do you think it is easy to change?*
> *Ah, it is very hard to change and be different.*
> *It means passing through the waters of oblivion.*
>
> (*CP*, p. 727)

The only consolation in these two poems is the hard fact of death. *Last Poems* works toward an end in which the poet, having stripped down to basic desires, may recover "with strands of down like floating ash"—the presumably happy moment of "Phoenix" (*CP*, p. 728). But in these last groups the experience of death is laced with needs unsatisfied, and we are forced to think of Lawrence in pain, caught in the interlude preceding death and rarely oblivious:

> *And we can be dying, dying, dying*
> *and longing utterly to die*
> *yet death will not come.*
>
> ("Difficult Death," no. 51, *CP*, p. 721)

The phoenix was practically Lawrence's trademark, representing the power for self-renewal, but the poem "Phoenix" does not invite us to a future paradise like that of the opening of *Last Poems:* "slim naked men from Cnossos, smiling the archaic smile / of those that will without fail come back again" ("Middle of the World," *CP*, p. 688). Aldington thought that "Prayer," the final poem in MS B, might have been the last poem Lawrence wrote (*CP*, p. 592). Although Aldington's guess could be right, the poem's imagery of moon and lion would place it in the third group of MS A. "Prayer," which ends unfinished with a comma (altered to a period in *CP*), is worth comparing with "Phoenix." It begins with a plea for cool lordliness, "O let my ankles be bathed in moonlight, that I may go / sure and moon-shod, cool and bright-footed"; it ends, facing an approaching fire, "For the sun is hostile, now / his face is like the red lion" (*CP*, p. 684), betraying the pain behind the myth. "Phoenix" wrestles more aggressively with pain, "burnt, burnt alive, burnt down," beginning with an unanswerable question, "Are you willing to be sponged out, erased, cancelled, / made nothing?" (*CP*, p. 728). And it confronts the reader, who must die or else "will never really change":

> The phoenix renews her youth
> only when she is burnt, burnt alive, burnt down
> to hot and flocculent ash.
> Then the small stirring of a new small bub in the nest
> with strands of down like floating ash
> shows that she is renewing her youth like the eagle,
> immortal bird.

Slight, redundant images of rebirth emerge, "the small stirring of a new small bub in the nest," then in the last two lines Lawrence gives up imagining the phoenix, praising her instead by comparing her to the eagle. While not reenforced elsewhere in *Last Poems* and likely to remind us of the tired eagle at the end of *Birds, Beasts and Flowers,* this last shift to yet another symbol—noble, lasting, and a bird—gives the poem a bluntly assertive ending. And while it is far less persuasive than "The Ship of Death" in suggesting that Lawrence actually changed, it is aimed more sharply at his reader, his most-desired opposite and object; like all his verse cycles, this one left its difficult propositions finally unbound.

—

CHAPTER SEVEN

Conclusion

Some final remarks about the scope and implications of my subject are in order, though these should not be substituted for the summary and methodological justification of the preface and chapter 1. Nearly half of this study is devoted to the books of *Rhyming Poems,* the early poetry of love, elegy, war, and the city: a body of work that has not received the kind of attention awarded to developmental periods in the careers of other major poets or to Lawrence's early novels. The last form this poetry took in the 1928 *Collected Poems* is in some ways an improvement on the original publications, especially in individual revisions, and when examined closely, volume 1 turns out to be a significant, imaginative work. But the rearrangement also obscured the nature of the earlier books, which were not all improved when merged in one collection. It is unfortunate even for prior versions of individual poems that these first books are not more readily available, for the final revisions disrupted and mixed different stages of style. Perhaps one day they may be reissued.

Making up less than half the poetry, the scope of these early books indicates how large the corpus actually is. Eight books, including *Collected Poems,* were published in Lawrence's lifetime, and the number of books of poetry is raised to twelve if we also count the unpublished "Bits," the poems of *The Plumed Serpent,* and the posthumously published books, *Nettles* and *Last Poems.* The juvenilia in many manuscripts, particularly in the extant notebooks, form another well of material, most of it now listed in the bibliographies of Lindeth Vasey and Carole Ferrier. General access to all that lies behind the books should soon be possible with publication of the Cambridge edition of the poems.

Close examination of the timing of Lawrence's poetic works indicates that while he was by no means the "spontaneous" writer he sometimes claimed to be, his reputation for writing rapidly is genuine. The speed of any particular production, or phase of production, however, is no key to its quality or importance in registering a new phase of thought or ability. The extent of the drafts, for example, in the *More Pansies* notebook alone suggests how much stands behind *Pansies,* but the enormous output of the last years could misleadingly suggest that these are less-considered works than they are. Like the four books of *Rhyming Poems,* collected from 1912 to 1919, the final works of 1927–30,—*Collected Poems, Pansies* and *Last Poems,*—are highly individual collections. Of course speed did not necessarily deliver a great book, if *Nettles* is any symptom. Lawrence wrote some of his most lasting pieces, nonetheless, under unusual conditions, rapidly and with a deceptively cavalier attitude. To cite yet another example, the production of "Poetry of the Present" was motivated by a letter from Benjamin Huebsch of 11 August 1919: "As [*New Poems*] is unprotected by copyright and may be reprinted by anyone who wishes to do so, I suggest that some slight change, substitution or addition be made; or you might include a short foreword if you can appropriately do so. This will make it possible to copyright the book because technically it becomes a different book than the one already published in England" (*Letters* 3 : 385 n. 2). Lawrence had received this letter by 23 August, when he wrote to Martin Secker with Huebsch's message. Six days later, Lawrence reported that "a little Preface" was ready. Written for the sake of the rights to the poetry and for financial reasons (subsequently he sold the essay to three different journals, *Voices, Playboy,* and *Evening Post Book Review*), "Poetry of the Present," is one of Lawrence's few significant statements on poetry, instantly recognized as such by the American reviewers of *New Poems* and widely quoted ever since.

The impressive scale of Lawrence's endeavors as a poet is not, of course, a measure of his excellence, though it should make one pause before judging him to be primarily a novelist. Since he began and ended his literary career writing poetry and composed books of poems along with the novels, it is clear that the poetry was prominent in his opinion, even when he judged the novel a higher form than "pietistic" verse ("The Novel" [1925], *Phoenix II,* p. 417). Given the range of his accomplishments in poetry, the diversity of subject and method, the number of effective poems from every period (when those periods are correctly understood), and his formal innovations especially in the development of the poetic sequence, Lawrence surely should be granted a larger place in the history of modern poetry. When a scholar can begin a summary essay with the comment that "as a poet, Lawrence had a high rate of failure," while believing that he is "the only English-born modernist poet of real importance to survive the First World War,"[1] then we should probably also ask that any reevaluation bring with it, if not a consistent description of his achievement, at least an intent reflection on the values that inform our readings of the poetry.

While working within Romantic traditions with which he felt wholly familiar, Lawrence was an eclectic and eccentric poet, shying away (audibly, for the most part) from the mainstream whenever he identified it. But time may show him thus more representative than others of the methods and concerns of his contemporaries. In evading what have since been gauged as the central habits of the literary modernists, Lawrence exhibits several modernist tendencies: to cut away from orthodox models, to vary stances, to search without rest for alternative modes of thought. Moreover, while shying away from received absolutes, from the good and true of yesterday, he nonetheless invested so entirely in his (modernist) counter-creeds, the imperfect, transient, and unknown, that these in turn became received absolutes in his writing. Perhaps as a result, Lawrence has since been used occasionally by new poets as a stick with which to beat both his contemporaries and their own drums. In the opinion of the editors of *Naked Poetry,* "nothing much new has happened in English poetry since Lawrence laid down his pen and died" (December 1968).[2] As opposed to the properties characteristic of "high" modernism—the cosmopolitan, masked, and apolitical; the complex, closed structures; the aggressive enlistment of a daunting tradition—we find in Lawrence a contrasting set: the local and plainspoken; lucid and "open" verse; the domestic and the political. But the debate goes on; we can overhear it, for example, in a preface by Donald Davie to the verse of Yvor Winters: "The fundamental distinction among English-language poets . . . is not any distinction between Romantic and Classicist, between rationalist and irrationalist, between a strict kind of formalist and the loose or "organic" kind. The fundamental, the radical split is between those who think that a poem is a considered utterance, and those who think it is unconsidered."[3] Davie then rebuilds this "fundamental distinction" into a defense of metered and rationalist verse. Though not "a strict kind of formalist" poetry, Lawrence's work was (as I believe I have demonstrated) amply "considered."

No matter how narrow his thoughts at any particular moment (and they appear most constricted when he was combatting what he perceived as the narrowness of others), Lawrence's recurrent stratagem was to awaken response, not to close it off, and this saved the literature he wrote from too much certainty. Neither madman nor messiah, he ranged freely between the poles he erected, unable or unwilling to take an easier path. One final case, an autobiographical account from the letters, is enough to suggest how and why there was no end to writing as long as Lawrence lived. In his well-known response to Jung (this might have been also to Freud, though Lawrence could not tolerate the tone Freud took), we catch him "in the middest":

> This Mother-incest idea can become an obsession. But it seems to me there is this much truth in it: that at certain periods the man has a desire and a tendency to return unto the woman, make her his goal and end, find his justification in her. In this way he casts himself as it were into her womb, and she, the Magna Mater, receives him with gratification. This is a kind of incest. . . . I have done it, and now struggle all my might to get out. In a way, Frieda is the devouring mother. —It is awfully hard, once the sex relation has gone this way, to recover. If we don't recover, we die. —But Frieda says I am antediluvian in my positive attitude. . . . [M]en must go ahead absolutely in front of their women, without turning round to ask for permission or approval from their women. (*Letters,* 3:301–2)

This letter is an admission of defeat and a renewed resolution. It is his "desire," his "goal and end" to return at times to his mother. But then, this is "a kind of incest" and must be combatted or "we die." Lawrence allows both needs, though they contradict each other. He is caught returning and leaving, never quite there or altogether apart. The mythic allusions refract his conflict: between the Magna Mater and Eurydice, who is Lawrence? These tendencies and identities are limited by what they cannot gain and where they cannot go; so was Lawrence, the man in the middle, always in relation to, rarely one with, his goal. Even death was a "passing through doors, / in the great hush of going from this into that" ("Silence," *CP,* p. 699). But this restlessness was not Lawrence's confusion or his sickness: it is a condition of our thought and a ground of our emotion.

Appendixes

Notes

Indexes

Order of poems in vol. I, *Rhyming Poems,* of *Collected Poems* (1928) and their order in the earlier books in which they first appeared

Order in *RP*	Poem title in *RP*	Earlier titles	Earlier placement		
1	"The Wild Common"		2	*AM*	33
2	"Dog-Tired"		24	*LP*	35
3	"From a College Window"		3	*NP*	35
4	"Discord in Childhood"		4	*AM*	36
5	"Cherry Robbers"		4	*LP*	36
6	"Dream-Confused"		19	*LP*	37
7	"Renascence"		23	*LP*	37
8	"Virgin Youth"		5	*AM*	38
9	"Study"		3	*AM*	40
10	"Twilight"	"Palimpsest of Twilight" (*NP*)	25	*NP*	41
11	"Love on the Farm"	"Cruelty and Love" (*LP*)	3	*LP*	42
12	"Gipsy"		12	*NP*	44
13	"The Collier's Wife"		28	*LP*	44
14	"Flapper"		4	*NP*	46
15	"Thief in the Night"		8	*NP*	46

NOTE: Column three provides titles of poems in earlier books when they were substantially different from those in *Rhyming Poems.* When titles vary only in spelling, capitalization, hyphenation, or definite and indefinite articles, I have supplied the final title as it appeared in *RP* in column one.

In column four, the number to the left of the book-title abbreviation refers to the position of the poem in that volume. The number that follows the title abbreviation refers to the page on which the poem appears in *Complete Poems.* Poems from earlier books that were dropped by Lawrence from *Rhyming Poems* include: "Song-Day in Autumn" (*LP,* no. 11); "Disagreeable Advice" (*AM,* no. 9; titled "Irony" in the American edition); "Restlessness" (*AM,* no. 22)—all these poems are inserted at the end of *Rhyming Poems* in Pinto and Roberts's edition of *Complete Poems.*

Order in *RP*	Poem title in *RP*	Earlier titles	Earlier placement		
16	"Monologue of a Mother"		6	*AM*	47
17	"The Little Town at Evening"		2	*B*	48
18	"In a Boat"		7	*AM*	48
19	"Last Hours"		3	*B*	49
20	"Flat Suburbs, S.W., in the Morning"		7	*NP*	50
21	"The Best of School"		31	*LP*	51
22	"Dreams Old and Nascent: Old"		10	*AM*	52
23	"Suburbs on a Hazy Day"		10	*NP*	53
24	"Weeknight Service"		8	*AM*	54
25	"A Man Who Died"	"Bitterness of Death" (*NP*)	32	*NP*	55
26	"Letter from Town: On a Grey Morning in March"	"Letter from Town: On a Grey Evening in March" (*NP*)	9	*NP*	57
27	"Letter from Town: The Almond-Tree"		6	*NP*	58
28	"Wedding Morn"		1	*LP*	58
29	"Violets"		26	*LP*	60
30	"Lightning"		10	*LP*	61
31	"End of Another Home Holiday"		7	*LP*	62
32	"Baby Running Barefoot"		14	*AM*	64
33	"Sigh No More"		15	*NP*	65
34	"Guards"		1	*B*	66
35	"Aware"		12	*LP*	67
36	"A Pang of Reminiscence"		13	*LP*	67
37	"A White Blossom"		14	*LP*	67
38	"Corot"		20	*LP*	68
39	"Michael Angelo"		25	*LP*	69
40	"Hyde Park at Night, Before the War: Clerks"		11	*NP*	70
41	"Piccadilly Circus at Night: Street-Walkers"		18	*NP*	70

Order in *RP*	Poem title in *RP*	Earlier titles	Earlier placement		
42	"After the Opera"		5	*B*	71
43	"Morning Work"		21	*LP*	72
44	"Transformations"		22	*LP*	72
45	"A Baby Asleep after Pain"		23	*AM*	73
46	"Last Lesson of the Afternoon"	"Afternoon in School" (*LP*)	32	*LP*	74
47	"School on the Outskirts"		28	*NP*	75
48	"A Snowy Day in School"		30	*LP*	75
49	"Whether or Not"		27	*LP*	76
50	"A Winter's Tale"		12	*AM*	85
51	"Return"		16	*LP*	85
52	"The Appeal"		17	*LP*	86
53	"Lilies in the Fire"		5	*LP*	86
54	"Red Moon-Rise"		15	*LP*	88
55	"Scent of Irises"		16	*AM*	90
56	"Forecast"	"Epilogue" (*AM*)	13	*AM*	91
57	"Prophet"		17	*AM*	91
58	"Discipline"		15	*AM*	92
59	"The Punisher"		25	*AM*	94
60	"Tease"		1	*AM*	95
61	"Mystery"		19	*AM*	96
62	"Repulsed"		18	*LP*	97
63	"Coldness in Love"		6	*LP*	98
64	"Suspense"	"Patience" (*AM*)	20	*AM*	99
65	"Endless Anxiety"	"Anxiety" (*AM*)	24	*AM*	100
66	"The End"		26	*AM*	100
67	"The Bride"		27	*AM*	101
68	"The Virgin Mother"		28	*AM*	101
69	"At the Window"		29	*AM*	102
70	"Reminder"		8	*LP*	103
71	"Drunk"		30	*AM*	104
72	"Sorrow"		31	*AM*	106
73	"Dolour of Autumn"		32	*AM*	107
74	"The Inheritance"		33	*AM*	108
75	"Silence"		34	*AM*	109

Order in *RP*	Poem title in *RP*	Earlier titles	Earlier placement		
76	"Listening"		35	*AM*	110
77	"Brooding Grief"		36	*AM*	110
78	"Last Words to Miriam"		18	*AM*	111
79	"Malade"		38	*AM*	112
80	"Lotus and Frost"	"Lotus Hurt by the Cold" (*AM*)	37	*AM*	113
81	"The Yew-Tree on the Downs"	"Liaison" (*AM*)	39	*AM*	113
82	"Troth with the Dead"		40	*AM*	114
83	"At a Loose End"	"Dissolute" (*AM*)	41	*AM*	115
84	"Submergence"		42	*AM*	115
85	"The Enkindled Spring"		43	*AM*	116
86	"Excursion Train"	"Excursion" (*AM*)	46	*AM*	116
87	"Release"	"Reproach" (*AM*)	44	*AM*	117
88	"These Clever Women"	"A Spiritual Woman" (*AM*)	48	*AM*	118
89	"Ballad of Another Ophelia"		21	*AM*	119
90	"Kisses in the Train"		2	*LP*	120
91	"Turned Down"	"Perfidy" (*AM*)	47	*AM*	121
92	"After Many Days"		52	*AM*	122
93	"Snap-Dragon"		54	*AM*	122
94	"Come Spring, Come Sorrow"	"Mating" (*AM*)	49	*AM*	126
95	"The Hands of the Betrothed"		45	*AM*	127
96	"A Love Song"		50	*AM*	129
97	"Twofold"		13	*NP*	129
98	"Tarantella"		19	*NP*	130
99	"Under the Oak"		14	*NP*	130
100	"Brother and Sister"		51	*AM*	131
101	"The Shadow of Death"	"Blue" (*AM*)	53	*AM*	132
102	"Birdcage Walk"		5	*NP*	133
103	"In Trouble and Shame"		56	*AM*	134
104	"Call into Death"	"Elegy" (*AM*)	57	*AM*	134
105	"Grey Evening"		58	*AM*	135

Order in *RP*	Poem title in *RP*	Earlier titles	Earlier placement		
106	"Firelight and Nightfall"		59	*AM*	135
107	"Blueness"	"The Mystic Blue" (*AM*)	60	*AM*	136
108	"A Passing-Bell"		55	*AM*	136
109	"The Drained Cup"		29	*LP*	137
110	"Late at Night"	"Phantasmagoria" (*NP*)	23	*NP*	140
111	"Next Morning"		24	*NP*	141
112	"Winter in the Boulevard"		27	*NP*	141
113	"Parliament Hill in the Evening"		17	*NP*	142
114	"Embankment at Night, Before the War: Charity"		22	*NP*	143
115	"Embankment at Night, Before the War: Outcasts"		26	*NP*	144
116	"Sickness"		29	*NP*	147
117	"In Church"		20	*NP*	147
118	"Piano"		21	*NP*	148
119	"The North Country"		31	*NP*	148
120	"Love Storm"		16	*NP*	149
121	"Passing Visit to Helen"	"Intime" (*NP*)	36	*NP*	150
122	"Twenty Years Ago"		35	*NP*	152
123	"Reading a Letter"		34	*NP*	152
124	"Seven Seals"		33	*NP*	153
125	"Two Wives"		37	*NP*	154
126	"Noise of Battle"	"Apprehension" (*NP*)	1	*NP*	159
127	"At the Front"	"Heimweh" (*NP*)	38	*NP*	159
128	"Reality of Peace, 1916"	"Débâcle" (*NP*)	39	*NP*	160
129	"Narcissus"		40	*NP*	161
130	"Tommies in the Train"		16	*B*	162
131	"On the March"		7	*B*	163
132	"Ruination"		14	*B*	164
133	"The Attack"		10	*B*	164
134	"Winter-Lull"		9	*B*	165

Order in *RP*	Poem title in *RP*	Earlier titles	Earlier placement		
135	"Bombardment"		8	*B*	166
136	"Rondeau of a Conscientious Objector"		15	*B*	167
137	"Obsequial Ode"		11	*B*	167
138	"Going Back"		6	*B*	169
139	"Shades"		12	*B*	169
140	"Town in 1917"	"Town" (*B*)	4	*B*	170
141	"Bread upon the Waters"		13	*B*	171
142	"War-Baby"		17	*B*	172
143	"Nostalgia"		18	*B*	172
144	"Dreams Old and Nascent: Nascent"		11	*AM*	173
145	"On That Day"		42	*NP*	176
146	"Autumn Sunshine"		41	*NP*	177

Transcription of holograph list of poems as they appear in vol. 1, *Rhyming Poems,* of *Collected Poems* (1928) (Ferrier MS 71; Vasey MS E214b)

A list of titles for *Rhyming Poems,* vol. 1 of *Collected Poems* (1928), appears in Lawrence's hand and in his own copy of *Love Poems and Others.* Lawrence developed this numerical list in November 1927 to January 1928 when preparing his *Collected Poems.* The list is now held by the Poetry/Rare Book Collection of Lockwood Memorial Library at SUNY, Buffalo.

No attempt has been made to reproduce the position of columns in relation to the original pages of *Love Poems and Others.* The different sections of the list are designated by page number (the holograph occupies four pages of the book) and column number (seven columns altogether), and descriptions of these pages, including any additional autograph markings, are presented at the beginning of each designated page. Several types of erasure occur in Lawrence's penciled list. He sometimes erased a group of titles without rubbing out the numbers assigned to each, then wrote in fresh titles; when the latter group exceeded the former in size, the titles no longer corresponded exactly to their numbered positions. These areas of erasure are indicated to the right of the list by vertical brackets. In addition, whole titles or parts of titles are often still visible despite erasure, and these are marked by angle brackets, as in ⟨Red Moon-rise⟩. If a gap is left in the document by erasure, but the words erased are illegible, this is marked ⟨*illeg.*⟩. Titles that are crossed out rather than erased are indicated as in ~~Dog tired.~~ If Lawrence wrote titles above, below, or beside these cancellations, their approximate positions are indicated accordingly. In two cases, however, an erased title can be read underneath its substitution, and here the new title appears above the erased title. In two other instances, Lawrence canceled a title, then decided to retain it and did so by writing the words over again in bold pencil; these are designated in bold letters. He usually altered numbers, not by erasure or through cancellation, but by superimposing a new number on the old. These are indicated in the transcription by a slash through the original number, and its replacement positioned directly above

(e.g., 1$\overset{2}{/}$).

All marginal notations in italics are editorial. Any other markings not mentioned here (arrows, balloons, underlinings) are Lawrence's.

PAGE I. COLUMN I.

[This is the verso of title page—representing p. iv in the front matter—and precedes the first contents page. At center of page is the inscription: "Several of these Poems have appeared in the 'English Review,' the 'Nation,' and the 'Westminster Gazette.'" Column I stands to the left of this inscription; column 2 stands to its right.]

    The Wild Common
  1. ~~Dog-tired~~
    Dog Tired
  2. ~~The Wild Common~~
    From a College Window
  3. ~~Study~~
    Discord in Childhood
  4. ~~Monologue of a Mother~~
  5. Cherry robbers
    Dream-Confused
  6. ~~Discord in Childhood~~
  7. Renascence
  8. Virgin Youth
    Study
  9. ~~From a College Window~~   New P
    Twilight ~~at home~~
10 ~~Palimpsest of twilight~~   "
11 Cruelty & Love

2
1~~1~~ Gipsy   ⟨stet⟩
  A Collier's Wife
    Flapper

3
1~~2~~ Thief in the Night
    Monologue of a Mother
        ⟨other⟩   *erasure*
                                        under list
4
1~~3~~ Little Town at Evening
        ⟨ing⟩
14. In a Boat

15 Last Hours
    Flat Suburbs S.W.   *erasure*
15. The Best of School   *under*
      Dreams Old   *list*
16 ~~Dreams Nascent~~ ⟨SW⟩
17. Suburbs on a Hazy day ⟨Day (New Poems)⟩
 8
17 Weeknight Service   ⟨ing⟩
19 A Man Who Died   ⟨ing⟩
20 Letter from Town—on a Grey Evening
21   "   "   "   The Almond Tree   ⟨NP⟩⟩
 2
21 Wedding-Morn
23 Violets
24 Lightning
25 End of Another Home Holiday
26 A Baby Running Barefoot
 7
26 Sigh no More
 8
27 Guards
 9
28 Aware   ~~Flapper~~
30
29 A Pang of Reminiscence
 1
30 A White Blossom
 2
31 Corot

PAGE 1. COLUMN 2.

 3
31 Michael Angelo
    Hyde Park at Night: Clerks
 4
33 Piccadilly Circus at Night   *erasure*
 5
34 After the Opera   *under*
    Morning Work
    ⟨Transformations⟩   *list*
 6
35 Transformations

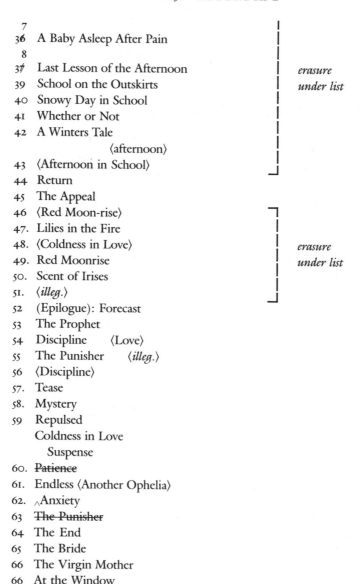

7
36 A Baby Asleep After Pain
8
37 Last Lesson of the Afternoon | *erasure*
39 School on the Outskirts | *under list*
40 Snowy Day in School
41 Whether or Not
42 A Winters Tale
                    ⟨afternoon⟩
43 ⟨Afternoon in School⟩
44 Return
45 The Appeal
46 ⟨Red Moon-rise⟩
47. Lilies in the Fire
48. ⟨Coldness in Love⟩   *erasure*
49. Red Moonrise   *under list*
50. Scent of Irises
51. ⟨*illeg.*⟩
52 (Epilogue): Forecast
53 The Prophet
54 Discipline   ⟨Love⟩
55 The Punisher   ⟨*illeg.*⟩
56 ⟨Discipline⟩
57. Tease
58. Mystery
59 Repulsed
     Coldness in Love
        Suspense
60. ~~Patience~~
61. Endless ⟨Another Ophelia⟩
62. ∧Anxiety
63 ~~The Punisher~~
64 The End
65 The Bride
66 The Virgin Mother
66 At the Window

PAGE 2. COLUMN 3.

[Table of Contents for *Love Poems and Others* (p. v of front matter): Lawrence has ticked all titles except "Wedding Morn," "Kisses in the Train," "Bei Hennef," and "Song-Day in Autumn" (his motives here are unclear: "Wedding Morn" and "Kisses in the Train" do appear in the list, though "Bei Hennef" and "Song-Day in Autumn" do not); he has crossed out "Bei Hennef" and "Song-Day in Autumn"; next to "Reminder" he has written, "Do you remember / How night after night." A single handwritten column of numbered titles appears in the righthand margin—squeezed next to the page numbers of the published contents for *LP*.]

67   Reminder
68   Drunk
69   Sorrow
70   Dolor of Autumn
71   The Inheritance
72. Silence
73   Listening
74   Brooding Grief
75   Last Words to Miriam
76   Malade
77   ~~The North Countrie~~
78. Lotus Hurt by the Cold
        Yew Trees
79   ~~Liaison~~
80   Troth with the Dead
81. Dissolute
82   Submergence
83. The Enkindled Spring
        ~~Another Ophelia~~
84   Excursion
85   Release
86   ~~A Spiritual~~   e
        These Clever Woman
        Another Ophelia
87   Kisses in the train
        Turned down
88   ~~Perfidy~~
89   After Many Days
90
8~~9~~   Snapdragon
  1
9~~6~~   Mating
  2
9~~1~~   The Hands of the Betrothed
  3
9~~2~~   A Love Song

4
9̸3 Two-fold
   Tarantella

5
94 Under the Oak
   Brother & Sister

PAGE 3. COLUMN 4.

[Second page of printed contents—representing p. vi of front matter—for *Love Poems and Others:* Lawrence has ticked off all titles. Autograph columns 4 and 5 appear below printed contents, though slightly overlapping with the last two printed titles, "II. The Best of School" and "III. Afternoon in School."]

⌐   Birdcage Walk
⌐95 Shadow of Death
   6
   9̸6 ~~Blueness~~
   97 In Trouble & Shame
        Call into Death
   98 ~~Elegy~~
   99 Grey Evening
  100 Firelight & Nightfall
        Blueness
  101 ~~The Mystic Blue~~
  102 A Passing Bell
  103 The Drained Cup (Dialect)
        Coming Home in the Night
  104 ~~Phantasmagoria~~   ⌐
  105. Next Morning | *erasure*
  106 Winter in the Bvd | *under*
        Parliament Hill | *list*
  107. ⟨Hyde Park at Night⟩ |
  108 ⟨Piccadilly Circus at Night⟩ |
  109 Embankment at Night Charity   ⌐
  110 ⟨Phantasmagoria⟩
  111. ⟨Next Morning⟩
  112 Embankment—Outcasts
  113 Sickness

PAGE 3. COLUMN 5.

In Church
Piano
The North Countrie
Love Storm
114   A Passing Visit (~~Intime~~)
115.   Twenty Years Ago
Reading a Letter
~~Apprehension~~   Noise of Battle
116   Seven Seals
                    Two Wives
            At the Front
117   ~~Heimweh~~
            Reality of Peace 1916
118   ~~Debacle~~
119   Narcissus
120   ~~Autumn Sunshine~~
121   ~~On That Day~~
            ~~Love Storm~~
            ~~Reading a Letter~~
            ~~Sigh no More~~

            ~~Apprehension~~
Tommies in the Train
On the March
Ruination
The Attack
Winter Lull
Bombardment
Rondeau of a Conscientious Objector
Obsequial Ode
Going Back
Shades

PAGE 4. COLUMN 6.

[This page represents p. 1 of the book: on it are printed the first three stanzas plus two lines of the poem "Wedding Morn." Below this poem appear two short handwritten columns.]

Town in 1917
Bread upon the Waters

War Baby
Nostalgia
Dreams Nascent

PAGE 4. COLUMN 7.

On That Day
Autumn Sunshine

Notes

Preface

1. I. A. Richards, *Practical Criticism* (New York: Harcourt, Brace, 1929), p. 108.

2. D. H. Lawrence, *Etruscan Places,* in *Mornings in Mexico and Etruscan Places* (1927, 1932; rpt. London: Penguin, 1971), p. 168. Subsequent page references will be to this edition and will be cited in the text. *Etruscan Places* copyright © 1972 by The Viking Press, Inc.; copyright 1921 by Thomas Seltzer, Inc.; copyright renewed 1949 by Frieda Lawrence. Reprinted by permission of Laurence Pollinger Ltd., the Estate of Mrs. Frieda Lawrence Ravagli, and Viking Penguin, Inc. Excerpts from *Mornings in Mexico* are quoted by permission of Laurence Pollinger Ltd., the Estate of Mrs. Frieda Lawrence Ravagli, and Alfred A. Knopf, Inc.

3. *The Letters of D. H. Lawrence,* vol. 2 (Cambridge: Cambridge University Press, 1981), p. 243. Citations of D. H. Lawrence's letters prior to July 1921 will refer to the Cambridge edition: vol. 1, Sept. 1901–May 1913, ed. James Boulton (1979); vol. 2, June 1913–Oct. 1916, ed. George Zytaruk and James Boulton (1981); vol. 3, Oct. 1916–June 1921, ed. James Boulton and Andrew Robertson (1984). After that date, citations of Lawrence's letters will refer to *The Collected Letters of D. H. Lawrence,* vol. 2, ed. Harry T. Moore (New York: Viking, 1962), unless otherwise noted. Subsequent page references for these sources will be cited in the text. *The Letters of D. H. Lawrence:* vol. 1, copyright © 1979; vol. 2, copyright © 1981; vol. 3, copyright © 1984. All copyrights held by Cambridge University Press, Laurence Pollinger Ltd., and the Estate of Mrs. Frieda Lawrence Ravagli; excerpts here are reprinted with their permission. Excerpts from *The Collected Letters of D. H. Lawrence,* Volume 2, edited by Harry T. Moore, copyright © 1962 by Angelo Ravagli, and C. Montague Weekley, Executors of the Estate of Frieda Lawrence Ravagli; copyright 1932 by the Estate of D. H. Lawrence, and 1934 by Frieda Lawrence; copyright © 1933, 1948, 1953, 1954, and each year 1956–1962 by Angelo Ravagli and C. Montague Weekley, Executors of the Estate of Frieda Lawrence Ravagli. Reprinted by permission of Laurence Pollinger Ltd., the Estate of Mrs. Frieda Lawrence Ravagli, and Viking Penguin, Inc.

4. "Study of Thomas Hardy," in *Phoenix: The Posthumous Papers of D. H. Lawrence,* ed. Edward D. McDonald (New York: Penguin, 1978), pp. 448–51. Subsequent page references from this volume will be cited in the text. Excerpts from "Pornography and Obscenity" (1929; rpt. in *Phoenix,* 1936), by D. H. Lawrence, copyright © 1930 by Alfred A. Knopf, Inc.; reprinted by permission. All other

excerpts from *Phoenix, The Posthumous Papers* (1936), by D. H. Lawrence, edited and with an introduction by Edward D. McDonald. Copyright 1936 by Frieda Lawrence, renewed © 1964 by the Estate of the late Frieda Lawrence Ravagli. Reprinted by permission of Laurence Pollinger Ltd., the Estate of Mrs. Frieda Lawrence Ravagli, and Viking Penguin, Inc.

5. Paul Zietlow, *Moments of Vision* (Cambridge: Harvard University Press, 1974), ix.

6. D. H. Lawrence, *The Complete Poems of D. H. Lawrence,* ed. Vivian de Sola Pinto and Warren Roberts (1964, corrected 1971; rpt., New York: Penguin, 1977), p. 720 (see also D. H. Lawrence, *Collected Poems,* 2 vols. [London: Martin Secker, 1928]). The citations that follow of Lawrence's poems and of the prose works that have been reprinted in *Complete Poems* will refer to the Pinto and Roberts edition (*CP*) unless otherwise indicated, and page numbers will be noted in the text.

Excerpts from *The Complete Poems of D. H. Lawrence,* collected and edited, with an introduction and notes by, Vivian de Sola Pinto and F. Warren Roberts, copyright © 1964, 1971 by Angelo Ravagli and C. M. Weekley, Executors of the Estate of Frieda Lawrence Ravagli. Introduction and notes copyright © 1964 by William Heinemann Ltd. Reprinted by permission of Laurence Pollinger Ltd., the Estate of Mrs. Frieda Lawrence Ravagli, and Viking Penguin, Inc.

Chapter One

1. R. P. Blackmur, "D. H. Lawrence and Expressive Form," *Form and Value in Modern Poetry* (New York: Doubleday, 1952), p. 255; Vivian de Sola Pinto, Introduction, in Lawrence, *Complete Poems,* pp. 1–10; Sandra Gilbert, *Acts of Attention: The Poems of D. H. Lawrence* (Ithaca, N.Y.: Cornell University Press, 1972), pp. 21–24; Harold Bloom, "Lawrence, Blackmur, Eliot, and the Tortoise," *A D. H. Lawrence Miscellaney,* ed. Harry T. Moore (Carbondale: Southern Illinois Press, 1959), pp. 360–69.

2. Gail Porter Mandell, *The Phoenix Paradox: A Study of Renewal through Change in the Collected Poems and Last Poems of D. H. Lawrence* (Carbondale: Southern Illinois Press, 1984). Any study of autobiographical methods, must, today, acknowledge the theoretical literature, growing increasingly abundant in books and periodical issues, represented by the collection, for example, of James Olney, ed., *Autobiography: Essays Theoretical and Critical* (Princeton, N.J.: Princeton University Press, 1980), or of *New Literary History* 9 (Autumn 1977). Among Lawrence studies, which frequently include biographical discussions, should be counted essays or chapters that have appeared in other contexts, for example, in Leo Bersani, *A Future for Astyanax* (Boston: Little, Brown, 1976); Robert Kiely, *Beyond Egotism: The Fiction of James Joyce, Virginia Woolf, and D. H. Lawrence* (Cambridge: Harvard University Press, 1980); Robert Langbaum, *The Mysteries of Identity: A Theme in Modern Literature* (New York: Oxford University Press, 1977); and Garrett Stewart, "Lawrence, 'Being,' and the Allotropic Style," in *Towards a Poetics of Fiction,* ed. Mark Spilka (Bloomington: Indiana University Press, 1977), pp. 331–56.

3. Sandra Gilbert, "Hell on Earth: *Birds, Beasts and Flowers* as Subversive Narrative," *D. H. Lawrence Review* 12 (1979): 256–74; Ross Murfin, *The Poetry of D. H. Lawrence: Texts and Contexts* (Lincoln: University of Nebraska Press, 1983), pp. vii–xiii.

4. See T. S. Eliot, *After Strange Gods* (New York: Harcourt, Brace, 1934), pp. 41–42, 63–66; W. H. Auden, "D. H. Lawrence," *The Dyer's Hand and Other Essays* (New York: Random House, 1962), p. 278; Blackmur, "D. H. Lawrence"; Bloom, "Lawrence."

5. For detailed discussions of the analogies between Whitman's works and Lawrence's, see James Miller, Karl Shapiro, Bernice Slote, *Start with the Sun: Studies in the Whitman Tradition* (Lincoln: University of Nebraska Press, 1963). See also John Colmer, "Lawrence and Blake," and Roberts W. French, "Whitman and the Poetics of Lawrence," in *D. H. Lawrence and Tradition*, ed. Jeffrey Meyers (London: Athlone, 1985), pp. 9–20, 91–114.

6. D. H. Lawrence, "Whitman," *Studies in Classic American Literature* (1923; rpt., New York: Penguin, 1977), pp. 171–87. Subsequent page references will be to this edition and will be cited in the text.

Excerpts from *Studies in Classic American Literature*, by D. H. Lawrence, copyright 1923, 1950 by Frieda Lawrence; copyright © 1961 by the Estate of the late Mrs. Frieda Lawrence. Reprinted by permission of Laurence Pollinger Ltd., the Estate of Mrs. Frieda Lawrence Ravagli and Viking Penguin, Inc.

7. Walt Whitman, *Leaves of Grass, Comprehensive Reader's Edition*, ed. Harold W. Blodgett and Sculley Bradley (New York: New York University Press, 1965), p. ix. Copyright © 1965 by New York University Press; reprinted by permission.

8. D. H. Lawrence, *Sons and Lovers*, (1913; rpt., New York: Penguin, 1977), p. 148. Subsequent page references will be to this edition and will be cited in the text.

Excerpts from *Sons and Lovers*, by D. H. Lawrence, copyright 1913 by Thomas Seltzer, Inc. All rights reserved. Reprinted by permission of Viking Penguin, Inc., Laurence Pollinger Ltd., and the Estate of Mrs. Frieda Lawrence Ravagli.

9. D. H. Lawrence, *Fantasia of the Unconscious*, in *Fantasia of the Unconscious and Psychoanalysis and the Unconscious* (1923, 1921; rpt., London: Penguin, 1977), p. 15; *Letters*, 1:544. Subsequent citations of *Fantasia* and *Psychoanalysis* will be to this edition and page numbers will be cited in the text.

As Keith Cushman has expressed this, "each work, whether expository or purely imaginative, as it succeeds its predecessor is an attempt to explore and annex new territory. Each new territory then provides a starting point for further exploration," in *D. H. Lawrence at Work: The Emergence of the Prussian Officer Stories* (Charlottesville: University Press of Virginia, 1978), p. 23.

Excerpts from *Fantasia of the Unconscious*, by D..H. Lawrence, copyright 1922 by Thomas Seltzer, Inc.; copyright renewed 1950 by Frieda Lawrence. Reprinted by permission of Laurence Pollinger Ltd., the Estate of Mrs. Frieda Lawrence Ravagli, and Viking Penguin, Inc.

10. Lawrence's sequences may be contrasted with Yeats's more esoteric books: see Hugh Kenner's "The Sacred Book of the Arts," in *Yeats: A Collection of Critical Essays*, ed. John Unterecker (Englewood Cliffs, N.J.: Prentice-Hall, 1963), pp. 10–22. For a general discussion of verse sequences, see M. L. Rosenthal and Sally Gall, *The Modern Poetic Sequence* (New York: Oxford University Press, 1983).

11. This document is described by Carole Ferrier as MS 71, in her "D. H. Lawrence's Poetry, 1920–1928: A Descriptive Bibliography of Manuscripts, Typescripts, and Proofs," *D. H. Lawrence Review* 12 (1979): 294, 299; and is listed as MS E214b by Lindeth Vasey, comp., "E. Manuscripts," in Warren Roberts, *A Bibliography of D. H. Lawrence*, 2d ed. (Cambridge: Cambridge University Press, 1982),

p. 478; no other scholar has cited this manuscript. A transcription of this holograph list of poems may be found in Appendix B. For permission to transcribe this document, I wish to thank Dr. Warren Roberts, Laurence Pollinger Ltd., and the Estate of Mrs. Frieda Lawrence Ravagli.

12. Mandell, *The Phoenix Paradox,* pp. 45–53, 144–45.

13. Lawrence Lipking, *The Life of the Poet: Beginning and Ending Poetic Careers* (Chicago: University of Chicago Press, 1981), pp. xii–xiii.

14. These comments may be found in mixed forms: for example, in the essays of A. Alvarez, "D. H. Lawrence: The Single State of Man," in his *Stewards of Excellence* (New York: Charles Scribner's Sons, 1958), pp. 140–61; Richard Ellmann, "Barbed Wire and Coming Through," in *The Achievement of D. H. Lawrence,* ed. Frederick Hoffman and Harry T. Moore (Norman: University of Oklahoma Press, 1953), pp. 253–67; Ronald Draper, *D. H. Lawrence* (New York: Twayne, 1964), pp. 149–60; Horace Gregory, *Pilgrim of the Apocalypse* (New York: Viking, 1933), pp. 3–16, 103–11; Graham Hough, *The Dark Sun* (London: Duckworth, 1956), pp. 191–216; Edward Lucie-Smith, "The Poetry of D. H. Lawrence—with a Glance at Shelley," in *D. H. Lawrence: Novelist, Poet, Prophet,* ed. Stephen Spender (New York: Harper & Row, 1973), pp. 224–33.

15. Ellmann, "Barbed Wire," p. 261.

16. Ibid., p. 264.

17. Draper, *D. H. Lawrence,* p. 153.

18. Jonathan Culler, *Structuralist Poetics* (Ithaca, N.Y.: Cornell University Press, 1975), pp. 164–70.

19. Auden, "D. H. Lawrence," p. 285.

20. Gregory, *Pilgrim of the Apocalypse,* p. 110.

21. Alvarez, "D. H. Lawrence," p. 158.

22. Gilbert, *Acts of Attention,* p. 6.

Chapter Two

1. Lawrence revised many poems in 1912 to sharpen their form and create more powerful narratives of conflict between men and women: see E. W. Tedlock, *The Frieda Lawrence Collection of D. H. Lawrence Manuscripts: A Descriptive Bibiliography* (Albuquerque: University of New Mexico Press, 1948), pp. 82–85. Mandell touches on some of these when she examines the incorporation of *Love Poems and Others* into *Collected Poems,* but her suggestion that the 1928 revisions "clarified" the conflicts of school poems (like "A Snowy Day in School") and love lyrics (such as "Lightning") is vague and even misleading (*The Phoenix Paradox,* pp. 55–56, 68–71). Lawrence's shift toward a poetry of conflict occurred early in his career; his later work resulted in further intensification and in subtle alterations of doctrine, including another stage of revisions in 1916–18, deserving more scrupulous study than they have received. Such a study will become feasible with the publication of the Cambridge University Press variorum edition of Carole Ferrier and Christopher Pollnitz. In the meantime, reference may be made to all stages of the pre-1920 poetry in Carole Ferrier, "The Earlier Poetry of D. H. Lawrence: A Variorum Text," Ph.D. diss., University of Auckland, 1971.

2. Lawrence's two college notebooks will be noted hereafter in the text as Ferrier MS 1, Vasey MS E317, and Ferrier MS 5, Vasey MS E320.1. For descriptions of

these and other early manuscripts, see Carole Ferrier, "D. H. Lawrence's Pre-1920 Poetry: A Descriptive Bibliography of Manuscripts, Typescripts, and Proofs," *D.H. Lawrence Review* 6 (1973): 333–59, and her "variorum" pp. 4–46; see also Vasey, "E. Manuscripts," pp. 431–540. Transcriptions of the manuscript sequences "Transformations," "Movements," and "A Life History in Harmonies and Discords" appear in Appendix I of my dissertation, "The Story of the Poetry: D. H. Lawrence's Struggle to Come Through," (Princeton University, 1982).

Egon Tiedje believes that Lawrence recorded poems in a roughly chronological sequence in his first college notebook (Vasey MS E317); see Tiedje "D. H. Lawrence's Early Poetry: The Composition-Dates of the Drafts in MS E317," *D.H. Lawrence Review* 4 (1971): 227–52. Carole Ferrier writes persuasively in rebuttal that since "none of the poems in MS E317 are in their first state (for, as Tiedje recognizes, it is plain that the notebook was used for the recording of fair copies), a dating of the drafts in the state in which they appear in MS E317 largely on the basis of biographical information must be misleading" (Carole Ferrier and Egon Tiedje, "D. H. Lawrence's Pre-1920 Poetry: The Textual Approach: An Exchange," *D.H. Lawrence Review* 5 [1972]: 149–50). Note, too, that the order of poems in both college notebooks (Vasey MS E317 and MS E320.1) has almost no correlation to the order in any of the books in which these poems reappeared.

3. Jessie Chambers, *D.H. Lawrence: A Personal Record by E. T.,* 2d ed., ed. J. D. Chambers (1935; rpt., New York: Barnes & Noble, 1965), p. 57.

4. Harry T. Moore, *The Priest of Love* (New York: Farrar, Straus and Giroux, 1974), p. 106. When Austin Harrison succeeded Hueffer as editor of the *English Review,* Lawrence published more poems there, including a small group entitled "Night Songs," but as Ferrier notes in her "variorum," Lawrence did not approve of Harrison's choices (p. 17), and he made no attempt to preserve these combinations. See "C4" in Roberts, *Bibliography,* p. 323.

5. D. H. Lawrence, *Women in Love* (1920, rpt., New York: Penguin, 1976, 1978), pp. 29–30, 122. Subsequent page references will be to this edition and will be cited in the text.

Excerpts from *Women in Love,* by D. H. Lawrence, copyright 1920, 1922 by D. H. Lawrence; renewed 1948, 1950 by Frieda Lawrence. Reprinted by permission of Laurence Pollinger Ltd., the Estate of Mrs. Frieda Lawrence Ravagli, and Viking Penguin, Inc.

6. "Art and the Individual," in *Phoenix II: Uncollected, Unpublished, and Other Prose Works by D.H. Lawrence,* ed. Warren Roberts and Harry T. Moore (New York: Penguin, 1978), pp. 221, 226. Citations to this source will hereafter be given in text.

Excerpts from *Phoenix II, Uncollected Papers of D. H. Lawrence,* edited by F. Warren Roberts and Harry T. Moore, copyright © 1959, 1963, 1968 by the Estate of Frieda Lawrence Ravagli. Reprinted by permission of Laurence Pollinger Ltd., the Estate of Mrs. Frieda Lawrence Ravagli, and Viking Penguin, Inc.

7. Richard Aldington originally called attention to the influence on Lawrence's poetry of Buddhist doctrine (for example, on "Dreams . . . Nascent" and "Corot") in *D. H. Lawrence: Portrait of a Genius but . . .* (New York: Duell, Sloan and Pearce, 1950), p. 88.

8. A transcription of the titles in the manuscript sequence "Transformations" is listed in Ferrier, "D. H. Lawrence's Pre-1920 Poetry," pp. 345–46 (final titles and the position numbers of the poems in *Collected Poems* follow in parentheses):

  1. "Evening" (no. 113, "Parliament Hill in the Evening")
  2. "Morning" (no. 20, "Flat Suburbs, S.W., in the Morning")
  3. "Men in the Morning" (no. 43, "Morning Work")
  4. "The Inanimate that Changes Not in Shape"
     "Oh stiffly shapen houses that change not . . ." (no. 23, "Suburbs on a Hazy Day")
     "The Town" (no. 44, "Transformations: I. The Town")
     "The Earth" (no. 44, "Transformations: II. The Earth")
  5. "The Changeful Animate / Men Whose Shape is Multiform" (no. 44, "Transformations: III. Men")
  6. "Corot" (no. 38, "Corot")
  7. "Raphael" (no. 39, "Michael Angelo").

See Appendix A for order of these poems in *Collected Poems* (1928).
   9. From MS E320.1, privately owned; see Ferrier, "variorum," nos. 113 and 23. All transcriptions of manuscript poems are checked against Ferrier's readings, and since her edition forms the basis for the Cambridge edition soon to be published, reference is made to her dissertation. Quoted by permission of Laurence Pollinger Ltd. and the Estate of Mrs. Frieda Lawrence Ravagli.
   10. A transcription of the titles in the manuscript sequence "Movements" is listed in Ferrier, "D. H. Lawrence's Pre-1920 Poetry," p. 342 (final titles and the position numbers of the poems in *Collected Poems* followed in parentheses):

  1. "A Baby Running Barefoot" (no. 32, "Baby Running Barefoot")
  2. "A Baby Asleep after Pain" (no. 45, [same title])
  3. "The Body Awake" (no. 8, "Virgin Youth")
  4. "A Man at Play on the River" (not published by Lawrence)
  5. "The Review of the Scots Guards" (no. 34, "Guards").

See Appendix A for order of these poems in *Collected Poems* (1928).
   11. D. H. Lawrence, *The White Peacock* (1911; rpt., London: William Heinemann, 1950), p. 107. Other references to Wordsworth may be found in *Studies in Classic American Literature*, p. 142, and Notes to "Ghosts" in *Birds, Beasts and Flowers, CP*, p. 406.
   12. Gilbert, *Acts of Attention*, pp. 79–84.
   13. Chambers, *D. H. Lawrence*, p. 122.
   14. From MS E317, held by the University of Nottingham Library; Ferrier, "variorum," no. 34. Quoted by permission of Laurence Pollinger Ltd. and the Estate of Mrs. Frieda Lawrence Ravagli.
   15. Christopher Heywood, "D. H. Lawrence's 'Blood-Consciousness' and the Work of Xavier Bichat and Marshall Hall," *Etudes Anglaises* 32 (1979): 401. A transcription of the titles in the manuscript sequence "A Life History in Harmonies and Discords" is listed by Ferrier in "D. H. Lawrence's Pre-1920 Poetry," p. 345 (final titles and the position numbers of the poems in *Collected Poems* follow in parentheses; otherwise these poems were not published by Lawrence):

"First Harmony"
"Discord"
"Second Harmony"
"Discord"
"Third Harmony" (no. 122, "Twenty Years Ago")

"Discord" (no. 4, "Discord in Childhood")
"Fourth Harmony"
"Baiser"
"Discord"
"Last Harmony"
"Kiss."

16. D. H. Lawrence, *A Collier's Friday Night*, in *The Complete Plays of D. H. Lawrence* (New York: Viking, 1966), pp. 497–98.

17. From MS E320.1; Ferrier, "variorum," no. 4. Quoted with permission of Laurence Pollinger Ltd. and the Estate of Mrs. Frieda Lawrence Ravagli.

18. From MS E320.1; Ferrier, "variorum," no. 302. Quoted with permission of Laurence Pollinger Ltd. and the Estate of Mrs. Frieda Lawrence Ravagli.

19. From MS E317; Ferrier, "variorum," no. 129. Quoted with permission of Laurence Pollinger Ltd. and the Estate of Mrs. Frieda Lawrence Ravagli.

20. For detailed discussion of Lawrence's cultural milieu, especially in connection with the Georgian poets, Imagism, and Pound, see Kim A. Herzinger, *D. H. Lawrence in His Time: 1908–1915* (Lewisburg, Pa.: Bucknell University Press, 1982).

21. John Synge, Preface to his *Poems and Translations* (Dublin: Maunsel, 1911), pp. 3–4.

22. [Lawrence], review of *Contemporary German Poetry*, in the *English Review* 9 (1911): 723; see also Carl E. Baron, "Two Hitherto Unknown Pieces by D. H. Lawrence," *Encounter* 33 (1969): 3–5.

23. Gilbert, *Acts of Attention*, pp. 50–51.

24. D. H. Lawrence, *Love Poems and Others* (London: Duckworth, 1913), p. 39. Citations of this source will hereafter be given in the text.

25. Ezra Pound, *Personae* (New York: New Directions, 1926), p. 188.

26. Ferrier, "variorum," p. 19.

27. *Maud*, in *Tennyson's Poetry*, ed. Robert W. Hill (New York: W. W. Norton & Company, 1971), p. 238.

28. See also *Letters*, 1:442, 444. To De la Mare, Lawrence's comments on his selection are full of gratitude.

29. Ezra Pound, "Review of *Love Poems and Others*" (1913), in R. P. Draper, ed., *D. H. Lawrence: The Critical Heritage* (New York: Barnes and Noble, 1970), p. 53.

Chapter Three

1. Amy Lowell, "Imagism Past and Present" (lecture delivered at the Brooklyn Institute on 27 March 1918), in S. Foster Damon, *Amy Lowell: A Chronicle* (Boston: Houghton Mifflin, 1935), p. 446.

2. W. B. Yeats, *The Autobiography of William Butler Yeats* (New York: Macmillan, 1965), p. 210.

3. John Stuart Mill, *Autobiography*, ed. Jack Stillinger (Boston: Houghton Mifflin, 1969), p. 3. For comparisons, see Carl Dawson, *Victorian Noon* (Baltimore: Johns Hopkins University Press, 1979).

4. Richard Jefferies, *The Story of My Heart* (London: Longmans, Green, 1898), pp. ix, 6–7.

5. Ibid., pp. 33, 43, 115, 201.

6. Helen Corke later wrote her own novel, *Neutral Ground* (London: Arthur Baker, n.d.), based on this diary. *The Freshwater Diary* is reprinted in Helen Corke, *In Our Infancy* (London: Cambridge University Press, 1975), pp. 222–35. One of Lawrence's published poems, "Coldness in Love," is based on Corke's poem "Fantasy," which is reprinted in the note to poem no. 63, in Ferrier, "variorum."

7. Contrary to Lawrence's assertion in this letter, he expresses fondness for Jefferies elsewhere (*Letters,* 1:137). See also *Letters,* 1:337, and W. J. Keith's discussion of the influence of *The Story of My Heart* on Lawrence, in *Richard Jefferies: A Critical Study* (Toronto: University of Toronto Press, 1965).

8. Lawrence modified these comments later in the "Study of Thomas Hardy," calling ideal moments "lyrical" in reference to choruses in the drama of Euripides (*Phoenix*, p. 477). In his essay "The Novel" (1925), he calls traditional verse "pietistic" as opposed to the novel, which represents the "whole man" (*Phoenix II*, p. 417).

9. *The Complete Works of Robert Browning,* ed. Roma A. King et al., vol. 5 (Athens: Ohio University Press, 1981), pp. 137–51.

10. Patricia Ball, *The Heart's Events: The Victorian Poetry of Relationships* (London: Athlone, 1976), p. 4.

11. Rachel Annand Taylor, Preface to *The Hours of Fiammetta: A Sonnet Sequence* (London: Elkin Matthews, 1910), p. 6.

12. Michael C. Sharpe, "The Genesis of *The Trespasser,*" *Essays in Criticism* 11 (1961):34–39.

13. Taylor, Preface to *The Hours of Fiammetta,* p. 5.

14. Mark Kinkead-Weekes, "The Marble and the Statue: The Exploratory Imagination of D. H. Lawrence," in *Imagined Worlds: Essays on Some English Novels and Novelists in Honour of John Butt,* ed. Ian Gregor and Maynard Mack (London: Methuen, 1968), p. 380.

15. Boulton notes (*Letters,* 1:544 n. 4) that Lawrence is probably recalling Lascelles Abercrombie, *Thomas Hardy* (London: Secker, 1912).

16. Cushman, *D. H. Lawrence at Work,* p. 23.

17. Thomas Hardy, "Where the Picnic Was," *The Complete Poems of Thomas Hardy,* ed. James Gibson (New York: Macmillan, 1976), p. 357.

18. "The Voice," ibid., p. 346.

19. This notebook is described by Ferrier as MS 27 in her "D. H. Lawrence's Pre-1920 Poetry," pp. 352–54; and is listed by Vasey as MS E320.2, in "E. Manuscripts," pp. 505–10.

20. Mandell, *The Phoenix Paradox,* pp. 13–14, 35, 238–39 n. 12.

21. *Letters,* 2:478, 498, 506, 521, (on *Amores*); 3:227 (on *Bay*); 3:86–87, 93–94 (on *Look!*); 3:229–33, 243–44 (on *New Poems* and *Bay*); 3:254–55 (on *New Poems*). Keith Sagar, *D. H. Lawrence: A Calendar of His Works* (Austin: University of Texas Press, 1979), pp. 68–69, 76–77, 85–86. Mandell bases her argument in part on the evidence of Ferrier MS 27, Vasey MS E320.2, a notebook Lawrence used in Cornwall to collect *Amores* and keep his accounts (see n. 19, above). Since he sent this to Ottoline Morrell immediately upon completion of *Amores* and apparently did not ask for its return until March 1918, it is unlikely that he revised verse for *New Poems* or composed any for *Bay* in January 1916, though he did so in this same notebook two years later. The poems for *Amores* occupy the back of this notebook: among more than forty-seven drafts, only five found their way into *New Poems* or *Bay* (three of these were elegies, and the other two "twilight" poems equally suitable

for *Amores*). His accounts occupy the front of the notebook, and many drafts for *New Poems* follow these. See *Letters*, 2:521; 3:230; for a description of this notebook, see Ferrier MS 27, "D. H. Lawrence's Pre-1920 Poetry," pp. 352–54; Vasey MS E320.2, "E. Manuscripts," pp. 507–10.

22. Chambers, *D. H. Lawrence*, pp. 184, 201–4.

23. Ferrier suggests that the addressees were, to a certain extent, interchangeable, and she supports this conclusion with evidence from Lawrence's revisions (Ferrier and Tiedje, "D. H. Lawrence's Pre-1920 Poetry," p. 151).

24. Ferrier, "variorum," nos. 56, 231, 301.

25. Ferrier, "variorum," nos. 101, 107, 318. Ferrier's "variorum" may be consulted for manuscript drafts of all poems in the discussions that follow: titles and numbering for these poems refer to *RP* (see Appendix A).

26. For multiple manuscript sources and early versions of these poems, see Ferrier, "variorum," nos. 105–6.

27. For a hint of Lawrence's views on troubadour verse, see his "Review of *The Minnesingers* by Jethro Bithell," *Phoenix II*, pp. 271–72.

28. *Amores* (London: Duckworth, 1916), p. 35. All references will be to the Duckworth edition; individual poems in the American edition (New York: B. W. Huebsch, 1916) occasionally vary from the English, and these should be consulted for a full history (collated also in Ferrier, "variorum").

29. Gilbert, *Acts of Attention*, pp. 62, 65–69.

30. These lines were omitted in the American edition of *Amores* as well as in *Collected Poems*, revised to dwell on his self-pity: "I shall get no answer in any hour. / To live alone is my doom" (*CP*, p. 106).

31. For a discussion of language and the psychological structures of elegies, see Peter Sacks, *The English Elegy* (Baltimore: Johns Hopkins University Press, 1985). Perhaps conscious of his dependence on language to bridge the gap, Lawrence revised one of the love poems in this sequence to read

Surely, ah not in words alone I'd spill
The vivid, ah, the fiery surplus of life
. . . to touch you.
("Come Spring, Come Sorrow," no. 94, CP, p. 127)

32. Mandell, *The Phoenix Paradox*, pp. 24–26. Lawrence incorporated classical allusions more directly into the revisions for *New Poems*, and these often set the pattern for his alterations of 1928.

33. Underscoring the theme of the Book of Hours, Lawrence originally wrote "Illuminations" for "records." (From Vasey MS E320.2, privately owned; "variorum," Appendix 1, vol. 2, p. 60. Quoted by permission of Laurence Pollinger Ltd. and the Estate of Mrs. Frieda Lawrence Ravagli.) He revised this inscription for the English edition of the undemonstrative, "To Ottoline Morrell," but for the American edition, he amplified his inscription: "To Ottoline Morrell in Tribute to Her Noble and Independent Sympathy and Her Generous Understanding These Poems are Gratefully Dedicated."

34. Bernice Slote, "The *Leaves* of D. H. Lawrence," in *Start with the Sun*, pp. 72, 81.

35. Poems sent to Edward Garnett are listed under MS 19 in Ferrier, "D. H. Lawrence's Pre-1920 Poetry," pp. 338, 349–50; Vasey lists them as MSS E319.2, E320.4, E446.5, in "E. Manuscripts," pp. 503–4, 511–12, 539.

36. Sagar, *Calendar*, pp. 27–78.

37. Laurence Sterne, *A Sentimental Journey through France and Italy*, ed. Ian Jack (London: Oxford University Press, 1968), p. 84. Quoted by Boulton in *Letters*, 1:398.

38. John Keats, "When I Have Fears That I May Cease to Be," *The Complete Poems*, ed. John Barnard (Harmondsworth: Penguin, 1973), p. 221.

39. Anaïs Nin, *D. H. Lawrence: An Unprofessional Study* (London: Neville Spearman, 1961), p. 104.

40. Auden, "D. H. Lawrence," p. 288.

41. Alvarez, "D. H. Lawrence," p. 159.

42. Frieda preserved an earlier version of these—which she preferred and which were therefore printed in the Warren Roberts memorial edition for her—in *Look! We Have Come Through!* (Cornwall: Ark, 1958).

43. Paul Delany, *D. H. Lawrence's Nightmare: The Writer and His Circle in the Years of the Great War* (New York: Basic, 1978), p. 287.

44. See also Sagar, *Calendar*, p. 78.

Chapter Four

1. Tom Marshall, *The Psychic Mariner* (New York: Viking, 1970), pp. 101–2. Sandra Gilbert discusses "Eloi, Eloi, Lama Sabachthani?" as a representative wartime poem in "Soldier's Heart: Literary Men, Literary Women, and the Great War," *Signs* 8 (1983):424. See also Keith Cushman, "D. H. Lawrence's *Bay:* The Noncombatant as War Poet," forthcoming in *The Spirit of D. H. Lawrence*, ed. Gamini Salgado and G. K. Das (London: Macmillan, 1987).

2. Paul Fussell, *The Great War and Modern Memory* (London: Oxford University Press, 1975), pp. 313–14.

3. Ibid., p. 312.

4. Sagar, *Calendar*, p. 57.

5. These magazine poems include "Eloi, Eloi, Lama Sabachthani?" "Erinnyes," "Resurrection," "Resurrection of the Flesh," "Labour Battalion," and "No News," which are reprinted in *Complete Poems*, pp. 737–49. David Farmer demonstrates the relationship between Lawrence's letters about the war and his conception of "The Turning Back" (reprinted in part and mistitled "We Have Gone Too Far" in *Complete Poems*, p. 736) in "D. H. Lawrence's 'The Turning Back': The Text and Its Genesis in Correspondence," *D. H. Lawrence Review* 5 (1972): 121–31.

6. Lawrence earlier claimed to have translated these cryptic poems into English from the German translations of Arabic poems. See Ferrier, MS 2, "D. H. Lawrence's Pre-1920 Poetry," pp. 343–44; and Ferrier "variorum," nos. 236–47, 330–45.

7. "All of Us" is listed by Ferrier in Appendix 1, "D. H. Lawrence's Poetry, 1920–28," pp. 302–3, and by Vasey as MS E49b, in "E. Manuscripts," pp. 444–45; "Bits" is Ferrier's MS 47 in "D. H. Lawrence's Pre-1920 Poetry," pp. 341, 357 and Vasey's MS E49a, in "E. Manuscripts," pp. 443–44. "All of Us" is an earlier version of "Bits," but neither manuscript was published by Lawrence. "All of Us" contains thirty-one poems, and "Bits" twenty-nine when the two parts of "Prisoner at Work in a Turkish Garden" are counted as one, as in Lawrence's numbered list of poems for "All of Us."

8. William Empson, *Some Versions of Pastoral* (New York: New Directions, 1974), p. 12.

9. Ferrier, "D. H. Lawrence's Poetry, 1920–28," p. 303.

10. Edgar Lee Masters, *Spoon River Anthology* (New York: Macmillan, 1919).

11. Ferrier, "variorum," nos. 34, 17, 19, 131, 135, 132, 136.

12. Ferrier, MSS 39, 40, 41, in "D. H. Lawrence's Pre-1920 Poetry," pp. 341, 355–56; Vasey's listing in "E. Manuscripts" is more complete, MS E40.5a-i, pp. 440–41.

13. D. H. Lawrence, *Movements in European History* (1921; rpt., London: Oxford University Press, 1971), p. 307. Subsequent page references will be to this edition and will be cited in the text.

14. "War-Baby," *Bay* (London: Beaumont, 1919), p. 40. Citations to this edition will hereafter appear in the text.

15. Masters, *Spoon River,* p. 249.

16. Thomas Carlyle, *On Heroes, Hero-Worship and the Heroic in History* (1841; rpt., New York: AMS, 1969), p. 154.

17. Cushman, *D. H. Lawrence at Work,* pp. 5–6, 27–46.

18. Barry Lydgate, "Mortgaging One's Work to the World: Publication and the Structure of *Montaigne's Essais,*" *PMLA* 96 (1981): 210–23.

19. Lawrence, "War Films," *Poetry* 14 (1919): 178–82.

20. Mandell, *The Phoenix Paradox,* pp. 24–25, 27–29.

21. From MS E317, held by the University of Nottingham Library; Ferrier, "variorum," no. 27. Quoted by permission of Laurence Pollinger Ltd. and the Estate of Mrs. Frieda Lawrence Ravagli.

22. From MS E320.4, held by the Berg Collection of the New York Public Library; Ferrier, "variorum," no. 40. Quoted by permission of Laurence Pollinger Ltd. and the Estate of Mrs. Frieda Lawrence Ravagli.

23. Ferrier, MSS 1, 5, 27, in "D. H. Lawrence's Pre-1920 Poetry," pp. 342–46, 352–54; Vasey MSS E317, E320.1, E320.2, in "E. Manuscripts," pp. 500–502, 505–10.

24. This document is described by Ferrier as MS 43 in her "D. H. Lawrence's Pre-1920 Poetry," pp. 341, 356; and is listed by Vasey as MS E269.5, in "E. Manuscripts," pp. 488–89. This manuscript is held by the Harry Ransom Humanities Research Center of the University of Texas at Austin. Cited by permission of Laurence Pollinger Ltd. and the Estate of Mrs. Frieda Lawrence Ravagli.

25. Note that "Song-Day in Autumn," "Disagreeable Advice," and "Restlessness" at the end of volume 1 of *Rhyming Poems* in *Complete Poems* (1977) were placed there by Pinto and Roberts and did not appear in *Collected Poems* (1928).

26. Thomas Carlyle, *Sartor Resartus,* ed. Charles Harrold (New York: Odyssey, 1937); *Past and Present,* ed. Richard Altick (New York: New York University Press, 1977).

27. Gilbert, "Hell on Earth," p. 259.

28. Ibid., pp. 261, 263.

29. Mandell, *The Phoenix Paradox,* pp. 104–5.

30. Gilbert, "Hell on Earth," pp. 258, 273.

31. R. P. Le Bossu, *Traité du Poëme* (Paris: Pierre Gandouin, 1708), p. 34.

32. Hymn 592, "Now the day is over," in *Hymns Ancient and Modern* (1861; rpt., London, William Clowes and Sons, 1904), p. 539.

33. Lawrence quoted in Damon, *Amy Lowell,* p. 577.

34. This description of the pantomime is based chiefly on the useful summary in David Mayer's "The Case for Harlequin: A Footnote on Shaw's Dramatic Method," *Modern Drama* 3 (1960): 60–74. See also Mayer, *Harlequin in His Element* (Cambridge: Harvard University Press, 1969).

35. For another discussion of Joyce's use of pantomime materials in *Ulysses,* see

David Hayman, "Forms of Folly in Joyce: A Study of Clowning in *Ulysses*," *English Literary History* 34 (1967): 277–79.

36. In an unpublished letter of 12 November 1929 to the illustrator Blair Hughes-Stanton (held by the Harry Ransom Humanities Reseach Center, University of Texas at Austin), Lawrence suggests that he compiled these notes only at Hughes-Stanton's request. His disavowal must be taken with a grain of salt, since he had an old interest in the bits of Greek philosophy that he picked up from John Burnet's *Early Greek Philosophy* (3rd ed., 1920) and that he mixed into his own invented proverbs. See *Complete Poems*, pp. 995–1000.

Unpublished letter of 12 November 1929 to Blair Hughes-Stanton from D. H. Lawrence is cited here by permission of Laurence Pollinger Ltd. and the Estate of Mrs. Frieda Lawrence Ravagli.

37. See Sagar, *Calendar,* for development, pp. 102–7, 125–30, 169, 189. A description of the manuscripts behind *Birds, Beasts and Flowers* may be found in Ferrier, "D. H. Lawrence's Poetry, 1920–28," pp. 291–99.

38. Although "The American Eagle" stands outside the last group, Lawrence once described it as "*last* in the *Birds Beasts* MS, among the *ghosts,*" in Gerald Lacy, ed., *D. H. Lawrence: Letters to Thomas and Adele Seltzer* (Santa Barbara: Black Sparrow Press, 1976), p. 79. Also see Sagar, *Calendar,* p. 127. Scholars of the poetry have failed to notice the organization of the table of contents for *Birds, Beasts and Flowers;* see, for example, Mandell, *The Phoenix Paradox,* pp. 107–8, 111.

39. Sagar, *Calendar,* pp. 101–27. Sagar records "The Mosquito" as probably written in May 1920 in Syracruse, prior to "Tropic" in June at Taormina. George Trail notes that Lawrence wrote "Humming-Bird" in Italy (not in Española, New Mexico) and previously published it in May 1921 ("West by East: the Psycho-Geography of *Birds, Beasts and Flowers*," *D. H. Lawrence Review* 12 [1979]: 243).

40. Lawrence's debts to Frazer are widely acknowledged. See John B. Vickery, *The Literary Impact of The Golden Bough* (Princeton: Princeton University Press, 1973); Sir James George Frazer, *The Golden Bough* (London: Macmillan, 1890); Frazer, *Totemism and Exogamy* (London: Macmillan, 1910). Another strong influence was Jane Ellen Harrison, *Ancient Art and Ritual* (London: Williams and Norgate, 1913).

41. George Borrow, *Lavengro: The Scholar—the Gipsy—the Priest* (London: J. Murray, 1851). Jessie Chambers has recorded Lawrence's great admiration for Borrow, noting that "he said that Borrow had mingled autobiography and fiction so inextricably in *Lavengro* that the most astute critics could not be sure where the one ended and the other began," Chambers, *D. H. Lawrence,* p. 110.

42. Gilbert, "Hell on Earth," pp. 269–70.

43. Wallace Stevens, "Sunday Morning," *The Collected Poems of Wallace Stevens* (1923; New York: Vintage, 1982), pp. 69–70. Copyright © 1923, 1931, 1935, 1937, each year 1942–52, and 1954 by Wallace Stevens. Reprinted by permission of Alfred A. Knopf, Inc.

44. Gilbert, "Hell on Earth," pp. 256–57.

Chapter Five

1. Moore, *The Priest of Love,* pp. 341–44.

2. Lawrence quoted in Mabel Dodge Luhan, *Lorenzo in Taos* (New York: Knopf, 1932), pp. 16–17.

3. Moore, *The Priest of Love*, pp. 354–405.

4. Lawrence quoted in Luhan, *Lorenzo in Taos*, pp. 13, 23.

5. *The Plumed Serpent* (1926; rpt., New York: Vintage, 1959), p. 21. All quotations from this work, including the poems, will be from this edition, and page numbers will be cited in the text. Quoted by permission of Laurence Pollinger Ltd., the Estate of Mrs. Frieda Lawrence Ravagli, and Alfred A. Knopf, Inc.

6. Bernard Malamud, *Dubin's Lives* (New York: Farrar, Straus, Giroux, 1979).

7. D. H. Lawrence, "Review of *A Second Contemporary Verse Anthology*" (1923), in *Phoenix*, pp. 322–26.

8. Lawrence's discussion of Whitman in these terms recurs in "Poetry of the Present," *Complete Poems*, p. 185; Joseph Foster, *D. H. Lawrence in Taos* (Albuquerque: University of New Mexico Press, 1972), pp. 242–45; D. H. Lawrence, "Whitman," in *Studies in Classic American Literature*, pp. 171–87.

9. Brother Antoninus [William Everson], *Robinson Jeffers: Fragments of an Older Fury* (Berkeley, Calif.: Oyez Press, 1968), pp. 74–75.

10. Lawrence quoted in Luhan, *Lorenzo in Taos*, pp. 6, 65.

11. Ibid., p. 238.

12. "The Woman Who Rode Away," in D. H. Lawrence, *The Complete Short Stories*, vol. 2 (1922; rpt., New York: Penguin, 1976), pp. 546–81.

13. "Change," in Luhan, *Lorenzo in Taos*, pp. 157–59; "Change of Life," *Complete Poems*, pp. 766–71.

14. L. D. Clark, *Dark Night of the Body* (Austin: University of Texas Press, 1964), p. 13 and passim.

15. D. H. Lawrence and M. L. Skinner, *The Boy in the Bush* (1924; rpt., New York: Penguin, 1981), p. 196. As Bruce Steele points out, "The Novel" and other essays written at this time (including "Surgery for the Novel—Or a Bomb," "Art and Morality, I and II," "Morality and the Novel, I and II") were triggered in part by discussions of the future of the novel and by publication of *Ulysses;* Lawrence was meditating his own role at this time in producing new approaches to the novel. See *Study of Thomas Hardy and Other Essays*, ed. Bruce Steele (Cambridge: Cambridge University Press, 1985), pp. xliv–l.

16. Gilbert, *Acts of Attention*, pp. 204–5; Hough, *Dark Sun*, pp. 136–38.

17. Clark, *Dark Night*, p. 88.

18. Lewis Spence, *Gods of Mexico* (London: T. Fisher Unwin, 1923). William York Tindall first noted this source in *D. H. Lawrence and Susan His Cow* (New York: Columbia University Press, 1939), p. 117. Also see Fray Bernardino de Sahagún, *General History of the Things of New Spain*, book 2, *The Ceremonies*, trans. Arthur J. O. Anderson and Charles E. Dibble (Santa Fe, N.M.: The School of American Research, 1981), pp. 221–45.

19. Clark, *Dark Night*, p. 89.

20. Gilbert, *Acts of Attention*, p. 202.

21. Josephine Miles, *The Continuity of Poetic Language: Studies in English Poetry from the 1540's to the 1940's* (Berkeley: University of California Press, 1951), pp. 161–222.

22. William Wordsworth, "She Dwelt among the Untrodden Ways," *The Poems*, ed. J. O. Hayden (Harmondsworth: Penguin, 1977), 1:366.

23. See Moore, *The Priest of Love*, p. 455.

24. Mandell, *The Phoenix Paradox*, pp. 3–7, 30.

25. Gilbert, *Acts of Attention*, pp. 7–8.

26. Ibid., pp. 6, 9–10.

27. Ibid., pp. 10–11.

28. Victor Shklovsky, "Art as Technique," *Russian Formalist Criticism: Four Essays*, trans. Lee Lemon and Marion Reis (Lincoln: University of Nebraska Press, 1965), pp. 12–13.

29. For an account of *transition* and Jolas's "revolution" in language, see Richard Ellmann, *James Joyce* (New York: Oxford University Press, 1977), pp. 600–601.

30. *Lady Chatterley's Lover* (1928; rpt., New York: Grove, 1982), p. 137. Further page references from this source will be cited in the text. Quoted by permission of Laurence Pollinger Ltd. and the Estate of Mrs. Frieda Lawrence Ravagli.

31. Frieda Lawrence, *"Not I, but the Wind . . ."* (New York: Viking, 1934), p. 255.

32. *Letters from D. H. Lawrence to Martin Secker, 1911–1930*, ed. Martin Secker ("Privately Published," 1970), p. 100.

33. Mandell's study should be consulted for descriptions of approximately twenty-five revised poems in Lawrence's collection, (*The Phoenix Paradox*, pp. 31–78). For an early study, see Phyllis Bartlett, "Lawrence's *Collected Poems:* The Demon Takes Over," *PMLA* 66 (1951): 583–93.

34. *Letters to Martin Secker*, p. 98.

35. Lawrence, "Verse Unfree and Free," *Voices*, Oct. 1919; pp. 129–34; Ferrier, "variorum," Appendix 1, 2:62–70.

36. Lawrence quoted in Luhan, *Lorenzo in Taos*, pp. 334–35.

37. *Letters to Martin Secker*, p. 106.

38. Blackmur, "D. H. Lawrence," p. 255.

39. Andrew Lang, Introduction to his *Selected Poems of Robert Burns* (London: Kegan Paul, Trench, Trübner, 1892), pp. xx–i; *Letters*, 1:487, 489, 504–5.

40. Even if Lawrence consulted his earlier notebooks, their arrangement in no way resembles that of *Rhyming Poems*. When he was revising poems for his collection, he altered them in his own copies of *Love Poems and Others* (Vasey MS E214b; Ferrier MS 71), *Amores* (Vasey MS E14.5d; Ferrier MS 72), *Look! We Have Come Through!* (Vasey MS E205.8c; Ferrier MS 73), and *Birds, Beasts and Flowers* (Vasey MS E47h; Ferrier MS 74). Lawrence's personal copies of *Look! We Have Come Through!* and *Birds, Beasts and Flowers* are held at the Humanities Research Center of the University of Texas, Austin, and his *Amores* is in private hands. *Look! We Have Come Through!* and *Birds, Beasts and Flowers* contain brief instructions directing the publisher where to place them in *Collected Poems*. Lawrence typed all the poems for *Collected Poems* except those from *New Poems*, which he asked Secker to have typed for him. For descriptions of these books and typescripts, see Ferrier, "D. H. Lawrence's Poetry, 1920–28," p. 299.

41. In *Collected Poems* (see Appendix A), Lawrence retained only three groups from *Love Poems and Others* ("Aware," "A Pang of Reminiscence," and "A White Blossom," nos. 35–37; "Return" and "The Appeal," nos. 51–52; "Morning Work" and "Transformations," nos. 43–44), but he created five new sets ("Cherry Robbers," "Dream-Confused," and "Renascence," nos. 5–7; "Wedding Morn," "Violets," "Lightning," and "End of Another Home Holiday," nos. 28–31; "Corot" and "Michael Angelo," nos. 38–39; "Lilies in the Fire" and "Red Moon-Rise," nos. 53–54; "Mystery" and "Repulsed," nos. 61–62). From *New Poems*, he retained five clusters ("In Church" and "Piano," nos. 117–18; "Late at Night" and "Next Morning," nos. 110–11; "Passing Visit to Helen," "Twenty Years Ago," "Reading a Letter," "Seven Seals," and "Two Wives," nos. 121–25; "At the Front," "Reality of Peace, 1916," and "Narcissus," nos. 127–29; and "Autumn Sunshine" and "On That Day," nos. 145–46), and he created five more clusters, including a long sequence

toward the end ("Flapper" and "Thief in the Night," nos. 14–15; "Letter from Town: On a Grey Morning in March" and "Letter from Town: The Almond-Tree," nos. 26–27; "Hyde Park at Night, Before the War" and "Piccadilly Circus at Night," nos. 40–41; "Twofold," "Tarantella," and "Under the Oak," nos. 97–99; poems 110–29, "Late at Night" through "Narcissus"—this long sequence includes at least three further sets of pendants, see Appendix A). Altogether, four sets of pendants match those of Ferrier MS 27 ("In Church" and "Piano"; "Twofold" and "Tarantella"; and two "Letters from Town"); and—joined as four poems in MS 27 under the title "London Nights"—the two "Embankment at Night" poems, "Hyde Park," and "Piccadilly Circus"). For further discussions of these books as well as the incorporation of *Amores, Bay,* and Lawrence's earliest verse sequences into *Collected Poems,* see the corresponding sections in previous chapters.

42. Ferrier, note to poem no. 129, "variorum."

43. Two stages in the arrangement of the first nine poems in the Buffalo holograph are particularly clear. Numbered 1–9, the order was first "Dog-Tired," "The Wild Common," "Study," "Monologue of a Mother," "Cherry Robbers," "Discord in Childhood," "Renascence," "Virgin Youth," and "From a College Window"; Lawrence reordered these to "The Wild Common," "Dog-Tired," "From a College Window," "Discord in Childhood," "Cherry Robbers," "Dream-Confused," "Renascence," "Virgin Youth," and "Study." Although erasures often make it difficult to discern successive stages, Lawrence reached his final decisions here (see Appendix B).

44. The Buffalo holograph does not help much with deciphering stages in *RP* nos. 21 to 63, although Lawrence reworked this section of the list carefully. Among his last decisions, he inserted "Hyde Park at Night," "Piccadilly Circus at Night," "After the Opera," "Morning Work," and "Transformations" after "Michael Angelo" (nos. 39–44); he moved "Last Lesson of the Afternoon" (no. 46) from below "A Winter's Tale" (no. 50) to above "School on the Outskirts" (no. 47), "Red Moon-Rise" from between "The Appeal" and "Lilies in the Fire" to between "Lilies in the Fire" and "Scent of Irises" (nos. 52–55), "The Punisher" (no. 59) from after "The End" (no. 66) to follow "Discipline" (no. 58), and "Coldness in Love" (no. 63) from after "Lilies in the Fire" (no. 53) to after "Repulsed" (no. 62). (See Appendix B.)

45. Mandell finds great continuity between the Note and Foreword and the poetry; in the numerical order of *Rhyming Poems;* and in the volume's mythology, especially toward the end of the *Rhyming Poems* (The Phoenix Paradox, pp. 18–24).

46. Mandell, *The Phoenix Paradox,* p. 23. "Noise of Battle" is the only poem in the Buffalo holograph that is not in the position listed in the published *Collected Poems;* instead, it is inserted there between "Reading a Letter" and "Seven Seals" (nos. 123–24). It is unlikely, however, that anyone but Lawrence made that final change. (See Appendix B.)

47. See also Mandell, *The Phoenix Paradox,* p. 38.

48. Richards, *Practical Criticism,* pp. 99–112, 241–54. For an account of the fascinating history of "Piano," its critical reception and revisions, see my article, "The Poems of 'Piano,'" *D. H. Lawrence Review* 8 (1985–86): 183–99.

Chapter Six

1. Davies quoted in Edward Nehls, ed., *D. H. Lawrence: A Composite Biography* (Madison: University of Wisconsin Press, 1959), 3:274.

2. Brewster quoted ibid., 3:421.

3. Richard Aldington, "Introduction to *Last Poems* and *More Pansies*," *Complete Poems*, pp. 591–93; Gilbert, *Acts of Attention*, chapters 4 and 5 and pp. 265–66 n. 3; Marshall, *Psychic Mariner*, chapters 4 and 5; Pinto, Introduction to *CP*, pp. 15–17. See also the description of this manuscript in David Farmer, "A Descriptive and Analytical Catalogue of the D. H. Lawrence Collection at the University of Texas at Austin," Ph.D. diss., University of Texas at Austin, 1970. Aldington labeled the two manuscripts *More Pansies* and *Last Poems* and classified them respectively as MS B and MS A (in what he considered their order of importance rather than chronology). The manuscripts are now listed and described as a single group, classified as MS E192 under the title *Last Poems* by Vasey, in "E. Manuscripts," p. 472.

4. T. A. Smailes, *Some Comments on the Verse of D. H. Lawrence* (Port Elizabeth, South Africa: University of Port Elizabeth, 1970), p. 102; Mandell, *The Phoenix Paradox*, pp. 133–38; Marshall, *Psychic Mariner*, pp. 232–33.

5. Aldington and Pinto represent antithetical attitudes on this issue, Aldington making the harsh judgment of these poems and Pinto, the appreciative one. Gilbert and Marshall steer between these two, though both believe that these poems represent a lesser effort than what precedes and follows them. See Aldington in *Complete Poems*, p. 595; Pinto, Introduction to *CP*, pp. 15–16; Gilbert, *Acts of Attention*, p. 208; Marshall, *Psychic Mariner*, pp. 165, 181–82. For a study of the relationship between satire and sympathy throughout Lawrence's works, see Ronald P. Draper, "Satire as a Form of Sympathy: D. H. Lawrence as a Satirist," in *Renaissance and Modern Essays Presented to Vivian de Sola Pinto in Celebration of His Seventieth Birthday*, ed. G. R. Hibbard (London: Routledge and Kegan Paul, 1966), pp. 189–97.

6. *The Riverside Shakespeare*, ed. G. Blakemore Evans (Boston: Houghton Mifflin Company, 1974), p. 1766.

7. Frieda Lawrence, *The Memoirs and Correspondence*, ed. E. W. Tedlock (New York: Knopf, 1964), p. 389.

8. Yvor Winters, *In Defense of Reason* (Denver: Swallow Press, 1947), pp. 578, 589.

9. Hymn 592, *Hymns Ancient and Modern*, p. 539.

10. *Pansies* (London: Martin Secker, 1929); *Pansies* (London: privately printed by P. R. Stephensen, 1929) (this private edition was actually printed by Charles Lahr; see David Farmer, "An Unpublished Version of D. H. Lawrence's Introduction to *Pansies*," *Review of English Studies* 21 [1970]: 182 n. 2). The expurgated poems were "The Noble Englishman," "Women Want Fighters for Their Lovers," "Ego-Bound Women," "There is No Way Out," "My Naughty Book," "The Little Wowser," "The Young and Their Moral Guardians," "What Matters," "What Does She Want?" "Don't Look at Me," "To Clarinda," "Demon Justice," "Be a Demon!" and "The Jeune Fille"; all of these are restored to their original positions in *Complete Poems* (with the exception of "Trust," which should be the last poem rather than preceding "Demon Justice"). The order of *Complete Poems* follows that of the expurgated *Pansies*, which varies from the unexpurgated edition in a few small ways that strengthen the internal groupings: for example, "Leda" is moved from below "Natural Complexion" to below "Swan," and "November by the Sea" is

moved from below "Good Husbands Make Unhappy Wives" to below "The Sea, The Sea."

11. For descriptions of this notebook (Vasey MS E302d), see Tedlock, *The Frieda Lawrence Collection,* pp. 104–12; and Farmer, *A Descriptive Catalogue,* pp. 125–27. Also see Vasey, "E. Manuscripts," MS E302a-h, pp. 495–96.

12. Those groups that correspond in Vasey MS E302d and the published book are as follows: "Our Day Is Over" to "To Let Go or to Hold On—?" (*CP,* pp. 425–29); "How Beastly the Bourgeois Is" to "When I Went to the Circus" (*CP,* pp. 430–46); "The Noble Englishman" to "Work" (*CP,* pp. 446–51); "Moon Memory" to "The Sea, The Sea" (*CP,* pp. 453–55); "Fight! O My Young Men" to "Beware, O my Dear Young Men" (*CP,* pp. 456–63); "The Gazelle Calf" to "Touch" (*CP,* pp. 466–68); "The Ignoble Procession" to "Nottingham's New University" (*CP,* pp. 484–89); "I Am in a Novel" to "When I Read Shakespeare" (*CP,* pp. 489–94); "Cerebral Emotions" to "Blank" (*CP,* pp. 500–501); "Elderly Discontented Women" to "Nullus" (*CP,* pp. 502–10); "Wages" to "Lizard" (*CP,* pp. 521–24); "Sun-Men" to "Immoral Man" (*CP,* pp. 525–29); "Cowards" to "Fate and the Younger Generation" (*CP,* pp. 529–34); "Energetic Women" to "What Ails Thee?" (*CP,* pp. 537–40). The group from "Salt of the Earth" to "Sick" (*CP,* pp. 495–500) corresponds in *More Pansies* and *Pansies.* There are, of course, additional groups, both smaller and larger, in the published book. Altogether, the changes behind these poems are more numerous and complex than for any previous book, but the details are less illuminating—when the poems became briefer, the choices became less significant.

13. Gilbert, *Acts of Attention,* pp. 256–59.

14. Ibid., p. 260.

15. *Letters to Martin Secker,* pp. 119, 122.

16. Smailes, *Some Comments,* p. 99. Marshall believes that "most of *Nettles* is on the same level as the most trivial of the pansies," *Psychic Mariner,* p. 182. Gilbert and Murfin do not discuss *Nettles* separately from *Pansies.* Mandell is the only critic to treat these apart and with tentative respect, *The Phoenix Paradox,* pp. 131–33.

17. For a listing of poems in *More Pansies,* see Farmer, "A Descriptive Catalogue," pp. 115–18.

18. Auden, "D. H. Lawrence," pp. 294–95.

19. Unpublished poem in Vasey MS E192a (Aldington MS B), held in the Harry Ransom Humanities Research Center, University of Texas at Austin; Mandell, *The Phoenix Paradox,* p. 132. This excerpt from Vasey MS E192a is quoted by permission of Laurence Pollinger Ltd. and the Estate of Mrs. Frieda Lawrence Ravagli.

20. Christopher Hassall, "Black Flowers: A New Light on the Poetics of D. H. Lawrence," in Moore, *A D. H. Lawrence Miscellany,* pp. 370–77; D. H. Lawrence, *Apocalypse* (1931; rpt., New York: Penguin, 1976). Subsequent page references will be to this edition and will be cited in the text.

Excerpts from *Apocalypse,* by D. H. Lawrence, copyright 1931 by the Estate of David Herbert Lawrence. Introduction by Richard Aldington, copyright 1932; copyright renewed © 1960 by The Viking Press, Inc. Reprinted by permission of Laurence Pollinger Ltd., the Estate of Mrs. Frieda Lawrence Ravagli, and Viking Penguin, Inc.

21. A third part, far less specific than these cycles, disclosed a cosmic man, woman, and dragon in conflict with each other, but this paradisal ending exceeded his vision even in *Apocalypse* (see pp. 46–47, 63–64).

22. Michael Kirkham, "D. H. Lawrence's *Last Poems,*" *D. H. Lawrence Review* 5 (1972) : 97, 108–9.

23. Wordsworth, "Ode: Intimations of Immortality," *The Poems,* 1 : 528.

24. Gilbert, *Acts of Attention,* pp. 280–84; Kirkham, "D. H. Lawrence's *Last Poems,*" pp. 112–16.

25. Elizabeth Cipolla, "The *Last Poems* of D. H. Lawrence," *D. H. Lawrence Review* 2 (1969): 111; Mandell, *The Phoenix Paradox,* p. 144.

Chapter Seven

1. Lucie-Smith, "The Poetry of D. H. Lawrence," p. 224.

2. *Naked Poetry,* ed. Stephen Berg and Robert Mesey (New York: Bobbs-Merrill, 1969), p. xii. Signs that the scholarly outlook on Lawrence's modernity may be changing appear in four recent essays: Roberts W. French, "Lawrence and American Poetry," in *The Legacy of D. H. Lawrence,* ed. Jeffrey Meyers (London: Macmillan, 1987); A. Walton Litz, "Lawrence, Pound, and Early Modernism"; Phillip Marcus, "Lawrence, Yeats, and 'the Resurrection of the Body'"; and Marjorie Perloff, "Lawrence's Lyric Theatre: *Birds, Beasts and Flowers*"—the last three essays all in *D. H. Lawrence: A Centenary Consideration,* ed. Peter Balbert and Phillip Marcus (Ithaca, N.Y.: Cornell University Press, 1985). One recent essay that argues for only limited influence of Lawrence's poetry on that of later writers is: William M. Chace, "Lawrence and English Poetry," in *The Legacy of D. H. Lawrence.*

3. Donald Davie, "The Poetry of Yvor Winters," Preface to *The Collected Poems of Yvor Winters* (Manchester: Carcanet, 1978), p. 1.

INDEX OF THE WORKS OF D. H. LAWRENCE

GENERAL INDEX

Monologue (*continued*)
    LP, 45; *see also* Dialogue, Dramatic
    verse, Lyric, *and* Victorian verse
Monro, Harold, 35
Monroe, Harriet, 40, 103, 112, 121, 167
Montaigne, Michel de, 121
Moore, Harry T., xii, 150, 151
Moore, Marianne, 203
Morrell, Ottoline, 61, 107; dedication to
    Amores, 77, 265 n.33
Mountsier, Robert, 126
Murfin, Ross, 4, 198
Myth: of opposition, 2, 32, 227; and autobi-
    ography, 7–8; in "Under the Oak," 20;
    and Lawrence's mother, 20, 65–66, 68,
    70–73; of renewal, 23, 24–25, 141; in
    juvenilia, 23–34 *passim;* of touch, 24,
    26, 29–31, 33–34; of relationship, 26,
    52–54, 55–56, 58–59; of sympathy, 26–
    29; and fall, 27–29, 38–39, 226, 227–28;
    in *The Plumed Serpent,* 141; and Amer-
    ica, 150, 152; of community, 151; of pro-
    phetic poet, 153–56, 166; of sacrifice,
    155; of discipline, 155–56; of chaos, 171–
    74; of *RP,* 185, 189–91; of death in *LP,*
    232–36

Nehls, Edward, xii
Nichols, Robert, 4, 103
Nietzsche, Friedrich, Lawrence on, 60
Nin, Anaïs, 87
Noguchi, Yone, Lawrence's debt to, 34

Opposition: in self, 3, 5–6; to Whitman, 7;
    centrality of, 8; in "Under the Oak,"
    17–19; and "states of blood," 33; of per-
    sonalities in "Cherry Robbers," 37–38;
    of male and female, 36, 37, 45–47, 58–
    59, 67–68, 93–94, 260 n.1; of "lyric"
    and "dramatic," 52–53, 264 n.8; of
    women, 55; of love and hate in *Look!*
    83–84, 97; in "Bits," 108–9; and "di-
    vided" hero, 128; of worlds after war,
    130–31; merging into separateness,
    131–32; in "Snake," 135; and *Collected
    Poems,* 175; and *RP,* 180, 186; and sanity,
    201–2; of body and mind, 201–3, 222–
    23, 224–27, 229, 231; and order of *Pan-
    sies,* 208; *see also* Dualism
Ovid, and *Birds, Beasts and Flowers,* 141
Owen, Wilfred, 107

Pascal, Blaise, 203
Persephone, 46, 122–23, 185, 227; in *LP,* 73;
    and Frieda, 87; in *RP,* 193

Phoenix, as emblem, 235–36
Pinker, J. B., 61, 100, 107, 122; Lawrence's
    dismissal of, 126
Pinto, Vivian de Sola, xii, 42, 80, 81, 83, 102,
    105, 175, 198, 207, 208, 216 n, 243 n,
    267 n.25; on Note to *Collected Poems,*
    3–4; on Lawrence and Wordsworth,
    20; on Lawrence and autobiography,
    128–29
Plato, 221, 224
Poe, Edgar Allen, 34
Pollnitz, Christopher, xii, 22
Pound, Ezra, 33, 35, 38, 40, 154, 263 n.20;
    "Hugh Selwyn Mauberley," 40; on
    LP, 47

Radford, Dollie, 61
Rananim, 100
Raphael, 27
Relationship: as central theme, 36, 52; and
    sequence, 53–54, 55–56; as opposition,
    37, 45–47, 58–59, 67–68, 93–94,
    260 n.1; and war in *Look!* 104–5; polar-
    ization in "Snake," 135; redefinition in
    Birds, Beasts and Flowers, 139–41; of na-
    tions, 154–55; and rejection of heroism,
    167; and love poems in *RP,* 187–88; *see
    also* Opposition *and* "Study of Thomas
    Hardy" in Index of Works
Repetition: as creative scheme, x; and
    change, xiii; of crises in *LP,* 23; in
    "Corot," 29; in *Pansies,* 209–11
Revision: for *RP,* 9–10, 17, 61–62, 73–77,
    117, 119, 181–85, 186, 188, 260 n.1,
    270 n.40; in "Raphael," 29; of Words-
    worth, 29–31; of "Transformations,"
    35; of fall, 38–39; of Christianity, 57–58,
    67, 158–59; in *Amores,* 62–65; of titles
    in "Bits," 107–8; for *Bay,* 112; for *NP,*
    122–26; of hymns in *Birds, Beasts and
    Flowers,* 134; for *Collected Poems,* 168–
    69, 265 n.31; of career in *Collected Poems,*
    169–70; *see also* specific titles of works
Richards, I. A., ix; on "Piano," 195
Roberts, F. Warren, xii, 80, 81, 83, 105, 175,
    207, 208, 216 n, 243 n, 267 n.25
Roe, Robert, 152
Romantic tradition, 16, 170; Lawrence's re-
    lation to, ix, 4, 13, 15, 31, 171, 239; and
    autobiography, 51; and diction in *The
    Plumed Serpent,* 165; and "The Wild
    Common," 182; and lyric, 194; and
    imagination, 200, 220; and "Butterfly,"
    226; *see also* Keats, Lyric, Shelley, *and*
    Whitman

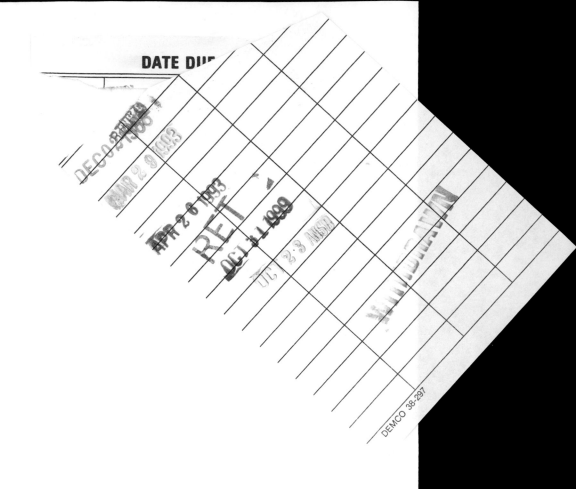